W0112543

Language Politics and Public Sphere
in North India

'A "language" may be a "dialect" with an army, but the historical, political, social, and conceptual processes involved in the transformation from the one to the other are far deeper than that famous quip allows. Few examples of such transformation in India are more salient than that of Maithili. Mithilesh Kumar Jha's thoughtful study shows that the army can be an imaginary one, but no less powerful for that.'

—Sheldon Pollock, Arvind Raghunathan Professor,
Sanskrit and South Asian Studies,
Columbia University, New York, USA

'This is an incisive and meticulous work that adds to the growing body of work on language politics, especially in the context of Hindi expansionism and its effort to colonize other vibrant and flourishing linguistic cultures like Maithili. It also tells us a larger story of the uncertain origins of languages and their fluid trajectories—seen for instance in Maithili's close relationship with Bangla and Ahomiya on the one hand, and Hindi on the other.'

—Aditya Nigam, Professor,
Centre for the Study of Developing Societies,

'An important and much needed work on the relationship of modern Hindi to Maithili, a richly literary language that it sought to reduce to "dialect" status in its own aspiration to be recognized as [a] national language. Jha's detailed and meticulous work on the history of the movement to restore status to Maithili is exemplary, opening the way for further studies on related languages that have suffered similar suppression.'

—Vasudha Dalmia, Professor Emerita,
Department of South and Southeast Asian Studies,
University of California, Berkeley, USA

Language Politics and Public Sphere in North India

Making of the Maithili Movement

MITHILESH KUMAR JHA

OXFORD
UNIVERSITY PRESS

OXFORD
UNIVERSITY PRESS

Oxford University Press is a department of the University of Oxford.
It furthers the University's objective of excellence in research, scholarship,
and education by publishing worldwide. Oxford is a registered trademark of
Oxford University Press in the UK and in certain other countries.

Published in India by
Oxford University Press
2/11 Ground Floor, Ansari Road, Daryaganj, New Delhi 110 002, India

© Oxford University Press 2018

The moral rights of the author have been asserted.

First Edition published in 2018

All rights reserved. No part of this publication may be reproduced, stored in
a retrieval system, or transmitted, in any form or by any means, without the
prior permission in writing of Oxford University Press, or as expressly permitted
by law, by licence, or under terms agreed with the appropriate reprographics
rights organization. Enquiries concerning reproduction outside the scope of the
above should be sent to the Rights Department, Oxford University Press, at the
address above.

You must not circulate this work in any other form
and you must impose this same condition on any acquirer.

ISBN-13 (print edition): 978-0-19-947934-4
ISBN-10 (print edition): 0-19-947934-8

ISBN-13 (eBook): 978-0-19-909172-0
ISBN-10 (eBook): 0-19-909172-2

Typeset in ITC Giovanni Std 9.5/13
by The Graphics Solution, New Delhi 110 092
Printed in India by Rakmo Press, New Delhi 110 020

To my parents
Karpura Devi and Ramanath Jha

Contents

Maps, Images, and Tables

Maps

Images

Tables

Acknowledgements

Writing this book has been a wonderful and very enriching journey both intellectual and emotional, for me. In due course of my research for this book, I have had the opportunities to interact and converse with a great many number of scholars, writers, and activists. I have greatly benefitted from their knowledge and their keen interest in my research always motivated me to undertake my work earnestly. I offer my heartiest thanks to all of them.

Above all, I wish to thank my PhD supervisor P.K. Datta. He has been a constant support. Without his able guidance and intriguing questions it would not have been possible for me to complete this work. He had not only enriched my understanding of the issue involved in this research with his extremely important and apt suggestions and comments but also have been a great support in developing the thesis into a publishable manuscript. I am greatly indebted to him.

Aditya Nigam and Veena Naregal have been great mentors throughout. They have enriched my thinking about the language issue in India and also the political and sociocultural aspects of this problem. They had always found time for me whenever I approached them and took keen interest in my research progress. I sincerely thank both of them.

I am also grateful to Nivedita Menon and Ravikant for their interests in my research. Menon Ma'am (as I call her) has always enlightened me. It is no exaggeration to say that she has been a great source of inspiration for many of us and has taught us the ethics of doing research. Ravikant too helped me in various ways not only with his critical remarks and insights but also by suggesting some absolutely critical works on my research problem. I am greatly indebted to both of them.

At different points of time, I have discussed my research progress with Ujjwal Kumar Singh, Bidyut Chakrabarty, Madhulika Banerjee, Satyajit Singh, Ashok Acharya, N. Sukumar, Saroj Giri, Mollica Dastider, Rajesh Dev, Sohini Guha, and Devika Sharma. I sincerely thank all of them for their comments, feedback, and suggestions.

I am grateful to Paul R. Brass for giving me an opportunity to discuss with him my research work. I have also benefitted from the valuable suggestions by Hetukar Jha, Uday Narayan Singh, Rakesh Pandey, Bhim Nath Jha, Amarnath Jha 'Bakshi', and Sadan Jha. I sincerely thank all of them for their interests in my work and their valuable suggestions.

I am also grateful to Ashok Dansana with whom I have shared light and difficult moments of research. I thank Lalit for his support at different stages of my work and help in translating many paragraphs from Maithili into English. I am also grateful to Kamal Nayan Chaubey, Indrajeet Jha, Anurag Pandey, Awanish Kumar, Pankaj Kumar Jha, Narrotam Vinit, Vinit Kumar, and Neeraj Mishra. They have always supported me. Particularly Kamal Nayan Chaubey, who has been a great support with his critical suggestions and feedback. I am also very grateful to my friends—Amarjyoti Mahanta, Debapriya Basu, Amit Kumar Sharma, Sushant Kumar Verma, Virendra Kumar, Chakravarti Mahajan, Chhatrapal, Santosh, Anusha Singh, Santana Khanikar, Subarta, Amya, Neelam, Avantika, Rinki, Devarati, Shivali, Vikramaditya, Kunal, Smriti, Kapil, Animesh Mohapatra, Narendra, Digvijoy, Faizal, Awadhesh, Sandeep, Heemanshu Shekhar Gogoi, and others. I always cherish their friendship. I warmly thank all of them.

I am grateful to the University of Delhi for granting me the University Teaching Assistantship that gave me the opportunity to teach in the Department of Political Science. I am also grateful to the University Grants Commission for Junior Research Fellowship and Senior Research Fellowship during the course of my PhD.

I am also very grateful to the Charles Wallace India Trust and the Indian Council of Social Science Research, New Delhi, for providing me a scholarship to visit London for a short duration in August–September 2012. It gave me the opportunity to consult the India Office Records Library at British Library, United Kingdom, which proved to be a great help in my research. It also gave me an opportunity to interact with eminent academicians like Peter Robb, Francesca Orsini, Eleanor Newbegin, Rochna Vajpayee, Shabnum Tejani, Aishwarj Kumar, and Rakesh Nautiyal. I sincerely thank all of them for their valuable inputs. My stay at the Indian YMCA Hostel, Fitzroy Square, London, was very pleasant. The company of friends like Abhishek Sarkar, Amitva Chatterjee, Mehar Tej Ravula, and Ghosh was wonderful during my stay in London. I thank them all.

I am also grateful to my friends and colleagues at the Department of Humanities and Social Sciences, Indian Institute of Technology, Guwahati, for their goodwill and welcoming gestures. It is here where I have mostly worked on the thesis. Particularly, I wish to thank Arup da, Debarshi Das, Pahi, John Tomas, and Sawmya Ray for their interests in my work.

For the collection of materials, I have visited the following libraries—Raj Post Graduate Research Library, Darbhanga; Central Reference Library, Lalit Narayan Mithila University, Darbhanga; P. G. Department of Maithili Library, Lalit Narayan Mithila University, Darbhanga; Kalyani Foundation, Darbhanga; Mithila Research Institute, Kabraghat, Darbhanga; Central Reference Library, Maharaja Kameshwar Singh Sanskrit University, Darbhanga; Bihar State Archive, Patna; K.P. Jayaswal Research Institute, Patna; Bihar Rashtra Bhasha Parishad, Patna; A.N. Sinha Research Institute, Patna; National Library, Kolkata; National Archive of India, Delhi; Parliament Library, Parliament House Delhi; Nehru Memorial Museum and Library, Teen Murti House, Delhi; Centre for the Studies of Developing Societies Library, Delhi; Sahitya Akademi Library, Delhi; Ratan Tata Library, University of Delhi; Central Reference Library, University of Delhi; South Campus Library, University of Delhi; D.S.A. Library, Department of Political Science, University of Delhi; British Library, United Kingdom; and Cambridge University Library, Cambridge, United Kingdom. I am grateful to the librarians and the staffs of these libraries for their cooperation. I would also like to thank the two anonymous reviewers for their comments and suggestions, and Oxford University Press for their cooperation and able assistance at different stages of this work.

I am thankful to my in-laws for their constant support and encouragement. Last but not the least, I owe my gratitude to my parents Karpura Devi and Ramanath Jha, to whom this book is dedicated. I thank them for their confidence in me and for providing a space to think freely and independently. I would also like to acknowledge the help and support of my wife Meenakshi Gogoi in completing this manuscript. She has read many chapters and provided some valuable suggestions. Thanks for her will neither be sufficient, nor required, I hope.

A Note on the Translation

This book contains a number of paragraphs in Maithili written in Devanagari script, although Maithili has its own script, namely, Mithilakshar or Tirhuta which is closer to modern Bengali and Assamese scripts. However, with the expansion of print technology, modern Maithili writers adopted Nagari; this was more so when they began to publish modern magazines and journals like *Mithila Moda*, *Maithil Hit Sadhan*, and *Mithila Mihir* in the early decades of the twentieth century. This adoption of Devanagari might have been possible due to three reasons. First, a modern printing font in Mithilakshar was not available; second, Mithila was the hub of Sanskrit learning where many scholars were already familiar with Devanagari; and finally, they might have been persuaded by the Nagari Pracharani Sabha to adopt Devanagari script in writing modern Maithili. In later years, there have been serious attempts to revive the use of Mithilakshar, but it has met with very little success and Devanagari has now become indispensable in modern Maithili writings.

All the translations from Maithili to English in this text, unless otherwise indicated, are mine. While using the Maithili or Hindi words in Roman, diacritics or transliterations are avoided. Instead, these words are italicized except for those proper names now widely used in English; and its nearest synonymous words in English is provided when such words are used for the first time.

Abbreviations

ABHSS	Akhil Bharatiya Hindi Sahitya Sammelan
ABMM	Akhil Bhartiya Maithili Mahasangh
ABMP	Akhil Bhartiya Mithila Party
ABMS	Akhil Bhartiya Maithil Sangh
ABMSP	Akhil Bhartiya Maithili Sahitya Parishad
ABMYS	Akhil Bharatiya Maithili Yuvak Samiti
AICC	All India Congress Committee
AIMC	All India Maithili Conference
AIMCC	All India Maithili Co-ordination Committee
AIMM	All India Maithili Mahasangh
AIMS	All India Maithil Sangh
AIMSP	All India Maithili Sahitya Parishad
AIMSS	All Indian Maithili Sahitya Samiti
AIMWC	All India Maithili Writers Conference
AIR	All India Radio
AIWA	All India Writers Association
AMP	Antarrashtriya Maithili Parishad
BBS	Bharatiya Bhasha Samiti
BCCE	Bihar Citizens Council on Education
BDM	Bharat Dharma Mahamandal
BHSS	Bihar Hindi Sahitya Sammelan
BJP	Bhartiya Janata Party
BPCC	Bihar Pradesh Congress Committee

BPMBS	Bihar Prantiya Maithili Bhashi Chhatra Sangharsha Samiti
BPSC	Bihar Public Service Commission
BRP	Bihar Rashtrabhasha Parishad
BRS	Bihar Research Society
BSEB	Bihar State Bengali Conference
BTBPCL	Bihar Text Books Publishing Corporation Limited
CPI	Communist Party of India
CS	Chetna Samiti
DCC	District Congress Committee
HPS	Hindi Prachar Sabha
IGNOU	Indira Gandhi National Open University
INC	Indian National Congress
JDU	Janata Dal United
LSI	Linguistic Survey of India
MBCS	Maithili Bhashi Chhatra Sangh
MCC	Mithila Chamber of Commerce
MDPL	Mithila Darshan Private Limited
MLA	Member of Legislative Assembly
MLC	Member of Legislative Council
MLS	Mithila Loka Sangh
MM	Maithil Mahasabha
MMCC	Mithila Mandal Central Committee
MMM	Maithili Mukti Morcha
MMP	Mithila Maha Parishad
MP	Member of Parliament
MPB	Mithila Pustak Bhandar
MPCC	Mithila Pradesh Congress Committee
MPS	Maithili Prakashan Samiti
MRA	Mithila Rajya Abhiyan
MRS	Maithili Rashtra Sabha
MRSS	Mithila Rajya Sangharsha Samiti
MSP	Maithili Sahitya Parishad
MSPPU	Maithili Sahitya Parishad Patna University
MSS	Mithila Sangharsha Samiti
MVP	Maithili Vikas Parishad
MYS	Maithil Yuvak Sangh
NBMBCS	Nikhil Bharatiya Maithili Bhashi Chhatra Sangh

NDA	National Democratic Alliance
NPS	Nagari Pracharini Sabha
PCC	Provincial Congress Committee
PLSI	People's Linguistic Survey of India
RJD	Rashtriya Janata Dal
RSS	Rashtriya Swayamsevak Sangh
SRC	State Reorganisation Commission
UP	Uttar Pradesh
UPSC	Union Public Service Commission
VSS	Vidyapati Seva Sansthan

Introduction

Language Politics in India and the 'Hindi Heartland'—
The Status of Maithili

Since the nineteenth and early twentieth centuries, with the enumeration processes of mapping and census, set on course by the colonial administration in India, languages have become an important tool for social and political mobilizations. After its association with religion and emergent Indian nationalism, language became a much more intense and a politically and emotionally charged issue in colonial north India. For the colonial administrators, language and its knowledge were important to consolidate their rule in India. But, for the speakers of native languages, the progress and standardization of their language came to be identified with the progress of their community.[1] And within a short span of decades, several linguistic communities with a sizeable number of speakers began to rally around their languages.

Most of the studies on language politics in north India are limited to the study of controversy surrounding the Hindi–Urdu debates and the making of Hindi as a 'national' language. For a long time, the Hindi–Urdu debate has provided an important source to critically asses the various facets of nationalist movements in north India. But an overemphasis on this debate undermines the developments that were simultaneously taking place in many other linguistic communities within the 'Hindi heartland', such as Maithili, Braj, Awadhi, Bhojpuri, Magadhi, and so forth. Therefore, in this book my attempt is—through a study of modern Maithili—to shed light on the politics of these minority linguistic communities. This includes a study of the ambiguous and often contradictory relationships between the 'national' language Hindi and its 'dialects'. I have examined this dynamic interrelationship in the context of Hindi and Maithili. While doing so, I have also tried to analyse the historical trajectory of the Maithili language and the movement that led to the formation of a modern Maithili community and various challenges to it. Maithili, as a distinct modern linguistic community, has evolved in ways that are different from its own traditional modes of existence—internally, through its negotiation with different castes, regions, and varieties of Maithili speakers; and externally, by its attempts to distinguish itself from other linguistic communities. This double movement has not been seriously studied. Through the study of the Maithili language and movement, I have also explored how a traditional community, such as that of Maithili speakers, engaged with 'our modernity' that emerged in colonial conditions but has outlasted the latter and articulated itself even more vigorously in independent India. This work, thus, is an attempt to problematize the process of such transformations, locating these in relationship to the various challenges of religion, nation, and nationalism—provincial or parochial. In general, the Maithili language movement has been studied as a community initiative which, at the height of the national movement, accepted and adapted to Hindi but at the same time fought relentlessly for its recognition as an independent language of modern India when it began to be classified as a 'dialect' of Hindi.

There is a conspicuous silence when it comes to critically engaging with the issues and challenges of these vernacular languages, particularly of north India. These processes and movements in the vernacular languages of north India are usually and conveniently dubbed as inconsequential or at the best, as merely caste-based movements. But this is only one aspect of these movements. Such frameworks do not allow us to interrogate and understand how nationalist feeling was emerging and expanding within these not-so-separate, albeit porous linguistic and cultural boundaries of the 'Hindi heartland'. How did these communities come to terms with nationalist ideas? How and on what points did they challenge or even oppose nationalist claims? In other words, how did traditional communities in India encounter modernity? What is the lingering life of that encounter? How did they assert themselves and put forward their demands in a postcolonial context?

Language, Print, and Nationalist Imaginaries in India

With the emergence of nation states, the role of language and print becomes far more important as a tool for social and political mobilizations. Language plays a critical role in the psychological and emotional integration of the heterogeneous people and communities into, what Anderson calls an 'imagined community'. For the germination of the idea of a nation, there was a need for a tool that could connect the people and tie them together in different ways than earlier affiliations, such as kinship, caste, clan, and religion. The development of 'print capitalism', according to Benedict Anderson, ended that search and made it possible to link 'fraternity, power, and time meaningfully together'. Commenting on the 'newer nationalisms' of Asia, Africa, and Latin American countries, Anderson argued, that there were two features of these nationalisms that 'changed the face of the old world'. First, in almost all of them, a 'national print language' was of central ideological or political importance. And second, these could work from visible models provided by their distant and not-so-distant predecessors.[2] Further, examining the rise of nationalism in modern Europe, he writes that print languages laid the basis for national consciousness in three distinct ways. The first was the creation of 'unified fields of exchange and communication below Latin and above the spoken vernaculars'. Thus, the speakers of the varieties of French, English, or Spanish, for whom it could have been difficult or even impossible to understand one another in conversation, became capable of comprehending one another via print and paper. Gradually,

> these fellow readers, to whom they were, connected through print, formed in their secular, particular–visible invisibility, the embryo of a nationally imagined community. Second, print capitalism gave a new fixity of language which, in the long run, helped to build that image of antiquity so central to the subjective idea of the nation. Third, print capitalism created languages-of–power of a kind different from older administrative vernaculars. Certain dialects inevitably were 'closer' to each print language and dominated their final forms. Their disadvantaged cousins, still assimilable to the emerging print language, lost

caste, above all because they were unsuccessful in insisting on their own print form.[3]

For Anderson 'the general growth in literacy, commerce, industry, communication, and state machinery' has also played a critical role in the unification of vernacular languages within each dynastic realm. Similarly, Seton Watson has also examined the crucial role language played in the growth of Finnish nationalism. According to him,

> the leaders of the burgeoning Finnish nationalist movement were persons whose profession largely consisted of the handling of language: writers, teachers, pastors, and lawyers. The study of folklore and the rediscovery and piecing together of popular epic poetry went together with the publication of grammars and dictionaries, and led to the appearance of periodicals which served to standardize Finnish literary (print) language, on behalf of which stronger political demand could be advanced.[4]

Thus we see, with the introduction of print, language—while providing a tool for sociopolitical mobilizations—went through a dramatic transformation. Its capacity to emotionally bind the people together became far more intensive with the publication of grammars, dictionaries, and literatures. In the case of India, like Latin, Sanskrit did provide a link language to the length and breadth of the country, but unlike Europe, the standardization of vernacular languages in India did not necessarily and always lead to the rise of smaller nationalisms. However, such ideas were not totally absent. With the introduction of print and standardization of vernacular languages, an exclusive sphere for each language was created. This in turn led to the creation of a linguistic sphere where even if there existed multilingual or bilingual speakers, one 'local' language became dominant or the lingua franca. Often, these vernacular languages also aspired for a separate political identity. This created an unresolved tension in India regarding its national and official language.[5] Here a great many number of languages are used simultaneously for official purposes.[6] The imaginary of Indian nationalism has been fraught with other identities, which are only recently cropping up and compel many political scientists to re-examine the very 'idea of India'. There are different imaginaries of the nation in India. And most of these scholars consider the origin of nation and nationalism in India as the by-product of 'colonial modernity'. The dominant view of India as a secular nation with its diversity and plurality came to be represented mainly by the Indian National Congress and most of the left parties. However, there are other imaginations of nation like Savarkar's Hindutva,[7] which takes the idea of the Indian nation prior to both pre-colonial and pre-Mughal times.[8] The idea of India as a secular nation enters a phase of crisis in contemporary times with the majoritarian turn in Indian politics. This led to a series of inquiries on the formation of the Indian nation and nationalism and its various fault-lines based on language, religion, caste, peasants, tribals, gender, and regional or subnational politics.[9] The other aspects of these debates are whether India is a plural multinational nation or whether is it a singular—'secular' or 'Hindu' nation. There are obvious tensions in both these formulations. And in many ways postcolonial politics in India tries to negotiate and reconcile with these identities. It would be interesting to explore the dialogic relationship of heterogeneous imaginations of Indian nation on these lines and homogenizing idea of Indian nation—secular or Hindutva—on the other.

Coming back to the question of language and its association with nationalist imaginaries in India, it is true that several linguistic communities undertook the task of social and political mobilizations from the middle of the nineteenth century.[10] And this was more so when the nationalist movement in India, led by Indian National Congress, took the character of a mass movement from the 1920s onwards. But the associations of these communities with their 'local forms of speech' and its worth are not that recent. The growing shift towards the vernacularization away from the cosmopolitan Sanskrit in India from the beginning of the tenth century is discussed in the latter part of this chapter. However, it is important to note that the increasing and exclusive creation of a literary sphere, and social and political mobilizations on that basis, is the result of nineteenth- and twentieth-century political developments. And many of these vernacular spheres in India did have their own imaginations of the nation and of the political. In other provinces, such as Bengal, Bombay, Madras, and Punjab, the exclusive provincial identity could not be appropriated with the growth of Indian nationalism. In fact, these provincial identities have often challenged Indian nationalism if it is perceived as a threat to their exclusive provincial identity. But in the 'Hindi heartland', also referred to as the heartland of Indian nation,[11] such formations of provincial identities based on language, except on the basis of Hindi, were not just discouraged but all the other languages in the region began to be classified as the 'varieties' of Hindi. Any attempt to create an independent identity based on language distinct from Hindi was dubbed as parochialism and hence a challenge to the 'national' language of India. In the first two or three decades after Independence, India did experience the reorganization of states on the linguistic lines. But even so, the political elites in the 'Hindi heartland' remained successful in maintaining the hegemonic status of Hindi by thwarting away any attempts by the other linguistic groups to demand their separate identities. However, they have not been entirely successful in these efforts as, time and again, such demands have kept haunting post-independent India. At the forefront of such demands have been the speakers of Maithili, Bhojpuri, and Bundelkhandi. Such voices are not totally absent among the speakers of Magadhi, Awadhi, Khari Boli, Braj, and so forth. And in post-independent India, with the growth and expansion of print, many newer linguistic groups are agitating for the official recognition of their languages. In the present work, I have tried to understand such tensions regarding the expansion of Hindi as the 'national' language and the rise of the Maithili language movement in north Bihar.

Language and 'Dialects': Conceptual Explorations

One common distinction that is drawn between 'language and dialects is that dialects are considered as mutually intelligible varieties of one language while languages are mutually unintelligible'.[12] Dialects have long been used; of course, to refer to a substandard form of speech deviated from a prestigious or standard language. The *Oxford English Dictionary* defines 'dialect' as 'one of the subordinate forms or varieties of a language arising from local peculiarities'. Sometimes, there are other criteria applied for this distinction based on the availability of grammar and literary production. If a speech form lacks these two features, then it is classified as a 'dialect' or 'varieties' of a standard language.

However, there are complexities involved in such distinction between language and 'dialects'. One can understand these complexities by the following two examples—first, Cantonese and Mandarin speakers, despite the lack of mutual intelligibility, are both considered to be the 'dialects' of Chinese, not only because they use the same script but also because the locations from which they arise are part of the

Chinese state. Second, Norwegian and Danish speakers, although they can understand one another perfectly well, are seen to be speaking different languages because of their different sociopolitical allegiances.[13] So, there are no inherent linguistic or aesthetic criteria per se for the distinction between language and dialects. It is often based on the social prestige and the power of their speakers. And therefore, the relationship between a language and dialects cannot be static. It always remains contingent. In this work, I have studied this changing relationship in the context of Hindi and Maithili in north India.[14] Our perceptions and opinion do not emerge in a vacuum. The case with language and 'dialects' is similar. What we consider a 'dialect' or a 'language' is conditioned more by the prevailing socio-historical and political conditions than by the innate qualities of a speech form. Of course, there exists a difference between language and 'dialects', but this very act of differentiation between the two is an exercise of power and can be explained historically; and is subject to change.

There are many ways to understand or conceptualize a language. In the general sense of the term, language is used for communicative purposes by a group of people who constitute the speech or linguistic community. It is basically understood as a means of communication among and between the members of a speech community. This is called the *communicative function* of language. But language is also understood as an emblem of 'groupness', as a symbol, a rallying point, which continues to play an important role in ethnic and nationalist sentiments of various kinds. This is called the *symbolic function* of language.[15] Here, the power of the language extends beyond the communicative function. In other words, language is very much related to concepts such as recognition, particularly when language is understood not just in written and spoken form but in association with culture, identity, and a whole way of life. So, then the struggle for recognition of a language is also a fight for the recognition of their culture, their identity and their ways of life.

Language occupied the attention of great minds in all the ages. In the early enlightenment era, the study of philology was more conducive to making sense of human beings, their outlook, their origin, their evolutions, their interconnectedness, and the possibility or impossibility of their reconciliation in the near future. It is also used to make sense of the world as it exists, its differences in culture, habits, and manners. In the first phase of this debate, philosophers and philologist were preoccupied with the idea of the origin of the language. After that, the contentious and still unsuccessful classifications of language into different families, followed. Many, perhaps because of the residue of religious thoughts, continued to believe in the principle of the divine origin of language. In his thesis on *Treatise on the Origin of Language*,[16] Herder, however, rejects the divine origin of the language and has explained in detail the human invention of language. For him, language is not something which is just a medium of expression or communication that is external to us. A human child invents his or her own language first to make sense of the bewildering world that s/he experiences; then depending upon the stages of his/her invention, s/he goes on to develop this language. And this is a progressive movement of language that is internal to the child.

For Herder, language in this sense is an expression of one's own nature, feelings, values, manners, character, and connected to the individual soul. Human reason and rationality function within it. Therefore, he refutes the claim that it is human reason or rationality that creates or invents language. On the contrary, in his opinion, it is reason and rationality that functions within that language which human invents or creates for oneself. He is critical of formal language teaching and the development of a language through its grammars and dictionaries. According to him, it obstructs the natural progress of a language and deprives it of its real expression of feelings and makes it artificial.

The most striking proposition of Herder is the connection he makes between language and the human soul, instead of with the intellect or reason. Language, according to Herder, when made too decorative obstructs the real feelings and emotions or felt experiences and becomes a means of manipulation. It produces an artificial construct. Such linguistic practices result in the loss of a language which we first learnt to understand both objects external to us as well as our own feelings. Perhaps this is the reason why we still believe—and on this, there is nearly universal consensus—that the mother tongue is the best medium to educate a child. The connection to other languages that one learns can never be the same as it is with one's mother tongue.

So everything, starting from becoming aware of our surroundings, to understanding and thinking about it, is done in a language which we invent inwardly and express it outwardly. And throughout our life our existence is oriented towards this understanding, that is, towards the progress of our language. Hence, according to Herder, language teaching in the classroom through grammars obstructs the progress of a language. It alienates language from its natural spirit. It shows the finality of a language. According to Herder, a human being is at the root of what is forceful, what is powerful, what is great, what is essential in a language and not grammars or textbooks. One interesting contrast he makes is between a human infant who is fragile, weak, and needier in the beginning than the offspring of an animal. Yet it is the human infant, through inventing a language and through constant practice and perfection in it, who may become 'inwardly united whole'. This capacity is not endowed, according to Herder, to the other species on the earth. He also refutes the singularity of a language. For Herder, there are differences and plurality in language use within a language system between a wife and a husband, teachers and pupils, father and son, mother and daughter, between the young and the old. Besides climate, air, water, food, and drink have an immense influence on the linguistic organs and naturally on language.

Language in this sense has an origin, spread, or expansion through human beings alone within a community and outside. But it is very difficult to classify them into different language families. Like any other objects, it has a life, it grows, and it dies depending upon the circumstances and transformations within and outside it. With every new generation, there is something new that is added to it; it does not pass through one generation to the other as it exists. Herder expresses it thus, '[t]he first thought in [the] first human soul is connected with the last soul in the last human soul'.[17]

Other theorists have argued that language is also deeply connected with the social and political forces in the society. Katerina Clark and Michael Holquist in *Marxism and the Philosophy of Language*[18] write that 'a word in the mouth of a particular individual is a product of the living interaction of social forces'.[19] Many terms in linguistic analysis, like 'heteroglossia', 'intertextuality', and the 'linguistic construction of the self' are closely associated with one of the most complex and original thinkers of the twentieth century, Mikhail Mikhailovich Bakhtin (1895–1975). He was a late discovery for the modern west in the late 1970s. He was taken seriously firstly in literary theories and cultural studies and then in linguistics. It is strange that the world takes him seriously in the age of post-structuralism and postmodernism, for he wrote during the high time of structuralism. Inspired by Kantian philosophy and neo-Kantian thought that focused on the dialectic relationship of mind and matter, Bakhtin's lifelong concern was to understand the perception that stems from this relationship. He wanted to study language independently, free from the clutches of grammarians and philologists, who tried to impose a system upon the languages through abstraction. He was critical of Saussure, who studied language as a system over which he gave little control to speakers. Saussure divides language into *langue* and *parole*, and he focused on langue as a systematic and scientific way to understand language. He considered parole as unsystematic and unworthy of scientific study. Contrary to this, Bakhtin made parole, in his term 'utterance', the central part of his study on language. For him 'the actual reality of language—speech—is not the abstract system of linguistic norms ... but the social event of verbal interaction implemented in an utterance'.[20] His whole work is based on two premises—first, the role of signs on human thought; and second, the role of utterance in language. He considered utterance as the most important part of a language. It is utterance which gives life to a language and combines the experience or consciousness of the speaker and materiality of the language. This leads to dialogism between the uttered words and meaning. Hence, for him, the word has no meaning and the same word may mean different things in different contexts. Even the same word may mean different things in the same context depending upon the intonation of the speaker.

In his understanding, an utterance and its meaning are thus context-dependent. This put the listener and speaker into a relationship but context itself is boundless and this form what he calls *heteroglossia*. Here an utterance is a step in a chain of communications between individuals—the meaning of which is an effect in an already existing eco-system of language. It 'is the effect of an interaction between speaker and listener produced via the material of a particular sound complex'.[21] So any understanding of an utterance is dialogic, essentially plural and not fixed, singular, or static. This is connected to his idea of polyphony. Thus, considering language as a social phenomenon, Bakhtin disagrees with those who emphasize on individual subjectivity in language use. For him, the right way to understand the self is from the social to the individual rather than from the self to the social. It is in language, not in the nation state, that social force finds its most realized expression. All societies and all cultures and their degrees of openness and boundedness can be classified, according to Bakhtin, based on the way they handle reported speech—by which he means the speech of the other, speech within speech, utterance within utterance, speech about the speech, and utterance about the utterance. In this way, we find in Bakhtin, the location of language in a wider and complex web of human existence. He was so sure about the heterogeneity of this existence that he refuted strongly any claim of homogeneity. His understanding of language not only questions the singularity of language but it also questions those systematic and scientific studies of language which look at it as an independent variable free from its social and cultural context.

Another extremely insightful and similar analysis of language is provided by a French social theorist, Pierre Bourdieu. In his *Language and Symbolic Power* (1991), he criticizes Chomsky's work on language where Chomsky gives greater emphasis to the 'generative capacity' of competent speakers. Chomsky makes a distinction between 'competence', that is, knowledge of a language possessed by an ideal speaker/hearer in a completely homogeneous speech community, and 'performance' which is the actual use of language in concrete situations. According to Bourdieu, this distinction leads linguists to take for granted an object domain which is, in fact, the product of a complex set of social, historical and political conditions of formation. Language cannot be understood in isolation from these social economic conditions. For him, the completely homogeneous language and speech community does not exist. So, the right approach to study the language phenomena would be by looking at the ways in which languages have emerged historically as dominant ones in particular geographical locales, often in conjunction with the formation of modern nation states.

The key concept that Bourdieu develops in his approach is *habitus*, that is, a set of dispositions which incline agents to act and react in certain ways. The dispositions generate practices, perceptions, and attitudes which are 'regular' without being consciously coordinated or governed by any 'rule'. These are acquired through a gradual process of inculcation. According to Bourdieu, religion and politics achieve their most successful ideological effects by exploiting the possibilities inherent in the social inequality of the 'legitimate' language. In his words 'specialized discourses can drive their efficacy from the hidden correspondence between the structure of the social space within which they are produced: the political field, the religious field, the artistic field, the philosophical field, etc. and the structure of the field of social classes within which the recipients are situated and in relation to which they interpret the message'.[22] So it is clear that the study of language in isolation from social and economic elements of space and time will not be a fruitful exercise. But he also believes that social science must consider the autonomy of language, its specific logic and its rules of operation. One cannot understand the symbolic effects of language without considering the fact, frequently attested, that language is an exemplary formal mechanism whose generative capacities are enormously infinite. This infinitely generative capacity of language provides it with the power to produce an existence for itself, by generating the collectively recognized and thus realized representation of existence. This, according to Bourdieu, is possibly the principal support of the dream of absolute power.

Regarding the production and reproduction of legitimate language, Bourdieu writes that 'language form(s) a kind of wealth which all can make use of at once without causing any diminution of the store and which thus admits a complete community of enjoyment; for all, freely participating in the general treasure, unconsciously aid in its preservation'.[23] For him integration into a single 'linguistic community, which is a product of the political domination, that is endlessly reproduced by institutions capable of imposing universal recognition of the dominant language, is the condition for the establishment of relations of linguistic domination'.[24] He also acknowledged the role played by dictionaries, the educational systems, and the nation building exercise in the production of standard language.

Thus, the use of language, the manner as much as the substance of discourse depends on the sociopolitical position of the speakers, which governs the access s/he can have to the language of the institution that is to 'the official, orthodox and legitimate speech'. The power of language, as many believe, does not reside within itself. According to Bourdieu it resides in the institutional conditions of their production and reception. The language of authority never governs without the collaboration of those it governs, without the help of the social mechanisms capable of producing this complicity, which is the basis of all authority.

Languages are also seen as 'different systems reflecting different varieties of human condition. Although they may be unequal in complexity at given points, this does not imply that some have, overall, greater expressive power. Environment differs and, therefore, the things that must be detailed in language differ'.[25] Discarding the view of language purity, Edwards believes that language changes—adapting to new conditions and requirements—but it does not do so in terms of linguistic purity. Different social, geographical, and other conditions determine this change. This is an important formulation that Edwards establishes and this is a critical insight used in exploring the contentious relationship between language and 'dialects' in the context of Hindi and Maithili in the present study. During the nationalist phase of the 1920s and even before that, Hindi was projected as the 'national language' in India. Although there were many controversies surrounding Hindi, that I will discuss later, here it is suffices to say that while Hindi did exist earlier, it was not the same modern print 'Hindi' that we know today. Secondly, it did not have the same power or dominance over other languages or 'dialects' in the region that it has achieved during this period. It has acquired an unprecedented capacity for social and political mobilization. One of the purposes of the present research is to analyse this process. How was a language created as a 'national' language? What was the politics involved in that process? Did socio-economic and political conditions and colonial legacies play a role in it? What was the role of print in the modernization and standardization of Indian language? How did it affect the growth and development of other existing independent languages in the 'Hindi heartland'?

Vernacular Politics in India

Although the language issue remains one of the most contested and politically and emotionally hotly debated topics in India since the colonial times, it is only in the recent times that 'language politics' is employed as an important category for scholarly inquiry into the political processes in modern India. So far it has been treated as a policy matters or at best as an identity issue. One of the books which establishes this category of 'language and politics' is Asha Sarangi's edited volume *Language and Politics in India*.[26] According to Sarangi, 'It is important to explore and examine the sites where language and politics interact. They mutually reproduce and reinforce scales of social hierarchies, political power, cultural and economic inequalities.'[27] And, it is important to examine how language is invoked in modern times in the name of culture, community, region, nation, and state and its underlying social and political histories.

Here, it is equally important to understand the ways in which the term 'vernacular'[28] have been deployed in India. This term became a rallying point for discussion among colonial and native scholars, when the British undertook the responsibility of 'educating' the natives and making it mandatory for their officials to learn the language *of* the people. The role of Christian missionaries in promotion of vernacular languages in India was equally important. Besides the classical languages like Sanskrit, Arabic, and Persian, the British also encountered numerous regional languages spoken by the common masses. The issue of the medium of instructions for imparting education was hotly debated among the colonial administrators and native reformers. On the one side of the debate the issue was whether any Indian classical languages like Sanskrit or English should be deployed and promoted. Whereas, on the other side, the debate was between whether English or Hindustani and other Indian vernaculars should be used for the purpose. And this debate remained a fiercely contested issue since then. Although it was English which gradually became the language of prestige, the British also promoted vernacular educations in India from the middle of the nineteenth century.[29] And this was the period when various vernacular spheres in India began to consolidate their regional, political, and literary space. Although, it is also true that this vernacular turn in Indian history began sometime prior to the tenth century (as discussed ahead) and more explicitly so with the beginning of the Bhakti movement, the creation of an exclusive vernacular domain is the result of nineteenth century.

It is equally important to note here that the modern social reforms movement in India first started in these domains[30] and the national movement was the outcome of the coming together of these vernacular elites from Maharashtra, Bengal, Madras, and Punjab. However, gradually these vernacular domains were dominated by national politics. Nationalist ideas and imaginaries began to be transmitted to these vernacular spheres through the provincial and bilingual elite. However, these 'nationalist' ideas and imaginaries were not understood in the same way as it was at the national level. And the actual story of continuity and change with the coming of modernity and its adaptation by the various communities in India will remain incomplete unless it includes the trajectories of how these vernacular spheres came into terms with modernity. Unfortunately, this remains more or less a neglected area of social and political inquiry in modern India and South Asia.

However, there are many new enterprises in the studies of languages in India. The mammoth exercise of the Bhasha Research and Publication Centre under Professor G.N. Devy to publish *People's Linguistic Survey of India* in 50 volumes, is one of the most extensive linguistic surveys after Grierson's. It has identified around 780 languages and 66 scripts in India. Unlike other estimates it does not differentiate among the languages based on numbers and is rooted in 'people's perception of language'. There are over 1,600 mother tongues reducible to roughly about 200 languages in India.[31] According to Annamalai, socio linguistic research in India has naturally concentrated on language maintenance, functional distribution, or communication pattern, convergence, and code mixing. The studies show that the multilingual scene in India is changing. The fundamental change is the transformation in the role of language for political control and social mobility. During colonial rule, English played the most important role for political control and social mobility. It was the sole dominant language and all the native languages were categorized as vernaculars in comparison to English. Now after Independence, these vernaculars began to compete for the dominant position at different levels of national and state politics and in administration. The minority languages sought protection from unfavourable dominations and appropriations. This lead to language conflicts at the societal level. The reorganization of provinces into linguistic states based on the principle of one language for one state made it possible for the emergence of the numerically largest language in the state as the dominant language. This changed the sociolinguistic relation between languages and the conflicts inherent in the struggle to attain an acceptable position, and led to linguistic tensions. Further, he claims, that the linguistic variables are manipulated to express social relations such as social distance, social control, social solidarity, and social identity. Undoubtedly, Annamalai gives an insightful analysis of inherent tensions in the linguistic scenario of India. Most of the existing research[32] shows that language politics had its strongest manifestation during the anti-colonial movement, especially during the 1920s, with the emergence of Gandhi as the mass leader. There was also a time when, along with the English-educated elite/leadership, there emerged a bilingual leadership which entrusted itself with the role of local/ vernacular as well as national leadership by their ability to correspond between the vernacular masses on the one hand and the colonial state and the *limited* 'public sphere' created by the English-speaking elite on the other. There was the emergence of a new leadership in vernacular languages as well, but they did find enormous difficulties in assert-ing their voice in the emerging 'public political sphere' in India. They mostly remained recipients of the language provided by the English or bilingual leadership. Yet they were never completely assimilated; these vernacular elites were constantly struggling in more subtle ways, though they largely remained marginalized for the time being, to assert their voice and their differences from the given/projected national lan-guage of India. India has witnessed these manifestations in the first and second decades after independence and these are continuing in one form or the other.

It is now extremely important to explore the simultaneous expan-sion of ideas like 'progress' and nation in the vernacular spheres of modern India. These remain an often neglected and conveniently ignored area of inquiry for a very long time, particularly in the 'Hindi heartland'. Although, there have been studies on the various 'dialects' of the region, such as Braj, Khari Boli, Maithili, Bhojpuri, Magadhi, and so on, such studies focused on the status of these 'dialects' vis-à-vis Hindi, their literature, history, and at times their grammar. These 'dialects' of the 'Hindi heartland', despite their separate literary histories began to be classified and clubbed together as 'dialects' or 'varieties' of Hindi. These literary spheres thus remained always marginal to the Hindi public sphere and what happened in the literary sphere of Hindi was always understood as happenings throughout the 'Hindi heartland'. Only recently are there growing interests in these other literary spheres of the region. And only such studies can unravel the layers of articula-tions and understandings of modern ideas like nation, progress, and community in the 'Hindi heartland'.

One of the frequently charted paths for the studies on/about the ver-nacular languages is to examine how these languages or 'dialects' were standardized with the coming of print and the introduction of modern vernacular education by the colonial administration. And then, to study how these vernaculars forged an identity and began to compete with other vernaculars. And further, these vernacular movements need to be studied based on their successful or unsuccessful negotiations for separate political identities. Mostly all the vernacular movements in India seek a distinct political identity for their linguistic communities within the larger political framework of *Bharatvarsha* (India). Here, it is important to note that demands and struggles for the creation of altogether a new sovereign political identity was not totally absent in such discourses.

The other possibilities of studying the vernacular politics in India are to take the studies of vernaculars well before the period of colonial modernity. This may give a greater historical understanding of vernacular politics in India and may allow us to reconfigure the relation between nation and region in modern India. And, again studies on such vernacularization processes in India, according to Sheldon Pollock, are least explored.[33] According to him, such a process, both in Asia and in Europe, entails 'a transformation in cultural practice, social identity formation, and political order with far reaching and enduring consequences'.[34] And, such a process did not just happen but there were people consciously involved in literary production in more localized languages and idioms which they knew would not travel across the regions like Sanskrit did. Some of the vernaculars were successful, according to Pollock, in the creation of their own cosmopolitan vision within their own regional world. The expansion of Braj from the middle of the fifteenth century is one of the classic examples of vernacular cosmopolitanism.[35] This vernacularization process that started a little before AD 1000 clearly shows the turn away from Sanskrit in the greater part of South Asia. Pollock has rightly argued that although such processes in different parts were 'disparate and complex' there were three commonalities. First, superposed literariness is appropriated and localized; second, 'the geocultural sphere of literary communication becomes itself a matter of literary representation, something we might call literary territorialization'; and finally, 'vernacular literary production becomes a central concern for royal court'.[36] Thus, what is obvious, is the decisive shift away from the translocal Sanskrit towards more localized form of literary productions from a little before AD 1000 and more so from the middle of the fifteenth century across South Asia.

And such processes were not devoid of the making of new literary communities and political ramifications, as the site of such productions was mostly royal courts.[37] It thus, I hope, will be interesting to explore as to why such processes led to the formations of modern nation states in Europe but in India nationalist ideas enter the sociopolitical discourse only during the colonial rule? However, it would be inappropriate to argue that such vernacularization had no effect here. It did give rise to strong provincial affiliations. But, the historical and political trajectories in India have been different. And again, where there is a plethora of studies on such historical and political trajectories, there are hardly any serious attempts to study how these emergent vernacular spheres were negotiating and reconciling with such historical and political developments in modern India.

The recent work by Raziuddin Aquil and Partha Chatterjee[38] shows yet another way of studying vernacular histories. They explain the inherent challenges of studying vernacular history that is different from the academic discipline of history. It requires methods that differ from the archival and documenting practices of the academic discipline of history. Such vernacular histories are often based on ethnologies, folklores, novels, cultural practices, and even poetry and openly display their prejudices. Such histories often give rise to identity politics and, at times, it becomes difficult to approve of everything that goes in the name of vernacular history. Therefore, it requires cautious and careful investigations. But such investigations, according to them, are worth the effort as these vernacular histories have the possibilities of uncovering the trajectories of modernity in south Asia. They have rightly argued that 'effective histories are being made in the vernacular'[39] and such histories constantly challenge the academic discipline of history. The real challenge, therefore, is to understand the vernacular as a sphere, which not only participated in the unfolding of modernity in south Asia but was also a site where most of the modern ideas were imitated, appropriated, and newer forms of identities constructed.

In the study of the Maithili language and movement one often encounters terms like *Desha*, *Appan Desha*, and *Mithila Desha*. But interestingly, articulations of these terms were quite distinct from its articulation in contemporary Hindi or any other modern vernaculars in India. The Maithili imagination of *Desha* in the beginning of the twentieth century was more in terms of the distinct social and cultural life of Mithila. But, in the political sense, they did consider Mithila as an integral part of *Bharatvarsha* (India). However, within the 'Hindi heartland' they were also struggling for a separate and distinct identity. The expansion of Hindi in the Maithili-speaking area and its willing adaptation by the Maithili coincided with the often suppressed but visible discomfort between Hindi and Maithili in the region. Thus, the forging of the modern identity of the Maithili community is intrinsically related to the resistance against the expansionist agendas of Hindi. However, the articulations of the modern Maithili community itself remained internally challenged and externally suppressed and suspected for a very long time. This study is an attempt to explore these layers of processes and politics through which a vernacular community does not just adapt to a new language but also attempts to create and assert the identity of its own.

Language Politics in the 'Hindi Heartland'

'Hindi heartland' is a common term often used to refer to Hindi-speaking regions of the north Indian states, particularly Uttar Pradesh, Madhya Pradesh, Bihar, and Rajasthan. Here, Hindi is the *standard* language and widely used in the press, markets, schools, colleges, courts, and administrations. The 'Hindi heartland' was at the forefront of linguistic agitations in colonial India. Its anti-English agitations and demand for the declaration of Hindi as the national language of India attracted both wide support within the region and a high degree of suspicion from outside the region, particularly from south India. This continued to haunt the political discourse of the region for many decades after independence. The Hindi–Urdu controversy that shaped much of the political discourse in colonial North India is widely explored by the social scientists and linguists. However, the 'Hindi heartland' was and still is very diverse in terms of the number of languages and 'dialects' spoken there. According to one estimate, Hindi has 48 varieties spoken throughout the 'Hindi heartland'.[40] But, these are classified often as 'dialects', or 'varieties' of Hindi, which was at times challenged by the speakers of these 'dialects' or 'varieties'. Some of these languages, like Maithili, have been successful in establishing its independence from Hindi. But others, like Bhojpuri, are still struggling for such a status. Similar concerns can also be observed among the speakers of Bundelkhandi, Braj, Awadhi, Khari Boli, and the speakers of 'varieties' of Rajasthani languages. Thus, we invoke these states when we imply the term 'Hindi heartland' but its exact boundary remains a contentious issue.

The question of language in the 'Hindi heartland' has always been associated with the issue of caste, class, gender, and of course religion. Religion was one of the fundamental reasons for the Hindi–Urdu divide. Krishna Kumar, while writing about the expansion as well as the standardization of modern Hindi, acknowledges the role of print, journalism, textbooks, schools, universities, and employment opportunities, and asserts that 'language had become, both among the Muslim landed and salaried gentry and the Hindu upper castes, the means as well as the symbol of community creation'.[41]

One can study or examine the language politics in the 'Hindi heartland' on three axes—a colonial enterprise; print and employment opportunities; and finally, the role of nationalist elites and debates over Hindi or Hindustani. These three axes are neither separate nor independent from each other but often are mutually reinforcing. Their interplay have made remarkable contributions in the expansion of Hindi and in the creation of the 'Hindi heartland'. The role of colonial linguistic policy and classificatory exercises in the language politics in modern India is discussed in greater details in the next chapter. Here, it is important to understand the major role colonial linguistic policy played in language politics in India. Bernard S. Cohn's remarkable essay 'The Command of Language and Language of Command'[42] critically examines how the establishment of Fort William College at Kolkata and Gilchrist studies of Indian languages led to the Hindi–Urdu divide and in the establishment of Hindustani as the language of command in India. David Lelyveld argues 'how language was construed by the power of a foreign regime into bounded institutions and communities with defined roles in an overarching political structure'.[43] Explaining the conditions in which India became a rich field of 'philological enterprise' Lelyveld writes that the British had developed through their extensive studies of Indian languages starting from William Jones, not only a practical advantage for their rule in India but also gave rise to an ideology of languages as separate, autonomous objects in the world which could be classified, arranged, and comparatively studied. Now these linguistic communities were expected to have 'different histories,

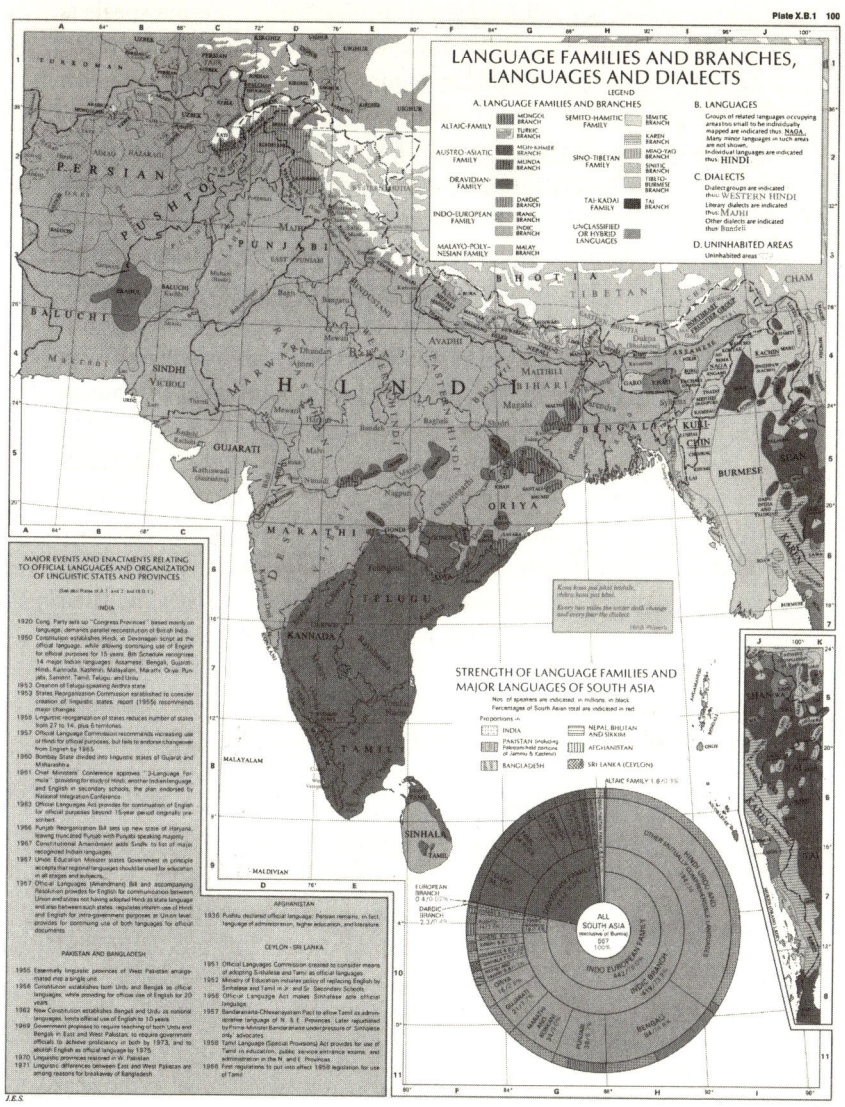

Map I.1 A Map of India Showing Language Families and 'Dialects'

Source: Joseph E. Schwartzberg. 1992. *A Historical Atlas of South Asia*, Oxford University Press, p. 100. The digital image from the Historical Atlas of South Asia is provided courtesy of the Digital South Asia Library, http://dsal.uchicago.edu.

Note: Map not to scale and does not represent authentic international boundaries.

the history of the people who spoke or used them to create literatures; and these could be studied comparatively and used to make sense of the advantages that nations had gained over other in the course of history.[44] Thus, the studies and classifications of Indian languages were an integral part of the colonial history of power and domination in South Asia. In India, the British hardly took any interest in the development of any provincial languages.[45] Their promotion of Hindustani was to make the task of governing smoother and easier. However, in that process they undermined and subordinated numerous varieties of other languages of Hindustan. And this process of undermining continued even when the nationalist leadership took over and language became the marker of Indian nationalism and unity. Some languages like Punjabi successfully recovered from this subordination and asserted its richness and literary competencies.[46] But many languages in the Hindustani-speaking region that we now refer to as the 'Hindi heartland' are still struggling to establish their independent status from Hindi.

Alok Rai's *Hindi Nationalism* is a critical voice on the subject of language and politics in the 'Hindi heartland'. He argues that the Hindi that we know today is the product of the nineteenth century and the awareness of its Hinduness have been almost imposed upon the populace by colonial intervention a good few decades before the Hindu elites themselves took up the cause of Hindu–Hindi. However, this was not a smooth transition. According to Rai, Hindi at the end of the nineteenth century had many battles to fight before it could establish itself as a full-fledged literary, social, and official language of India. For Rai, when MacDonnell on 18 April 1900 declared, 'permissive but not exclusive use of Hindi in courts', it was explicitly a political move. This was done not to promote Hindi or Hindustani but to curb the 'Muslim threat' posed by their greater presence in the administration, about which the British became more suspicious. Despite the colonial intervention, Rai believes that language question was a result of the power struggle among the elites which had little to do with the common people. He also argues that standard Hindi was yet to become the language of widespread domestic use in the cities. It had very little rural presence. But by the first decade of the twentieth century there were widely held beliefs amongst the propagators of 'Hindi' that it was indeed being spoken (almost) everywhere in north India. Thus, from Rai's account one can clearly infer the incongruities in the real use of the languages in the 'Hindi heartland' and its imaginary construct by the supporters of Hindi.

Another critical work on the language politics in the region is by Francesca Orsini—*The Hindi Public Sphere*—where she has documented the role of print in the production of new literary journals in Hindi and how it created a new literary but limited public sphere in the 'heartland'. She has also discussed the role of school curricula and teaching methods, as well as *Kavi Sammelans* in the expansion of this public sphere. She has not only studied the making of Hindi in modern India but also asserts that 'Hindi's claim to be the national language of India was an ideological construct'.[47] She shows how this construct was developed and its claims forcefully invoked at the expense of Braj, of Urdu, of the other local languages and oral traditions, while clearly undermining the historical facts of linguistic diversity and pluralism in the region.

> The issue of national language is thus embedded in rhetoric of an all-inclusive religious community along devotional lines. Just as the path of devotion is open to all and are both a means and an end. So, the national language is presented as the means to create a national community open to all and conferring a sense of unity.[48]

Orsini also examines the role of literary figures like Mahavir Prasad Dwivedi in popularizing Hindi, who had also helped in the making of an ideological construct which linked the issue of *nij bhasha* with that of *rashtra bhasha*. By critically looking at the works of Hindi literary figures like Madan Mohan Malviya, Purushottam Das Tandon, Ganesh Shankar Vidyarthi, Acharya Narendra Dev, and Babu Sampurnananda, she concludes that their conscious efforts in promoting Hindi helped in projecting Hindi as the national language of India.

Vasudha Dalmia's *The Nationalization of Hindu Traditions*[49] examines the construction of modern Hindi, first as the language of all the Hindus and later as the language of all the nationalists in India and how the personality of Bharatendu Harischandra and his literary works in nineteenth-century Banaras played a critical role in such a construct. In her analysis, she has also examined the contributions of the merchant class in language agitations in nineteenth-century India. She writes that, 'it was largely from the ranks of the merchant then, that the agitation for the recognition of Hindi as the language of the courts was carried out, making Allahabad and Banaras the joint centres of the

Hindi movement'.[50] She further stresses that 'in the actual substantive development of modern Hindi ... the terrain was at first occupied by missionaries and schoolbook writers. After the mid-century, however, the concept of Hindi as the language of the Hindus, with vast territorial and ideological aspirations, was appropriated by nationalists and henceforth developed almost exclusively by them'.[51] Locating the Hindi language agitation in the social, cultural, and religious milieu of nineteenth-century India, Dalmia suggests that the study of the development of Hindi cannot be studied by separating it from its cultural and religious identification with Hindus at a supra-regional and later at the national level. For her, the development of modern Hindi, throughout the nineteenth century, involved threefold interrelated processes:

1. It was first and foremost a process of dichotomization, that is, separation from Urdu, coupled with the claim of absolute autonomy for Hindi.
2. The language thus separated was standardized by means of grammars, dictionaries, and school primers, which not only represented autonomy but also cultivated and increased it, by introducing new vocabulary and stressing those phonological and grammatical alternatives that were different from those of Urdu.
3. Along with standardization came historicization, that is, the process of establishing historical links with literary works connected with great ideological movements of the past. Speech communities create myths and genealogies concerning the origin and development of standard varieties of language. The archivization thus constructed, provides for respectable ancestry. The origin of Hindi from Sanskrit as the ancient mother tongue of the Aryans was supported by the nineteenth-century discovery of historical regularity. The great ideological movement, which Hindi came to be associated with, was offered by the devotional Bhakti movement, which came to be seen as the Hindu response to the threat posed by Islam.[52]

In these processes, she does acknowledge the role of British administrators and missionaries but its ideological and political projection as the 'national' language of India according to Dalmia was largely an indigenous affair led by the nationalist elite. This work by Dalmia is extremely helpful in understanding the ideological construct as well as the socio-religious and cultural basis of the Hindi language movement in nineteenth-century India. In this work, I have extended this critical scrutiny of the Hindi movement to understand the ways through which the modern 'national' language Hindi interacts, appropriates, and subordinates the other languages in the region. And, also how these languages responded to such developments.

The other major work on the language politics in the 'Hindi heartland' is Christopher R. King's *One Language and Two Scripts*.[53] He studies the cumbersome and contentious language politics and its role in shaping the discourse of communalism and nationalism in India. King does not agree with many studies which conclude that the villain in the act of partition of British India is to be found among the protagonists of the Urdu language and Muslim League. Instead, he proposes that the Hindi movement motivated a communal consciousness in pre-independence India. He emphasizes that this movement 'not only expressed but reinforced' a communal awareness which can be seen as culminating in the birth of Pakistan in 1947. King argues that the Hindi movement in the nineteenth century consciously distinguished between people in terms of religion and language—and language was determined by its script and vocabulary, not by its actual linguistic configurations.

In his study of the Hindi movement, King has applied Karl Deutsch's method of social mobilization, assimilation, and differentiation. Here, by social mobilization, he means 'a process of change occurring in areas undergoing modernization, which brings increasing members of the more isolated portions of population into an ever denser net of social communication'.[54] He justifies Deutsch's formulation that the rate of assimilation—'a process of change which brings different peoples or ethnic groups within the same political system or into the same network of social communication'[55]—must keep ahead of that of social mobilization, if differentiation is not to be the result. King argues that a conscious attempt was made at the college of Fort William to differentiate language in terms of script and vocabulary. In his view, Hindu ideologues tried to differentiate everyday use of Hindi or Hindustani from Urdu through the process of Sanskritization and standardization of Hindi. He described how this process leads to a change in the equation Hindi or Hindustani = Hindu + Muslim, written in both Nagari and Persian script; into Hindi = Hindu, and Urdu = Muslim.[56] He also discusses the internal tensions in the process of assimilation within the Hindi movement—especially among the supporters of the Braj and Khari Boli Hindi.

Taking Hindi versus Urdu as a model, he explored the role of organizations like *Nagari Pracharin Sabha* and *Anjuman-e-Urdu*. To 'purify' their separate languages of alien words, these organizations played a critical role in the process of differentiation. King also explains the economic factor—employment, especially in the government sector, as the major motivation for the language politics in the 'Hindi heartland'. Further, he observes that Sanskritized Khari Boli Hindi went through a process of assimilation and differentiation to establish its supremacy among the other languages of north India. It particularly distinguished and distanced itself from Urdu and gradually arrived at a point where it could set itself up as the 'national' language of India. This form of Hindi not only undermined the position of Braj Bhasha as the literary medium, but also proceeded to claim other languages then in circulation in North India as its 'dialects'. Thus, he shows the limitation of Hindi which somehow managed to create 'a loosely unified nation' but failed to create 'a coherent nation'.

From the second decade of the twentieth century, Hindi's claim as the national language of India became widespread. Congress also supported such demands. Gandhi was closely associated with the Hindi or Hindustani movement and he was the president of the eighth *Hindi Sahitya Sammelan* meeting in Indore in 1918. There, he announced that 'until all public activities take place in Hindi the country can't progress. Until Congress conducts all its activities in the rashtra bhasha, we shall not attain swaraj'.[57] The Congress session at Nagpur (1920) decided to set up its units in the provinces based on linguistic regions. In 1928, the all parties' conference, presided over by Motilal Nehru, appointed a committee to draft a constitution for a full and responsible government in India. The committee recommended that the principle governing the redistribution of provinces should be partly geographical, and partly economic and financial, but the main considerations must necessarily be the linguistic unity of the area concerned. The Calcutta Congress Session, in 1937, reaffirmed its policy of forming linguistic states, and recommended the formation of Andhra and Karnataka.[58] Thus, it was Hindi which was mostly used in the mainstream politics of nationalist mobilizations. However, there was a huge controversy surrounding what would be *the* national language of India—Hindi or Hindustani. Several national leaders like Gandhi, Nehru, and Rajendra Prasad were in favour of Hindustani but they were vehemently opposed by the *Hindi Sahitya Sammelan* and many other leaders like Govind Ballabh Pant, Purushottam Das Tandon, Seth Govind Das, Amarnath Jha, and others. And this issue remained highly contentious during the constituent assembly debate, which completely undermined the issues related to the other independent languages of the 'Hindi heartland'.[59] The other issue surrounding language politics in the 'Hindi heartland' that got popular support in the post-independence period was the *Angrezi virodhi andolan* or *Angrezi hatao andolan* (Movement against English). The political leadership of the region fought against the English *politically*; as they considered it a colonial hangover that must go. They hold it responsible for depriving the Hindi-speaking masses of better opportunities and employment. These political masters also made policies to the effect that ordinary students were deprived of English education but they unapologetically sent their children to English-medium schools. This makes the 'Hindi heartland' in India a fascinating linguistic scene to investigate the political economy of the languages; to investigate the politics of language through the contours of culture, mother tongue, political identity, and sociopolitical mobilizations. In this linguistic scene of the 'Hindi heartland' we have a nationalist, English-educated, middle-class, bilingual elites (English and Hindi; a few of them trilingual also with tacit support to Hindi), local or provincial bilingual elites (Hindi and their vernaculars also and not just Hindi), and then the large masses with little or no knowledge of Hindi let alone English. So, when nationalist consciousness and awakening were taking place, Hindi nationalism combined with Hinduism was also expanding its social and political base in the region. But apart from this, there existed and still exist many vernacular spheres which challenge the claims of Hindi nationalism by asserting their distinct and independent identity. This kind of linguistic politics creates a unique condition where at least three layers of linguistic interactions or assertions—English, Hindi, and local vernaculars—were/are taking place simultaneously and at times independently from each other. In the present study, I have tried to explore these in the context of Hindi and Maithili. In the Maithili linguistic sphere, there had been a simultaneous presence of Hindi and English and of Sanskrit and Urdu. Still, Hindi enjoys a privileged position in public spaces—such as schools, markets, universities, offices, public transport, and so forth. But, this status of Hindi was often envied and at times challenged by the Maithili protagonists. Although Hindi does enjoy more prestige as the rashtra bhasha in the Maithili-speaking region, its opposition is stiffer when the legitimate status and spaces of Maithili are usurped by the supporters of Hindi.

Social Expansion of Hindi and the Maithili Movement

In India, there has been identity formations on the basis of language to an unprecedented scale during the anti-colonial struggle and immediately after the first and second decade of independence. Since then, there has been a succession of linguistic movements which have at times seemed to be on the point of challenging the unity of the country. However, most of the existing literatures on language politics in India is confined to Hindi versus Urdu or Hindi versus Hindustani or Hindi versus English. There is hardly any critical scrutiny of the language politics in the 'Hindi heartland' when it comes to the interrelationships between the 'national' language Hindi and its so-called 'varieties'; or the processes of linguistic 'assimilation'.[60] How did these other existing languages respond to the challenges of the social and political expansion of Hindi in the region?[61] Was there any resistance to such an expansion? In this study, I have tried to understand these in the context of the dynamic interrelationships between Hindi and Maithili. Here, the relationship between the two can be seen as not of complete opposition but that of ambivalence. In other words, as such there has not been enmity between the two. However, Maithili speakers have been very conscious of the independent and distinct identity of Maithili since the very beginning and have been resisting any attempts to classify it as a 'dialect' of Hindi.

The present work is undertaken with an objective to explore the newer aspects of the language politics emerging within the 'Hindi heartland'. During the late nineteenth century and throughout the twentieth century, various kinds of identity formations were taking place. One such important formulation was based on language. At times, many identities were put together to give it a more acceptable and authoritative status. One such important combination was that of the language, religion, and nation. And these identities have been hierarchized and

re-hierarchized since then. Within the 'Hindi heartland' this combination of *Hindi, Hindu, Hindustan* gave rise to a new discourse on the
linguistic identity and political mobilizations based on language.
Throughout the twentieth century there have been various political
polarizations on this basis. This remains one of the most complex and
challenging issue since then. As I have mentioned, there have been several studies on the formation of such discourses and its correlation with
Muslim and Urdu debate particularly within 'Hindi heartland'. Recent
studies by Dalmia and Orsini put a historical perspective on such formations more critically. However, in the present work, I have studied
the dynamics that were at work when Hindi was expanding its social
and political base in the region and how the other linguistic communities responded to it. Secondly, throughout the history of the Maithili
movement, what we find is not just an opposition to Hindi's claim
of Maithili being its 'dialect' or the ambivalent relationship between
the two. But more appropriately, one can see a double movement. The
authority of Hindi was strengthening with its adaptation and promotion as the 'national' language. It was a language of opportunity too
within the Maithili-speaking region, at the same time as the Maithili
assertion was becoming more powerful with the making of a separate
Maithili linguistic community distinct from Hindi.

The text of Paul Brass, 'The Maithili Movement in North Bihar' in his
Language, Religion, and Politics in North India (1974) remains so far the
most brilliant work on the Maithili movement.[62] Broadly, studying the
movement during the first two decades after the independence of India,
Brass argues that, although, the objective conditions for differentiation
from the other movements in terms of language and culture was available to the Maithili movement, it lacked the subjective consciousness
amongst its leaders and speakers. According to him, in the absence of
a strong political organization, the Maithili movement remained very
weak and unorganized. However, Brass's study is not only limited in
terms of its engagement with the historical trajectories of the Maithili
movement but he also fails to understand how the Maithili identity
has been evolving and disseminating, cutting across the boundaries of caste, gender, and religion for more than a century. Secondly,
taking the instrumental approach to study linguistic movements like
Maithili and considering it merely as an instrument in the hands of the
elite for political manipulations clearly undermines the cultural and

psychological roots of these movements which sustain them over the long period. How can one explain the existence of the Maithili movement for more than a century if it was/is merely an instrument in the hands of the elite? Of course, it is difficult to argue that there were/ are no such aspirations of the elite attached with this movement but certainly there exists something more than that in such struggles for recognition of a language.

In this work, I have studied the trajectories of the Maithili movement historically, from the middle of the nineteenth century, to its recognition as an independent modern Indian language and its inclusion in the eighth schedule of the Indian Constitution in 2003. I have studied its success and challenges in terms of the inclusion of various castes and classes of Maithili society within the fold of the movement. And finally, I have examined the gradual assertion of the movement for a separate statehood for Mithila in its most recent and contemporary phase.

Thus, through the study of Maithili language and movement in the 'Hindi heartland', I have sought to revisit the dynamic hierarchy that was produced during the expansion of 'national' language in the region, that is, between Hindi and other languages like Maithili, Braj, Awadhi, Bhojpuri, Magadhi, and so forth. I have also explored the formation and evolution of the modern Maithili community—distinct from its own traditional self; and externally, how it distinguishes itself from other emerging linguistic communities like Hindi. In this way, I have tried to explore how a community engaged with 'our modernity' and in the process, recreated itself and how that process is fraught with the various challenges of religion, nation, and nationalism—provincial or parochial. In other words, the Maithili language movement is studied from the point view of a community which, at the height of national movement, when Hindi was expanding its social and political base in India, accepted Hindi as the 'national' language but at the same time, fought relentlessly for its own recognition as an independent language. And this movement has been quite successful in getting such recognition, although Hindi's expansion in the region is still unabated.

It is essential to engage more seriously with the language issue as a social and political phenomenon, particularly the way in which it was played out in the context of the nation state in India and how it continues to raise consciousness among the people about their linguistic, cultural, and community identity. The study of language politics is also deeply connected with the important issues in a society like power, intersection of leaderships and sociopolitical structure, and finally politics. It is interesting to note how a speech categorized as 'language' or 'dialects' is not based on the sole criteria of linguistics per se, but it depends mostly on the level of consciousness within that speech community, the mobilization skills of its leaders/elite, wider national politics, and the development of other languages in the region. Whether Maithili was/is a mass movement or not is difficult to answer. The answer to it is somewhat complicated. Perhaps, it can be classified as a cultural and literary movement, although political demands have been always part of the Maithili movement. But, if one looks at its organizational set-up, mass support, leaderships, and demands, which have been so weak, loose, and inconsistent, that it can be hardly classified as a movement in the broader sense of the term. However, there has been a persistent mobilization and politicization of the Maithili issue since its inception. In the contemporary phase when the demand for separate statehood is increasingly being asserted and many people are associating with the movement, there are also several people who distance themselves from it claiming that they are activists of the literary movement and the statehood vis-à-vis political movement in Mithila is separate from the literary movement. It is interesting, though, to note that although they do not actively participate in the movement for separate statehood for Mithila, but they do not oppose such demands.

Most Maithili speakers remained indifferent towards the Maithili movement. Politically they are still less conscious about these demands—though things have been changing now; even the Hindi dailies in the Maithili-speaking region report about Maithili and Mithila demands. However, within Maithili-speaking regions in public places like markets, railway stations, universities, schools, and colleges, it is Hindi which has the upper hand in comparison to Maithili. There is also some degree of social prestige that is usually associated with Hindi or for that matter the 'foreign' language English. However, in informal speech and discussions it is Maithili which is mostly used. In the villages, and in the households, even in the cities it is Maithili which is widely in use. These include all the castes, classes, and religious groups, including the Muslims in the Maithili-speaking region. However, the younger generations in urban households are increasingly 'switching over' to Hindi even in their households and informal speeches.

Unlike the linguistic movements in the Deccan and south India, like Tamil, Telugu, Marathi, we do not find the Maithili movement ever coming as close to these movements in terms of their mass support and agitations to the extent of self-immolations and linguistic riots. The major strategies of the Maithili movement have been very different. By resorting to methods like petitioning, presenting memoranda, and putting pressure on the government through mass mobilizations, the Maithili movement remained a peaceful literary cultural movement for a very long time. It was operating under a very knotty situation where it had to face challenges from the supporters of Hindi on the one hand, and persistent indifferent attitudes of the large number of Maithili speakers on the other. Even the rich landlords, including the Maharajas of Darbhanga, were in favour of Hindi despite their affinities with Maithili. The emerging middle class of Maithili speakers shared an ambiguous relationship with Hindi. Although, they were aware of the richness and distinct identity of Maithili, they sided with Hindi and considered it as not just a national language but also as a language of opportunities. In this situation, the struggle for the recognition of Maithili as an independent language distinct from Hindi was carried out by a small section of Maithils, most of whom were also Sanskritists. In addition to this, its assertion and development as an independent Indian language had not only been discouraged but also suspected. However, the character of the movement began to change from the 1980s and mass protests, demonstrations, and protest marches became the major strategies in its struggle for inclusion in the eighth schedule of the Indian Constitution.

The other important feature of the Maithili movement has been its accommodative approach to Hindi. It appears that Maithili speakers have reconciled with the status of Hindi as 'national' language of India. They opposed Hindi only when it posed a threat to the independent status of Maithili. Thus, unlike Tamil or Telugu movements in the South, speakers of Maithili never became the exclusive subject of Maithili. And yet it would be wrong to argue, as Paul Brass did, that Maithili speakers lacked the subjective consciousness and therefore despite the favourable objective conditions they failed to create a separate Mithila state based on Maithili. If that were the case, the Maithili movement would not have survived for more than a century now. In fact, contrary to Brass's arguments, I wish to argue that the Maithili movement in 'Hindi heartland' remains a very successful movement. Given the political and historical conditions of the 'Hindi heartland', the Maithili movement has been successful not only in meeting all its demands, but it has been increasingly politicized and presently it continues to mobilize the masses for separate statehood for Mithila. I also wish to argue that movements like Maithili or for that matter Bhojpuri, Awadhi, Khari Boli, Magadhi, Bundelkhandi and so forth can be better explained and understood through the application of the theoretical framework of James Scott's[63] *Weapons of the Weak*, rather than by comparing them with any other 'successful' language movements and then pointing out the lack of one or the other elements for their 'failures'. These movements may or may not succeed but they do resist and their form of resistances differs depending upon the conditions of their existence. More nuanced and critical explorations of these linguistic movements, no matter how small, against all forms of dominations and appropriations, will, I believe enrich our understanding of language politics and how they have engaged with the trajectories of modernity and nationalist imaginations in modern India.

Notes and References

1. For example, see a poem by the founding father of modern Hindi, Bhartendu Harischandra, 'Matri bhasha ke Prati', available at http://www.anubhuti-hindi.org/dohe/bhartendu.htm; accessed on 24 January 2016, 10 a.m. Here, he declares that progress of one's language is key to all progress (*nij bhasha unnati ahai sab unnati ki mool*).
2. Benedict Anderson, *Imagined Communities: Reflections on the Origin and Spread of Nationalism* (London: Verso, 1991), p. 66; for the critique to this second feature of nationalism see Partha Chatterjee, *Nation and Its Fragments* (Delhi: Oxford University Press, 1995); here he criticized Anderson by arguing that if the 'model' were already available for the newer nationalism then what was left for them to imagine?
3. Anderson, *Imagined Communities*, pp. 44–5.
4. Seton H. Watson, *Language and National Consciousness* (London: British Academy, 1981); cited in Anderson, *Imagined Communities*, pp. 74–5.
5. For debates on the official and national language in India and controversy surrounding it, see Granville Austin, *Indian Constitution: Cornerstone of a Nation* (New Delhi: Oxford University Press, 2009) and Jyotindra Das Gupta, *Language Conflict and National Development: Group Politics and*

National Language Policy in India (Berkeley, CA: University of California Press, 1970).

6. The eighth schedule of the Indian Constitution now contains 22 scheduled languages. Originally it had only 14 languages. The most recent inclusions in the list are the Maithili, Santhali, Dogri, and Bodo languages in 2002. There are many linguistic communities which are still struggling for such recognition. Bhojpuri, the other major language in the 'Hindi heartland', is currently struggling for recognition as an independent language and demanding its inclusion into the eighth schedule of the Indian Constitution. It has a considerable social support base and also the back-up of such demands from the various political parties.

7. Vinayak Damodar Savarkar, *Essentials of Hindutva* (first published in 1923), available at http://www.savarkar.org/en/hindutva-hindu-nationalism/essentials-hindutva; and also, Dhananjay Keer, *Veer Savarakar* (Mumbai: Popular Prakashan, 1966).

8. A. Raghuram Raju, 'Problematising Nationalism,' *Economic and Political Weekly*, vol. 28, nos 27/28 (3–10 July 1993).

9. Chatterjee, *Nation and Its Fragments*; Orsini, *The Hindi Public Sphere*; Dalmia, *Nationalization of Hindu Traditions*; Rai, *Hindi Nationalism*; just to name a few major studies done on these lines.

10. Lisa Mitchell has argued about how the language of the region became the language of the masses in her recent work on the Telugu language; see Lisa Mitchell *Language, Emotion, and Politics in South India* (Ranikhet: Indiana University Press, 2010).

11. It is true to some extent that for a very long time this region did dominate the political life of the nation, both in the executive and in the legislature. And it did lead to a sense of exclusion in south and north-east India.

12. John Edwards, *Language, Society, and Identity* (Basil Blackwell in association with Andre Deutsch, 1985), p. 18.

13. Edwards, *Language, Society, and Identity*, p. 20.

14. For details on the complexities involved in the classification of Indo-Aryan languages as language and dialects, see Colin P. Masica, *Indo-Aryan Languages* (Cambridge: Cambridge University Press, 1991), pp. 23–7.

15. Edwards, *Language, Society, and Identity*, pp. 17–18.

16. Johann Gottfried Herder, 'Treatise on the Origin of Language', in Michael N. Forster (ed.), *Herder Philosophical Writings* (Cambridge: Cambridge University Press, 2002) (1772), available at http://www.marxists.org/archive/herder/1772/origins-language.htm; accessed on 22 July 2012.

17. Herder, 'Treatise on the Origin of Language', in Michael N. Forster (ed.), *Herder Philosophical Writings*, p. 48.

18. Katerina Clark and Michael Holquist, 'Marxism and the Philosophy of Language', in their eds., *Mikhail Bakhtin* (Cambridge, MA: Harvard University Press, 1984), pp. 212–37. This same text *Marxism and the Philosophy of Language* was published by Bakhtin in 1929 under a pseudonym, Volosinov.

19. V.N. Volosinov, 'Marxism and the Philosophy of Language', trans. Ladislav Matejika and I.R. Titunik, New York, *Seminar Press* (1973); 24; cited in Clark, Katerina and Michael Holquist, 'Marxism and the Philosophy of Language', p. 220.

20. Clark and Holquist, 'Marxism and the Philosophy of Language', p. 221.

21. Clark and Holquist, 'Marxism and the Philosophy of Language', p. 232.

22. Pierre Bourdieu, *Language and Symbolic Power* (Cambridge MA: Harvard University Press, 1991), p. 41.

23. Bourdieu, *Language and Symbolic Power*, p. 43.

24. Bourdieu, *Language and Symbolic Power*, p. 46.

25. Edwards, *Language, Society, and Identity*, p. 19.

26. Asha Sarangi (ed.), *Language and Politics in India* (Delhi: Oxford University Press, 2009).

27. Sarangi (ed.), *Language and Politics in India*, p. 1.

28. The relation between a vernacular and language is as difficult to ascertain as between a language and 'dialects'. Its definition in socio-linguistics is far from settled. It is generally understood as a language form which is used by the common people in their day-to-day informal conversations and is different from the cultivated, standard, or literary language. So, the same people may use one language in literary expressions or in formal administrative set-ups and another in their informal day-to-day conversations. This linguistic scenario is also termed as *diglossia*.

     However, it is equally true that with the passage of time a number of vernaculars have developed, particularly after its association with the idea of nation and nationalism, into standard and cultivated literary languages. The history of modern languages in Europe—English, French, German, and Italian—are major examples of this. In the Indian context too, this process started much earlier, but its consolidation and assertion for distinct identity began from the middle of the nineteenth century. And the colonial exercise of enumerations and classifications formed the basis for such consolidations. For more on this, see Chapter 2, and also Asha Sarangi, 'Enumeration and the Linguistic Identity Formation in Colonial North India', *Studies in History*, vol. 25, no. 2, n.s. (2009): 197–227.

29. For more on this see, John D. Windhausen, 'The Vernaculars, 1835–1839: A Third Medium for Indian Education,' *Sociology of Education*, vol. 37, no. 3 (Spring 1964): 254–70.

30. Dennis Dalton, *Indian Idea of Freedom: Political Thought of Swami Vivekananda, Aurobindo Ghose, Mahatma Gandhi, and Rabindranath Tagore* (Cambridge, MA: The Academic Press, 1982).

31. E. Annamalai, *Managing Multilingualism in India: Political and Linguistic Manifestations* (Delhi: Sage Publications, 2001), p. 35.

32. Christopher King, *One Language Two Scripts: The Hindi Movement in Nineteenth Century North India* (Mumbai: Oxford University Press, 1994); Alok Rai, *Hindi Nationalism* (New Delhi: Orient Longman, 2001); Veena Naregal, *Language Politics, Elites and the Public Sphere* (New Delhi: Permanent Black, 2001); Francesca Orsini, *The Hindi Public Sphere: Language and Literature in the Age of Nationalism* (Delhi: Oxford University Press, 2002).

33. Sheldon Pollock, 'The Cosmopolitan Vernacular', *The Journal of Asian Studies*, vol. 57, no. 1 (1998): 6.

34. Pollock, 'India in the Vernacular Millennium: Literary Culture and Polity, 1000–1500', *Daedalus*, vol. 127, no. 3, Early Modernities (Summer 1998): 41.

35. Pollock, 'The Cosmopolitan Vernacular'.

36. Pollock, 'India in the Vernacular Millennium', p. 49.

37. Pollock, 'The Cosmopolitan Vernacular'; 'India in the Vernacular Millennium'.

38. Raziuddin Aquil and Partha Chatterjee (eds), 'Introduction', in *History in the Vernacular* (Ranikhet: Permanent Black, 2008).

39. Aquil and Chatterjee, 'Introduction', in their eds., *History in the Vernacular*, p. 23.

40. According to the Census of India 1991, the list also included Maithili here but later it was added to a special category with a total number of speakers 7,776,597, which is less than the total number of Magadhi speakers of 1,056,642; cited in Anvita Abbi, 'Vanishing Diversities and Submerging Identities: An Indian Case', in Asha Sarangi (ed.), *Language and Politics in India* (Oxford: Oxford University Press, 2009).

41. Krishna Kumar, 'Quest for Self-Identity: Cultural Consciousness and Education in Hindi Region, 1880–1950,' *Economic and Political Weekly*, vol. 25, no. 23 (9 June 1990): 1247; here, Krishna Kumar also discusses the role of journalism in creating a distinct sense of community among the heterogeneous urban middle class. This middle class 'consisted of salaried professionals and office clerks, merchant groups, property owners in towns, and rural landowners with urban links. Heterogeneous though this educated town-based society was in terms of its economic character, it was mainly upper caste, dominated by Brahmins and Kayasthas'. Also see

his *Political Agenda of Education: A Study of Colonialist and Nationalist Ideas* (New Delhi: Sage Publications, 1991).

42. Bernard S. Cohn, 'The Command of Language and Language of Command', in his *Colonialism and Its Forms of Knowledge* (Princeton: Princeton University Press, 1996).

43. David Lelyveld, 'Colonial Knowledge and the Fate of Hindustani', *Comparative Studies in Society and History*, vol. 35, no. 4 (October 1993): 668.

44. Lelyveld, 'Colonial Knowledge and the Fate of Hindustani', 669–70. For more on this important formulation, see Michel Foucault, *The Order of Things* (New York: Vintage, 1973).

45. Lelyveld, 'Colonial Knowledge and the Fate of Hindustani', p. 668.

46. For more on this, see Farina Mir, *The Social Space of Language: Vernacular Culture in British Colonial Punjab* (Berkeley, CA: University of California Press, 2010).

47. Orsini, *The Hindi Public Sphere*, p. 126.

48. Orsini, *The Hindi Public Sphere*, p. 126.

49. Vasudha Dalmia, *The Nationalization of Hindu Traditions* (Delhi: Oxford University Press, 1997).

50. Dalmia, *The Nationalization of Hindu Traditions*, p. 94.

51. Dalmia, *The Nationalization of Hindu Traditions*, p. 147.

52. Dalmia, *The Nationalization of Hindu Traditions*, pp. 147–8.

53. Christopher King, *One Language Two Scripts: The Hindi Movement in Nineteenth Century North India* (Mumbai: Oxford University Press, 1994).

54. King, *One Language Two Scripts*, p. 2.

55. King, *One Language Two Scripts*, p. 2.

56. King, *One Language Two Scripts*, p. 15.

57. Cited in Orsini, *The Hindi Public Sphere*, p. 358.

58. Sajal Basu, *Regional Movements Politics of Language, Ethnicity-Identity* (New Delhi: Manohar Publishers, 1992), p. 28.

59. See Austin, *Indian Constitution*.

60. The process of assimilation can be understood as absorbing the difference into a particular kind of identity and also as re-hierarchizing the existing status of different identities; for example, see Dalmia, *The Nationalization of Hindu Traditions*.

61. In the context of Bihar, how regional languages played a crucial role in the promotion of modern standard Hindi and how their voices were marginalized and suppressed in the canonical history of modern Hindi, see Aishwarj Kumar, 'A Marginalized Voice in the History of Hindi', *Modern Asian Study*, vol. 47, no. 05 (September 2013): 1706–46.

62. Another work on this subject by Richard Burghart, 'A Quarrel in the Language Family: Agency and Representations of Speech in Mithila', *Modern Asian Studies*, vol. 27, no. 04 (October 1993): 761–804 is a serious attempt to understand the relationship between power culture and speech form in the context of Maithili. He also studied why for almost ten generations of census Maithili had been classified as a 'dialect'. This article is discussed in some detail in the next chapter.

63. James C. Scott, *Weapons of the Weak: Everyday Forms of Peasant Resistance* (New Haven, CT: Yale University Press, 1985).

1

British Rule and Classifications of Indian Languages

Making of Modern Enumerated *Communities*

Census, mapping, and the processes of enumerations and classifications provided the basis for many communities in India to organize, agitate, and demand more political power during the colonial and in the postcolonial times, based on language, religion, caste, and so on. The political trajectories in India have continuously witnessed and continue to witness such movements. As language proved to be more resilient in terms of binding the heterogeneous population emotionally and psychologically together, sometimes all other identities based on caste, gender, and religion are put together to make it a more authoritative and effective identity. The successes and failures of these movements depend on other factors as well, such as the consciousness of their speakers, but the structure for the possibilities of such imaginations as well as mobilizations were already put in place very effectively during the colonial rule in India.

This chapter explores the various ways through which Christian missionaries and the British officials attempted to classify Indian languages. How did these exercises form the basis for many groups in India to forge various identities? How did that lead to competing claims and counter claims by various communities and groups in modern India? Language turns out to be a powerful marker of group identity. The question of 'chaste' versus 'standard', 'written' versus 'oral', and language with or without grammar and literature became a politically and emotionally charged issue since the early nineteenth century. It has also led to the politics of linguistic dominations and subordinations as well as resistances to such processes.

During the colonial era, with the European discovery of Sanskrit and their increasing familiarities with its rich literary traditions and history, along with the introduction of comparative philology by Sir William Jones, a new kind of discourse began about the languages in India. It gave rise to a new zeal for learning various 'native' languages of India and of the world. The more important purpose for such an exercise was to convert something that was heterogeneous and bewildering into something that could be mapped and compared. And this was the reason that the questions of language and race were deeply connected and at times these two were used interchangeably too. These were at the centre of philological discourse in the eighteenth and nineteenth centuries.[1] Based on such a study, the objective was to create a world family of languages as one of the major language families in the world which eventually led to the formation of the Indo-European languages. Various languages hitherto unrelated and unknown to each other came to be categorized as part of the Indo-European language family. In this chapter, the following questions are explored—how do these classifications and the categories produced and affected various social and political groups under colonialism, and continue to do so in the postcolonial era? Have these groups overcome this colonial legacy or the grip of the latter have further strengthened?

British Rule and Classifications of Indian Languages

The British conquest of India was a conquest based on knowledge;[2] with the territorial conquest they also conquered an epistemological space[3] through which they legitimized their rule by producing knowledge for and about India not only for the non-Indians abroad but for the Indians as well. It was this victory at the epistemological level that provided the basis for the durable sustenance of British rule in India. Through the practices of census, mapping, and district gazetteers, the colonial government established the 'logic of numbers' in Indian social, cultural, and political discourse.[4] And through it they also produced newer categories to make sense of this vast unfamiliar world to govern them better. This logic was applied to the classifications of languages too.

The knowledge produced by the Christian missionaries, colonial administrators, and orientalists[5] was considered to be superior in the

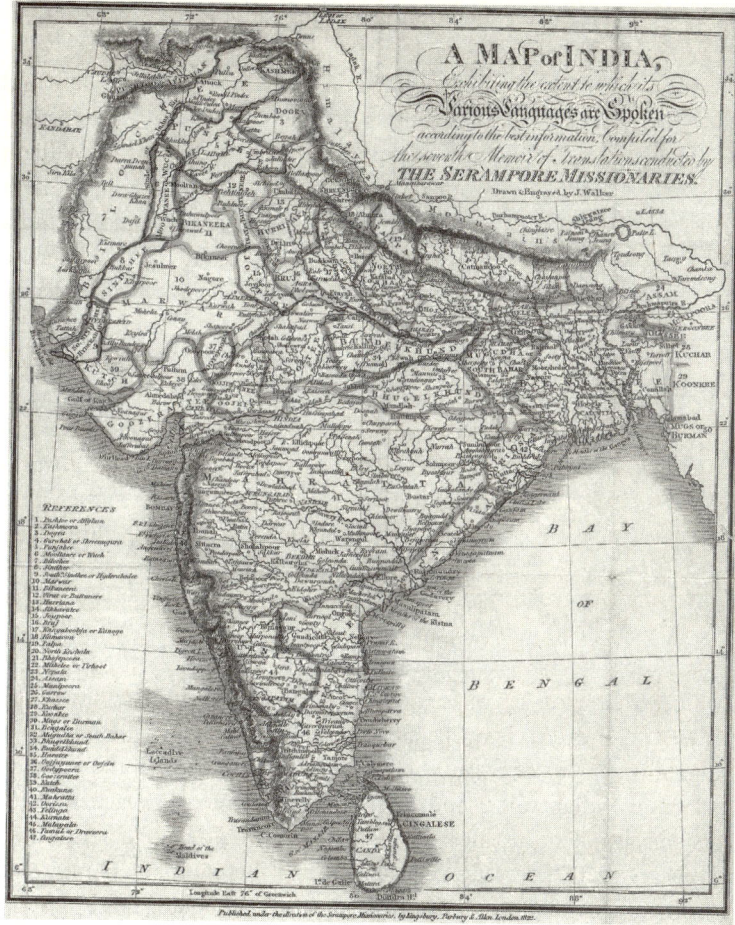

Map 1.1 A Map of India Exhibiting the Extent to which Its Various Languages Are Spoken, 1822

Source: Centre for the Study of Life and Work of William Carey, D.D. (1761–1834). Hattiesburg, Mississipi: William Carey University.

Note: Map not to scale and does not represent authentic international boundaries.

hierarchy of knowledge.[6] The mastery over the languages was inevitable in the production of such knowledge. In the process, language acquired a new form, and became a powerful tool, not only for the missionaries, administrators, or orientalists and Indologists but for Indians too. In the beginning, the missionary and non-missionary linguistic works 'resulted in representations of languages as powerful icons of spiritual, territorial, and historical hierarchies that emerged in the colonial societies'.[7] This new avatar of language continues to haunt society and politics in postcolonial India as well.

The British, for their part, did not have a consistent linguistic policy in India as such. Their approach to Indian languages varied and was purely based on the calculation of their interests. At different junctures of their rule in India, they promulgated different policies towards Indian languages. Gradually, by the end of the nineteenth century, they undertook the mammoth exercise of mapping, classifying, and fixing the boundaries of each language and putting them in one or the other linguistic family. Before that, it was mostly the Christian missionaries, particularly the Serampore Mission at Kolkata, which played a critical role in the classifications of and publications in Indian languages. The colonial exercises of mapping and classifications were always embodied in the larger politics and policies of the colonial rule in India. These exercises not only 'enumerated' the earlier 'fuzzy' world (more on this later) for the colonialists and hence made its rule more effective, but it also played an important role during the nationalist movement and continues to influence the postcolonial Indian politics and society.

Since their status as a major mercantile European company, the British realized the need to learn Persian—the court and official language of Mughal India—to carry out their trade negotiations with the Mughals and other Indian rulers and to seek their favour. However, learning Persian was not an easy task.[8] Thus, before the battle of Plassey (1757), it appears that there were very few among the company's employees having sufficient knowledge of Persian or any other languages of India. Even Robert Clive (1725–1774) did not know any Indian language with the exception of the Portuguese trade language.[9] It was only after the battle of Plassey that the British began to seriously study Indian classical languages—Arabic, Persian, and Sanskrit, and also various 'vulgar' languages of India.[10] According to Cohn, it was during the period of 1770 to 1785, when the colonialists seriously began to 'study' Indian languages in order to make their rule durable. Through the apparatuses of grammars, dictionaries, treatises, class books, and translations about and from the Indian languages, the British initiated a larger process in India besides consolidating their rule. The introduction of grammars and dictionaries to learn Indian languages was not just for Europeans;

even the native speakers of that language had to follow the same if they were to use their own language 'correctly'.[11]

However, it was the Christian missionaries and evangelists, who were at the forefront of mapping and classifying Indian languages. They also published voluminous works in local languages/dialects and scripts. It included mainly the translations of the Bible and many other religious books, including those of the local culture, history, and community.[12] They also prepared fonts for various scripts and made print available in various modern vernacular languages and 'dialects' in India. When the British rulers in India undertook the task of 'studying' and 'classifying' Indian languages more 'objectively' and 'systematically' at the larger level, covering all of India through census and mapping under the supervision of George A. Grierson, they were in many ways extending the work done by these Christian missionaries. Of course, there were lots of complexities, contradictions, and contestations involved in such processes. The making of 'standard' languages led to endless tensions and confrontations often among the speakers of the same language.

The British, especially the company officials, were not learning the languages of India out of curiosity but due to compulsions. For them, the knowledge of Persian became necessary precisely because they had to carry out trade negotiations with the Mughals and other Indian princely states in this language. They had considered it as the language of politics. Now, after the battle of Plassey, the British were trying to consolidate their rule in India; they realized it was necessary to know the other languages, religions, and culture especially of the 'Gentoos' (Hindus), who were in the majority. There may be some scholarly curiosity among a few British administrators to learn the languages of India to unlock its 'mysterious past', but largely they were motivated to learn Sanskrit out of an immediate practical necessity of running a smooth administration of justice in Bengal. Sir William Jones' initial reluctance and later enthusiasm to learn Sanskrit make this point even clearer. He started learning the language to better administer justice in India. They were suspicious of Maulvis and Pandits as the intermediaries in the administration of justice. According to Warren Hastings' plan of 1792, 'India should be governed by Indian Principles, particularly in relation to law. Following current practice in Bengal, which was a Muslim-ruled state, the British accepted Muslim criminal law as the law of the land, but civil law was to be Hindu for Hindus and Muslim for the Muslims.'[13]

With the inspiring studies of Sanskrit and other classical works of India by Sir William Jones, a new curiosity developed about learning the languages of the world in the form of comparative philology. There were systematic and sincere attempts to establish the relationships between and among the languages and races of the world. There also developed a new category in the study of the languages—the Indo-European language family. A family tree of the world language was created in which all the languages of the world were classified and hierarchized. Jones in 1786, clearly articulated the concept of an Indo-European language family 'as a group of related languages consisting of Sanskrit, Latin, Greek, Gothic, Celtic, and Old Persian, condescended from a lost ancestral language, although he did not give this language family a name. The "original stock" that spoke the ancestral language he simply called Indian or Hindu'.[14] There were also various contestations regarding the name of this language family. According to Thomas R. Trautman, in the early nineteenth century, there were at least four different names for this language family and the people who spoke this language:

> from the Bible narrative of Noah and his three sons, Shem, Ham, and Japheth, came the name Japhetic for this family; unlike the coordinate names Semitic and Hamitic, which are still in use for language families, the name Japhetic did not last long. German Philologists preferred 'Indo-Germanic' devised by Heinrich Klaproth in 1823, but non-Germans resisted. The English linguist Arthur Young proposed 'Indo-European' as early as in 1813, and it eventually displaced the other terms.[15]

This kind of development had a lot to do with the legitimization of the colonial rule. The study of the Indo-European languages family went hand in hand with the establishment of affinities among various languages and races, and 'colonial linguists' became a mediator between the colonizer and colonized people. There also emerged a new kind of study among Europeans, especially among the 'German Romantics' (*wissenschaft*) to bridge the gap between the 'occident' and the 'orient', considering them as the lost brothers who had to reunite again, and to establish the Aryan as the common ancestor of both the civilizations. This also led to a new kind of political formulation in Europe, especially in Germany, where the concept of the 'superiority of the Aryan race' provided an impetus for the politics of exclusion and reaffirmation of this superiority through conquering other nations within Europe and bringing them under one 'superior empire'.[16]

The study of comparative philology and 'classical Sanskrit' enhanced European power in Asia. In India, Jones's whole project was to study its classical language Sanskrit to provide 'authentic' and 'pure' laws through which Indians can be better governed. In the process, there emerged an 'ideology of antiquity' in which the ancient period was considered to be the golden period in Indian history and successive periods were regarded as degenerations and perversions from that golden past. This project of classical studies was also in continuity with the Europeans' discovery of the classical Greek texts of Plato and Aristotle, among many others. This was applied to the mythical texts as well, the more antique the texts were the more pure and authoritative they were regarded. Those texts written in the later periods were considered to be either 'impure' or 'perverted'.

G.A. Grierson's *Linguistic Survey of India* was a major development and culmination of the colonial project of classification and standardizations of the Indian languages. Many anti-colonial and postcolonial linguistic movements derive their strengths and weaknesses from this epoch-making work, the significance of which can be understood from the words of the author himself, who writes that, 'what has been done in it for India has been done for no other country in the world'.[17] One of the striking examples of the influence of such classifications is the Maithili language movement in north Bihar. In this work, Grierson classified Maithili as a 'dialect' of the no-one's language which he named *Bihari*. According to Grierson, the Bihari language consisted of Maithili, Bhojpuri, and Magadhi. Although in his other works,[18] Grierson did consider Maithili as having its own independent and distinct literary history and culture. However, his classification in the linguistic survey became the authoritative, official stand on the status of the Maithili language for many years to come. I shall explore the consequences of this on the Maithili language and the movement, and how it has emerged from that status and asserted its independence, in other chapters. Here it is very important to understand the rationale underlying the linguistic survey; how it categorized the past works on the subject; and compiled and classified the languages of India.

Grierson writes that in the seventeenth and eighteenth centuries, there were serious misconceptions about the number of Indian languages.[19] According to him, there were serious attempts to systematically and objectively classify Indian languages and every decade, data on or about the Indian languages were collected, but no scientific study of these was possible. Before Grierson, William Carey (1761–1834), Joshua Marshman (1768–1837), T.H. Colebrook (1765–1837), John Beams (1837–1902), Hoernle (1841–1918), and Hodgson (1800/01–94) made sincere attempts to scientifically study and classify Indian languages. And these, according to Grierson, had significantly improved the European understanding about the existence of various vernaculars and the complex linguistic scenario in India.[20] Grierson's *Linguistic Survey of India* was the first systematic and comprehensive study of Indian languages undertaken by the colonial government to cover almost the whole length and breadth of the country. Interestingly, this was also a period when census and mapping was simultaneously undertaken by the British government, which produced an enormous amount of 'objective' knowledge on and about India.

The main method applied in the *Linguistic Survey* of Grierson was the collection of three specimens—a standard passage to be translated into every known dialect and subdialect of the area covered under operation; a piece of folklore or some other passage in narrative prose or verse, selected on the spot and taken down from the mouth of the speakers; and the list of words and sentences. The total number of the languages and dialects reported from the survey area was 231 and 774, respectively. However, after scrutiny, Grierson reduced it to 179 for the languages and 544 for the dialects. Grierson writes that the same languages were reported more than once and the same form of speech was reported many times under different names. It is interesting to note that he cited the Census of 1921, which listed 188 languages, the number of dialects being unknown. Now the major problem that he faced was the preparation of the list. He first collected the local lists of dialects and subdialects through the local officers and from this list, provincial lists were compiled and printed. These compilations, he himself claimed, were far from accurate as the officers who collected these numbers 'did not pretend to be philological experts'. Then,

> when the lists were printed, the dialects were divided into two main
> classes, distinguished by a difference of type, viz., (1) those which were
> vernaculars of the localities from which they were reported, and (2)
> those which were spoken by the foreigners in each locality. The latter

were once for all excluded, and attention was thenceforth devoted only to the former.[21]

He also confessed the difficulties in deciding,

> where a given form of speech is to be looked upon as an independent language, or as a dialect of some other definite form of speech. In practice, it has been found that it is sometimes impossible to decide the question in a manner which will gain universal acceptance. .... [I]n common use we may say that, as a general rule, different dialects of the same language are sufficiently alike to be reasonably well understood by all whose native tongue is that language, while different languages are so unlike that special study is needed to enable one to understand a language that is not his own.[22]

However, he was not convinced by this explanation regarding the Aryan languages of north India, and he writes:

> mutual intelligibility cannot always be the deciding factor, for the consideration is obscured by the fact that between Bengal and the Punjab every individual who received the very slightest education is bilingual. In his own home, and in his own immediate surroundings he speaks a local idiom, but in his intercourse with strangers he employs or understands some form of that great lingua franca, Hindi or Hindostani.[23]

Given this complexity of the linguistic scenario, for the linguistic survey, Grierson classified the languages based on their grammatical systems into three groups, each of which is given the dignity of a language—Bihari, Eastern Hindi, and Western Hindi. This kind of division was based on the grammatical structure and nationality factor, although he was in favour of separating the philology from the ethnology. He was also aware of the difficulties in fixing the boundaries of the language. He writes:

> As a rule, unless they are separated by great ethnic differences, or by some natural obstacles, such as a range of mountains or a large river, Indian languages gradually merge into each other and are not separated by hard and fast boundary lines. When such boundaries are spoken of, or are shown on a map, they must always be understood as conventional methods of showing definitely a state of things which is in its essence indefinite.[24]

After British colonial administrators established 'Hindustani as the language of command'[25] in India, they began to impose it throughout north India, considering it as the lingua franca of the region. They hardly took any further interest to understand or develop any other language of the region, be it Bhojpuri, Braj, Awadhi, Maithili, or Magadhi. It was largely the native speakers of these languages who continuously strove to forge a collective community identity based on their languages. In doing so, they did rely upon colonial practices. In fact, the association of each language with a community or region was the outcomes of the colonial practices of census and mapping. The association of language and script with a religious community was initiated by the Christian missionaries and was tacitly promoted by British rule as well. Of course, later developments of linguistic politics in India were led by the nationalist elites themselves. However, the process for the growth of such practices and perceptions were already set.

In the 'Hindi heartland', the politics of language took a different turn where an increasing polarization took place on the issue of the Hindi–Urdu controversy.[26] Clearly the language divide led to a communal divide where Hindi now became the language of all the Hindus and Urdu that of the Muslims. This was clearly a move to transform the multilingual social and cultural milieu of colonial North India into a model where a community spoke only one language, and was confined to a region. In this model, all the other languages of the region, no matter how old their literatures were or how distinct their speech was, began to be classified as 'varieties' of Hindi. Ramchandra Shukla's *Hindi Sahitya Ka Itihas*[27] provided the much needed historicity for making such claims. The speakers of these other languages of the region now had to face an enormously tough situation in which they were struggling to maintain and preserve the distinctiveness of their languages. So, while many of them had the consciousness of such distinctiveness, very few made such claims openly and assertively. Does it allow us to think that they were only conscious of Hindi and wanted to learn it even at the cost of their own languages? If that were the case then how can we understand the case of Maithili, or Bhojpuri, or for that matter Awadhi and Khari Boli or any other 'varieties' of Hindi in the region?

Thus, for the colonialist, generally the question of language was important so long as it helped them in the consolidation and maintenance of the Raj. They increasingly denied, particularly in the 'Hindi heartland', the suitability of any languages other than Hindi/

Hindustani or Urdu for the language of administration and of educa-tion. The division of Hindi and Urdu was not the result of colonial linguistic policy alone. However, the British recognition of Hindi and Urdu as two separate and mutually exclusive languages was consistent with their overall strategy of the maintenance of colonial rule. In fact, after their relentless and tumultuous pursuit of 'studies' on or about Indian languages and its diversity, it was eventually Hindustani which turns out to be the 'language of command'. Many nationalists, such as Gandhi, Nehru, and Rajendra Prasad were also in favour of mak-ing Hindustani the national language of India and they vigorously but unsuccessfully mobilized public opinion for the same.

Debates over the Status of Language: Classical versus Vernacular and Oral versus Written

The more institutionalized and systematic study of Indian languages was inaugurated with the establishment of Fort William College at Kolkata in 1800. The college was established to train the young staff of the company in the history, customs, languages, laws, and religions of India. Initially, there were four departments—Sanskrit–Bengali; Arabic; Persian; and Hindustani. It was during this time that a debate started about the study of classical languages or the spoken vernaculars[28] of India. Gilchrist and William Carey both wanted the spoken vernaculars to be studied, explored, and classified. According to Cohn, the 'battle between classicists and vernacularists in relation to Hindustani was to continue throughout the nineteenth century. Each new dictionary or grammar that would appear caused argumentation. The missionary soon joined the officials of the company, and questions of scripts and source of borrowings or lexical items and for grammatical refinements became a politically charged issue.'[29] In this debate over the vernacular and clas-sical status of a language, often the status of a classical language began to be understood as a language which is no longer in popular use.[30]

John Gilchrist was appointed as the Professor of Hindustani; beside him there were a few Indian scholars. The notable among them were Inshallah Khan, Sadal Mishra, and Lalooji Lal. It was here that numer-ous books on languages, literature, grammars, and lexicography in the Indian vernaculars were published. The study of Hindustani—the lan-guage of command—was the most favoured subject at the institute, but it gradually led to the creation of two separate languages—Hindi and Urdu. According to Alok Rai,

> The important thing that emerged from Fort William is the idea of two-ness, of linguistic duality. Fort William College gave institutional recognition to the notion that there were in-fact two ways of doing Hindustani–One which used the available and mixed language, and another from which the Arabic-Persian words had been removed in order to produce a language more suitable to Hindus.[31]

Fort William instantly acquired an authoritative status on the languages of India. Soon, it was seen both as the visible symbol of the imperial policy of divide and rule through linguistics and other divisions including religion and caste; or alternatively, as the official recognition of the 'neglected' linguistic tradition which came into its own as modern Hindi—the language of most Hindus.

The actual process of replacing Persian—the language of Mughal administration—with the local vernaculars, shows considerable local variations. This decision to replace Persian with the vernaculars was the main reason for the standardization of modern Indian languages. Rai argues that,

> modern Bengali, or modern Marathi, or modern Tamil, must all recall the replacement of Persian (in 1832 in the Bombay and Madras Presidencies, in 1837 in Bengal Presidency, with the exception of Bihar, which was then a part of the Bengal Presidency) as a crucial moment. But their subsequent histories were subject to the specific cultural and demographic topographies of those regions.[32]

He further writes that '[i]n Bihar and in the central Provinces (now Madhya Pradesh), Hindustani in the Persian script began to be replaced by Hindi in the Nagari script in the 1870s and 1880s, while in the Punjab, Urdu (or Hindustani) and the Persian script retained their dominance until well into the twentieth century'.[33] For Alok Rai and many other scholars, the most crucial region for the linguistic division and identification of religion and culture with the language was the North Western Province and Oudh (that is, roughly modern Uttar Pradesh). 'It is here that the resistance was strongest, the struggle more intense, the cultural consequences most profound'.[34]

Another significant debate over the language status in the region was about the written, print, and hence 'standard' language on the one hand; and popular, uncultivated, and spoken language of the 'unlettered' and rustic people, mostly in the villages and in vicinities of the town, on the other. To study and classify the bewildering varieties of oral languages into a set model of a linguistic family and to scientifically organize them all to enable the comparative studies of languages and linguistic groups in India was one of the biggest challenges before the philologists. Such classifications of languages led to fierce debate and heated exchanges among the philologists as well as among the company officials. Despite their love for written and standard print languages, they were acutely aware of the rich oral traditions prevailing in regions which often encompass the exclusively defined linguistic boundaries. Hence, many of them supported oral against written and vernaculars against the classical language. Writing about the pre-modern and pre-print communities Alok Rai, believes that the

> pre-modern community ... was crucially an oral community. Unaffected by the imperatives of print-standardization, it was a community which worked through local 'borrowings' and 'neighbourly intelligibility', recognized and affirmed in flexible acts of oral communication that necessarily implicate both parties, communicator and communicate, in the labour of finding common ground. Printed communication, on the other hand, is intrinsically fixed–and unilateral.[35]

For S.W. Fallon (1817–1880), a great supporter of Hindustani and other vernaculars of India, languages in its written forms with their grammars are artificial and corrupt the natural growth of a language. He considered language in its written form as a privilege for the lettered class. These lettered classes admired the structural and constructed language over the rustic vernacular, and for them that was more real and expressive. But contrary to this, Fallon believed words uttered by rustics embody his thoughts, feelings, and sentiments, which he acquired through experience; and hence, it was more real and expressive. Regarding the Hindustani as used in written and spoken forms in nineteenth-century India, he writes:

> the wealth of the language is in the spoken tongue; and how rich and expressive that is, those best know who are familiar with the diversified phases of every-day speech of the impressionable and imaginative Oriental. The best part of the language cannot be left out, if the language is to be represented in its integrity. The living utterances of the people

are almost absent from the Dictionaries. Their place is filled instead by a great many Arabic, Persian, and Sanskrit words which are seldom or never used in written or spoken Hindustani...learned Moulvis and Pandits. These are the autocrats who have banished the people's mother tongue, and forged in its place the artificial language which divides the people and the ruling class. With might and main they have laboured to keep out the spoken vernacular from the written language of books and legal procedures and official correspondence; ... They refuse to admit these earliest friends of their youth into the new-found courts and palaces in which they have been installed by the royal favour. They speak one language in their houses, and another when they appear in the Public.[36]

One major tradition which was prevalent widely in the country before the penetration of printing technology during colonial era, were the strong oral traditions. This continues to exist in many parts of the country even today, including in Mithila. In these traditions, there are special relations between the *vakta* (speaker, scholar, or lettered person) and the *srota* (listener or unlettered person). There was little or no use of grammar and dictionaries to learn their own language and there was also less segmentation between the lettered and unlettered class. Transmission of knowledge was more direct and comprehensible in the concrete and localized community in comparison to the impersonal and imagined communities produced by the rapid publications of books, journals, magazines, and newspapers supported by print capitalism. Written texts were available, not in the form of books but in the form of manuscripts, which used to command a very different kind of value and possession than the publication of the finest book in the era of print. The relevance of this knowledge system was judged based on its applicability to the social, moral, and politico-economic betterment of the local community. 'Pathshala education was predominantly vocational, consisting of simple arithmetic, commercial, and agricultural accounts....'[37] Now with the introduction of modern education (English education; not only the language but also its contents and patterns) it seems to create a divide in the complementary role between education and its societal relevance, between lettered and unlettered masses that existed in oral traditions. Now the certificate given by the (colonial/postcolonial) government, rather than the societal test of knowledge through public debate, had/have become the sole criterion for judging 'merit'. It leads to a new kind of educational system, cut off from day-to-day social lives, where the relevance of any kind of knowledge is really tested. Through the new educational institutions of schools and universities, textbooks, literary spheres, quite distinct from the traditional modes of learning and dissemination of knowledge, a new literary elite have emerged who are not only cut off from their 'own traditions' but have also developed a sense of disgust for the same. Again, according to Fallon,

> (w)hile the pedantry of scholars, growing with the artificial wordiness it feeds on and the wide distinctions which it continually strives to make between themselves and the mass of the people, had caused the written language to diverge more and more from the spoken tongue—destined, however, with the return of a sounder taste, to converge again towards its prototype—the perennial stream of living speech of the unlettered mass has followed on ever in its own bed, self-sustained, self-moving, and apart.[38]

The oral and spoken forms of a language are its real treasure. These give the language longevity and allow it to adapt to newer challenges. Here, I wish to talk about Vidyapati (1350–1448), Sanskrit scholar, poet, musician, writer, diplomat, who is popular even today not because of his erudite Sanskrit texts but because of his innumerable songs that he composed in the vernacular language of the region—Maithili. For many scholars, it is his songs which keep him alive even today and he is remembered as *Kavikantahar* (people's poet). It was through his innumerable songs that Vidyapati could break literary barriers and directly touched the lives of the masses. His songs are deeply embedded in the day-to-day social and cultural lives of Mithila even today. This is one of the major reasons that Maithili withstood the pressure of expansionist Hindi.

Fallon criticized Maulvis and Pandits alike, because they bring strange words, known to them in the language they use, which keep them isolated from the masses. He also gave the example of Kabir—a sufi poet. How did his poems become very popular? It was due to his use of the words—Persian, Hindi, and Sanskrit—which were more commonly in use. So, it is evident from these explanations that a living language in the forms of oral speech was considered more real than a written or dead language. And yet, all the struggles over the issue of language in the nineteenth and twentieth centuries was the struggle over the written or published works in a language that became the criteria for a language's worth and not its rich oral traditions.

Maithili in Pre-colonial India

The earliest reference to the language of Mithila was *Avahatta* or *Mithila Apabhransha*.[39] This *Mithila Apabhransha* was distinct from Sanskrit and *Prakrit* both and referred to as *desil bayna*.[40] As the Mithila region was also called Tirabhukti and more popularly as Tirhut during the colonial era, its language was also referred to as Tirhutiya. It was also referred to as *Taurutiana* (*Tirhutiya*) in the *Alphabetum Brahmanicum* (1771). In this work Maithili was considered as one of the eight languages in India. Colebrook (1801) classified the language as Mythili. Thus, we find the close association of language and region here. Even when the term Maithili was popularized by Grierson for a very long time Maithili was referred to as Mithila Bhasa.[41]

Like many other modern vernaculars in India—Assamese and Bengali—Maithili speakers also trace the origin of their language to the texts of the *Charya Padas*.[42] Some scholars of Maithili—Jayakant Mishra (1922–2009) and Subhadra Jha (1909–2000)—claim it to be the ancient form of Maithili. Suniti Kumar Chatterjee (1890–1977) believed it to be the ancient form of Bengali. Many scholars of Assamese and Hindi also trace the origin of their languages to these *Charya Padas*. However, taking a cue from the recent works of Pollock,[43] one can argue that these claims and counter-claims cannot be resolved by either accepting or refuting any claims. The development and growth of modern Indian vernaculars that we use and know today, were part of a larger process when there was a gradual shift away from Sanskrit more decisively from the beginning of the tenth century. The development of each of these vernaculars took different trajectories; colonial rule and the introduction of modern print played a crucial role in shaping the modern forms of these languages.

Maithili, although claimed to be originated from the *Ardha-Magadhi*; and *Charya Padas* are reminiscent of ancient Maithili, is like Bengali and Assamese. It is also claimed that the scripts of all these three languages have originated from one common source. There are amazing similarities between these three scripts. The history of Maithili is divided into three parts—ancient (AD 1300–AD 1600), medieval

(AD 1600–AD 1860), and modern (AD 1860 onwards). This division of Maithili, as Jayakant Mishra has argued, is based on the political developments in Mithila. However, there are considerable differences among the Maithili scholars about the exact periodizations of Maithili literary history.[44] The period prior to AD 1300 is considered to be a period of proto-Maithili. As with the case of any other modern Indian languages, the forms of Maithili were also changing. But literary production continued unbroken, from Jyotirishwar's *Varnaratnakar*[45] to Vidyapati, Manabodh, Saheb Ramdas, Harshanath Jha, and Chanda Jha.[46] In Mithila, even when there were literary productions in Maithili, Sanskrit was still regarded as the language of learning and high philosophy. A great many number of treatises on philosophy, religion, laws, and politics were written in Sanskrit. In many Sanskrit dramas, dialogues were written in Maithili as well. Thus, Maithili was always in use but Sanskrit had a higher status. Even after the beginning of Islamic control, the rulers in Mithila remained somewhat autonomous, and philosophy and religious discourses continued to flourish.[47] But gradually the traditions of scholarly inquiry and debates declined and by the end of the nineteenth century there developed a lot of evil practices and social evils.[48] The social and cultural life of Mithila became utterly orthodox and static.

During the reign of the Mughal emperor Akbar, the authority to rule over the *Sircar-i-Tirhut* was given to Mahesh Thakur, the founder of the Khandawal dynasty (the last ruling dynasty of Mithila). Its last ruler was Maharaja Kameshwar Singh (1907–1962). This dynasty did provide a relatively stable and peaceful rule in Mithila. During the colonial period, after the permanent settlement, it was reduced to a zamindari. In 1860, when the Court of Wards took over the administration of the Darbhanga Raj, attempts were made to introduce Urdu and Hindi in the administration of the Raj and in the vernacular school education in the region.

Maithili did share affinities and intelligibility with the other languages of Bihar and Eastern India—Magadhi, Bhojpuri, Bengali, Oriya, Assamese, and Hindi.[49] Therefore, there were always confusions about classifying it as a dialect of Hindi or Bengali or Bihari. It continued to haunt the Maithili movement for recognition of Maithili as an independent language for many decades. Maithili has its own script—Mithilakshar or Tirhuta. It was once widely in use and a number of

Sanskrit texts were written in this script.[50] It is during the colonial rule and with it the introduction of modern print and the *Nagari Pracharani Sabha*'s attempts to promote the Nagari script for all modern Indian languages that Maithili adopted the Nagari script.[51] But this adoption of the Nagari script proved counterproductive as despite of such a rich and long literary history, Maithili had to fight a hard battle to get recognized as an independent language of modern India. One important basis for the denial of such a position to Maithili was that, 'it did not have a script of its own'. There were numerous attempts to classify it as a dialect of Hindi. The history of modern Maithili is thus a struggle against such appropriations by asserting its independence and adapting to and engaging with our 'colonial' modernity.

The Status of Maithili in the Colonial Classifications of Indian Languages

In the colonial estimates about Maithili, there are contradictory and at times ambiguous statements about its status as a language. Richard Burghart accurately observes this. He says that throughout the company rule, and in the early colonial period, Maithili remained poorly understood by European scholars. Looking westward from the company seat at Kolkata, Maithili (sometimes called Tirhuti) for Colebrook and William Carey appeared to be a dialect of Bengali. However, looking eastward from the Mughal Imperial seat at Delhi for philologists like Kellog and Hoernle, Maithili appeared to be a dialect of eastern Hindi. But this estimation of Maithili being a dialect of eastern Hindi was not without some misgivings. Therefore, a more accurate and precise perception about Maithili required the arrival of Grierson in Mithila.[52]

Although George Grierson spent considerable time in Mithila, enjoyed a first-hand experience of the spoken varieties of Maithili and its rich literary history, which not only enabled him to bring scholarly attention to its rich literary culture, write a *Grammar and Chrestomathy* (1881) of the language, and revive an interest in the language among its speakers, he was not consistent on his stand on Maithili. A number of leaders and activists of Maithili language movements acknowledged his role in the development of modern Maithili language. In fact, there is a market in Madhubani named after Grierson, which exist even today and is called *Gileshan* Bazar. But in his *An Introduction to the Maithili*

Language of North Bihar (1881), he referred to Maithili as a dialect and a spoken language.[53] However, in the same book he further writes:

> Maithili *is* a language and not a dialect. It is a custom to look upon it as an uncouth dialect of untaught villagers, but it is in reality the native language of more than seven and a quarter millions* of people, of whom, as will be borne out by every official having experience of North Bihar, at least five million can neither speak nor understand either Hindi or Urdu without the greatest difficulty. It differs from both Hindi and Bengali, both in Vocabulary and in Grammar, and is as much a distinct language from either of them as Marathi or Uria. It is a country with its own traditions, its own poets, and its own prides in everything belonging to itself.[54]

Grierson goes on to argue that Maithili is spoken by all the inhabitants of Mithila—Hindus as well as Muhammadans. Of course, he states that Muslims used more Persian and Arabic words in their conversation but they considered themselves speakers of Maithili. Grierson described the geographical boundaries of Mithila to be the Himalayas in the north, the river Ganges in the south, the river Kosi in the east, and the river Gandak in the west.[55] He considered the language spoken around the Madhubani subdivision as the 'standard' form of Maithili. Thus, it is obvious that Grierson was not very sure about the status of Maithili as an independent language. And yet he considered Maithili as a distinct language spoken by over seven million people who 'could not speak either Hindi or Urdu without great difficulty'. This estimation of Maithili by Grierson was possible because of his long stay at Madhubani as subdivisional magistrate. Then, it is surprising that he persisted to characterize Maithili as a dialect. In his *Linguistic Survey of India*, he classified Maithili as a 'dialect' of the Bihari language. And he also classified Magadhi and Bhojpuri, along with Maithili, to be 'dialects' of the Bihari

*Population of:	
Champaran	1,440,815
Tirhut	4,384,706
Begusarai Sub-Division of Munger	537,725
Supaul Sub-Division of Bhagalpur	565,747
Madhaipura Sub-Division of Bhagalpur	391,086
Total:	7,320,079

[These figures are mentioned by Grierson; for details, see Grierson, *An Introduction to the Maithili Language of North Bihar*, p. 2.]

language. This became the authoritative official positions about the status of these three languages in Bihar. During the nationalist movement, none of these languages were promoted and Bihar came to be identified as 'Hindi *Pradesh* (Province)'. How speakers of Maithili negotiated with this precarious situation and successfully asserted its independent status is discussed in the next chapters. However, other languages of Bihar remain marginal to Hindi. Bhojpuri in contemporary times is increasingly demanding recognition as an independent language and not a dialect of Hindi. So, I suppose the story of adoption of Hindi as well as resistance to it by the speakers of various linguistic communities in the 'Hindi heartland' will open an exciting debate on the language politics as played out in the context of nation and nationalism and its revival in post-independence India.

Of course, there are reasons to believe that Maithili was used in the administrative structure of Mithila. However, the extant of its use is not very clear and Mithila remained a seat of Sanskrit learning for many centuries. With the Islamic interventions from the thirteenth century onwards, Persian and Arabic also entered the linguistic scene. And therefore, Mithila had the simultaneous existence of Sanskrit, Persian, Arabic, Maithili, and Hindi too.[56] It was in 1861, the year in which the Darbhanga Raj came under the administration of the Court of Wards, that English became the official language of the state; prior to that year the records were maintained in Persian.[57] All the efforts on the part of the government to spread English education in Mithila or in the district of Tirhut, failed until the beginning of the Court of Wards rule. The region being a stronghold of orthodox Brahmans, it resisted the introduction of a foreign language in the domain of learning. They were suspicious of this move by the government and to study English was considered to be an act of irreligion. The Muhammadans and Kayasthas of Mithila, who usually went in for Persian and Arabic education, were equally averse to English education. Although, Maharaja Rudra Singh and other Zamindars made liberal donations to the Anglo-Vernacular School when it was established in 1844 at Muzaffarpur, no upper-caste parent would send their children to this institution. Again, when a similar school was started at Darbhanga in 1855, on the initiative of some local government officials, it had to be closed within two years for want of students. The credit for opening of an Anglo-Vernacular School at Darbhanga on a sound footing goes to the first General Manager,

James Forlong. The school was opened in September 1861 and proved to be quite popular. And by 1867, the number of students rose to 100. The Darbhanga Raj began to bear the entire cost of its running. By 1871, another Anglo-Vernacular School was started at Madhubani, which received aid both from the Raj and the government. Gradually the prejudices against English education had begun to disappear in Mithila.[58] In the annual report of 1875, it was noted that, 'Tirhootias both Kayasthas and Brahmins who are as a rule averse to English education have begun appreciating the same'. This point was further emphasized in the annual report of the following year. 'The fact of the Tirhoot Brahmins attending the school is an encouraging sign because the tenets of their religion have hitherto led them to regard any attempt to educate the people in English, with distrust and suspicion, in the ignorant belief that the teaching of English is indirectly intended to discourage the teaching of Sanskrit....'[59] Does this mean that it was all due to the Court of Wards' rule that English education was introduced and promoted in Mithila? What were the conditions that made the Maithils appreciate English education, about which they were once so suspicious? However, there was again a shift to Sanskrit studies with the accession of Maharaja Rameshwar Singh (1860–1929) to the throne. 'Within a year he created twenty scholarships for the revival and encouragement of Vedic education.' He also established *Maharani Rameshwar Lata Vidyalaya*, July 1907 'To encourage conversation in Sanskrit he passed an order to the effect that the teachers and students of the *vidyalaya* should talk among themselves in Sanskrit only'. 'But all the efforts proved to be a movement against the spirit of the time. Sanskrit education failed to secure even a bare livelihood for scholars'. Although there were as many as 26 schools started for vernacular education under the jurisdiction of the Raj, these remained a failed exercise as Brahmins and Kayasthas, who usually pursued study beyond the middle school, were unwilling to enroll themselves in these schools as there was no provision for English teaching.

Colonial Modernity and the Making of Enumerated Communities in India

It is widely acknowledged that the languages, their relationships with their own 'dialects' or 'varieties' and other languages and their 'dialects', and their explicit geographical boundaries are something which began to be drawn, sometimes correctly and sometimes arbitrarily (though it can be argued that it was always done arbitrarily), with the arrival of Europeans and especially after the establishment and consolidation of British rule in India. This is not to say that these languages and dialects did not exist earlier; these certainly did exist but not in the same way that they emerged during and after the colonial rule. Using Kaviraj's idea of 'fuzzy' and 'enumerated' communities,[60] it is possible to argue that before the introduction of enumeration processes like census, mapping, and surveys, these communities did exist, for Kaviraj in its fuzziness, but certainly not with the idea of their exact number of speakers, their boundaries, the exact differentiations with other linguistic groups, their grammatical, phonological, and morphological difference and so on. So, after the processes of enumeration, the speakers develop different kinds of consciousness about themselves and their languages. They began to imagine and develop a new kind of inter and intra-group relationships.[61] And above all, they could form an identity based on language, which made it possible to untie and assert their claims—social, political, and economical—by subsuming other identities like caste, class, gender, region, and religion. In the practices of these linguistic politics, all these other identities were also used, especially in the politics of Hindi and Urdu linguistic nationalism. In this whole process, a great stress is placed on the co-relationships of territory and the existence of (mono) language divisions to produce linguistic parochialism and hierarchization. It is possible to argue that the creation of linguistic groups and communities; and the politics of language that developed in India during the colonial times, were the outcome of the colonial enumerations. Now it is even more important to not to recognize that, 'newly emerging linguistic movements' are the result of 'parochial and backward-looking mentalities' or 'uneven economic development'. It is equally important not to completely negate these charges against all the linguistic groups and communities in post-independent India, but we must recognize that these movements are/were the outcome of the same processes of enumeration, which gave rise to modern Indian nationalism and particularly Hindi's and Urdu's linguistic nationalism. However, the making and growth of these movements cannot be explained through the 'logic of the numbers' alone. There are many factors—social, cultural, and political—that need to be taken seriously to explain the phenomenal rise of these linguistic movements in India since the nineteenth century. The present study of the Maithili movement is an inquiry in this direction.

These linguistic movements are resurfacing now and shall continue to do so in the future, depending upon the assertiveness of their speakers, their political and cultural leaderships, the history of their cultural and literary selfhood, the consciousness of these among the speakers, and the developments in regional and national politics. The most important among these are, and shall be, their level of interaction and experience of the modern technicalities of enumeration processes, in other words with 'our modernity'.[62] All the communities did not have the same kind and level of experience and engagement with this modernity. Then, the nature of movements and their scope and strategies are, and shall be, determined by these processes and the ability to interact with 'our modernity' which is 'colonial modernity' as well.

Notes and References

1. Thomas R. Trauttman, *Aryans and the British India* (Berkeley, CA: University of California Press, 1997); Romila Thapar, 'The Historiography of the Concept of Aryan', in Essays by Romila Thapar, Jonathan Mark Kenoyer, Madhav M. Deshpande, Shereen Ratnagar, *India: Historical Beginnings and the Concept of Aryan* (New Delhi: National Book Trust, 2006); G.A. Grierson, *Linguistic Survey of India vol. I, part I* (Delhi: Motilal Banarsidas, reprint, 1967 [1927].

2. Bernard S. Cohn, 'The language of command and the command of language', in R. Guha (ed.), *Subaltern Studies IV* (Delhi: Oxford University Press, 1985), p. 276.

3. Epistemological space refers to a methodological standpoint from and through which knowledge about something is produced. There can be different methodologies for the production of knowledge; but the British, by claiming their methodology as scientific and objective, considered their knowledge of Indian history, languages, and culture more accurate. Knowledge produced in this way alone was considered authoritative knowledge; for details, see E. Said, *Orientalism* (New York, Pantheon Books, 1978); J. Errington, 'Colonial Linguistics', *Annual Review of Anthropology*, vol. 30 (2001): 19–39.

4. For how 'logic of numbers' and formulations of newer categories through census, surveys, gazetteers, and other enumerative practices helped in increasing differentiations between Hindi and Urdu in colonial India, see Asha Sarangi, 'Enumeration and the Linguistic Identity Formation in Colonial North India', *Studies in History*, vol. 25, no. 2 (2009): 197–227. She has also analysed the inconsistencies and internal challenges to such enumerative practices and how these practices led to construction of discourse about various identities and politics in India.

5. Said, *Orientalism*, pp. 1–28.

6. R. Inden, 'Orientalist Constructions of India', *Modern Asian Studies*, vol. 20, no. 3 (1986): 401–46.

7. Errington, 'Colonial Linguistics', p. 19.

8. To discover how difficult it was for the British to learn Persian and what the blockages in its learning were, see Bernard S. Cohn, 'The Language of Command'.

9. M. Jones, *Clive in India* (London, 1974), p. 225; cited in Cohn, 'The Language of Command, p. 282.

10. Cohn, 'The Language of Command'.

11. Cohn, 'The Language of Command', p. 283.

12. For example, for the role of Christian missionaries in the promotion of Punjabi language and Gurumukhi script, see Farina Mir, *The Social Space of Language: Vernacular Culture in British Colonial Punjab* (Berkeley, CA: University of California Press, 2010).

13. Cohn, 'The Language of Command', p. 290.

14. T.R. Trautman, *Aryans and the British India* (Berkeley, CA: University of California Press, 1997), p. 13.

15. Trautman, *Aryans and the British India*.

16. S. Pollock, 'Deep Orientalism Notes on Sanskrit and Power Beyond the Raj', in Peter van der Veer and Carol A. Breckenridge (eds), *Orientalism and the Postcolonial Predicament: Perspective on South Asia New Cultural Studies* (Pennsylvania: University of Pennsylvania Press, 1993); Trautman, *Aryans and the British India*.

17. Grierson, *Linguistic Survey of India vol. I, part I*, p. ii.

18. Grierson, *An Introduction to the Maithili Language of North Bihar Containing a Grammar, Chrestomathy & Vocabulary* (Kolkata: Asiatic Society, 1881).

19. For details, see Grierson, *Linguistic Survey of India* vol. I, pp. 9–12.

20. Important works by these writers are: John Beames, *Outlines of Indian Philology* (Calcutta: Wyman Bros., 1867); R.F. A. Hoernle, *Comparative Grammars of the Gaudian Language* (Trubner & Co., 1880); B.H. Hodgson, *Essays on the Languages, Literature and Religion of Nepal and Tibet* (Trubner

& Co., 1874); For more on this, see Grierson, 1967; Errington, 'Colonial Linguistics', *Linguistic Survey of India*, Vol. I, Part I, pp. 19–39.

21. Grierson, *Linguistic Survey of India*, p. 19.

22. Grierson, *Linguistic Survey of India*, p. 22.

23. Grierson, *Linguistic Survey of India*, pp. 22–3.

24. Grierson, *Linguistic Survey of India*, pp. 30–1.

25. Hindustani was considered to be spoken in Persian mixed with Hindi and written in both Devanagari and Persian script. It was also a language that was supported by many nationalist leaders like Mahatma Gandhi, Rajendra Prasad, and others. To know what is Hindustani and how it came to be established as the language of command in India, see Bernard, 'The Command of Language'.

26. For the historical and political context of this controversy, see Christopher King, *One Language Two Scripts: The Hindi Movement in Nineteenth Century North India* (Bombay: Oxford University Press, 1994); Alok Rai, *Hindi Nationalism* (New Delhi: Orient Longman, 2001).

27. Ramchandra Shukla, *Hindi Sahitya Ka Itihas* (Delhi: Vani Prakashan, 2011). This book was first published in 1927.

28. It is important to note that the ways in which the vernacular was invoked by the colonial scholars had less to do with uncultivated and informal speech forms. It was uniformly used, contrary to the classical languages, for the spoken language of the natives.

29. Cohn, *Colonialism and Its Forms of Knowledge* (Delhi: Oxford University Press, 1986), p. 45.

30. Many linguistic communities were not in favour of getting a classical status for their language, as it was understood as a 'dead' language, which is no longer in use. In the context of the struggle for the recognition of the Maithili language, when Patna University agreed to recognize Maithili as a classical language, it was fiercely opposed by many Maithils like Babu Bhola Lal Das. For him Maithili was a '*jeevit bhasha*' (living language) and hence he insisted that it be recognized as a vernacular and not as a classical language in the curriculum of the university. For details on this, see Das, Babu Bhola Lal, *Sansmaran*, cmpl. and ed., Phoolchandra Jha 'Praveen', Babu Bhola Lal Das Rachnavali, vol. I (Darbhanga: Mithilendu Prakashan, 2008).

31. Rai, *Hindi Nationalism*, pp. 22–3.

32. Rai, *Hindi Nationalism*, p. 27.

33. Rai, *Hindi Nationalism*, p. 27.

34. Rai, *Hindi Nationalism*, p. 27.

35. Rai, *Hindi Nationalism*, p. 25.

36. S.W. Fallon, *A New Hindustani-English Dictionary, Hindustani Literature and Folk Lore* (Benaras: The Medical Hall Press, 1879), pp. i–ii.

37. A. Ghosh, 'An Uncertain "Coming of the Book": Early Print Cultures in Colonial India', in *Book History*, vol. 6 (2003): 23–55.

38. Ghosh, 'An Uncertain "Coming of the Book": Early Print Cultures in Colonial India'.

39. Jayakant Mishra, *A History of Maithili Literature*, vol. 1 (Allahabad: Tirabhukti Publications, 1949), p. 39. Vidyapati also wrote in *Avahatta*. His famous texts *Kirtilata* and *Kirtipataka* are said to be written in *Avahatta*.

40. Mishra, *A History of Maithili Literature*.

41. See Chapter 2, for more on this.

42. *Charya Padas* are influenced by Buddhist literatures. See Radhakrishna Chaudhary, *A Survey of Maithili Literature* (Deoghar: Shanti Devi, 1976); Mayanand Mishra, *Maithili Sahityak Itihas* (Supaul: Kishun Sankalp Lok, 2014); Bhimnath Jha, *Parichayika* (Patna: Bhawani Prakashan, 1985).

43. Pollock, 'The Cosmopolitan Vernacular', *The Journal of Asian Studies*, vol. 57, no. 1 (February 1998); Pollock, 'India in the Vernacular Millennium: Literary Culture and Polity, 1000–1500', *Daedalus*, vol. 127, no. 3, Early Modernities (Summer 1998).

44. For details, see Jaykant Mishra, *A History of Maithili Literature*, vol. 1 (Allahabad: Tirabhukti Publications, 1949); Chaudhary, *A Survey of Maithili Literature*; Durganath Jha, *Maithili Sahityak Itihas* (Darbhanga: Bharati Pustak Kendra, 1983); Mishra, *Maithili Sahityak Itihas*.

45. Suniti Kumar Chatterjee and Babuaji Mishra, *Varnaratnakar of Jyotirishwar Kavishekhara Carya* (Delhi: Sahitya Akademi, 1998); Anand Mishra and Govind Jha (eds), *Varnratnakar* (Patna: Maithili Akademi, 1980). This was the first known text in prose so far in any other Indian languages.

46. For details about these and many other Maithili writers, see Appendix.

47. It is considered that the first serious confrontations between the Hindu ruler of Mithila, Harisingh Deva, and the Delhi Sultanate took place during the time of Vidyapati. Vidyapati has also written about the influence of Islamic rule in his *Kirtilata*, and *Kirtipataka*; For details on the political rule and dynasties of Mithila, see Parmeshwar Jha, *Mithila Tattvavimarsha* (ed.), Govind Jha (Patna: Maithili Akademi, 1977); Upendra Thakur, *History of Mithila* (Darbhanga: Mithila Research Institute, 1988); Indrakant Jha, *Vidyapati Kalin Mithila* (Patna; Maithili Akademi, 1986).

48. For details, see Jha, *Mithila Tattvavimarsha*; Although, to what extent such scholarly traditions declined requires further explorations. But it is true that gradually Nadiya in West Bengal overtook Mithila as a seat of Navya Nyaya learning. It needs to be asserted here that Nyaya along with four schools of Indian philosophy originated and flourished in Mithila—Nyaya,

Vaisheshika, Mimansha, and Sankhya. But soon Mithila became a seat of orthodoxy with an extremely rigid and static social and political outlook. Even Ganganath Jha (1872–1941) in his autobiographical notes writes that by his time only four scholars of Mimansha were alive, whereas earlier there were more than hundreds. This was the result of a gradual and continuous decline of Sanskrit learning. With the establishment of Islamic rule, Persian and Arabic did attract scholarly attention. Even the first two histories of the region were written in Urdu, see Chapter 2. Later Urdu was also used in the urban centre of Mithila and *mushaira* culture became an integral part of urban life in Mithila.

49. For details, see Mishra, *A History of Maithili Literature*, pp. 49–67.

50. Personal Interview, Sureshwar Jha, Darbhanga, 25 June 2011.

51. Many other modern Indian languages like Marathi and Gujarati also adopted the Nagari script for their respective languages.

52. Richard Burghart, 'A Quarrel in a Speech Family', *Modern Asian Studies*, vol. 27, no. 4 (1993): 772.

53. See Grierson, *An Introduction to the Maithili Language of North Bihar*.

54. Grierson, *An Introduction to the Maithili Language of North Bihar*.

55. Grierson, *An Introduction to the Maithili Language of North Bihar*.

56. This is discussed in Chapter 2.

57. J.S. Jha, *Beginnings of the Modern Education in Mithila Selections from the Educational Records of Darbhanga Raj 1860–1930* (Patna: K.P. Jayaswal Research Institute, 1972), p. ii.

58. For the nature and development of English education in Mithila see, Jha, *Beginnings of the Modern Education in Mithila Selections from the Educational Records of Darbhanga Raj 1860–1930*, pp. xvi–xx.

59. Cited in Jha, *Beginnings of the Modern Education in Mithila*, p. xvii.

60. S. Kaviraj, 'The Imaginary Institution of India', in Partha Chatterjee and Gyanendra Pandey (eds), *Subaltern Studies VII Writings on South Asian History and Society* (Delhi: Oxford University Press, 1992), pp. 1–39.

61. Paul R. Brass, *Language, Religion and Politics in North India* (Cambridge: Cambridge University Press, 1974).

62. Chatterjee, *Our Modernity*, Rotterdam/Dakar, South–South Exchange Programme for Research on the History of Development (SEPHIS) and the Council for the Development of Social Science Research in Africa (CODESRIA), 1997.

2 Language, History, Nation, and the Imaginary of Maithili Identity

Although the understanding of nation and nationalities are too complex to be condensed into language and literature alone, it is primarily through language and literature that one can map the contours of the formations of nationalist imaginations of various kinds. This chapter is an attempt to explore this interrelationship between language and nation in the context of India, particularly the imaginings of Maithili identity in the 'Hindi heartland'. This chapter also seeks to understand why imaginings of nation and nationalities necessarily require language in a newer form—written, standard, secular, and universally applicable to all the inhabitants of the community. This is quite distinct from the traditional use of the same language.

History is yet another theme, which has played an important role in such imaginaries of nation and nationalities in modern India. It remains a highly contentious and politically charged area of inquiry. In this chapter, I have examined how a new sense of writing the scientific and objective history of Mithila emerged among the scholars in the region. What kind of roles did these historical narratives play in the formation of Maithili identity? What kind of Mithila had been imagined? What role, if any, did print and journalism play in such a context? Was this a hindrance for the Maithili imaginary or not?

The interrelationship between the nation and language is relatively less explored in India. Although, there have been fascinating studies on the subject, yet, these are mostly limited to the issue of the Hindi–Urdu controversy and the nationalization of Hindi or at best, language based politics (for example, about Tamil, Marathi, Telugu, and so on) in association with the other markers of identities such as region, culture, caste, and religion.[1]

The nation, according to Benedict Anderson's *Imagined Communities* (1991 [1983]), understood as an *imagined community*, requires a group of people who associate with each other, struggle, and aspire together to form a community in a profoundly new way which was inconceivable in earlier times. Print capitalism made it possible for rapidly growing numbers of people to think about themselves, and to relate themselves to others, in profoundly new ways. It also opens a new way of linking fraternity, power, and time meaningfully together. Anderson goes on to point out two features of 'newer nationalisms' that 'changed the face of the old world'. First, in almost all of them, a 'national print language' was of central ideological or political importance. Second, all could work from visible models provided by their distant and not so distant predecessors.[2] Further, he also writes, in the context of Europe, that print languages laid the basis for national consciousness in three distinct ways: First,

> 'they created unified fields of exchange and communication below Latin and above the spoken vernaculars. Speakers of the varieties of Frenches, Englishes, or Spanishes, who might find it difficult or even impossible to understand one another in conversation, became capable of comprehending one another via–print and paper'.[3]

In the process, they gradually became aware of the hundreds of the thousands or millions, who spoke and read the same language. According to Anderson,

> These fellow readers, to whom they were connected through print, formed in their secular, particular–visible invisibility, the embryo of a nationally imagined community…Secondly, print capitalism gave a new fixity of language, which in the long run helped to build that image of antiquity so central to the subjective idea of the nation…Thirdly, print capitalism created languages-of-power of a kind different from older administrative vernaculars. Certain dialects inevitably were 'closer' to each print language and dominated their final forms. Their disadvantaged cousins, still assimilable to the emerging print language, lost caste, above all because they were unsuccessful in insisting on their own print form.[4]

There was an assimilation process of different vernacular languages into a single common secular language. In many ways, Anderson has rightly observed that 'the general growth in literacy, commerce, industry, com-munication, and state machinery that marked the nineteenth century created powerful new impulses for vernacular linguistic unification within each dynastic realm'.[5] One can apply this theory of Anderson, to some extent, in studying the formations of modern secular identities, such as nation and nationalities in India. But, its limitations become obvious when we find that in India, the creations of such identities are challenged at two levels. Firstly, it is challenged from the existing identi-ties of caste and religion, which reconsolidate itself in newer forms, with the beginning of census and enumeration processes in modern India.[6] Thus, it was difficult to forge a pan-Indian national identity based on a singular secular language. A second process is concerned with the co-option or marginalization of regional identities within a larger pro-cess of pan-Indian identity formation and resistance to such processes. Within the 'Hindi heartland', we do not find any serious challenges to this pan-Indian identity formation, at least not in the beginning. But, a weak, even suppressed but obvious and often visible discomforts against such formation was not totally absent. I will discuss in the later part of this chapter how such pan-Indian identity formations were contested by the speakers of Maithili language within the 'Hindi heartland'.

Historical Narratives and Imaginaries of Mithila and Maithili

Modern history writing is recognized as part of a wider 'struggle for political power' and as 'an agenda for self-representation'[7] by vari-ous communities. In the context of Mithila, its history and language, Maithili, provided the tool for such a struggle for power and self-representation. Here, it is important to distinguish between these two terms—Mithila refers to a region, which is present-day North Bihar in India; and Maithili denotes a language, which is spoken in that region (a sizeable number of Maithili speakers also live in the Terai/Madheshi region of Nepal). But, there have been considerable debates and con-troversies surrounding these two terms. How these two terms came into being and were gradually used in the popular discourse is a subject of exploration in this chapter. These are discussed subsequently. There were numerous attempts to mobilize all the inhabitants of Mithila. Writing its history was a significant step in that direction. Therefore, the unfolding of the Maithili movement should be understood, not merely as a struggle for its recognition as an independent language in modern India, but also as a deeper struggle within—to organize a divided society based on caste, sects, and gender, into a modern secular community.

The imaginaries of modern Mithila and Maithili developed with a new approach to its past. How and under what circumstances did they deem it essential to have a history of their region? What were the different kinds of history that were produced and in which languages? How did Maithili become an important category in such narratives? Why does a kind of history get promoted in the region and how did it get legitimacy over many other histories, which were marginalized and even suppressed? What could be the consequences of a renegotiation by 'regional' histories for their legitimate space against the hegemonic claims of nationalist history? I have discussed these questions, in the context of history writing in Mithila during the second half of the nineteenth century to the 1920s. I have also explored how these texts have contributed in the formation of modern Maithili identity.

Like many societies prior to the coming of print, Mithila too had a very rich oral tradition. Its history was mostly based on the myths and legends of Smritis, Samhitas, Upanishads, and Puranas. Such modes of remembering the past were beginning to be seriously challenged and interrogated from the middle of the nineteenth century. Therefore, conscious efforts were made to write its history using modern 'scientific methods'. However, initially such historical texts were written not in Maithili and not even in the widely considered language of learning, Sanskrit, which was also the language of the cultural elite of the region. The first two texts on the history of Mithila were written in Urdu. These are *Riyaz-i-Tirhut* (1868) of Ayodhya Prasad 'Bahar' and *Aina-i-Tirhut* (1883) of Bihari Lal 'Fitrat'. In Maithili, such texts were written only after the publication of *Mithila Darpan* in Hindi by Ras Bihari Lal Das in 1915. It was individuals like Chanda Jha (1831–1907) who made sincere and conscious efforts to produce such works in Maithili as well. For this purpose, he visited many parts of Mithila. But, it was Parmeshwar Jha (1856–1924) who wrote *Mithila Tatva Vimarsha*, the first book on the history of Mithila in Maithili. He completed the writing of this book in 1919, but it was published much later in 1949 from Vidyapati Press, Laheriya Sarai.[8] Such a delay in publication of this book is difficult to explain. By then, there was a sizeable Maithili readership and Maithili's consciousness was in ferment. Print was also accessible and at least three Maithili journals[9] were published. Then, a possible reason for such delay might be the fact that, in the 1920s there was more emphasis on learning Hindi in Mithila, and there were shifts in focus towards pan-Indian nationalism. So, it is possible that such an important text in Maithili remained unpublished for so long. The next book on the history of Mithila was written in English, by Shyam Narayan Singh. It is entitled *History of Tirhut* and was published from the Baptist Mission Press, Calcutta (now Kolkata) in 1922. It is still considered as the most comprehensive and authoritative work on the history of Mithila. Another such text in Maithili is *Mithila Bhashamaya Itihas* by Mukund Jha 'Bakshi'.

Riaz-i-Tirhut of Ayodhya Prasad 'Bahar' begins by paying tribute to 'Allah, the almighty'. Then, it provides a very rich account of kings, their palaces, people, their lands, lives, and culture in Mithila in the second half of the nineteenth century. He chose Urdu for writing this book and not Maithili or Hindi. This was because Urdu was the language used in the administration of the courts. At that time, knowledge of Urdu was desirable for employment. Urdu was also part of urban social and cultural life in Mithila. This was particularly so among the literary elites in the towns like Darbhanga.

Ayodhya Prasad was the son of Babu Gopal Lal, and was a Khatri by caste. He used to live at Maner Sharif of Pargana Maner in the district of Patna. His father, Babu Gopal Lal worked as thana-in-charge of different thanas in the district of Tirhut for about twenty to twenty-two years from 1846.[10] Later, he settled in Muzaffarpur. Ayodhya Prasad too served in the British administration in various capacities, from 1853.[11] When, in 1860, the Maharaja of Darbhanga, Maheshwar Singh, died and the Darbhanga Raj came under the administration of the Court of Wards, he was appointed as a subordinate officer in-charge of records. About the functioning of the Darbhanga Raj administration in those days, it is stated that:

> (t)here were thirty-three offices, all haphazardly containing records in Maithili, Devanagari, and other scripts right from the beginning of the Raj. There were *firmans*, deeds of purchase, decisions regarding bound-aries, papers of borrowing loan, horoscopes of Maharajas, and other papers regarding festivals, etc. All of them were collected and compiled

and brought to the notice of authorities. They were impressed and gave Ayodhya promotion.[12]

Ayodhya Prasad worked in the administration of Darbhanga Raj for six years, and then he was removed from the service, according to his own declaration, due to the jealousy of others through conspiracy. Here, it is important to emphasize that the author and his family were working in the colonial administration. They had access to English language and literature and might have felt the need to write a history of Mithila. And it is also possible that he got this opportunity when he was removed from the service. Thus, the need to have a 'scientific record' of the history was felt by those who came into the close contacts with the colonials and their administration. Secondly, that Maithili and its script were used, besides Devanagari or Hindi, in the administration of the Darbhanga Raj, is evident from his narrative. Although, to what extent Maithili and its script were used is not very clear. However, it leads naturally to the question as to why Maithili was not promoted in the Darbhanga Raj administration during the Court of Wards administration? Why was it that Hindi and not Maithili was used as a medium of instruction in the vernacular schools? Was it because of the Court of Wards administration of Darbhanga Raj? Or, was it due to their unfamiliarity with Maithili as a vernacular of the region? In this context, Ayodhya Prasad gives the details of a meeting, where he mentions that there were various attempts to impart education in the vernacular language of the region by the locals as well as by the colonial administrators. According to Prasad, a meeting for that purpose was organized in the premises of the government school at Muzaffarpur on 27 February 1868. All the Zamindars, money lenders, and cultural and literary elites of the region were invited. This meeting was presided over by William Stuart Fallon, the Inspector of Schools, Bihar. In this meeting, it was resolved that a representation should be made to the Governor-General in Council about making the vernacular the medium of higher education and examinations in the province.[13] He also mentions that the government approved the promotion of the vernacular language in school education in the region. But which vernacular language was to be used and promoted is not clearly mentioned by Prasad. Whether it was Hindi, or Urdu, or Maithili is not clear. However, the language that gradually took root and was promoted in the region was Hindi and not Maithili.

Aina-i-Tirhut by Bihari Lal 'Fitrat' is another important work on the history of Mithila. It was first published in 1883, from the Bahar Kashmir Press, Lucknow. Bihari Lal acknowledges the role of Maharaja Lakshmishwar Singh in its publication. In this book, Bihari Lal is very conscious and quite assertive about the distinct history, culture, and identity of Mithila. He writes: 'सुबा बिहार में तिरहुत जिसे मिथिला देश कहते है।'[14] (In the Province of Bihar there is Tirhut which is called Mithila nation.) So, we find that the idea of Mithila as a *desha* began to be conceptualized and expressed explicitly. Many journals, such as *Mithila Moda*, described Mithila as *desha* (country) or *appan desha* (own country) in the social and cultural sense; politically, most Maithili speakers considered themselves as part of *Bharatvarsha* (India). So, the word *desha* did not refer to the same entity in the social-cultural and political domain alike in this part of the region, as late as until the second decade of the twentieth century.

However, there was, as it appears from the account of Bihari Lal, not a very clear understanding developed by then, about the language of the region. Bihari Lal himself classified the vernacular of the region as *Ganvari* (uncultured) Hindi that he believed to be spoken by the illiterates; and Sanskritised Hindi, which he considered to be the language of the literates. However, the examples he gave for *Ganvari* Hindi is Maithili:

अहाँक नाम की छी ? (What is your name?)
कोन गाम घर अछि? (In which village do you live?)
कोन काजक हेतु आएल छी ? (For which work have you come?)
कै दिन रहब ?[15] (How many days will you stay?)

He also described the visit of Lord Northbrook to Darbhanga in 1874 for monitoring the relief works for the famine victims. For this visit, a letter of gratitude was given to him in Sanskrit and Urdu by Babu Guneshwar Singh and Murshid Hasan Kamil, respectively.[16] However, there was no such representation in Maithili. Surendra Gopal believes that from 'the second half of the eighteenth century ... Urdu began to occupy the space vacated by Persian in people's day-to-day life, in their literary outpourings, in their educations and in their administrative practices'.[17] This clearly establishes the point that prior to Urdu, it was Persian, which was the language of administration. Sanskrit remained the language of high learning among the Maithil Pandits. But prose writings in Urdu acquired unprecedented intellectual prestige, particularly after the establishment of Fort William College at Calcutta. Many texts on history and culture were published in that language. Hindus and Muslims both contributed in this kind of literary enterprise.

In the context of Mithila in the late nineteenth century, we have Bihari Lal 'Fitrat', who was well versed in Persian, Arabic, and Urdu. He considered these languages to be a significant part of Mithila's cultural and intellectual life. He devoted as much attention, in his book, to Persian and Arabic scholarship as he devoted to traditional Sanskrit learning and scholars in Mithila.[18] According to him, there were many Hindu scholars of Persian and Arabic. He mentioned the name of Munshi Sambhu Datta, Lala Bodh Sen Singh, and Lala Gopal Lal. All of them were Ambastha Kayasthas.[19] However, according to Hetukar Jha, education in Arabic, Persian, and Urdu was virtually confined to the Muslim community alone, apart from these three above-mentioned names. But he agrees that Muslim culture was deeply rooted in Darbhanga town and the south-western part of Tirhut.[20]

Bihari Lal also presents a vivid account of the formation and rise of Muzaffarpur as the most important town and a centre of modernity and western education in north Bihar. According to him, the city was established by Muzaffar Khan of Pargana Bisra. He developed his seven bighas of land for residential purposes and later developed it as a modern city that very soon overshadowed Darbhanga as an administrative centre of the colonial administration.[21] Gradually, English became a language of social prestige and many of the English-educated lawyers in the town were Bengalis. But, according to Bihari Lal, English was not the only language required, and many established lawyers used to discuss their cases in Urdu, which was still an acceptable and commonly used language in the court.[22] According to an estimate, there were seventy-six lawyers in those days in the district of Tirhut. Out of these, eleven conducted their practice in English. Of these, seven were Bengalis, two Srivastavas, and two Muslims.[23] None of these were Maithili Brahmins, many of whom were still devoted to Sanskrit learning. Thus, it appears that Persian and Urdu were still the court languages and these were gradually replaced by English. Hindi was a late entrant and Maithili was nowhere on the scene.

The book also describes the socio-economic condition of Mithila in the second half of the nineteenth century. It describes the growing discontents among the distressed farmers against the British policy of indigo plantation in the region. It says that by:

> the second half of nineteenth century European indigo planters had become a powerful force in the economy of Tirhut. The largest indigo factory in India, the Pandaul indigo factory, was based in the estate of Darbhanga. In 1860s a powerful anti-Indigo-planter movement—the first against the European indigo-planters in Bihar—had emerged in the vicinity of Pandaul and had been crushed by the government after much effort.[24]

There were growing resentments among the peasants in Mithila. According to Bihari Lal, indigo planting on fertile land was one of the chief reasons for the famines of 1866 and 1873 in Mithila. The government failed to help the distressed masses in the first famine but their role in second famine of 1873 was widely acknowledged and appreciated.[25] This was also a time when modern English and vernacular education were promoted in the Raj Zamindari, but, the spread of English education remained very limited. Under the rule of the Court of Wards (1860–79) and the administration of Maharaja Lakshmishwar Singh English was promoted in the administration of the Darbhanga Raj. After the Court of Wards undertook the administration of Darbhanga Raj, it was organized on modern bureaucratic lines. Most of the higher officials in the administration were either Bengalis or Europeans and not Maithils.[26] Bihari Lal also describes the rich classes of Maithili society. It included many Brahmins, Rajputs, and Bhumihar Zamindars; but it was the Khatris, Agarwals, and Shahus, who were financially more powerful. He mentions one Rai Nandipat Mahatha of Muzaffarpur, whose annual income was estimated to be rupees eight to nine million. It was much more than the estimated income of Maharaja Lakshmishwar Singh, the biggest Zamindar in the region, with an annual income of about rupees two and a half million.[27] Rai Banwari Lal Sahu Agrawal and Rai Govardhan Lal Bahadur of Darbhanga had annual incomes of rupees seven to eight million and rupees four to four and a half million, respectively.[28] So, to say that it was Maithili Brahmins and Karna Kayasthas alone, who were the leaders of Mithila, is to undermine the fact that at least in trade and financial matters, other castes were also dominant. But whether these castes had any influence on the social and cultural life of Mithila and in what way they contributed to the growth of Maithili culture and language, is hard to ascertain. However, it can be argued, that in the socio-cultural sphere of life in Mithila, the leadership of the Brahmins and Kayasthas were unchallenged and it continued to be so in many decades to come.

Ras Bihari Lal Das[29] in the beginning of *Mithila Darpan* writes that 'there was no historical account available to the people of Mithila which could make them aware of their past glories and conditions of existence. Therefore, Mithila had fallen to a precarious situation'.[30] Supporting this argument, Hetukar Jha writes, 'there was no historical account of this region available in Hindi or Maithili in the beginning of the twentieth century. Books written before in this context were in Urdu. For all those who could read and write at that time, it must have become very difficult to find out and read *Aina-i-Tirhut* or *Riaz-i-Tirhut*'.[31] Bihari Lal wrote *Mithila Darpan* in Hindi, which he calls *rashtra-bhasa* (national language). Its stated objective was to make non-Maithils aware of the rich history and culture of Mithila. He calls *Mithila bhasa* (referring to Maithili) a *gharau bhasha* (household language).

These historical works tried to demarcate the territory of Mithila as well. But, such demarcations remained highly contentious. In popular imagination, the existence of Mithila and Maithili was a relatively recent development, although Mithila is mentioned in the Puranas, in particular the *Brihad Vishnu Purana*—its second chapter is called *Mithila Mahatmya*. However, this knowledge was restricted to the tiny elite of educated Maithils and not revealed to the masses. In the historical works on the region, the administrative letters and papers, and also in the intercultural interactions, Tirhut was still more popular a term than Mithila, until the late nineteenth century and even in the first two decades of the twentieth century. In *Mithila Darpan*, Ras Bihari Lal Das states that by the beginning of the twentieth century, it was Darbhanga alone that had come to be known as Mithila. Even in Darbhanga, the areas under Madhubani, Khajauli, and Benipatti thanas were especially considered to be Mithila. It was Madhubani which was considered the centre of Mithila.[32] However, he did mention the six districts—Purnea, Bhagalpur, Munger, Darbhanga, Muzaffarpur, and Champaran—as constitutive of old Mithila, which was under the jurisdiction of Government of India.[33] It might be possible that the shrinking space of Mithila was the result of Brahminical orthodoxy and partly due to continuous administrative redistributions of the region. Sarkar Tirhut was ruled by the Maharajas of the Khandawala dynasty, but when the British got the right to collect the revenue of Bengal, Bihar, and Orissa, they appointed Franko Grand as the first collector of Tirhut District in 1782. But, because of his corrupt practices, he was soon replaced by Robert Bath. Lord Cornwallis first surveyed the district during 1790–3.[34] Until 1877, district Tirhut consisted of Darbhanga and Muzaffarpur. In 1878, it was divided into the separate districts of Darbhanga and Muzaffarpur.[35] Now, even Darbhanga's three old subdivisions— Darbhanga, Madhubani, and Samastipur—have been reconstituted as independent districts (1972). These administrative divisions and re-divisions of the region, prior to the growth of a standard common language or any other marker of collective identity, did obstruct the rise of any regional or political consciousness of linguistic unity among the inhabitants.

However, the development and organization of the region based on modern technology began to take place from the second half of the nineteenth century. According to Ras Bihar Lal Das, during the reign of Maharaja Chhatra Singh, the system of postal stamps, money orders, and book posts was introduced in 1840–2.[36] Four municipalities were formed in Darbhanga—Darbhanga (1864), Madhubani (1869), Samastipur (1897), and Rosera (1869).[37] Darbhanga, during the author's time had four major hospitals—Darbhanga Raj Hospital, Rai Banwarilal Hospital, Railway's Hospital, and one veterinary hospital, as well as many clinics.[38] Railways were introduced in the region between Patna to Darbhanga in 1874.[39] From November 1875, rail journeys were regularized.Then from February 1877, another railway line was laid down between Samasuddinpur (Samastipur) and Muzaffarpur.[40] Along with railways, it was the introduction of printing technology that helped in connecting different regions of Mithila. According to Das, there were six presses in Mithila—Union Press, Katahalwari; Darbhanga Raj Press, Kaidarabad; Mithila Mihir Press, Nai Bajar; Rameshwar Press, Kanhaiyalal Barabajar; Chitragupta Press, Mirzapur; and Mithila Press, Madhubani.[41] However, Ras Bihari Lal Das regretted the fact that despite the existence of so many presses, only one weekly newspaper—perhaps *Mithila Mihir*—was published.[42] And, despite these technologies and means of communications, the growth of Maithili remained a chequered one.

The case of scripts was no different. During the time of Ras Bihari Lal Das, three scripts were used in Mithila—Devanagari, Kaithi, and Tirhuta or Mithilakshar. Devanagari was already known in the region due to the high respect attached to the Sanskrit learning. Kaithi was mostly used by the Kayasthas for keeping records, particularly related to land. And Tirhuta or Mithilakshar was widely used in socio-cultural and ritual practices; even many Sanskrit texts had been written in this script. However, after the rule of the Mughals and then of the British, Persian and English/Roman were used. And after the introduction of print, gradually it was Devanagari, which became popular and usage of other scripts gradually declined, particularly that of the Maithili script Tirhuta or Mithilakshar and Kaithi.

Parmeshwar Jha in his *Mithila Tatvavimarsha*—the first work in Maithili on the history of the region—gave an account of not just *Bharat* (India) but also of the British Emperor from the viewpoints of a loyalist. He considered Hindi as the main language of India, which was understood by all. Then, according to him, there were many provincial languages too—Bangla, Maithili (Tirhutiya), Nepali, Panjabi, Brajbhasha, Maarbari, Marhatti, Gujarati, Dravir, Telangi, Madrasi, Oriya etc [emphasis mine].[43] Thus, although he considered Hindi to be the main language, he classified Maithili as an important provincial language in India. He further writes that Hindi was introduced in the courts of Bihar by Sir Ashley Eden from 1 January 1881. This, he considered, provided a great relief to the common people, as now they did not have to travel a long distance in search of those with the knowledge of Urdu. He mentions that there were oppositions to such decision. And these were published in *Bihar Bandhu* and *Masir Bihar*, weekly journals in Hindi and Urdu respectively in the 1880s.[44] This showed that Urdu as a court language of Bihar was a burden on the majority. So, when Hindi was introduced, the decision was welcomed by them. However, Parmeshwar Jha is silent about the claims of Maithili for such a status. It indicates that Maithili as a language of the courts and administrations was not sufficiently thought about by then. There is no evidence of such demands on behalf of Maithili. It might be possible that Hindi was welcomed because of the incomprehensibility of Urdu by most of the population. Secondly, the cultural elite in the region were drawn mainly from Sanskrit scholars. They already had the knowledge of Devanagari (as it was used in Sanskrit writings too). So, they might have found it easier to comprehend Hindi than Urdu. Again, when on 18 April 1900, Hindi was introduced along with Urdu in the courts of *Samyukt Prant* (United Province) by Sir Anthony Macdonald, it was also opposed but the decision prevailed. Parmeshwar Jha has commended the *Nagari Pracharani Sabha*, Kashi for its efforts that got Hindi an elevated position.[45]

Thus, the process of replacing Urdu and Persian with Hindi was enthusiastically taken up by the colonial administration. It was supported by the many nationalist leaders as well. But the identity of Mithila or Maithili, although germinating, had not yet developed sufficiently. Even when Shyam Narayan Singh published his book[46] in 1922, he used Tirhut to denote the region and did not use Mithila in the title of his book. This was so even when he was familiar with the earlier works, such as Riaz-i-Tirhut, Aina-i-Tirhut, Mithila Darpan, and Mithila Tattvavimarsha. However, his book was successful in catching the attention of Indologists such as Sylvain Levi and others. His account of Mithila is extremely rich in terms of the subjects it deals with. Along with the historical narrative of the region, it also provides an account of Sanskrit scholars in Mithila, a classification of Maithili literary activities, ancient and modern; Mithila Dialect; Brahman Marriage in Mithila; of the Darbhanga Raja and Bettiah Estate; and also, an account of European factories for indigo and sugar manufacturing together with a map of *Tirbhukti* (Mithila region was also referred to as *Tirbhukti*).

Although he stated that Mithila was a much older name, along with Tirhut and Tirbhukti,[47] he used mostly Tirhut for Mithila. It may be because during the Mughal period, the area was known as *Sircar Tirhut* and during the British for a long time there was a separate Tirhut Collectorate and then a Commissionary. So, Tirhut was still fresh in the popular imagination. Further, giving a *Puranic* and other oral descriptions about the boundary of the region, he considered the then districts of Muzaffarpur, Darbhanga, Champaran, and parts of the districts of Monghyr, Bhagalpur, and Purnea as part of Tirhut.[48] He has also included the history of Vaishali in his history of Tirhut.

However, this book, despite being the most comprehensive account of the history of Mithila, contains surprising discrepancies. First, instead of Mithila, the author preferred to use Tirhut even when at least two prior works *Mithila Darpan* and *Mithila Tattvavimarsha* had been already written. Further, journals like *Maithil Hit Sadhana*, *Mithila Moda*, and *Mithila Mihir* were also published and circulated. In that context, the fact that he preferred Tirhut to Mithila is surprising. Secondly, although, he described the antiquity of Maithili and demonstrated its richness and closeness with Bengali and even considered classical Bengali and Maithili to have originated from some common language, he nevertheless, classified Maithili as a dialect, instead of seeing it as a language.[49] Why did he use dialect for Maithili? Was it to subscribe to the official position on language? Third, the book does give a brief account of the Maithili Brahmin marriage ceremony but hardly says anything about other caste groups. The book is comprehensive in many aspects and helped in developing a geographic unity among the inhabitants. But it fell somewhat short of developing a political identity based on Maithili and Mithila, which was already in ferment. This was also a period when the identity of the region, language, and populace was shifting from Tirhut, Tirhutiya (used for the language and population both), to Mithila, Maithili, and Maithils, respectively.

There is another interesting story about the classification of the vernacular of the region as Maithili. Hetukar Jha, in the introduction of *Maithili Chrestomathy* of Grierson[50] writes that it is to the credit of Sir George A. Grierson that, for the first time, Maithili was recognized as the language spoken in the region.[51] Grierson is also attributed as the author of the first book of grammar of Maithili, which was published in 1880–1.[52] The language was earlier known as Tirhutiya. William Adam, while he was conducting a survey of vernacular schools of Tirhut in the third decade of the nineteenth century, did classify the dialect of Mithila, as having a distinct character. He called it *Tirhutia*. This dialect, according to him, was used as a medium of instruction in the village schools of the north-eastern part of the district of Tirhut.[53] Buchanan, in his Purnea and Bhagalpur reports of 1809–10 and 1810–11, respectively, mentioned the *Des Bhasha of the Maithilas* as a dialect of Hindi.[54] Thus, Maithili was classified unfavourably by the colonial administrators and scholars. None of them considered it as a language and Maithili as a term used by none of them to refer to the dialect of the region. Although William Adam reported in his survey that Tirhutia was used as a medium in the village schools, but when the modern education system was introduced in Mithila, it was Hindi which was favoured. Textbooks were not locally produced but imported from Allahabad, much to the difficulty of pupils and the teachers alike.[55] In matters of languages in North India, colonial administrators too, were preoccupied with the Hindi–Urdu debate; and took very little or no interest in the promotion of other vernaculars of the region, including Maithili. The imposition of Hindi, through modern school education, left very little prospect for the development of local vernaculars. However, it was to the credit of Grierson that the rich literary traditions of Maithili came to light, especially for the English-speaking public and philologists. Grierson was quite optimistic about the capacity of Maithili for literary expressions. But, he too, classified it along with Magadhi (Magahi) and Bhojpuri as a dialect of his imaginary Bihari language.

However, it was not just the colonials who were to be blamed for the misrepresentation of Maithili. Many native scholars also took different stands on the issue of regional vernaculars. Bihari Lal 'Fitrat' classified Maithili as *Ganwari Hindi* and *Sanskrit mixed Hindi*;[56] Chanda Jha called it *Mithila Bhasha*;[57] Ras Bihari Lal Das also called it *Mithila Bhasha* or *Gharao Boli*;[58] Parmeshwar Jha in his *Mithila Tattvavimarsha* and Mukund Jha 'Bakshi' in his *Mithila Bhashamaya Itihas* did not refer to Maithili as the vernacular of the region;[59] Gangapati Singh in an article published in *Mithila Mihir* in 1916 called it *Mithila Bhasha*.[60] Shyam Narayan Singh in his celebrated book *History of Tirhut*[61] used the word Maithili for the language of Mithila. According to Hetukar Jha, it is only after 1922 that Maithili was widely used as a name for the language of Mithila.

Thus, we find that by the 1920s, with the publications of historical works, the imaginary of Mithila and Maithili became somewhat consolidated. But before it could fully develop, Hindi entered in the courts and in the administrations. It was also made the medium of instruction for the vernacular education in the region. These historical texts on Mithila later discarded as the 'regional' history, and therefore, were not taught in the schools. These works remain largely absent in the popular imaginary. However, these texts are/were constantly referred to in the intellectual discourse of or about Mithila.

Darbhanga Raj, George A. Grierson, and the Growth of Maithili

In 1860, the management of Darbhanga Raj was brought under the supervision of Court of Wards.[62] They introduced Persian as the court language and persuaded Maharaja Lakshmishwar Singh to use Hindi as the language of administration. It appears that the officers of the Ward were not aware of the linguistic or literary traditions in the region, except perhaps Sanskrit. Therefore, they used both Hindi and Urdu as the medium of instruction in modern vernacular schools. The problem for Maithili and the other vernaculars of the region was compounded when the learned elite of the region complied with the administration in promoting Hindi. This might also be because of the increasing prospect of employability and publications in Hindi.

Another important development was that these Hindi- and Urdu-medium books were not locally produced but were brought from Allahabad. These books were published in Allahabad and perhaps written by the same authors. The most important among them were those prepared jointly by Munshi Suraj Mull and Pandit Radha Lal.[63] The teaching of Hindi was difficult in this region. And many inspecting officers have pointed out that for the most students, Hindi would be more convenient to learn than Urdu. So, steps should be taken to improve Hindi and not the local vernacular Maithili, they argued. When the attempt to bring Hindi teachers from western Uttar Pradesh failed, Hindi teaching was left to the local teacher with little or no knowledge of Hindi. However, G. Campbell, the Lieutenant Governor in 1871, favoured vernacular languages in school education. Regarding the use of the language in Bihar schools, he stated:

> I was astonished on lately visiting Bihar to find this bastard language not only flourishing in its fullest course in our official proceedings but that we are perpetuating it by teaching it in our schools... I found that in all our so-called vernacular schools this monstrous language, if it can be called a language, is being taught by Maulvis instead of vernacular... I am determined to put a stop to the teaching of this language in our schools.[64]

Unfortunately this view of Campbell was not taken seriously by the administration and combined with the indifferent attitude of the regional elite, there was hardly any space left for Maithili to develop and flourish. Although the learned elite used Maithili in their literary works, they did not act or fight in public for a political space for Maithili, because Hindi was patronized by the colonial administration and knowledge of Hindi meant better opportunities for employment. However, when Hindi was promoted in the region, most of the inhabitants were not comfortable with it. This was acknowledged by the colonial administrators as well. In 1869, the Inspector of Schools, Tirhut Division, said that 'most of the teachers, called Hindi teachers, know not even the Barnamala, the first Hindi Book' (sic).[65] Again in 1873 A. Keally, the Deputy Collector and Magistrate of Sitamarhi noted in his diary:

> the Brahmins of the village said they had their boys taught Sanskrit at home, but if they had a Pandit who would teach them Sanskrit and Hindee they would send the boys to the schools. Some Brahmins I met at the school said Hindee was of no use to them. One who repeated a 'shloka' in Sanskrit admitted he could not write a chitti or his signature in Hindee.[66]

Maharaja Lakshmishwar Singh and his younger brother Rameshwar Singh received a modern English education at Benares under the supervision of the Court of Wards. The maharajas took a keen interest in the promotion of English education in Mithila. It was only after the persuasion of Maharaja Lakshmishwar Singh, that the parents of Sir Ganganath Jha (1871–1941), a renowned Sanskrit scholar, allowed him to take up the study of the English language. However, in the beginning, he was taught Sanskrit to which he remained committed to all his life. He translated and interpreted many classical and rare Sanskrit texts into English. In his childhood, he was also put under some Maulvi to learn Persian, but he left it soon for want of interest. He supported the demand for the progress and development of Maithili and himself wrote in Maithili as well. So, while English education and Hindi were making a slow but gradual start in the Maithili-speaking region, Sanskrit was still revered. Later, a circular of Maharaja Lakshmishwar Singh, dated 14 July 1880, did everything required for the promotion of Hindi in Mithila. Through the circular, he ordered:

> I have given orders for introduction of Hindi character and language in my office a very long time ago. This, however, cannot take place till our vernacular amlas get thoroughly to understand the character to read and write fluently. This, however, I am sorry to say that none of our amlas know how to do.
>
> I have, therefore, been obliged to pass tho(e)se orders. That, all amla should at once, set to work to master the Hindi character and language. That, I give them another three months to learn it. That is, in November

they will have to master it thoroughly to save me from the painful necessity of pensioning or dismissing old hands.

—Lakshmishwar Singh

14 July 1980

Within three weeks from the publication of this circular, he also announced three prizes of rupees 200, 150, and 150 for works in Hindi on science, poetry, and novel, respectively. Also, a fourth prize of rupees 100 was announced for an essay in Hindi.[67] Thus, we find him decisively in favour of Hindi in the region. According to Jayadeva Misra:

> Maharaja Lakshmishwar Singh, who could have raised the status of his mother tongue by promoting its all-round cultivation and by enabling it to find a place in the school curriculum, threw away a golden chance. He even drove away Maithili from his office. This did not only render the knowledge of Maithili Language and script unnecessary for those seeking employment in Raj office but what was more important, it made lakhs of Raj tenants regard Maithili as of no consequence.[68]

Why did Maharaja Lakshmishwar Singh do this? Firstly, it may be said that he did so, because, he studied at Benares under the guidance of Europeans, who took very little or no interest in the languages of North India, except perhaps Hindi and Urdu. Secondly, he knew of Maithili as a household language or as a language used in informal conversations among courtiers. Finally, it may be because of his personal involvement in all-India politics where Hindi came next only to English. All these factors might have influenced the Maharaja to undertake the task of promoting Hindi. His preference for Hindi over Maithili had a crippling effect on the growth of Maithili as a modern vernacular language.

However, Maharaja Lakshmishwar Singh did take interest in the promotion of Maithili. But, his priority remained Hindi. He gave patronage to Chanda Jha, Parmeshwar Jha, and Harshanath Jha whose contributions to modern Maithili are critical. He asked Chanda Jha to translate Vidyapati's *Purush Pariksha* (originally in Sanskrit) into Maithili and to write a *Mithila Bhasha Ramayana*. He established Darbhanga Raj Press which published many Maithili books. According to Hetukar Jha, the Urdu and Kaithi scripts were in use in the administration of Darbhanga Raj during those days. Maharaja Lakshmishwar Singh preferred Devanagari over Kaithi because the knowledge of Kaithi was limited to one caste—Kayastha. Therefore, the Maharaja did not select

Devanagari over Mithilakshar, as by his time, according to Hetukar Jha, the use of Mithilakshar was already limited to a very small circle of Maithil Pandits alone.[69] However, it is obvious that for Lakshmishwar Singh, Hindi was essential for the Maithils to learn.

Maithili did find more favourable patronage under Maharaja Rameshwar Singh, successor to Maharaja Lakshmishwar Singh. However, he was more interested in the revival and promotion of Sanskrit. The Maharaja also played an active role in the promotion of Hindu Dharma at an all-India level. He was the life-time Chairman of the *Sanatan Dharma Mahamandal* and toured extensively all over India for its propagation. He took a very keen interest in reviving Sanskrit learning in Mithila. In this connection, he established many Sanskrit colleges and *pathshalas*—Rameshwar Lata College, Darbhanga; Kapileshwar Sthan Sanskrit School, Lohna Vidyapeeth, Lakshmipur Sanskrit School, and Rajangar Sanskrit School. Thus, he was more inclined towards the revival of Sanskrit and Vedic learning than the promotion of Maithili. Nevertheless, he ordered the publication of Mithila Mihir and played a critical role in the formation of the Maithil Mahasabha. So, what we find in the efforts of the Darbhanga Raj is that, when it could have promoted Maithili and could have brought it on par with any other modern Indian languages, it sided with Hindi and Devanagari. And even when it undertook the task of promoting Maithili, it was still trying to revive Sanskrit learning. Therefore, in my opinion, the efforts of the Raj were against the spirit of that time and resulted in the promotion of Hindi at the cost of Maithili.

However, during the same period, there were many scholars and administrators who championed the cause of Maithili and many of them were patronized by the Raj. The most important among them were Harshanath Jha, Chanda Jha, Bhanunath Jha, Jeevan Jha, Raghunandan Das, Parmeshwar Jha, and others. Sir George A. Grierson, the sub-divisional magistrate of Madhubani at that time, not only awakened the Maithils about the significance of their mother tongue Maithili, but also brought it firmly in the philological discourse of his time. Between 1880 and 1884, he published *Maithili Chrestomathy and Vocabulary*, *Twenty-One Vaishnava Hymns*, and Umapati's *Parijataharana*.[70] Although, starting from Jyotirishwar's *Varn-ratnakar*,[71] there was a long lineage of Maithili poets who were also Sanskrit scholars, it was only during this period that serious attempts were made to study the literature, grammar, and vocabulary of the Maithili language. Hali Jha, while assisting Grierson, is attributed to have written the first grammar of Maithili. Grierson also published a grammar of the Maithili language. Thus, the works of Grierson provided a kind of impetus for the Maithils, who did not regard Maithili in high esteem. Sanskrit was still revered. Now, with the publications of Grierson's works, these Pandits began to take keen interest in the growth of Maithili. This led to the establishment of the Mithila Printing Works at Madhubani for the sole purpose of publishing Maithili books.[72] For a very long time, it was these Sanskrit scholars in Mithila who provided the leadership for the Maithili movement.

Maithili Journalism, Hindi–Maithili Debate, and the Imaginings of Mithila *Desha*

Journalism in Maithili began with the publication of journals like *Maithil Hit Sadhana* (1905) from Jaipur and *Mithila Moda* (1905) from Benares, and *Mithila Mihir* (1909) from Darbhanga. *Mithila Mihir* (published until the 1980s) proved to be the longest circulating magazine in Maithili. All these magazines were bilingual in the beginning. Essays and poems were published in both the languages—Hindi and Maithili. In the case of *Mithila Moda*, it was trilingual, since it also included Sanskrit. All these papers were committed to social reforms and to resolve the problems of Mithila. Although there were very strong and harsh internal confrontations[73] among the editors of these journals, and all of them had an orthodox approach.[74] According to them, the root cause of all the social evils in Mithila was the *dharmabrhrstha acharana* (irreligious conduct) of the Maithils.

In these journals Mithila is usually referred to as *Desha, Swadesh, Appan Desha,* and *Mithila Desha.* Their use of the term *Desha* did not refer to India; or produce the same imagination as it does today in almost all the modern Indian vernaculars. In these Maithili journals, the word is used to refer to a specific geographical entity—Mithila, with its peculiar and distinct cultural and social life, its traditions and habits. Thus, one finds the imaginary of Mithila desh/nationality was germinating in the beginning of twentieth century. But, before it could take its proper shape, the region was brought within the fold of pan-Indian nationalism and this process was subsequently marginalized. However, this idea could not be completely erased from the popular memories. It resurfaced repeatedly in different contexts and in different forms during the 1930s, the 1950s, and throughout the post-independent period in India.

Religion and religiosity were defining features in such an imaginary of Mithila. It was thought that Mithila could only progress through the preservation and restoration of the 'eternal religion', that is *Sanatan Dharma*. The *Bharat Dharma Mahamandal* and its branch in Darbhanga named *Janak Dharma Mandal* were supposed to uphold this 'pure' *Sanatan Dharma*. All the prevailing social evils were the results of irreligiosity and because of the decline of *Sanatan Dharma*.[75] Their orthodoxy can be understood from the fact that when the Dayanand Sarasvati-led Arya Samaj propagated the widow remarriage in Benares, Maithil Pandits were against such a campaign. They even cautioned the *Nagari Pracharin Sabha* against their support for this programme.[76] Other new revivalist reform movements within Hinduism, such as the Radhaswami Sect, Kaviraha Sect, Shivanaraiya Sect, and Theosophists as well, were considered by these Pandits as an attack on *Sanatana Dharma*.[77] Although, there were some followers of the Arya Samaj in Mithila, they were negligible in numbers and influence. They were also ridiculed.[78]

To preserve *Sanatan Dharma*, the Shri Janak Mandal was established in Mithila. It was closely associated with the Bharat Dharma Mahamandal and Maharaja Rameshwar Singh was the chairman of both the organizations. It was surprising that the mouth-piece of these institutions *Nigamagamchandrika*, was published in Bangla, Gujarati, and many other provincial languages; even in the *atinindya* (disgraceful) Urdu, but not in the language of the Chairman, that is Maithili. In an issue of *Mithila Moda*, it was expressed that, although it was not desirable that Devakshar or Devanagari should be replaced by Mithilakshar, but it was necessary that religious texts and socially relevant essays should be published in Maithili to make the Maithils aware about the condition of Mithila and the relevance of contemporary education.[79]

The social behaviours of Maithils were highly conservative and extremely rigid. Interactions among and between different castes were extremely limited. The *Panji* system of Mithila created a unique hierarchy in Maithil society. This system divided even the Brahmins in Mithila into high and low, supposedly based on purity, although it was believed that this hierarchy was based on the cultivation of knowledge, on *Kula* (family); purity of conduct, and finally, based on wealth. However, following the religious mode of thinking, it was considered that in the age of *Kaliyuga* wealth had become more important than the first three. So, they thought it would be appropriate to abandon the whole system and treat everybody equally. Its maintenance was considered even more difficult as the British rulers gave equal consideration to all. Although the system was considered valuable, its observance in the modern context was thought to be difficult.[80] This argument indicates a move towards social reform that concerned a single caste and the problems of other caste groups were hardly mentioned. Besides, the literate sections of Maithils were divided into two groups. They were divided between those with the knowledge of Sanskrit and those who were English-educated. The Sanskrit-educated were larger in numbers but they were unfamiliar and suspicious of modern social norms and were still harping on the importance of *Sadachar* (righteous conduct). On the other hand, the English-educated were limited in numbers. However, they were familiar with the modern laws and regulations, were well-placed in the administration, and were economically better off. But it is alleged that they used to take *Sadachar* very lightly.[81] Being numerically smaller in numbers, they were forced to follow *Sadachar*, even if they did not fully subscribe to it.

Through these journals attempts were made for reforming the Maithili society. Practices of *Bikaua Vivah*[82] and *Jati bhed* were challenged. And at times the progress of one's caste (*Jatonnati*) was equated with the progress of society and of the *Desha* as well.[83] However, there were attempts to mobilize all the castes in Mithila. For example, there was an attempt to establish a residential *Janaknandini Mahavidyalaya* for the students of all castes. For the establishment of this institution, twenty-eight-thousand signatures were collected. People from all castes—Ojha, Upadhyaya, Mishra, Thakur, Singh, Rai, Das, Mandal, Raut—were invited to help in this cause.[84] To launch this signature campaign, a request was made that those who would send a thousand signatures with their consent letter would be given rupees 5 as a reward together with a pair of dhotis.[85] Another instance of non-Brahmins joining the cause of Maithili is provided by an essay of Shrimant

Narayan (Gopavanshiya, a non-Brahmin caste) of Khirahari village in Bhagalpur District. In this essay, he expressed his gratitude for the publication of *Mithila Moda* and *Mithila Mihir*, but regretted the fraught progress of Maithili. He requested educated Maithils to take the cause of their mother tongue more seriously, as *Mithila's progress was impossible without the progress of Maithili* (emphasis added).[86]

Maithil Hit Sadhana—the first Maithili journal—was published from Jaipur (Rajasthan). Madhusudan Jha and the Chief Justice of the Alwar State, Rambhadra Jha, were respectively its proprietor and editor. The approach towards this publication is captured in a *pada* by Kavishwar Chanda Jha. When his opinion was sought for the publication of *Maithil Hit Sadhana*, he expressed it, thus:

लिखल जाय मिथिला इतिहास । नहि हो तहिमे शिथिल प्रयास ।।
विषय विशेष हमहुं लिखि देव । सपनहुँ एक टका नहि लेब ।।
गुण रत्नाकर थिक जयपूर । आग्रह ग्रह नहि एको क्रूर ।।
पण्डित सभ्यक नियत निवास । बहुत पड़त नहि अनकर आस ।।
पत्र बहुतजन हर्षित लेत । नियमित मूल्य पूर्व दय देत ।।
मासिक मिथिला पत्र प्रचार । मैथिला भाषैं विहित विचार ।।
सभ तकइत अछि पत्रक बाट । पौषक दिवस रहल अछि खाँट ।।
नमस्कार लिखइत छथि चन्द । सत्वर लिखब कुशल आनन्द ।।[87]

[A history of Mithila should be written; there should be no indolence in this matter. I will write on a particular subject and will not ask to be paid to do so, not even in my dreams. Jaipur, as a city, is jewel-like in its virtues; people here are neither obstinate, nor cruel, nor unfortunate. It is the home of pandits and gentlemen; help from others will not be required. Many people will buy the paper, and they will even pay in advance. This monthly Maithili paper, and its writings in Maithili, should be well-promoted. Everyone is looking forward to such a publication; the month of Paush should be ideal for it. Greetings from Chandra; do write back with news of your well-being.]

Maithil Hit Sadhana had a serious approach towards Maithili journalism. It had declared in the very beginning that:

जनिका सबहिकैँ हा-हा-ही-ही, लझ्झो चप्पो, गीत-कवित्तक अतिरिक्त गम्भीर लेख सबहिक रसास्वादक योग्यता नहि छैनि तादृष व्यक्तिक ग्राहक नहि रहलासँ हित साधनक कोनोटा त्रुटि नहि ।[88]

[*Hit Sadhan* would not mind losing subscriptions from those who prefer cheap buttering songs and lack the intelligence to comprehend serious essays.]

It took the task of providing elementary books in Maithili for all the branches of learning—grammar, hygiene, philosophy, geography, mathematics, history, poetry, and music. The other ambitious task that it undertook was the improvement of Mithila through modern education. Hindi was not excluded in this journal and interestingly it was also used as a medium to teach Maithili to those Maithils who went outside Mithila—Agra, Ajmer, Jhansi, Aligarh, Ferozabad, and Mathura—and were settled there.[89] *Maithil Hit Sadhana* was very cautious about its writing style. It followed a format and paved the way for the standardization of Maithili. A new culture of discussion and debate through print was established in the Maithili language. Although it was a short-lived journal, often contemptuously called *Maithil Pandit Hit Sadhana*,[90] it nevertheless, set a trend for the other magazines that followed it, like *Mithila Moda* and *Mithila Mihir*.

Mithila Moda—the second journal in Maithili published from Benaras—made *Desha Sudhar* (reform of the country) as one of its stated objectives. The respected members of Mithila (referred to as *Shreeman*, and who were mostly wealthy landlords) were reminded by this journal of their duty to contribute generously for the publications in Maithili. The editors of the journal claimed that they were doing that job over and above their usual work of teaching and learning.[91] But they thought that their efforts would be insufficient, unless wealthy Maithils also contribute to the cause of Maithili. Its main objective was to refine and promote the mother tongue of all Maithils, by which they meant 'all the inhabitants of Mithila':

हमहिँ नहिँ, किन्तु सभहिँ मैथिलवृन्द काँ धन्यवाद देव उचित थिक जैं हेतु सभहिँ मैथिल क अर्थात् सम्पूर्ण 'मिथिला – निवासी' क मातृ–भाषा क संशोधन ओ प्रचार करबा मध्य उक्त महानुभाव लोकनि यत्नपुरस्सर प्रवृत भेल छथि ।[92]

[It is not my duty alone, but the responsibility of all Maithils, to thank these gentlemen, who are committed to improve and promote the mother tongue of all Maithils, the inhabitants of Mithila.]

But all these journals faced enormous challenge in terms of subscriptions. The readerships of these periodicals were very limited. Almost all the editors and publishers faced this crisis and most of them stopped publications due to insufficient subscribers. It also appears that the uppermost section of the society—Zamindars, including the Maharaja of Darbhanga—was more concerned about pan-Indian politics and only reluctantly responded to the demands of the Maithili litterateurs. However, the protagonists of the Maithili movement continued with the arduous task of developing their language. Parmeshwar Sharma, Head Librarian, Rajakiya Sanskrit Library, Darbhanga, praised the efforts of *Mithila Moda* and made some suggestions to improve the writing style of Maithili. For this, he felt the need of writing some novels in Maithili. He believed that Hindi had also faced this problem but within the span of thirty years it had improved a lot. But, in the case of Maithili, it would be difficult, as it faced too much antagonism. So, according to him, some educated Maithils should initially write novels in Maithili in their own styles and this would gradually lead to development of a standard writing style in Maithili. He believed that the way Maithili was spoken and written, in his times, was different from the earlier times. And there was also a difference between the language of the gentle villagers and others which also needed to be considered.[93] Thus, there were yearnings for the standardization of Maithili duly expressed in these journals and magazines.

Although, the circulation of magazines and newspapers was limited, three magazines were published—*Mithila Hitsikhsa* from Muniyari, *Tirhut Akhabar* from Muzaffarpur, and *Mithila Mihir* from Darbhanga.[94] *Mithila Hitsiksha* was published from Khadagvilas Press, Bankipur and distributed free of cost. Its language was Hindi. This effort was commended by *Mithila Moda*, as it sowed the seed for Hindi as a public language in Mithila.[95] But it also criticized *Hitsiksha*, for using Hindi. It said:

पुस्तक मेँ तँ सब विवृत विषय मैथिलसमाजिके अछि तखन मैथिली काँ त्याग कै नागरी (हिन्दी) आश्रय क कोन प्रयोजन भेल ? ई नहिँ बुझना जाइत अछि । बंगालीप्रभृति प्रान्तिक भाषा सभहि मेँ अनेकानेक उत्तमोत्तम सर्व-विषयक पुस्तक प्रकाशित भेल अछि ओ होइत जाइत अछि किन्तु मैथिल काँ अपन आन्तरिक विषयहु क विचार (जाहि हेतु प्रांतिक भाषा क मुख्य प्रयोजन) हु मेँ अपन मातृभाषा मैथिली (जे बंगभाषा ओ नेपाल 'नेबाड़' भाषा क जननी थिक) क व्यवहार करैत लज्जा वा अक्षमता बोध होइत अछि ? कहू ओ विचारु जे एहि सँ अधिक खेद क विषय की भ सकैत अछि ।[96]

[Since every subject discussed in the book relates to Maithil society, what was the need to use Nagari (Hindi) instead of Maithili? It is hard to comprehend this. High-quality texts are published in all the provincial languages, such as Bengali. However, Maithils are ashamed and incapable of using their own mother tongue, from which Bangabhasha and the Newari language of Nepal were born, to discuss the problems afflicting their society, a function for which provincial languages are ideal. Think of this and let me know what could be worse.]

Thus, we find that although there was no strong opposition against Hindi, Maithils were aware about its implications and use. In *Bihar Bandhu* (12 June 1909), Babu Jayanarayan Lal of Ara had criticized *Mithila Mihir* and wrote of Maithili as an oral language. It was challenged by *Mithila Moda*. It is important here to recall that to propagate Hindi in Mithila articles were published in Hindi as well in *Mithila Moda*, which was mostly in *Mithila-Bhasha*. But, such attempts by Hindi journals, like *Bihar Bandhu*, infuriated many Maithils. It was thus asserted by a Maithili protagonist that

हम लोग अभी 'नागरी' सागरी कुछ नहीं सुनैंगे और न देखेंगे ।[97]

[At present, we will not hear or see at 'Nagari' or Sagari (sic)]

Again, at a *Prantiya Sabha* (provincial conference) of the Maithil Mahasabha at Kashi, Trilochan Jha reasserted, that although Hindi should be adopted, Maithili should be used to discuss social issues (*Samajik Bhasha*).[98] It shows, the aspirations of Maithili speakers; although they did not oppose Hindi completely but they were against the use of Hindi in discussing the social issues of Mithila. In this way, they also contested the idea of Maithili as the household language of the womenfolk. The assertion of Maithili identity was becoming more and more vocal. However, Hindi was not completely boycotted. There are some essays in *Mithila Moda* in which Maithili and Hindi are both used. Interestingly, the writers and his protagonists in these essays, who were the officials of Raj Darbhanga, used Hindi—although many other Sanskrit Pandits used Maithili.[99] Babu Brajnandan Sahay of Ara wrote a biography of Vidyapati in Hindi, which shed some light on the kings of Mithila and their dynasties.[100] Although, this shows the attempts by the Hindi supporters to replace Maithili with Hindi, such attempts were welcomed by the Maithils.[101]

In an essay in *Mithila Moda*[102] Baidyanath Mishra of Basaith who was living in Kanpur at that time, emphasized the point that the progress of language and *Desha* were the same. When language acquires the capacity to describe many new and diverse things not comprehended so far, it reflects the progress of the country as well. According to him, a well-developed language could help in many ways to do things in a better and profitable ways; for instance, the cultivations of crops could be more profitable for the farmers, if scientific knowledge about them was available in their own language. The growth of one's own language and publications would provide knowledge about other societies, their culture, places, markets, and so on, which they could use for their own benefits.[103] So, standardization of their local language was considered to be extremely useful in the social, cultural, and economic spheres of life of the speakers. Thus, there were attempts to develop a standard form of Maithili, which would cut across the caste- and region-based varieties of Maithili. They also believed that the main reason for the marginalization of Maithili was due to the lack of a grammar. It is reported that Pandit Baidyanath Mishra of Basaith prepared a small *Mithila Bhasha* grammar.[104] They also stated that the Maithil Samaj could develop only when all the speeches given at *Maithil Mahasabha* were delivered in Mithila Bhasha. Hindi supporters were not expected to oppose this. They gave the example of Bengali in which not only literature but even history and other texts had been prepared. Many Maithils were now putting in efforts to do the same for Maithili. They also believed that without the progress of their mother tongue, social reforms would never be successful. Further, they felt that Maithili literature need to be developed and this should not be considered as a boycott of Hindi. Even the Maharaja of Darbhanga was requested to change *Mithila Mihir* from a Hindi paper with very little space for Maithili, to a *Mithila Bhasha* paper. The reason they gave was that there were so many Hindi journals and magazines already in existence but there were very few in Maithili.[105] The contestation between Hindi and Maithili were also reflected in some journals. The *Bharati*, a Hindi journal published from Ara, wrote the following about Maithili:

मैथिलों ने अपने उद्धार का विचित्र मार्ग अपनाया है । ... अबकी वारकी मैथिल कान्फरेन्स में यह प्रस्ताव भी स्वीकृत हुआ है कि, यथा साध्य मैथिल-भाषा में पुस्तकें लिख कर मैथिलों में विद्याप्रचार किया जाय । "मिथिला मिहिर" के चौथे प्रकाश का अर्द्धांश मैथिल-भाषा से भरा

हुआ है । ऐसी दशा में कहना अनुचित नहीं है कि मैथिल लोग पीछे से अपने अन्यान्य भाईयों को खींच रहे हैं । मिथिला मिहिर में जैसी मैथिली लिखी जाती है उससे सभी विचारवान समझ सकते हैं कि इसके द्वारा विद्याप्रचार नहीं हो सकता । क्योंकि क्रियापद और विभक्तियों के अतिरिक्त यह हिन्दी ही है । इससे मैथिलों में विद्याप्रचारका स्वप्न देखना शेखचिल्लीयों के सिवा दुसरों को नहीं सोहाता ।[106]

[Maithils have followed a strange path to empower themselves … this time in the Maithil Conference a resolution has been passed with regards to publication of books in Maithil-Bhasha in order to promote education among the Maithils. More than half of the fourth issue of 'Mithila Mihir' is filled with Maithil-Bhasha. In this condition, it is not inappropriate to say that Maithils are supporting other Maithils from the backdoor. Looking at the kind of Maithili written in Mithila Mihir any knowledgeable person may believe that it is not possible to promote education in this language. Because, except verbs and syntax, it is nothing but Hindi only. Promoting education in this language among the Maithils is merely day dreaming.]

This journal—*Bharati*—was criticized not only because of its opposition to Maithili but also for its 'poor' Hindi. The Maithili protagonists believed that there were many languages in India and all of them should flourish. So, Hindi supporters were requested not to object to publications in Maithili at least for five seven years, if they want the Maithils, to support the expansion of Hindi. The *Bihar Bandhu*, regarded as an older brother (बुढ़बा भाई) was asked by them to take these considerations seriously.[107] Maithil writers, who were living in Mithila, were requested to write in Maithili instead of Hindi. The supporters of Maithili expressed that theirs should not be considered as an anti-Hindi stand, but as the acceptance of Hindi with the preservation of the mother tongue *Mithila Bhasha*. There were few Maithils who believed that the knowledge of Hindi was necessary for Maithils. They also considered that the knowledge of Hindi among the Maithils will allow them to better represent themselves and the conditions of Mithila, before the government officials.

Against all these beliefs, Maithili supporters expressed that if this support for Hindi was at the cost of the mother tongue *Mithila Bhasha*, then the desired social progress might never be achieved. Second, if government officers were to be made aware of Mithila's condition, then why was not English recommended for such use? *Mithila Mihir* was rebuked for its reasoning that because of the subscriber's preference for Hindi it would be difficult to publish it as a Maithili paper. It was mentioned that this argument was wrong, as at the most there were not more than 40 to 50 subscribers of Hindi; but because of them, Hindi was imposed on 200–250 subscribers who would prefer Maithili.[108] The growing cleavage between supporters of Hindi and Maithili was widened in this period. It was widely covered in *Mithila Moda*, and gradually Hindi's space in the journal was reduced; later only Maithili was preferred and contributors were asked to send their essays *only* in *Mithila Bhasha*.[109]

Mithila Moda not only supported modern education in Mithila, but it asserted that without the growth of Maithili, Mithila would not progress. Sanskrit education was equally supported. They wanted the students not to waste time in *Shastrartha* (oral debates and discussions, which had lost its intellectual fineness and had been reduced to using derogatory remarks against each other) but to learn correct writing, reading, and speaking in Sanskrit. It was expressed that pupils should learn to translate Sanskrit into other languages.[110] They also believed that the condition of *desha* could not be improved without education.[111] The decline of the pathshala system of education in which all the shastras and puranas were taught (and for which some villages were renowned such as Ranti, Mangarauni, and Koilakh) in Mithila was also pointed out.[112] It led to the decline of Sanskrit education, while the modern system of education was still not adequately accepted by the society. Examples of the failures to revive Sanskrit pathshalas were given. Kaushlendra Chaudhary of Koilakh established a pathshala in his village. Its contributions were admired. But in the neighbourhood, it was not taken seriously. Instead, when he sought the support of the locals and went to *Sabhagachhi*[113] in Saurath for this purpose, he was criticized and ridiculed.[114] It reflects their attitude towards education, particularly traditional pathshala education.

Although there was growing discontent between the supporters of Hindi and Maithili, *Bihar Bandhu* was called *sahayogi* (colleague) by *Mithila Moda*. It shows the non-confrontationist attitude of Maithili towards Hindi. But when it started to support Hindi and to impose it upon the Maithils, it was fiercely opposed:

... एना झोकने 'हिन्दी' तथा 'नागरी' चलै त चला लिअ । अपन दशा के स्मरण करू, अस्तु जे हो, किन्तु हम येह कहब जे यावत मातृभाषा नहिं स्थिर होएत ओ 'बालशिक्षा' मातृभाषा मेँ

नहिँ होएत तावत् घोलघाल करैत रहब किछु नहिँ सुनब.....हमर मिथिलादेषवासिजनसमुदाय क मातृभाषा 'हिन्दी' नहिँ थिक।[115]

[If the use of Hindi and Nagari could expand by imposition alone, then by all means do it. Whatever happens, remember your condition. All we have to say is that, as long as the mother tongue is not stabilized and children's education is not imparted in it, we will listen to nothing you have to say, no matter how much you try to distract us. Hindi is not the mother tongue of our people of Mithila *desha*.]

The ideal of *Deshonnati* (progress of the country) was repeatedly invoked in the many issues of *Mithila Moda*. And, it was distinguished from the progress of one's village, self, caste:

देशोन्नतिक अर्थ ग्रामोन्नति तँ नहिँ, व्यक्त्युन्नति नहिँ, जात्युन्नति नहिँ, केवल देश अर्थात् मिथिला–देश, तकर उन्नति = बाढ़ि एतबा.....[116]

[The development of the country does not merely mean the development of one's village, nor of a person, nor of a caste, but that of the *Desha* that means *Mithila Desha* and its development, that's all....]

For the progress of *Desha* (referring to Mithila) it was considered that there was a need for conscious human efforts. Without such efforts, to think of *Deshhonnati* alone was merely a dream. Financial and other contributions from the Maharaja of Darbhanga and other leaders were solicited.[117] But it appears that this met with little success. In almost every issue, editors made a request for contributions particularly from the Maharaja of Darbhanga, who used to pay Rs 100 annually for the publication of *Mithila Moda*. Even after the completion of one year, the total number of subscribed readers of the magazine remained at less than fifty.[118] It was believed that even if each village in Mithila subscribed to at least one copy of the magazine, the total number of the subscription could reach a thousand easily. And that would have a positive impact on society.[119] An appeal was also made to the Maharaja of Darbhanga to provide the requisite leadership in social reforms. He was requested to protect the interests of all the Maithils and not just the Shrotriya.[120] This also explains, that, till then there was not a suf-ficiently strong middle class in Mithila to undertake the responsibility of social reforms. Although there were debates on social reforms, edu-cation, religious reforms, women's education, and moral education, but this took place only among the Sanskrit-educated Pandits and their debates had very limited or no influence on the everyday lives of the Maithils.

In their discourse on social reforms, one can easily find a division between those who wanted to revive the old and thoroughly followed the traditional 'orthodox' conduct (*Prachin Paripati*) and others who were relatively few in numbers and who wanted to introduce changes in the modes of conduct and to learn modern ways (*Naveen Paripati*). The latter were a tiny voice and were not totally opposed to the 'orthodox' conduct. On the contrary, they wanted to preserve 'Maithil distinctiveness' without missing out on the fruits of the modern way of life.[121] With regard to the language use, Hindi (referred to as Nagari in *Mithila Moda*) was considered appropriate for *par-desha bhasha* (foreign-nation language), popular throughout the country. But within one's own *Desha*, Maithili must be used and promoted.[122] There were resentments against the recruitment of English-educated non-Maithils in the service of the Darbhanga Raj. Many Maithils claimed that earlier almost all the staff were Maithils and certainly all the superior positions were held by them. But now, due to the lack of English education among the Maithils, and the introduction of the bureaucratic system in the Darbhanga Raj administration, all the superior positions were held by the Europeans, Bengalis, and other non-Maithils. To overcome this situation, they requested that proper arrangements should be put in place for the greater participation of Maithils in the administration. Second, there were also demands for removing untouchability, although in a defensive and cautious tone.[123] So, there was a gradual move to extend the identity of Maithils to include other castes within its fold. But, such attempts were so defensive and weak in the context of an all-pervasive orthodoxy that it met with very little success.

Modern Sabhas and Samitis in Mithila and Hindi Sahitya Sammelan at Bhagalpur

Modern Sabhas and Samitis in Mithila begun to be formed from the beginning of the twentieth century. The *Mithila-Anusandhan-Samiti*[124] is considered to be the first modern organization, established for the promotion of Mithila and Maithili. An advertisement tells us about the existence of the Mithila Research Society (*Mithila Tatva Vimarshini*

Sabha). According to Chandranath Mishra 'Amar', it was established in 1905.[125] The declared objectives of this society were the promotion of Sanskrit teaching and learning; research on and publication of popular texts on Mithila; writing the exact (यथार्थ) history of Mithila *Desha* and about the Maithil scholars and other renowned personalities; and investigating on and working for the restoration of historically important sites in Mithila. It might be possible that Parmeshwar Jha, in writing his book *Mithila Tatvavimarsha*, might have taken the help of this Sabha. This Sabha became inactive shortly and sarcastically it was called *Murda Club* (Dead Club). However, this so-called *Murda Club* made a beginning in the process of formations of modern Sabhas and Samitis in Mithila. This name was so fascinating that when Ramanath Jha formed an association in 1939 for the promotion of Maithili, he named it *Murda Club*.[126]

Maithil students also embarked on this new spirit of Mithila. Around 1910, many Maithil students of Tejnarayan Jubilee College, Collegiate School, Zila School, Mission School, Marwari-Sanskrit Pathshala and many other schools formed the Matihil Student's Association (मैथिल-छात्र-समिति)[127] in Bhagalpur. The main objectives of the Association were to develop fraternity among the Maithil students; encourage their social, religious, and intellectual progress; and work for the promotion of Mithila and Hindi languages.

These efforts created a small readership for Maithili. But without the patronage of the state and the administration, this readership was mostly usurped by Hindi magazines and journals. In 1912, to propagate Hindi, a branch of the *Hindi Sahitya Sammelan* was established at Laheria Sarai, with the efforts of Jeevanand Tripathi.[128]

The second annual conference of the *Hindi Sahitya Sammelan* was held at Bhagalpur in 1914. Girindra Mohan Mishra[129] writes that the issue of Hindi and Maithili was fiercely debated in this conference. He himself wrote an essay for this conference, in which he considered Maithili as a part of Hindi. Prior to this conference, a controversy in Bihar surfaced on the issue of the medium of instruction in primary schools. Most Maithili speakers wanted that at least in Mithila, Maithili should be the medium of instruction. And to this effect, they published their demands in the newspapers as well. But many people from other parts of Bihar were opposed to such demands. Despite their mother tongues being Magadhi and Bhojpuri, they were not opposed to Hindi as the medium of instruction in primary schools. Among the Maithils, opinions were divided. The residents of Bhagalpur and Munger were convinced that in comparison to Maithili, getting a Hindi-medium education from primary school onwards offered better prospects of employability in the future. For them, the different languages of Bihar were merely 'varieties' of Hindi. Many members of the *Sammelan* were also opposed to the demands of Maithils. Prior to the main conference, during the session of the Election Committee, a proposal was tabled, in which it was recommended that Hindi be made the medium of instruction in the province of Bihar. The next day, when Rajendra Prasad geared himself up to present that recommendation, it was Girindra Mohan Mishra, a Maithili speaker, who introduced it for the discussion. It was passed unanimously. However, many Mathils registered their protest against such a move by abstaining, like Raja Kirtyanand Singh Bahadur, who was also the chairman of the reception committee of the *sammelan*. But, such protests could not do much for Maithili, and Hindi was adopted as the medium of instruction.

Thus, the growth of Hindi was almost nearly smooth in the province of Bihar. It soon usurped the space of other languages. The greater chance of employability in Hindi was also one of the reasons for its expansion. Finally, its association with the national movement and many of the nationalist leaders taking the side of Hindi, made the prospect of other languages in Bihar even weaker. Hindi soon became the language of prestige. However, as we have seen above, resistance to such an expansion of Hindi was not totally absent.

The Maithil Mahasabha and Its Idea of Mithila

Formation of the Maithil Mahasabha[130] by the maharaja of Darbhanga, Rameshwar Singh in 1910, was foundational for the development of the Maithili and Mithila movement in later years. This was an institution, organized on modern lines, with traditional authorities like caste and religion still dominating the psyche of the members of this institution. The maharajas of Darbhanga were its chief patrons. The organization was staffed by the usual *sabhapati*s (chairmen); there was a committee headed by a *mahasachiv* (president), for which elections were held regularly. There was a constitution of the Mahashabha which was amended many times. It had provincial and district-level branches. In the beginning, it helped in developing a new consciousness and a sense of pride in Maithili culture among the Maithils, who were divided on different lines. The Mahasabha, from the beginning, made it a point to be an 'apolitical' institution, but its policies and decisions were never free from the influence of the Darbhanga Raj family. Even its first objective was to foster loyalty towards the Raj. Its other objectives were promotion of education in Mithila (for which scholarship were provided to many students); improvement of the socio-economic conditions of Maithils; preservation of Maithili culture; and protecting the interest of Mithila, Maithils, and Maithili. This institution was quite successful in promoting education in Sanskrit as well as modern western education in Mithila. The use of the Maithili language in primary education was debated in the Mahasabha, but did not met with much success. In the first session of the Maithil Mahasabha, held in Madhubani from 26–8 March 1910,[131] Pandit Murlidhar Jha (editor of *Mithila Moda*) proposed that in primary education, Mithila Bhasha should be used. But, it was decided that as there was a lack of grammar, history, and geography textbooks in Maithili, and so long as that situation continued, the use of Hindi would be permitted. However, the ambivalent relationship of Maithili with Hindi continued in this period and Hindi began to be considered as a threat for Maithili in *Mithila Moda*–हिन्दी = अंकुरितमिथिला–भाषा–प्रचार–विघातिनि[132] [Hindi = Destroyer of emerging *Mithila Bhasha* (language) and its expansion].

The above citation proves that, there was a growing discomfort with Hindi. The use of Hindi was permitted only as a temporary measure, because textbooks were not available in Maithili. The same argument was used in the context of Oriya and Assamese as well when Bengali alone was considered to be a suitable language for the medium of instruction in the schools.[133] Only when the imposition of Bengali was resisted from below, were textbooks prepared in these languages. This proved decisive for the development of modern Oriya and Assamese. But in the case of Maithili, it was not just the colonial administrators but also sections of the elites of Maithili society that permitted and even encouraged the use of Hindi. What, if the claims for Maithili were strongly put forward? The status of Maithili would have been different today, if textbooks in Maithili had been written[134] and if it had been introduced as the medium of school education in Mithila during that period.

However, it was to the credit of the Maithil Mahasabha that new schools were opened and there was strong demand for the establishment of a Mithila college in Darbhanga. But, according to Babu Bhola Lal Das, Maharaja Rameshwar Singh was of the view that an Arts College could not serve the purpose of 'true' education. In fact, he believed that it could only produce 'slaves' and based on this assumption, he undertook the task of reviving Sanskrit learning in Mithila. Even the membership of the Maithil Mahasabha was not open to all the inhabitants of Mithila. It was restricted to Maithili Brahmins and Karna Kayasthas. The other caste groups formed their own separate institutions like Rajput Sabha, Gopa Sabha, and Vaishya Sabha to improve their social and economic conditions. This decision of the Mahasabha not to include the other castes as members seriously damaged the development of the Maithili language and identity. It was from then on that Maithili was considered to be the language of Maithil Brahmins and Karna Kayasthas alone. The other caste groups were reluctant to call themselves Maithili speakers. This was a grave historical error on the part of the Mahasabha and the popular imaginary of Maithili identity signified these two castes alone, although the language is spoken by all the inhabitants of the region. The participation from other castes in the Maithili movement remained limited for a very long time. The Maithili movement has not adequately recovered from this predicament and caste consciousness remains greater than language consciousness among the inhabitants. Instead of Maithili being elevated to the position of the common marker of regional identity, the Mahasabha paved the way for the increase in the power of caste associations and caste consciousness. The other caste groups in Mithila looked at every activity of the Mahasabha with contempt and mistrust.

The growth of Maithili was obstructed not only by the British administrative policies but also by the emergent nationalist movement in India. In 1860, when Maharaja Lakshmishwar Singh succeeded to the throne, being a minor, he was made subject to the authority of the Court of Wards. The administration of the Court undertook the task of promoting Urdu and Persian as the language of public life. Surmising that Urdu might violate the religious sensibilities of the royal family, the British advised the young ruler, upon coming of age, to make Hindi the courtly language along with Urdu, and Persian remained the language of the lower courts.[135] The Maithil intellectuals, who wished to participate in the public life of upper India, adopted Nagari Hindi and even the Benares-based advocates of Maithili cultural movement, adopted Devanagari, when they began to publish a journal like *Mithila Moda*.[136] Although the consciousness about Maithili as a language was always there, it was not explicitly invoked. This was partly due to the supremacy of the Sanskrit language in all the branches of learning; and partly, because they did not perceive any threat to the prospects of Maithili. But, when modern education was introduced in Mithila in Hindi medium, and many leaders, including the Maharajas of Darbhanga, sided with nationalist politics and supported Hindi, many Maithils felt the threat to their mother tongue. Initially, they did not have any problem with Hindi *per se*. This is evident in the use of Hindi in almost all the magazines in Maithili—*Maithil Hit Sadhana, Mithila Moda,* and *Mithila Mihir*. But, gradually when *Hindiwallas*, to use the phrase of Granville Austin, started to appropriate the Maithili language, its literary figures, and its literary space and tried to reduce it to the household language, Maithili elites became much more vocal and assertive to such an extent that they became anti-Hindi at times. Although these movements failed to deliver a strong leadership and organization, it is to the credit of these intellectuals and activists that they were able to strengthen and to raise the consciousness about Maithili. They could do so against extremely knotty situations, such as the unavailability of print and publishing houses; a small reading public already affiliated to Hindi; apathy of the government; and mass education even at primary level in Hindi.

They also made numerous attempts to forge a modern-secular identity based on Maithili. But before it could take its proper shape, it had to compete with the Hindi and the emergent Indian national-ist identity. There were willing adaptations of Hindi, as the 'national' language, but not so at the cost of the mother tongue Maithili. The struggle to recognize Maithili as an independent language became far more intense in the following decades, when attempts were made to appropriate it as a 'dialect' of Hindi. Therefore, from the beginning of the twentieth century, Maithili did not develop independently, just by pulling its past and its spoken varieties together in 'a meaningfully new way'. But, its re-articulations and developments in many ways was a result of its response or resistance to the imperialist tendencies of Hindi language in India as well.

Notes and References

1. Some of the important works on these issues are Dalmia (1997); King (1994); Naregal (2001); Orsini (1999); Orsini (2002); Amrit Rai (1991); Alok Rai (2001); Alok Rai, 'Thinking through Hindi', in Rajeev Bhargava and Helmut Reifeld (eds), *Civil Society, Public Sphere and Citizenship: Dialogue and Perceptions* (New Delhi: Sage Publications, 2005); Ramaswami (1997); and Mitchell (2010).
2. Anderson, *Imagined Communities*, p. 66.
3. Anderson, *Imagined Communities*, p. 44.
4. Anderson, *Imagined Communities*, pp. 44–5.
5. Anderson, *Imagined Communities*, pp. 75–6.
6. For details, see Kaviraj, *The Imaginary Institution in India*.
7. Partha Chatterjee, *Nation and Its Fragments: Colonial and Postcolonial Histories* (Delhi: Oxford University Press, 1995), p. 76.
8. Jha, *Mithila Tattvavimarsha.*
9. These were *Maithili Hit Sadhan, Mithila Moda,* and *Mithila Mihir.* A more in-depth discussion on these journals is undertaken in the later part of this chapter.
10. Hetukar Jha (ed.), *A Glimpse of Tirhut in the Second Half of the Nineteenth Century: Riyaz-i-Tirhut of Ayodhya Prasad 'Bahar'*, Kameshwar Singh Heritage Series–3 (Darbhanga: Maharajadhiraja Kameshwar Singh Kalyani Foundation, 1997), p. 5.
11. Jha (ed.), *A Glimpse of Tirhut in the Second Half of the Nineteenth Century*, p. 6.
12. Jha (ed.), *A Glimpse of Tirhut in the Second Half of the Nineteenth Century*, p. 7.
13. Jha (ed.), *A Glimpse of Tirhut in the Second Half of the Nineteenth Century*, p. 26.
14. Jha, Hetukar (ed.), *Mithila in the Nineteenth Century: Aina-i-Tirhut of Bihari Lal 'Fitrat'*, Kameshwar Singh Bihar Heritage Series–5 (Darbhanga Maharjadhiraja Kameshwar Singh Kalyani Foundation, 2001), p. 51.
15. Jha (ed.), *Mithila in the Nineteenth Century*, p. 112.
16. Jha (ed.), *Mithila in the Nineteenth Century*, p. 164.
17. Jha (ed.), *Mithila in the Nineteenth Century*, p. 1.
18. Jha (ed.), *Mithila in the Nineteenth Century*, p. 28.

19. Jha (ed.), *Mithila in the Nineteenth Century*, p. 29.
20. Jha (ed.), *Mithila in the Nineteenth Century*, pp. 77–8.
21. Jha (ed.), *Mithila in the Nineteenth Century*, p. 38.
22. Jha (ed.), *Mithila in the Nineteenth Century*, p. 40.
23. Jha (ed.), *Mithila in the Nineteenth Century*, p. 94.
24. Jha (ed.), *Mithila in the Nineteenth Century*, p. 44.
25. Jha (ed.), *Mithila in the Nineteenth Century*, pp. 149–60.
26. Jha (ed.), *Mithila in the Nineteenth Century*, p. 69.
27. Jha (ed.), *Mithila in the Nineteenth Century*, p. 194.
28. Jha (ed.), *Mithila in the Nineteenth Century*, p. 195.
29. Jha, Hetukar (ed.), *Tirhut in Early Twentieth Century: Mithila Darpan of Ras Bihari Lal Das*, Kameshwar Singh Bihar Heritage Series–8 (Darbhanga: Maharajadhiraja Kameshwar Singh Kalyani Foundation, 2005).
30. Jha (ed.), *Tirhut in Early Twentieth Century*, p. iv.
31. Jha (ed.), *Tirhut in Early Twentieth Century*.
32. Jha (ed.), *Tirhut in Early Twentieth Century*, p. 105.
33. Jha (ed.), *Tirhut in Early Twentieth Century*.
34. Jha (ed.), *Tirhut in Early Twentieth Century*, p. 94.
35. Jha (ed.), *Tirhut in Early Twentieth Century*, p. 106.
36. Jha (ed.), *Tirhut in Early Twentieth Century*, p. 98.
37. Jha (ed.), *Tirhut in Early Twentieth Century*, p. 110.
38. Jha (ed.), *Tirhut in Early Twentieth Century*, p. 109.
39. Jha, *Mithila in the Nineteenth Century*, p. 159; although according to Ras Bihari Lal Das the year was 1873; see Jha, *Tirhut in Early Twentieth Century*, p. 100; but as Bihari Lal 'Fitrat''s *Aina-i-Tirhut* was published much earlier in the year 1883, his account appears to be more correct.
40. Jha (ed.), *Tirhut in Early Twentieth Century*, p. 160.
41. Jha, *Tirhut in Early Twentieth Century*, p. 128.
42. Jha (ed.), *Tirhut in Early Twentieth Century*.
43. Parmeshwar Jha, *Mithila Tattvavimarsha*, pp. 19–20.
44. Jha, *Mithila Tattvavimarsha*, p. 32.
45. Jha, *Mithila Tattvavimarsha*, 33.
46. Shyam Narayan Singh, *History of Tirhut* (Kolkata: Baptist Mission Press, 1922).
47. Singh, *History of Tirhut*, p. 3; it is believed that Mithila is named after King Mithi, son of Maharaja Nimi, and this term is mentioned in many puranic texts, such as the *Mithilakhanda* of the *Brihad Vishnu Purana* and Valmiki's Ramayana. Chanda Jha, attributed as the father of modern Maithili literature, describes the region as:

गंगा वहति जनिक दक्षिणदिशि पूर्व कौशिकिधारा। पश्चिम वहति गंडकी, उत्तर हिमवत वल विस्तारा।।

कमला त्रियुगा अमबृता घेमुरा वागवती कृतसारा । मध्य वहति लक्ष्मणा प्रभृति से मिथिला विद्यागारा ।।

[To the south of which flows the river Ganga, to west flows Gandaki, and in the north, exist gigantic Himalaya. Where Kamla, Triyuga, Ambrita, Ghemura, Bagwati flow from the length and breadth, and in the middle of which flows the river Lakshmana, that habitat of learning is Mithila.]

48. Singh, *History of Tirhut*.
49. Singh, *History of Tirhut*, pp. 202–5.
50. Jha, Hetukar (ed.), *Maithili Chrestomathy and Vocabulary by George A. Grierson*, Kameshwar Singh Bihar Heritage Series 13 (Darbhanga: Maharjadhiraja Kameshwar Singh Kalyani Foundation, 2009). Although, I have doubts regarding this attribution to Grierson, but it is true that it was Grierson who brought the attentions of the philologists of his time to the richness and literary traditions of Maithili.
51. Jha (eds), *Maithili Chrestomathy and Vocabulary by George A. Grierson*, p. ii.
52. Jha (eds), *Maithili Chrestomathy and Vocabulary by George A. Grierson*.
53. Basu (ed.), *Report on the State of Education in Bengal (1835 and 1838) by William Adam* (University of Calcutta, 1941), p. 248; cited in Jha, *Maithili Chrestomathy*, p. iii.
54. Francis Buchanan, *An Account of District of Purnea in 1809–10* (ed.), V.H. Jackson (Patna; Bihar and Orissa Research Society, 1928), pp. 170–2; *An Account of the District of Bhagalpur in 1810–11* (Patna: Bihar and Orissa Research Society, 1939), p. 201; cited in Jha, Hetukar, *Maithili Chrestomathy*, p. iii.
55. Jayadeva Mishra, *Chanda Jha* (Delhi:, Sahitya Akademi, 2007 [1977]). p. 18.
56. Jha, *Mithila in the Nineteenth Century*, p. 112.
57. Jha, 'Vijnapan', *Purush Paiksha* (Darbhanga; Darbhanga Raj Press, 1888); cited in Jha, *Maithili Chrestomathy*, p. iv.
58. Jha, *Tirhut in Early Twentieth Century*, p. xxv.
59. Jha, *Maithili Chrestomathy*, p. iv.
60. 'Raman', Ramanand Jha, Personal communication with Hetukar Jha; cited in Jha, *Maithili Chrestomathy*, p. iv.
61. Shyam Narayan Singh, *History of Tirhut*, pp. 81, 185.
62. There had been many changes introduced in the functioning of the Raj administration. From 1860 to 1871, they managed the Darbhanga house with *Thekedari* system; then from 1871 to 1876 through *Tahsildari* system; and finally, through bureaucratic system from 1876 which remained at work even after the Court of Wards administration was over; see Henningham, *A Great Estate and Its Landlords in Colonial India,*

Darbhanga 1860–1942 (New Delhi: Oxford University Press, 1990), pp. 34–40.

63. Misra, *Chanda Jha*, p. 18.
64. Misra, *Chanda Jha*, p. 21.
65. Misra, *Chanda Jha*, p. 18.
66. Misra, *Chanda Jha*, p. 20.
67. Misra, *Chanda Jha*, p. 22.
68. Misra, *Chanda Jha*, p. 21. Here, lakhs stand for more than one hundred thousand.
69. Hetukar Jha, 'Lakshmishwar Singh (1858–98) aur Hamara Samaj', *Maharaja Lakshmishwar Singh Memorial Lecture*, 30 December (Darbhanga: Maharaja Lakshmishwar Singh Memorial College, 2009), p. 4.
70. Mishra, *Chanda Jha*, p. 23.
71. Jayakant Mishra, *History of Maithili Literature* (Allahabad, Tirbhukti Publications, 1950).
72. Misra, *Chanda Jha*, p. 24.
73. For details on these confrontations between *Mithila Moda* and *Maithili Hita Sadhana*, see *Mithila Moda*, Udgar–3, Saal 1313, Shake (1827), Benares, Prabhakari Yantralaya, p. 56; *Mithila Moda*, Udgar–5, Saal 1313, Shake (1827), pp. 81–4; *Mithila Moda*, Udgar–6, Saal 1313, Shake (1827), pp. 105–6; *Mithila Moda*, Udgar–11–12, Saal 1313, Shake (1827), pp. 224–5; later this confrontation started between *Mithila Moda* and *Mithila Mihir* as well. And it was believed that *Mithila Mihir* in its then format could not serve the interest of Maithil society. There was a proposal for publishing a separate and independent paper for the Maithil Mahasabha as well; see *Mithila Moda*, Udgar–59, Bhadra, Saal 1319, Shake (1833), pp. 1–5.
74. Here, by orthodox approach I mean orthodox Hinduism, particularly Brahminism. It is interesting to note that even the Brahmins of the area were divided into–Shrotriya, Yogya, Panjibadha, and Jaibar or Grihasthas. Shrotriyas were the highest in the hierarchy. They themselves were again internally divided into *Pubairpar* and *Pachhvairpar* (east and west part of the region) where *Pachhvairpar* were considered inferior to *Pubairpar* based on their rituals, practices, and followings; see Rabindra Ray, *The Indianization of The Maithils* (Allahabad: Govind Ballabh Pant Social Science Institute, 1987); *Mithila Moda*, Udgar–2 to 59 (covers the period between 1906–7 to 1920s).
75. *Mithila Moda*, Udgar–5, Magh Purnima, Saal 1313, Shake (1827), p. 93.
76. *Mithila Moda*, Udgar–5, Magh Purnima, Saal 1313, Shake (1827), p. 114.
77. *Mithila Moda*, Udgar 28–29, Falgun Chaitra, Saal 1315, Shake (1829–30), pp. 64–5.

78. *Mithila Moda*, Udgar 28–29, Falgun Chaitra, Saal 1315, Shake (1829–30), pp. 66–7.
79. *Mithila Moda*, Udgar–17–19, Magh Purnima, Saal 1314, Shake (1828), pp. 380–1.
80. *Mithila Moda*, Udgar–6, Paush Purnima, Saal 1313, Shake (1827), pp. 98–9.
81. *Mithila Moda*, Udgar–49, Kartika, Saal 1318, Shake (1832), p. 22.
82. In this marriage Brahmins of the lower ranks used to pay money in the marriage of their daughters to the Brahmins of higher ranks to improve their social status.
83. *Mithila Moda*, Udgar–9 and 10, Chaitra, Vaisakha Purnima, Saal 1313, Shake (1827), pp. 159–64.
84. *Mithila Moda*, Udgar–58, Shrawan, Saal 1319, Shake (1833), pp. 6–7.
85. *Mithila Moda*, Udgar–58, Shrawan, Saal 1319, Shake (1833), pp. 7–8.
86. *Mithila Moda*, Udgar–58, Shrawan, Saal 1319, Shake (1833), pp. 21–3.
87. Shambhunath Mishra, *Maithilik Dadhichi Babu Bholalal Das* (Kolkata: Karnagoshthi, 1991). Some printing errors in this *Padas* of Kavishwar Chanda Jha were corrected with the help of Prof. Bhimnath Jha, Darbhanga, personal communication, dated 26 September 2013.
88. *Maithili Sahityak Ruprekha*, Part–2 (Patna, Chetna Samiti), p. 81; cited in Chandranath Mishra, 'Amar', *Maithili Patrakaritak Itihas* (Patna, Maithili Sahitya Akademi), p. 27.
89. Mishra, 'Amar', p. 34.
90. Mishra, 'Amar', p. 34.
91. *Mithila Moda*, Udgar–3, Ashwin Purnima, Saal 1313, Shake (1827), pp. 47–8.
92. *Mithila Moda*, Udgar–5, Magh Purnima, Saal 1313, Shake (1827), p. 92.
93. *Mithila Moda*, Udgar–11–12, Jyestha, Ashadh, Saal 1313, Shake (1827), pp. 272–3.
94. *Mithila Moda*, Udgar–30–31, Vaishakh, Jyestha, Saal 1316, Shake (1830–31), p. 107.
95. *Mithila Moda*, Udgar–30–31, Vaishakh, Jyestha, Saal 1316, Shake (1830–31), pp. 116–21.
96. *Mithila Moda*, Udgar–30–31, Vaishakh, Jyestha, Saal 1316, Shake (1830–1), p. 135.
97. *Mithila Moda*, Udgar–32, Ashadh, Saal 1316, Shake (1831), pp. 161–2.
98. *Mithila Moda*, Udgar–40, Magh, Saal 1316, Shake (1831), pp. 9–19.
99. *Mithila Moda*, Udgar–52–53, Magh–Falgun, Saal 1318, Shake (1832), pp. 40–8.
100. *Mithila Moda*, Udgar–54, Chaitra, Saal 1318, Shake (1833), pp. 3–4.

101. *Mithila Moda*, Udgar-54, Chaitra, Saal 1318, Shake (1833), pp. 3–4.

102. *Mithila Moda*, Udgar-52–53, Magh–Falgun, Saal 1318, Shake (1832), pp. 10–15.

103. *Mithila Moda*, Udgar-52–53, Magh–Falgun, Saal 1318, Shake (1832), pp. 10–15.

104. *Mithila Moda*, Udgar-54, Chaitra, Saal 1318, Shake (1833), p. 3.

105. *Mithila Moda*, Udgar-56, Jyestha, Saal 1318, Shake (1833), pp. 9–11.

106. Mithila Moda-56, Jyestha, Saal 1318, Shake (1833), pp. 11–12.

107. *Mithila Moda*, Udgar-56, Jyestha, Saal 1318, Shake (1833), pp. 11–13.

108. *Mithila Moda*, Udgar-57, Ashadh, Saal 1318, Shake (1833), pp. 14–16, 21.

109. *Mithila Moda*, Udgar-58, Shrawan, Saal 1319, Shake (1833), p. 24.

110. *Mithila Moda*, Udgar-8, Falgun Purnima, Saal 1313, Shake (1827), pp. 136–7.

111. *Mithila Moda*, Udgar-8, Falgun Purnima, Saal 1313, Shake (1827), pp. 136–7.

112. *Mithila Moda*, Udgar-9–10, Chaitra and Vaisakha Purnima, Saal 1313, Shake (1827), pp. 159–60.

113. There used to be an annual fair called Sabhagachhee in Mithila of the bridegrooms in which most of the marriages were solemnized.

114. *Mithila Moda*, Udgar-9–10, Chaitra, Vaisakha Purnima, Saal 1313, Shake (1827), pp. 179–80.

115. *Mithila Moda*, Udgar-59, Bhadra, Saal 1319, Shake (1833), pp. 22–3.

116. *Mithila Moda*, Udgar-5, Magh Purnima, Saal 1313, Shake (1827), p. 76.

117. *Mithila Moda*, Udgar-8, Falgun Purnima, Saal 1313, Shake (1827), pp. 139–41.

118. *Mithila Moda*, Udgar-11–12, Jyestha, Ashadha, Saal 1313, Shake (1827), pp. 287–8.

119. *Mithila Moda*, Udgar-13–14, Shrawan, Bhadra Purnima, Saal 1313, Shake (1827), pp. 242–51.

120. *Mithila Moda*, Udgar-13–14, Shrawan, Bhadra Purnima, Saal 1313, Shake (1827), pp. 242–51.

121. *Mithila Moda*, Udgar-17–19, Magh Purnima, Saal 1314, Shake (1828), pp. 339–42.

122. *Mithila Moda*, Udgar-11–12, Jyestha, Ashadha, Saal 1313, Shake (1827), pp. 67–70.

123. *Mithila Moda*, Udgar-25–27, Magh, Saal 1315, Shake (1829), pp. 11–21.

124. Jha, *Mithila Tattvavimarsha*.

125. Chandranath Mishra 'Amar', p. 43. The custodians of this society were Maharaja Rameshwar Singh and Justice Babu Shardacharan Mitra of Kolkata High Court and the members were Babu Tulapati Singh,

Vindhyanath Jha, Ganganath Jha, Vindheshwari Prasad Singh, Kalibabu Doctor, Pandit Chitradhar Mishra, Kavishwar Chanda Jha, Parmeshwar Jha, and others.

126. Jha, *Mithila Tattvavimarsha*.

127. *Mithila Moda*, Udgar–56, Jyestha, Saal 1318, Shake (1833), pp. 19–20.

128. Girindra Mohan Mishra, *Kichhu Dekhal Kichhu Sunal* (Laheria Sarai: Nava-Bharati Press, n.d.), p. 68.

129. Mishra, *Kichhu Dekhal Kichhu Sunal*, pp. 77–80.

130. For details on the working and contributions of the Maithil Mahasabha in the Maithili movement, see Chandranath Mishra 'Amar', *Akhil Bhartiya Maithili Mahasabhak Sankshipta Itihas* (Darbhanga: Akhil Bharatiya Maithili Mahasabha, 1999).

131. For the details on the functioning, and proposals in this Mahasabha, see *Mithila Moda*, Udgar–42 Chaitra, Saal 1317, Shake (1832), pp. 1–20; *Mithila Moda*, Udgar–43, Vaisakh, Saal 1317, Shake (1832), pp. 1–8.

132. *Mithila Moda*, Udgar–42, Chaitra, Saal 1317, Shake (1832), p. 3.

133. M. Kar, 'Assam's Language Questions in Retrospect', *Social Scientist*, vol. 4, no. 2 (1975): 21–35; F.G. Bailey, 'The Oriya Movement', *The Economic Weekly* (26 September 1959): pp. 1331–8.

134. Writing textbooks in Maithili was not very difficult. It was claimed that within a month or two, these texts could be prepared. For writing *Mithila Bhasha* grammar Pandit Chandrasekhar Jha of Harinagar; for history Pandit Parmeshwar Jha; for moral education Pandit Janardan Jha of Bajitpur; for translation of primers in *Mithila Bhasha* Babu Harinand Das Vakeel; and for mathematics there were many who were considered appropriate. And it was also claimed that they would not take much time in preparing them if the members of the Mahasabha so wished; see *Mithila Moda*, Udgar–42, Chaitra, Saal 1317, Shake (1832), p. 3. The issue of Maithili as a medium of primary education and the need for the preparation of the history of Mithila were raised and debated again and again in other meetings of the Mahasabha. It was also proposed that all the papers of the Mahasabha should be in Maithili and the speakers incapable of speaking in Maithili should use Hindi or any other language with the permission of the Sabhapati (chairman). This proposal was accepted, but it was still not included in the rule book of the Mahasabha; see *Mithila Moda*, Udgar–49, Kartik, Saal 1318, Shake (1832), p. 7; many textbooks in Maithili were prepared and published by *Maithil Hit Sadhana* also.

135. J. Mishra, *A History of Maithili Literature* (Allahabad: Tirbhukti Publication, 2nd edn., 1976 [1949–50]), pp. 221–2; cited in Burghart, 'A Quarrel in

the Language Family' *Modern Asian Studies*, vol. 27, no. 4 (October 1993), p. 773.

136. Mishra, J., *A History of Maithili Literature*, pp. 2–9; cited in Burghart, '*A Quarrel in the Language Family*'.

3 Maithili Language and the Movement, Part–I

Maithils became far more assertive about the rightful place for the status of their language, Maithili, from the early 1920s. An exclusionary form of Maithili identity began to take shape with an attempt to develop a geopolitical identity based on language. The contestation between Hindi and Maithili was more intense in this period, with the expansion, as well as assertion, of Hindi as the national language of India. All the attempts to classify Maithili as a dialect of Hindi were fiercely opposed. Yet, Hindi was not completely boycotted.

Several journals and magazines were published solely to furthering the cause of Maithili and Mithila. The Maithili Sahitya Parishad was established exclusively for the promotion of Maithili language and literature. This period was important in the history of the Maithili movement because, on the one hand, Maithili protagonists were resisting the claims of Hindi advocates of Maithili being its dialect; and on the other, they were also fighting against the appropriation of several Maithili literary figures, such as Vidyapati and Govinda Das, by Bengali scholars.

Support for the Maithili movement was increasing along with the rise of a modern educated middle class in Mithila. Babu Bhola Lal Das, Pandit Umesh Mishra, Ramanath Jha, Maharaja Kameshwar Singh, Sir Ganganath Jha, Dr Amarnath Jha, Tantranath Jha, Baldev Mishra, and many others played significant roles in the assertion of Maithili as one of the modern Indian languages. A sense of Maithili identity had already arisen over the past three to four decades within the tiny middle class that emerged after the advent of modern education in Mithila. But in the 1920s and 1930s this class of Maithils become far more assertive; through cultural celebrations, such as Vidyapati Parva, *Kavi Sammelans,* and Janaki Navami they could mobilize many Maithils as well. This chapter discusses how Maithili identity was evolving in comparison to Hindi and the kind of the antagonism that was developing between the speakers of the two languages. How did the social constituency of the Maithili movement broaden? How did other caste groups in Mithila respond to Maithili and the Mithila movement? What was the status of women in the Maithili discourse? What kind of newspapers and magazines were published and what was their stand on Maithili vis-à-vis Hindi?

Cooption and Cooperation: Maithili and Bengali Literary Elite

The classification of Maithili has always been contentious. It was often seen as a 'variety' or 'dialect' of Bengali and at times also of eastern Hindi. It created a lot of confusions and misconceptions among the philologists and language activists about the status of Maithili in the nineteenth and early twentieth century. Historically, there have been closer affinities between Maithili and Bengali speakers in comparison to Hindi speakers.[1] In modern times, the contributions of many scholars of the Bengali language in support of Maithili's rightful claims are widely acknowledged by the Maithili scholars and language activists.[2] Narendra Nath Gupta, a Bengali scholar, was the first to publish *Vidyapati Padawali.* They were also aware of the rich literary heritage of Maithili. Suniti Kumar Chatterjee reminded Maithili speakers about the rich literary history of Maithili at a meeting at Patna College of the Maithili Sahitya Parishad. He said that fifty or sixty years ago, the condition of Maithili literature was far better than Bengali. But since then, Bengali had been developing at a greater pace while Maithili was lagging.[3] He further said that

> we have an unbroken literary record in Maithili from the beginning of the fourteenth century, probably even earlier down to the present day. The earliest Maithili work which we have is the 'Varna Ratnakar' of Jyotirishwar Thakur, who wrote during the last quarter of the fourteenth century. Vidyapati Thakur (end of fourteenth early fifteenth century) is the greatest writer of Maithili. Vidyapati's songs, on the love of Radha

and Krishna, are among the fairest flowers in Indian lyric poetry. These exerted a tremendous influence on the Vaisnava lyric of Bengal. They spread into Bengal and were admired and imitated by Bengali poets from the sixteenth century downwards.[4]

Despite these close cultural and linguistic affinities between Maithili and Bengali, from the early decades of the twentieth century, there were attempts to co-opt many Maithili cultural and literary figures like Vidyapati and Govinda Das as Bengali poets. It gave rise to a great controversy and assertion of claims and counterclaims by the scholars of the Maithili and Bengali languages.

Many of Govinda Das's poems were collected and published in Bengali; to prove that he was a Bengali scholar, poet, and *Vaishnav Bhakta* and the contemporary of Shri Krishna Chaitanya Goswami, an imaginary biography of him was also published.[5] But then again, there were many Bengali litterateurs who clarified, through research, that Govinda Das was a Maithili poet. Ganganath Jha, a Sankritist and supporter of Hindi as well as Maithili, expresses a sense of pride that scholars of Bengali literature were claiming Maithili poets such as Vidyapati and Govinda Das as their own, since Bengali, compared to Maithili, was a better-developed language at that time He also appreciated the keen interest of many Bengali scholars in Maithili whose works proved that these poets were Maithils. And he thought of it as embarrassment for Maithils who, in his opinion, were not investigating seriously enough about their own literary figures. In this regard, he commended the effort of Mathura Prasad Dikshit (a Bengali) for collecting and editing the *Padas* of Govinda Das and providing a biographical account as well.[6]

Cultural Celebrations: Vidyapati Parva Samaroha and Janaki Mahotsava

Vidyapati Parva had played a key role in the expansion of Maithili movement particularly among the Maithili-speaking unlettered claasses. Its celebrations were used as a cultural tool for social and political mobilizations. Although the growth of Maithili literature had been remarkable over the years, it was Vidyapati Parva which provided a platform for the many Maithils to come together and fight for the cause of Maithili and Mithila. Over time, the *Parva* had expanded the social base of the Maithili movement. Bab   la Lal Das and Rajpandit

Baldeva Mishra were the main instigators of Vidyapati Parva. For the first time, it was celebrated on 14 and 15 November 1929 at Saraswati Vidyalaya, Laheria Sarai. In the beginning of the *Parva* only the life and works of Vidyapati—whether he was a *Shringari* poet or *Bhakta, Shaiva* or *Vaishnava* or *Shakta,* and so on—were discussed. But after the promulgation of the Indian Constitution, cultural programmes, particularly Vidyapati songs and Maithili dramas, were also included.[7] This period also witnessed the expansion and growth of Vidyapati Parva Samarohas (celebrations). In the beginning this celebration was mainly to commemorate the contributions of Vidyapati to the Maithili language and literature. But gradually the Parva began to symbolize the richness of Maithili culture and way of life. The Parva began to play a significant role in the cultural life of Mithila, more so among those Maithils who lived outside Mithila. The objective of the Vidyapati Parva was also to display to the other linguistic groups the richness and the independence of Maithili language. Now, it is celebrated all around the country and abroad wherever a sizeable number of Maithils live.

There was also an attempt to use a symbolic figure—in the form of Janaki (Sita, wife of Rama and daughter of King Janaka of Videha)—to which all inhabitant of Mithila could emotionally connect. This kind of symbolic image has played a crucial role in the formation of imaginary of modern identities in the form of nation states in the different part of the world—like the idea of Bharat Mata in the context of Indian nationalism. Similarly, in Mithila, the image of Janaki was used to form an identity of Maithilness among all the inhabitants of Mithila. The celebration of Janaki Mahotsava[8] in Mithila began in the 1930s. Soon, it began to be celebrated in many parts of the region, which continues till date. The other cultural programmes, such as Maithili Drama, Rangmanch, and Kavi Sammelans often organized during these Parvas had all played an influential role in the construction of the cultural sense of Mithila and Maithili.

Expansion of Maithili Journalism and Its Reading Public

The 1920s witnessed a phenomenal growth in Maithili journals and magazines. It produced many towering figures in Maithili journalism and literature—Babu Bhola Lal Das, Bhuwaneshwar Singh 'Bhuwan', Surendra Jha 'Suman', Ramanath Jha, Professor Krishnakant Mishra, and Lakshamipati Singh and among others. They not only worked for the expansion of Maithili journalism but also provided leadership to the Maithili movement. Many magazines like *Mithila Mihir*, *Mithila Moda*, and *Maithil Hit Sadhana* were published earlier. But these, particularly *Mithila Mihir*, were not limited to Maithili. These magazines also included articles, news, and stories in other languages besides Maithili, like Hindi and Sanskrit. The publication of *Shri Maithili* from 1925 onwards, under the editorship of Udit Narayan Das and Nand Kishor Das from Laheria Sarai, marked a visible and clearly decisive shift in Maithili journalism. These journals and magazines were not only exclusively in Maithili but its tone for the reforms of Mithila and Maithili became much more radical. The editor of *Shri Maithili*, for instance, proclaimed:

मैथिली प्रकाशनक प्रथम उद्देश्य थीक मिथिलाभाषाक प्रौढताक सम्पादन । .....जाहि भाषाक मध्य सर्वप्रथम हृदय मध्य हर्ष शोक, गौरव, घृणा आदि नाना भावक उत्थान होइत अछि, ताहि भाषाक रक्षा ओ बृद्धि करब हमरा लोकनिक प्रथम कर्त्तव्य ।[9]

[The primary objective of *Maithili* publications is to publicise the richness of Mithilabhasha. …it is our primary duty to protect and promote a language through which different emotions of pleasure, mourning, pride, and hate first arise in our heart.]

Although *Shri Maithili* was a short-lived magazine, mainly due to the untimely death of its editor Udit Narayan Das, it set a new trend in Maithili journalism. The space for Hindi in Maithili magazines of this era was done away with. The next magazine that succeeded *Shri Maithili* was *Mithila* from Vidyapati Press, Laheria Sarai. It was published since 1929 under the editorship of Babu Bhola Lal Das and Kusheshwar Kumar. The editorial policy of the magazine is reflected in the very first issue of *Mithila*, that includes the controversy in Mithila between old (*Puran*) and the modern (*Naveen*). In the words of the publisher:

वादि प्रतिवादि दुनू क हम, खण्डन मण्डन छापब ।
उचित दोष गुण जे क्यौ लिखता, नहिं तकरा हम झाँपब ।।
'कुमर' पुरातन नीति निरत छथि, 'दास' नवीन समाजी ।
अछि आशा, दुनू दुनू कैं, राखथि सब दिन राजी ।।[10]

[We will publish the comments and remarks of both those who are pro and against,

We will not hide the apt appraisal, whosoever may write,
'Kumar' is an adherent of tradition, but 'Das' is a modern socialist,
We hope that both persuade and convince each other ever.]

Its editorial comments reflect a peculiar interplay of linguistic identities between Maithili, Hindi, Bengali, and Bihari. The editor, sensing the perceived threat to Maithili, stated that the loss of language was worse than political defeat. In their opinion, through the loss of a language, a community can be totally defeated, which might not be possible through a political defeat. Maithili, they believed, had richer literary traditions in early and medieval times in comparison to Bengali. But in modern times, it was lagging behind Bengali. Many Bengali poets

Image 3.1   Cover Page of *Mithila* Portraying the Interrelationships between Bharat Mata and Maa Janaki

Source: *Mithila*, Year-1, Issue-9.

they thought were influenced by or imitators of Maithili poets like Vidyapati. If such was the case, then the editor asks, in surprise, how within sixty or seventy years, had Bengali become a leading modern language in India, while the status of Maithili was diminishing? The editor did not agree with the proposition that Maithils had any lesser attachment to Maithili.

The editor claims that he himself had shown many documents in Mithilakshar and Mithila Bhasha[11] fifty to sixty years ago. The medium of Sanskrit Tolas was Maithili and people used Maithili in all their activities. The chief reason, according to him, for the unprecedented growth of Bengali was that Kolkata—being the capital of colonial India—had an advantage over other languages and regions. Marathi was also believed to have developed in the same way. But the very existence of Maithili was being threatened. Gradually English, Urdu, and Hindi consolidated itself in courts, schools, pathshalas, stations, hospitals, market, committees, and associations, in other words, in almost all the public institutions and places. Maithili was further pushed into the household and to other social occasions. This led to the belief about Maithili being a household language with very little or no relevance in public-political life. Even in the household it was increasingly believed to be a language of the womenfolk. Thus, Maithili was also being feminized. There were many Bihari scholars and Hindi supporters who were trying to classify Maithili as the dialect of Hindi and even in Mithila, Hindi was seen as the mother tongue of the people. This created confusions among many Maithils who were made to believe that Maithili was merely a dialect.

Against such appropriations, these journals and magazines and their editors reasserted the rich and older literary traditions of Maithili. And while doing so they also began to expand the support base of Maithili movement among the various caste groups of Mithila. They also expressed that Maithili was not the language of Maithil Brahmins alone but of all the inhabitants of Mithila—Shakaldwipi, Bhumihar, Rajput, Vaishya, Shudra, Muslims, Christians, Bengali, Marwari, and even Englishmen. However, they considered it a different (internal) matter that many of these castes did not accept Maithili as their mother tongue. For them, the greater threat to Maithili was from those Maithils who believed that Maithili was a dialect of Hindi.

However, this does not mean opposition to Hindi. The editors of these magazines had stated that there was no struggle between Hindi

and Maithili per se. Interestingly, in their opinion, it was more appropriate if Vidyapati was to be considered a Bihari than a Bengali. It
clearly indicates their conscious attempts to align with Hindi. However,
they were not willing to accept Hindi supporters' claim of Maithili as
its dialect. And those Hindi supporters, who were afraid that the growth
of Maithili could threaten the expansion of Hindi, were cautioned that
this kind of attitude could only give rise to an opposition to Hindi and
not the other way around.

One important and bold move made through the publication of
these magazines was gradually moving away from a reliance on the big
landlords and the Maharajas (though there were attempts to seek their
patronage as well). Instead, they sought the support of the common
Maithili speakers. This was possible due to the rise of the middle class
in Maithili society and their growing self-confidence and belief in the
common Maithils. This shift also reflects their aspiration for directly
engaging with the Maithili speakers and garnering their support. The
main purpose of the *Mithila* was said to be the struggle for the proper
place of Maithili among the modern Indian languages. However, it
covered social and religious issues as well.[12]

Among the many Maithils who studied Hindi, Sanskrit, and English,
there were only two castes—Maithil Brahmins and Karna Kayasthas—
who were anxious about the status of Maithili and were tirelessly
working for its growth. The Maithil Mahasabha was held responsible
for that. Although the other castes spoke Maithili, they did not enthusiastically associate themselves in the Maithili movement. Hence, it was
felt that an effort should be made to get their co-operation.[13] Among
the other regions in Bihar, the main opposition to Maithili came from
the people of Ara and Chhapra, which was based, as claimed in these
magazines, mainly on their jealousy of Maithili and Mithila-*Desha*.[14]
The people of Ara and Chhapra had already adopted Hindi as their
mother tongue at the cost of their own vernaculars. Thus, they thought
of the insistence by the Maithili speakers to consider their language
independent of Hindi unwarranted. They were of the view that Maithili
as a modern language was not 'cultivated' enough to be fit for modern
education. There were other instances for such oppositions. When the
number of Maithili students increased in Patna University, a committee was formed to get Maithili recognized as a subject of study in the
University. To oppose such a move, an essay, *'Bihar me Mithila Bhasha'*

(Mithila Bhasha in Bihar) was published in the magazine *Desha*, which was published from Patna. In this article, it is stated that there was no existence of a Mithila province let alone the language. It also asserted that a contemporary Maithil was not the same as the ancient Maithil. Although it acknowledged the existence of Maithil, the author asserted that during the Magadh annexation of Mithila, they all became one; now they were all Biharis, Hindi was their mother tongue, and Bihar was their desh. It is interesting to note that the author of this essay claimed himself to be a Maithil.[15] For those who opposed Maithili, the main reasons of such oppositions were:

1. Maithili is part of Hindi and its progress will hamper the growth of Hindi;
2. Maithili literature is poor and for the people of Bhagalpur, Champaran, and others, learning Maithili would be as difficult as learning Hindi;
3. There is a possibility that Maithils on the basis of their different language would claim a separate province and because of the similarity of scripts with Bengali, they could even be included in Bengal.[16]

This opposition to Maithili was not just because of their support for Hindi but also due to apprehensions about the difference of Maithili and Mithila. Compounded with this was the fear that Maithils might demand territorial separation, a suspicion that stiffened their political opposition to Maithili. Against this background, the Patna Maithili Samiti sought the opinions of seven reputed scholars to dispel such misconceptions about Maithili. Sir Ganganath Jha was one among the invited scholars.[17] These scholars unanimously supported the claim of Maithili to be recognized as an independent language. They believed that the sacrifice of one's mother tongue for the sake of the national language would threaten the very existence of the Maithils, especially when the literary traditions in Maithili have been so rich. To further the cause of Maithili, the following demands were made:

1. The Maithili Sahitya Parishad at Darbhanga should be formed and Maithili scholars were requested to write books in Maithili and give it to the *Parishad*.

2. As the *Maithil Mahasabha* was the only big organization for Maithils, it should pass a resolution to ask the government to include the teaching of Maithili in Patna University.

3. Associations should be set up in different parts of Mithila and demands be made to the government for the same purpose and the Darbhanga District Board should be requested to open at least one primary school in Maithili medium.

4. If necessary, a deputation should be sent to the Minister of Education and Vice Chancellor of Patna University for the recognition of Maithili on behalf of the *Maithil Mahasabha*.

5. A *Maithil Samiti* should be established in every city and everyone should participate in its activities.[18]

Besides demands for the promotion and recognition of Maithili as an independent language, these magazines also raised voices for social reforms. In the issues of *Mithila*, concerns related to women's education, child marriage, polygamy, and unequal marriage were unequivocally expressed. The famous novel of Harimohan Jha, *Kanyadan*, was first published in a serialized from in *Mithila* (Darbhanga, 1929). This novel created the much-needed sizeable readership in Maithili. It also helped in the further expansion of the Maithili literary sphere and common speakers of the language began to associate themselves with literary productions in Maithili.[19] *Mithila* has a report about the constitution of the Akhil Bharatiya Maithil Yuvak Samiti, Calcutta (Kolkata) under the chairmanship of Kumar Ganganand Singh and Pandit Rambhadra Jha. The apparent purpose of this committee was to bring equality in Maithili society through social, political, and economic growth. How far this attempt was successful is hard to assess due to lack of any report on this in the later issues of *Mithila*. However, such an attempt shows the willingness of the leaders to bring about social reforms in Mithila.[20]

In the twentieth session of the Maithil Mahasabha at Munger, Pandit Janardan Mishra, a Professor at Patna College, refuted the importance of Maithil, Mithila Bhasha, Mithila Desha, and Mithilakshar in his speech and said that to make efforts for the progress of these would be a worthless exercise.[21] By this time, the Maithil Mahasabha had lost its popularity. Very few people had come to this session from the other districts of Mithila. It was even called Munger-Zila-Sabha. *Searchlight* and *Desha* were very critical of this session and in *Desha* it was mistakenly written that the demand of Maithili was rejected and the Maithil Mahasabha ended with the triumphant acceptance of Hindi.[22] Contrary to this report, resolutions regarding the promotion of Mithila Bhasha and publication of Maithili books and magazines were passed besides others relating to social and religious reforms in Mithila. Even a subcommittee was constituted for that purpose.[23] In his presidential address, the Maharaja of Darbhanga stressed the need to preserve and promote Maithili and Mithilakshar, but he also acknowledged the necessity of learning Hindi. He said:

मैथिल क मैथिली क उन्नति करथु एकर ई तात्पर्य कदापि नहिं भय सकैछ जे हिन्दी कोनो वस्तु नहिं थिक वा ओकर अनादर करैत जाउ। समय आबि रहल अछि जे सब सँ प्रधान स्थान साहित्यिक क्षेत्र में हिन्दी कें देल जयतैक। ओकर उन्नति समय पाबि अनिवार्य रूप सँ सबहि काँ कर्त्तव्ये अछि संगहि मैथिली कें विसरने मैथिलत्वहु सँ वंचित रहब। तैं मैथिली तथा तिरहुता पर मैथिल कें ध्यान देव अत्यन्त आवश्यक।[24]

[Maithils should promote Maithili. But it does not mean that Hindi is of no value and we should disrespect it. The time is coming when Hindi alone will be accorded the major place in the field of literature. Its growth, as per available time, is the compulsory duty for everyone; at the same time, forgetting Maithili will deprive us of our Maithiliness. So, it is necessary for the Maithils to focus on Maithili and Tirhuta.]

There were many Maithil writers who used to write in Hindi as well and Babu Bhuwaneshwar Singh 'Bhuwan' was trying to compile a directory of Maithil poets and writers of Hindi.[25] However, how Hindi was understood by the Maithils, especially women, can be understood from the following exchange in *Kanyadan*, a novel written by Harimohan Jha. A postman in khaki dress approached a household where the male members were absent. Merely his dress and appearance terrified the women of the household. When he asked: "पं भोलानाथ झा के नाम से एक तार आया है। कोइ अन्दर से आकर ले जाइए?" [in Hindi—A letter has come for Pandit Bholanath Jha. Someone should come from inside and collect it], an old lady replied to this: "तार आया है त दरबज्जे पर रह दीजिए। एकसरि आङन में क के उठा आनेगा।"[26] [in Maithili mixed Hindi—If the letter has come then let it remain at the door. Someone will bring it to the inner courtyard of the house.] Here it is evident that, although the women of the household understood the Hindi statement of the postman, they were unable to reply in Hindi. And in her reply Maithili words, syntax, and sentence structure is quite evident.

Mithila criticized the Darbhanga Raj for their *symbolic* sympathy for Maithili. It observed that contributions of the Raj in the promotion of Maithili were very little. However, in the Munger session of the Maithili Mahasabha, Maharaj Kumar Kameshwar Singh, who was present on behalf of his father, Maharajadhiraja Rameshwar Singh, made two points which became the guiding force for the Maithili movement. The first was: क्रियाकेवलमुत्तरम् (work alone is the answer); while the second demanded: संघषक्ति: कलौयुगे (organization is the only power in *Kaliyuga*).[27] Against those educated Maithils, who became critical and indifferent towards Mithila and Maithili, there was growing contempt, which is well captured by the poet Janardan Jha 'Janaseedan' in the following words:

जे निज देष क ज्ञान न रखलन्हि, नहिं किछु उन्नति कैलन्हि।
निजभाषा-प्रचारदिषि कहियो, ध्यान कनैको देलन्हि।।
उलटे निजदेष क निन्दा कै अयष भार सिर लेलन्हि।
"जनसीदन" से वृथा जन्म लै, माता कैं दुख देलन्हि।।
जौं मिथिलावासी चाहथि, निजदेषमहत्व क रक्षा।
जौं चाहथि हो उच्च सबहिसों अपन समाज क कक्षा।।
जौं निजभाषा भेष भाव पर राखथि अनुदिन ध्यान।
'जनसीदन' तैखन बुझकथिक निज देष क उत्थान।।[28]

[Those who did not preserve the knowledge of their country, did not develop at all;
Those who did not care for the promotion of their own language,
And instead condemned their own country, they earned contempt;
For 'Janseedan' their births were worthless, and only caused pain to their mothers;
If Mithilavasis want the protection of the importance of their country,
If they want to raise the status of their own country higher than that of the others,
Only when they consider the importance of their own language, apparel, and emotions consistently,
For Janaseedan, only then it is to be understood that the country will progress.]

In this period, we also find that Magadhi was often considered as a branch of Maithili.[29] The Maithili protagonists were claiming that, in principle, Maithili alone could be considered as a language in Bihar and

Hindi was certainly not a language of the province. 'Pure' Maithili was supposed to be spoken both in the north and south part of Madhubani subdivision but the total number of Maithili speakers was considered to be more than a crore. They claimed that in North Bhagalpur, West Purnea, East Muzaffarpur, North Munger, and in all Darbhanga, a pure form of Maithili was in circulation. But in south Bhagalpur, Munger, and in some parts of the Santhal Pargana, a perverted form of Maithili was spoken. It was called the *chhika chhiki* dialect of Maithili.[30] Referring to the census report of 1921, they demanded that the speakers of Maithili, Magadhi, and Bhojpuri should be clubbed together and this would take their total number to more than two and half crores.[31] Ironically the editor was aware that the refined form of dialect could be developed into a language and so the language, through perversion over time, might be reduced to dialects. He also believed that the transformation of language into 'dialects' and dialects into 'language' were common and obvious.[32] Again and again, it was claimed that in Bihar, although the total number of Oriya, Bengali, and Urdu speakers were 77 lacs, 16 lacs, and 18,000, respectively, these languages were recognized by the Patna University but Maithili, having more than a crore of speakers, had been denied such recognition.[33] Its supporters believed that, for the progress of Maithili, four things were important: first, recognition of Maithili in the provincial University and creation of a syllabus; second, establishment of a Mithilakshar press; third, publication and propagation of Maithili books; and finally, management of magazines and journals.[34] On the occasion of the coronation of Maharajadhiraja Kameshwara Singh Bahadur, the *Maithil Mahasabha* sent an *abhinandan patra* (felicitation letter) in which he was requested to help in fulfilling two extremely important demands of Maithils: first, an 'English' college for higher education in Darbhanga; and second, recognition of *Mithila Bhasha* in Patna University.[35] Demands were made about defining a uniform writing style in Maithili. But in response to that, it was asserted that what was needed at that time were more and more writings in Maithili, and over a period of time, a distinctive, standard Maithili style would develop on its own.[36]

The sixth issue of *Mithila* was very important. The tussle between tradition and modernity revived between the editors, Kumar and Das. Kumar seemed to support traditional mores, the *purdah* system, *Varnashrama*, and accommodating 'modern' elements in such a way as to not to challenge tradition. On the other hand, Das was radical in his approach. He went on to criticize *Varnashrama* system, the present condition of women, and lack of education in caste Hindu society, which according to him, were major reasons for their degraded condition. He went on to discuss the socialist revolution and its appropriateness. He emphasized the role of youth in social upliftment.[37] In his opinion, society could no longer be controlled through religion. The standardization of language was thought to be necessary for social organization.[38] The growing consciousness about Maithili was reflected in the following assertion of Ramanath Jha, and it also gives a glimpse of the Hindi–Maithili relationships of that period:

मातृभाषा प्रचार सँ शिक्षा में वृद्धि होयत । दिल्ली में हम हिन्दू कहाय हिन्दी बाजब परंच पटना में मैथिल कहाय मैथिली कियैक नहिं बाजब ?[39]

[With the promotion of the mother tongue, there will be an expansion of education. In Delhi, being called Hindu, we will speak in Hindi, but why should we not speak in Maithili and be called Maithils in Patna?]

Mithila was very radical and courageous in its opinion about social reforms. It consistently supported the cause of women's education. Similarly, issues like the abolition of *purdah*, unmatched marriages, child marriages, and the institution of widow remarriage, were raised against stiff challenges from the traditional orthodox forces in society. There was an interesting episode regarding the Sharda Act (1929) and the response to it in Mithila. Maithil Brahmins were very critical of this act as it raised the minimum age of marriage for girls. Their critique of this act was supposedly based on the scriptures. They did not oppose the Act in any organized way as some other groups did. But due to the fear of this act, it was reported that more than 300 marriages were to take place in December 1929 among the Shrotriya Brahmins in Mithila. All the girls above three years of age were to be married. *Mithila* categorically criticized this action of the Maithil Shrotriya Brahmins.[40]

For a discussion on the literary traditions of Maithili, a meeting was organized by Patna University on '*Maithil Kavi Govindadas Jhak Kavita Kshetra mei Mahatva*' (Importance of Maithil poet Govindadas in poetry). This meeting was chaired by Sachidananda Sinha and the Patna University Registrar was also present. Narendra Nath Gupta presented his essay on the topic. In this meeting, no renowned Maithils took the trouble to attend while many Maithil students were present. More importantly, Dr Sinha in the meeting said that, in Bihar if litera-ture was available to any language, it was *Mithila Bhasha*.[41] But his later opposition to Maithili's recognition by Patna University made Maithili speakers suspect the political motives of the Bihari elite and its leader-ships. In fact, Sachidananda Sinha later went on to say that Maithili was merely a language of a few Lals and Dases (चंद लाल दासों की भाषा है ।). This infuriated Maithil representatives and encouraged many to make serious efforts for the recognition of Maithili; an important activist among them was Babu Bhola Lal Das.

Akhil Bharatiya Maithil Yuvak Sammelan Adhaidenga (Maldaha) on 9, 10, and 11 November 1929 saw a new development in the Maithili movement. This Sammelan was attended by the Maithil representatives of Bihar, Samyukta Pranta, Bengal, Assam, Madhya Pradesh, Rajputana, Bombay, and Madras. Kumar Ganganand Singh was the chairman of the Sammelan. It developed a new interest among the Maithils of Bhagalpur, Purnea, Munger, and the Santhal Parganas. The Maithil Yuvak Sangha was organized on a large scale. All the proceedings of the Sammelan were conducted in Maithili and there were many reso-lutions passed for the promotion of the Maithili language. However, the Sammelan was not confined to discussions on Maithili language and literature. The social, political, and economic condition of Mithila and its improvements were also discussed. The focus of the Sammelan was on the social reforms—particularly reforms in marriages, untouch-ability, and the prospect of alignment with the Hindu Mahasabha. It should be noted that Maithil activists, in the beginning, were very criti-cal of the reformist policies of the Hindu Mahasabha.

Mithila Mitra, another important Maithili magazine of the period, was published from Patna. In an article entitled '*Maithili Sahityonnatik Upay*', Pulakit Lal Das 'Madhur'[42] provided a plan for the promotion of Maithili and the protection of the interests of Maithils and Mithila. According to him, Maithili was reduced merely to an oral language by the increasing use of Hindi and English. In a magazine called *Desha*, a series of essays by the name of '*Bihar mei Mithila Bhasha*' sought to prove the inappropriateness of Maithili. And it was only Babu Bhola Lal Das who tried to respond to such misgivings; other Maithils did not take any serious note of that. The need for an independent literary orga-nization was also felt by the Maithili protagonist that was supposed to work on the line of Hindi Sahitya Sammelan. There was a plan for the establishment of branches of such an organization in all the main towns of Mithila. Provisions for the distribution of awards, certificates, and titles were also sought and discussed. The provisions for the conduct of examinations at government colleges, high and middle schools, and other appropriate places were also demanded. The organization was supposed to have the following branches: *Nibandha* (Essay), *Sahitya* (Literature), *Prachar* (Publicity), *Pariksha* (Examination), and *Anveshan* (Research). Then there was a focus on the publications of all genres of literature in Maithili, including translations and textbooks for other subjects of learning. The organization was supposed to launch a movement for the recognition of Maithili by Patna University and by the Sanskrit Association. They also raised the demand for inclusion of Maithili as a medium of instruction in primary education. The need for the publication of Maithili songs and *Keertans* and authoritative editions of Vidyapati's and Chanda Jha's writings; the preparation of a list of older and more recent unpublished Maithili manuscripts and their publications; the preparation of a detailed history and geography of Mithila, as well as a history and geography of India in Maithili; and the establishment of a Maithili-Natak-Mandali were also discussed. Like Bangla language books and Sasta Sahitya Mandal Ajmer, Maithili books were also to be published and distributed at relatively low prices. To attract common Maithils to study Maithili, a compilation of essays on its utility was also expected to be prepared by the Maithili-speaking Sanskrit and English scholars in Mithila. And it was believed that with the support and contribution of rich Maithils, within a year, thousands of good books could be published in Maithili.[43] But one can observe that while there were discussions on these issues, hardly any serious attempts were made for its accomplishments.

Bharati was another very important Maithili magazine. It was published by the Maithili Sahitya Parishad and Babu Bhola Lal Das was its editor. The magazine came to be identified with the Maithili movement in this period. It played a significant role in the fight for the recognition of Maithili in Patna University. There is an essay, '*Maithilik Maang*' (Maithili's Demand), in the very first volume of *Bharati*, which was written by Thakur Surya Narayan Singh.[44] He was the headmaster of the Training School, Muzaffarpur. In this essay he mentions the following demands of Maithili speakers: the establishment of a *Rashtrasabha*;

free primary education through Maithili medium; appointment of preachers for the promotion of Maithili; the need to make Maithili the official language of the Darbhanga Raj; and to make the knowledge of Maithili compulsory for each member of the official staff of the state; the establishment of a registered Maithili *Vidvatparishad* (Committee of the scholars) for the translation into Maithili of texts from different languages; and finally, the creation of a one lakh rupees' fund, was suggested to the Maharaja, for the development of Maithili language.[45] These only suggest the growing consciousness among the Maithils about their language and the formulation of the demands on the basis of that. But it is difficult to ascertain how far such demands were pursued by them.

When the Wardha Scheme—in which the significance of mother tongue in primary education was deliberated—was set up, the Maithili Sahitya Parishad was also asked to share its view on the matter. The Parishad gave its opinion in favour of the use of mother tongue in primary education. When this was accepted as a policy, *Bharati* considered it as a golden opportunity for Maithili. It also cautioned Maithili supporters. For *Bharati*, it was an opportunity for the Maithils to assert that their language was Maithili and not Hindi or Bengali. It cautioned the Maithils that if they miss this opportunity, then it would pave the way for the hegemony of Hindi supporters in the Maithili-speaking area.[46] But such pleas of these magazines were largely ignored. There is a column by the name of *Jhajiki Chitthi* in *Bharati*, which gives glimpses of the indifferent attitude of common Maithili speakers and rivalry among Maithili magazines in that period. It was about the policies and status of *Mithila Moda*, *Mithila Mihir*, *Bharati*, and *Vibhuti*:

मिहिर के विशुद्ध मैथिलीक पत्र कोना बनाओल जाय ? एक बात और छैक केवल मैथिली रहने लोक केँ हिन्दी सिखबाक अवसरे कोना भेटतैक ? हमर विचार पूछल जाय त मिहिर मे अंग्रेजी, उर्दू, बंगला सबकेँ जोड़ी देबाक चाही अन्यथा ओकरा सब समाज पर एक रंग कृपा रखनिहार राज दरभंगाक पत्र कहैबाक योग्यते की रहतैक ? अन्यान्य तीनु पत्र यदि केवल मैथिलीकेँ अपनौने अछि, त ओकर कारणो प्रत्यक्षे छैक जे विभूति सोतिक पत्र थीक, मोद ब्राह्मणक और भारती कायस्थक और मिहिरक बात भिन्न छैक ।[47]

[How could *Mithila Mihir* be made into a purely Maithili newspaper? There is one more thing, if there were only Maithili, then how would people get the opportunity to learn Hindi? If my views are solicited, then

I would suggest that English, Urdu, and Bangla should also be included in *Mihir*, otherwise, how can it protect its credentials of being the Raj Darbhanga newspaper, with equal respect for all? If the other three newspapers are to stick to Maithili, then their reasons are also obvious— *Vibhuti* is the Shrotriya's newspaper, *Moda* is for Brahmins, *Bharati* is for Kayasthas, and *Mihir's* status is different.]

Mithila Mihir was criticized for its linguistic policies. It was believed that it was a Hindi paper with marginal space for Maithili. From 1930 onwards, English was also incorporated in it. It was ridiculed by saying that this trilingual—world language, national language, and provincial language—paper now should also include Urdu.[48] In this period, a film on Vidyapati was shown by New Theatres in which his character was apparently ridiculed. In protest, a subcommittee was formed. In its meeting on 23 November 1937, a protest letter was sent to New Theatres and the Censor Board, Bengal and Bihar.[49] These all show the growing sense and assertion of identity among the Maithils.

Mithila Moda was published again under the editorship of Upendranath Jha. He was the nephew of the former editor of *Mithila Moda*, Mahamahopadhyaya Murlidhar Jha. He was earlier associated with *Mithila Moda*. It again tried to form the required cooperation among the different magazines published in Maithili, which it thought extremely important for the development of Maithili literature. In one of the issues it stated:

करू 'विभूति' माथ पर राखू जिह्वा उपर 'भारती' थीर ।
सेबू 'मिहिर' क किरण, किन्तु हो बिनु मोदक नहि पुष्ट शरीर । [50]

[Keep 'Vibhut' on the head and let 'Bharati' remain on the tongue,
Serve the rays of 'Mihir', but growth will be incomplete without *Moda*']

Mithila Moda refuted all the attempts to reduce Maithili to a particular caste,[51] which shows the growing aspiration to forge a collective identity based on language. Published from 1936 to 1941, *Mithila Moda* provided the platform for Baidyanath Mishra 'Yatri', Dr Kanchinath Jha 'Kiran', Upendra Thakur 'Mohan', Kashinath Thakur 'Kalesh', and others. They all became major figures in Maithili journalism and the movement. *Mithila Moda* received the cooperation of all renowned Maithili writers of that time and played a critical role in the development of the Maithili movement through the celebrations of Maithili Divas,

Janaki Navami, and Vidyapati Smriti Divas, and so forth. In the presidential speech of the special session of the Maithili Sahitya Parishad at Sitamarhi, Rajpandit Baldeva Mishra, a champion of Maithili, expressed the interdependent relationship between the readership and standard literary works. He went on to assert that without considering the interest of masses, in Maithili, no publishers and writers could flourish. And according to him this could be done through proper publicity. Although, he was not satisfied with the standard as well as the number of publications in Maithili, he acknowledges the gradual growth of it. He envied, in this regard, the publication of Oriya magazines and journals, which, according to him, were publishing more than one hundred and fifty journals and magazines within one and half years of its separation from Bihar (in 1936). He was also not satisfied with the strategies of some Maithili magazines (here he was referring to *Vibhuti* published by Bhuwaneshwar Singh 'Bhuwan' where the editor brought his personal enmity with the Maharajadhiraja of Darbhanga in the magazine and published some disgraceful remarks against him). He did not want such magazines to do well. However, he stated that other magazines in Maithili needed promotion and protection. Expressing his opinion about the Maithili movement, he said:

यद्यपि हमरा सभक आन्दोलन विलम्ब सँ उठल अछि, कार्यो थोड़े भेल अछि, तथापि प्रान्त भरिमे एकर चर्चा पसरि गेल अछि आओर राष्ट्रियताक आड़मे किछु व्यक्ति आबहु विरोध करितहि छथि। हालमे मुजफ्फरपुरक समीप जे जिला हिन्दी साहित्य सम्मेलन भेल अछि तकर सभापति प्रसिद्ध विद्वान राहुलजीक (राहुल सांकृत्यायन) भाषण देखू। एहने बुझि पड़त जे मैथिलीकैँ स्वीकृति भेल आओर बिहारक प्रान्तियता भंग भेल। हमर विरोधी सभक ई आपत्ति बड़ प्राचीन छन्हि। हम एहिसँ भीत नहि छी। यदि बिहारक अन्यान्य लोक मैथिलीक आदर नहि करताह, यदि ओ सभ हमरा लोकनिसँ सहानुभूति ओ सहयोग नहि रखताह तँ हमरा ओहि प्रान्तसँ कोन लाभ? हम सब कियैक नहि स्वतन्त्रक आन्दोलन करब। आशे नहि, विश्वासो अछि जे बिहारक प्रबुद्ध नेतागण ई परिस्थिति उत्पन्न नहि करताह।[52]

[Although our movement has begun late, and very little work has been done, yet it is discussed throughout the province and some people still protest against us under the sway of nationalism. Look at the speech of Rahulji (Rahul Sankrityayan), the President of the recently held District Hindi Sahitya Sammelan in nearby Muzaffarpur. He wants us to believe that as soon as Maithili is recognized, the provincial status of Bihar would be jeopardized. This objection of our opponent is quite old. We are not frightened by that. If the people of Bihar do not respect Maithili, if they do not sympathize and cooperate with us, then what is the use of such a province for us? Why should we not launch a movement for separation? It is not just my hope, but I believe that the wise leaders of Bihar would not let such a situation arise.]

He was clearly explaining not just the status and gradual development of the Maithili movement but also cautioning the leaders of Bihar and Hindi supporters that if they did not recognize and appreciate the Maithili language, then it could lead to the demand for separate statehood for Mithila. *Mithila Moda's* contribution in this sense was commendable as it fearlessly gave coverage to such issues and expressions.

Vibhuti was published by Bhuwaneshwar Singh 'Bhuwan' from the Vaishali Press, Muzaffarpur. It too was a short-lived magazine, published from 1937 to 1938. The stated objective of the magazine was to contribute to the social progress of Mithila and Maithili through impartial and fearless publications.[53] But it soon entered into rivalry and its very first issue categorized the Maithili Sahitya Parishad as a Kayastha organization and its magazine *Bharati* as a *Kaithini Patrika* (Kayastha's magazine). It also criticized their false claims and hollowness.[54] It also criticized the Maithil Mahasabha and the Maharaja of Darbhanga. On the reader's page, it was written:

स्मरण राखू 'विभूति' ककरो सँ नहिं डैरनिहार सभक पोल खोलनिहार एके निर्भिक पत्र थीक। लल्लो-चप्पो में ई नहिं पड़त। सभक विषय में निरपेक्ष बात कहत। अधिकार क हेतु शक्ति भरि लड़त।[55]

[Remember that *Vibhuti* is not afraid of anyone, and is a whistleblower, a fearless newspaper. It will not indulge in false admiration. It will publish unbiased reports on every issue. It will fight for rights to the best of its ability.]

It gave the details of the further special issues of *Vibhuti*, which were— Kathank, Kavitank, Sahityank, Sharadank, and Mithila Rajyank.[56] [Special issue on prose, poetry, literature, Sharda (the goddess of learning), and on Mithila State] This fifth issue of *Vibhuti* was planned to cover the Mithila State. This showed that the demand for the separate statehood of Mithila had already entered the public discourse of Maithils in the 1930s. But he himself was not completely impartial in his approach. And this was perhaps the reason that the publication of magazine had to be stopped soon. The publication of *Maithili Sahitya*

Patra from 1937 to 1939 by Ramanth Jha in many ways opened up a new direction in Maithili publications. Its contribution to Maithili literature, particularly in standardizing and enriching the language, was immense though some scholars believe that it cannot be considered a *Patrika* (magazine)[57] as it did not have any editorial column and carried no news, Chandranath Mishra preferred to call it a *Granthmala* (book-series). *Sahitya Patra*'s main contribution was the publication of some valuable literary works[58] and it made an attempt to standardize Maithili prose by following a uniform style of writing in Maithili.

Swadesh was the first magazine in Maithili published after the political independence of India from British rule.[59] Only six issues of this magazine were published. But its contribution in terms of circulation and literary production was valuable. When Maithili was recognized as a mother tongue by the government of Bihar and a *Gadya Sangraha* (prose collection) of Maithili was compiled for the matriculation examination, most of the essays were taken from this magazine. It created a new class of readership in Maithili. According to Chandranath Mishra 'Amar', its readerships included betel sellers, cobblers, and the less educated *Grihasthas* (householders) of rural Mithila. Its circulation was more than 2,000. Another achievement of this paper was that it managed to keep the controversy and rivalry with other groups and magazines away. Through this paper, we also come to know about the policies and programmes of the Maithili movement. It included protection and promotion of culture and literature, preservation of the Maithili language and its scripts, question of separate statehood, establishment of Mithila University, solution to the Koshi problem, etc.[60] From 1955, the *Swadesh* was published as a daily newspaper for three months. According to Chandranath Mishra 'Amar', it was published due to the commitment and the enthusiasm of many Maithili supporters. But without sufficient economic support, it had to be closed very soon. This was followed by many magazines and papers, such as *Vaidehi* published from Sitamarhi as a fortnightly, *Mithila Jyoti* published from Patna, and a monthly magazine for the children, *Batuk*, published from Allahabad. There was also a growing enthusiasm for the publication of Older and more recent Maithili manuscripts.[61]

However, publications in Maithili in this period were caught in a condition where Maithili speakers were not very enthusiastic about Maithili magazines and journals. In such a situation, its publications were seriously handicapped due to economic considerations and editors were dependent on the patronage of rich landlords. Besides, there were serious threats from newly emerging Hindi zealots of Bihar to subsume Maithili within Hindi as its dialect. And finally, Maithili's recognition as an independent language of study was granted in Kolkata University and then Banaras University, but in its home state, Bihar, it had to fight almost for two decades to get such recognition by Patna University.

Even the educated Maithils did not take very keen interest in the cultivation of Maithili literature.[62] A letter by an unknown Maithil reader that was published in *Vaidehi*, edited by Bhuwaneshwar Singh 'Bhuwan', gives a sense of the perception of the common Maithils towards Maithili magazines as late as the 1930s:

क्यौ मिथिलाक 'मिहिर' बनि क पहुँचैत छथि, क्यौ मोद बनि विनोदक बात बनबैत। क्यौ 'भारती' क दुहाउ(इ) दैत छैथि। क्यौ 'विभुति' क यश गबैत छथि। सब गयाक प्रेत थिकाह। सभक दक्षिणाक भुख छैन्हि। पुराण नहिं, गीता नहिं, बान्हु की त अखबार। ई कलियुगी अवतार लोकनि जे नै चाहथि। किन्तु हमहु पुरान ठक्क छी। 'तर्पण' त अपन पितरहुक नहिं करैत छी, एजेन्टक तृसि साधनक तखन बाते की। हँ, नमुनाक रूप में सभ स एक एक दु-दु अंक धरि अवश्ये ठकने छियैन्ह। ज कल्याण चाहथि त ई लोक आबहु चेतथु।[63]

[Some reach us as *'Mihir'* of Mithila, some talk of entertainment by being *'Moda'*. Some talk of appreciation about *'Bharati'*. Some sing of praise about *'Vibhuti'*. All are ghosts of Gaya. All are desperate for charity. This is not the Purana, nor Saptashati Geeta, but what they ask us to read is a newspaper? These sons of Kaliyuga, nothing is impossible for them. But I am also an old *thug* (spoof). I don't even perform the libation of my forefathers; why should I try to satisfy agents? But yes, as a sample, I have swindled all, of one or two copies. If they want their wellbeing, then they must be cautious even now.]

It is obvious from the use of words like *Kaliyugi Avatar, Durgasaptasati, Geeta, Tarpan,* and *Pitarahu* that this response was from a Maithil Brahmin and not the other castes of Mithila. This kind of response also exhibits the Brahminic and Sanskritic hold on the minds and practices of the Maithils. The reading of *Durgasaptasati* and *Geeta* was permissible and praised, but the reading of newspapers was looked down upon with contempt. To purchase these newspapers and magazines, in their eyes, was sheer wastage of money. They did not mind reading free samples but purchasing subscriptions of these magazines was not what they were looking for. All the magazines and newspapers of that time were suffering from this discouraging attitude of not only the common speakers of Maithili but also of many literate ones. These all were suffering from critically low number of subscribers. Hence, even the best magazines by some of the committed writers of Maithils met with their untimely death.

One of the crucial moments in this period was the publication of a special issue of *Mithila Mihir's Mithilank*, in 1936 by its editor Surendranath Jha 'Suman'.

The editor used both Hindi and Maithili in the issue. In fact, following the policies of *Mithila Mihir*, in this special issue also there are 192 pages in Hindi but only 100 pages in Maithili. However, Hindi is used to explain the distinctive features of Mithila and Maithili. It contains a storehouse of information about Mithila and Maithili. And many distinguished scholars of the time (writers in Hindi and Maithili

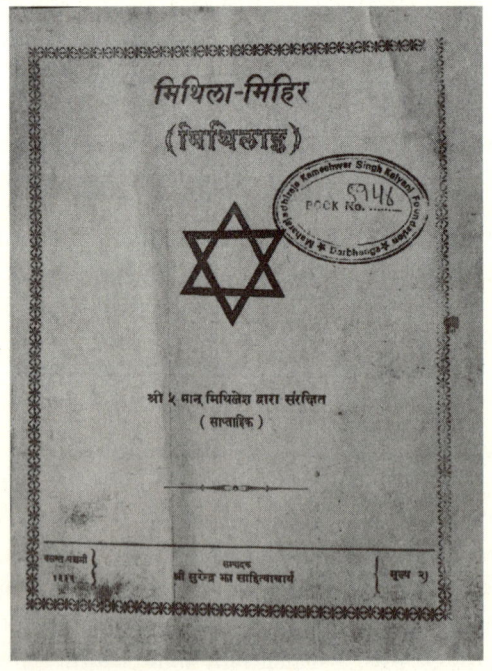

Image 3.2   *Mithila Mihir: Mithilank*

Source: Maharajadhiraja Kameshwar Singh Kalyani Foundation, Darbhanga.

both)[64] contributed in this compilation, covering different aspects of Mithila, its culture, its history, its language, the relationship of Maithili to Bengali and Hindi, and Sanskrit scholars and their traditions. S.M. Ane, Sachidanand Sinha, and Bhai Parmanand had a very high opinion about this issue and accepted the importance and contribution of Mithila in Indian culture and civilization.

Suniti Kumar Chatterjee in his *Maithili Bhasha aur Sanskriti* not only acknowledged the independence of Maithili but was critical of many Maithils who supported Hindi at the cost of their mother tongue Maithili. Although he supported Hindi as the national language and wanted every Indian to learn it, he also felt that it should not be at the cost of their mother tongues. He said:

मैं उन मैथिलों के तर्क को नहीं समझ सकता जो किसी बड़े हित के विचार से इसको दबाना चाहते हैं। भारत माता की भलाई की धुन में क्या कोई अपनी जननी को भूल सकता है ?[65]

[I do not understand the rationale of those Maithils who suppress this (referring to Maithili) for the larger good. In serving the interests of Bharat Mata, can anyone forget his own mother?]

Rambriksha 'Benipuri', a famous Hindi poet, in his *Vidyapati aur Hamara Kartavya* raised the issue of language, particularly of Hindi and Maithili. He avoided the question whether Vidyapati was a Hindi or Maithili poet. But he said that Vidyapati's language was Avahatta which was called '*adhunik Maithili*' (Modern Maithili). He made the following suggestions for the Maithils:

1. His (Vidyapati's) works should be published, but its language should be kept as it was and not made into modern Maithili.
2. A Vidyapati-Sahitya-Mandir should be established in Darbhanga, where all the manuscripts of Vidyapati should be collected. And not just Maithili but works of other poets should be collected as well.
3. Some events should be organized in the memory of Vidyapati in his village at Bisafi.
4. *Vidyapati-Jayanti* celebrations should not be left to individuals but it should be organized systematically and collectively.
5. A literary trip should be organized at least once a year to places associated with Vidyapati.[66]

Although *Mithilank* was a very informative issue of *Mithila Mihir*, there existed certain apprehensions regarding its usefulness as well. In a satirical essay on *Gonu Jhaki Nasdani*, the very purpose of *Mithilank* was ridiculed. It was said that what would be the worth of the issue as 'we' (Maithils) have little faith in newspapers; who then would read *Mithilank*? Would it be the other castes (non-Brahmins and non-Kayasthas) of Mithila, who lived there but did not call themselves Maithils? Why would they read it? The essay went on to assert that there was a general opinion even among many Maithils that if you talk about Maithili and Mithila it might be considered anti-national. According to this essay if, *Mithilank* was meant for the outsiders (non-Maithils) to give them some glimpses of Mithila, how it would be of any interest to them as for them Mithila was either merely a colony of Bengal and Maithili was merely a part of eastern Hindi.[67] This satirical essay acutely provides a glimpse of trivialities in which the issues of Mithila and Maithili were caught and had to cope up with in that period.

The slogan of Mithila-Maithil-Maithili enters the public discourse prominently after the publication of Umesh Mishra's essay in *Mithilank* by the same name—*Mithila-Maithil-Maithili*. Mishra discussed the growth of Maithili and Mithila from ancient times, its contemporary relevance, and the necessity to preserve it for the Maithils. Unless this was done, he believed, national or world service by the Maithils would not be valuable.[68] Here the relationships with selfhood, nationhood, and larger human community for the Maithils are well articulated by Mishra. Babu Bhola Lal Das in his *Maithili: Bhashak Rupme* writes that though some Hindi supporter acknowledged the literary capacity of Maithili, but as a language it was considered a part of Hindi. The author of *Hindi Bhasha Vigyan* Babu Shyam Sunder Das and Jayachandra Vidyalankar, author of *Bhartiya Itihas ki Ruprekha* classified Maithili as part of Hindi and Mithila as a Hindi-speaking region. He also shows that how, even in the census, Maithili was classified as a part of Hindi. Rambriksha 'Benipuri' and Mathura Prasad Dikshit also did not consider Maithili as independent of Hindi. For Babu Bhola Lal Das, this was the greatest misunderstanding of the time. Although, he said it was fortunate for the Maithils and Mithila that scholars like Grierson, Suniti Kumar Chatterjee, Pandit Mahavir Prasad Dwivedi, and many others considered it as an independent language. He was very critical of the fact that, despite having all the requisite qualities, Maithili was denied its rightful place in Bihar. According to him, the main quality of Maithili was that it had preserved its culture from the onslaught of many external attacks and yet it had been successful in maintaining its distinctiveness.[69]

Promotion of Mithilakshar—Maithili Script

Mithila also covers a report about the Mithilaksharankan Prabandhak Samiti Laheria Sarai, Darbhanga. Its chairman was Pandit Jeevanath Rai. The committee was involved in getting a Mithilakshar typesetting prepared from Kolkata based on modern Bangla script.[70] There was also a report about the existence of a Maithil Karna Kayastha Mahasabha in Darbhanga.[71] This was probably on the lines of the Maithil Mahasabha, but it was meant for Kayasthas only. This shows that caste remained the organizing principle in Mithila even when the Maithili language movement was increasingly gaining ground. In its meeting of 16 March 1930, the Mithilasharankan Samiti stated that though many Bengali letters were used in the Mithilakshar font, yet there were more than 200 letters and combined letters in Mithilakshar alone. It was decided as soon as the entire font was ready, 50,000 books would be published in it with the Devanagari (Hindi script) and it would be distributed at lower rate. It was also proposed that as soon as the font was ready, *Mithila* should give Mithilakshar its appropriate place. However, nothing much could be achieved in this direction, particularly in a context when many Maithili journals and magazines were struggling to get a sufficient number of subscribers. Ramlochan Sharan, founder of the *Mithila Pustak Bhandar* and publisher of *Mithila*, on the proposal of promoting Mithilakshar said that, first efforts should be made to make *Mithila* a widely and permanently circulated magazine and only thereafter promotion of Mithilakshar should be undertaken. His suggestion was referring to low subscriptions for *Mithila*. This was due to its too critical approach towards orthodoxy. These orthodox were unsupportive of *Mithila*. The radical essays, unacceptable to the orthodoxy, were promoted by Babu Bhola Lal Das. Therefore, it was decided that he should go on leave for a year. But, the other editor of the magazine, Kumar, did not agree to the proposal. As a result, Babu Bhola Lal Das continued to work as its editor; however, it was decided that orthodox viewpoints should also be given more space in *Mithila*.[72]

Mithila undertook the challenge of the promotion of Mithilakshar as well. The editorial in the eleventh issue of *Mithila* was written in Mithilakshar.[73] In the next issue of *Mithila* all the titles of the essays and poems were given in Mithilakshar.[74]

In the 21st session of the Maithil Mahasabha at Darbhanga, Babu Bhola Lal Das made a proposal with regards to the promotion of *Mithila* which was opposed. Although, it was discouraging, Babu Bhola Lal Das considered it beneficial for *Mithila*. He began to think that Maithili belonged to all the Maithils and not just Maithil Brahmins and Kayasthas whose interest the Maithil Mahasabha used to represent. However, in a situation when Devanagari already had an upper hand, this unenthusiastic support for Mithilakshar could not help in the promotion of the Maithili script. Those who opposed this proposal by Das

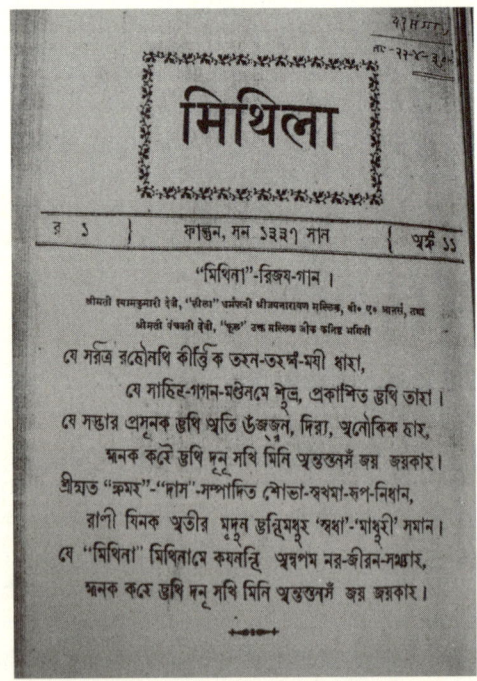

Image 3.3   A Specimen of Mithilakshar—1

Source: *Mithila*, Year-1, Issue-11.

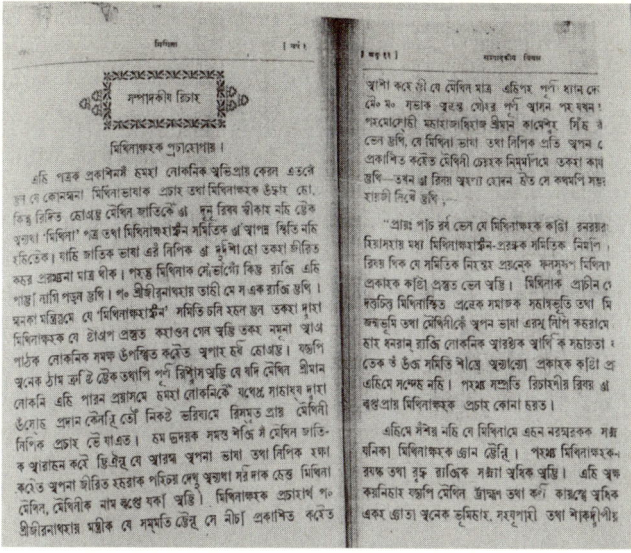

Image 3.4 A Specimen of Mithilalkshar—2

Source: Mithila, Year-1, Issue-11.

believed *Mithila's* policy was too radical and it adversely affected the youth. Gradually, the publication of *Mithila* also was short-lived and with that, any hope of the promotion of Mithilakshar died down. Had the promotion of Mithilakshar been successful, the story of the Maithili movement would have been different.

The Maithili Sahitya Parishad and Recognition of Maithili in Patna University

The Maithili Sahitya Parishad was established in 1930 to promote Maithili language and literature. It was the first institution constituted solely for such purpose. Maithili's inclusion in the syllabus of Patna University was the result of the enthusiastic efforts of this institution. This institution was born out of the Maithil Mahasabha. Kalikumar Datta, Nageshwar Mishra, Shashinath Chaudhary, Bhola Lal Das, and Dhanushdhari Das played key role in its formation.[75] The objectives of the institutions were: preservation and promotion of the Maithili language and Maithili (Tirhuta) script, Maithili literature, and Maithili culture. The means to achieve those objectives were: collection of early works in Maithili and the promotion of a modern Maithili literature with facilities to help the publication of new works; second, the establishment of museums and libraries; third, provision for the examination in Maithili; and finally, efforts through legal means to get appropriate recognition for Maithili by the government.[76] For many reasons, the second session[77] of the Parishad at Ghonghardia was extremely important.

This session of the Parishad was held along with the Maithil Mahasabha and was chaired by Mahamahopadhyaya Umesh Mishra.[78] His speech in this session was in many ways historical for the Maithili movement. In this speech, he explained the origin of Maithili literature,

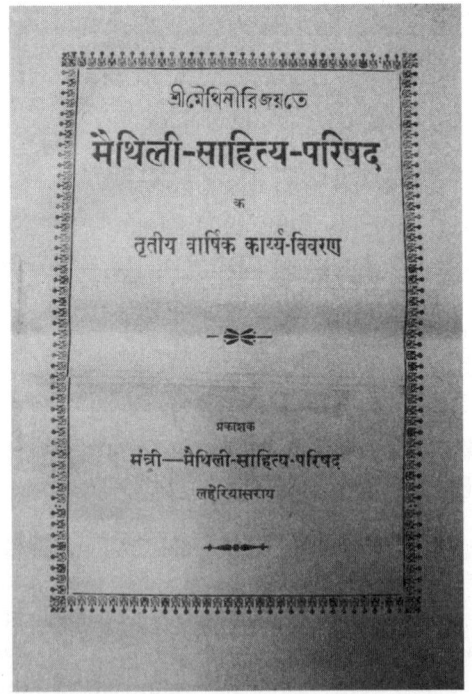

Image 3.5 *Maithili Sahitya Parishadak Triteeya Karya Vivaran*

Source: British Library, United Kingdom (IOR MSS EUR E223/231).

its progress and development, and the geographical boundaries of the Maithili speaking province. He also explained how Maithili literature and Mithilakshar affected the growth of many eastern languages in India.[79] He thoroughly rejected the claims of many scholars about Maithili being a 'dialect'.

The Parishad also began to work for the institutional recognition of Maithili as an independent language. In one of its standing committee meetings in 1933, a resolution was passed to express gratitude towards Banaras Hindu University (Hindu Viswavidyalaya) for recognizing Maithili as a subject of study from matriculation to B.A. They also decided to place the evidence before Patna University about the competency of Maithili.[80]

The Parishad with its branches in different parts of Mithila—in Pahitola under the chairmanship of Pandit Deenbandhu Jha, and in Samastipur under Babu Modeshwar Singh,[81] also made sincere attempts to cultivate a new sense of attachment to Maithili among different castes of Mithila. The President of the *Swagat Karini Samiti* (Reception Committee), in his speech at the third session of the Maithili Sahitya Parishad, cautioned that the other castes of Mithila, though speaking Maithili, do not consider themselves as Maithils. He also asserted that all the castes of Mithila were Maithils and at least on the basis of Maithili, Maithils of all castes should be mobilized. In this speech, he asserted the essence of Maithili culture as integral to Indian culture. Therefore, its progress and preservation was thought to be important. Unless its language was promoted, *Maithiliness* could not be preserved. Regarding the demand of Maithili, he vociferously said that:

यावत् मैथिलि क द्वारा हमरा लोकनि क शिक्षा नहिं होएत वा मैथिली कैं यावत् सरकारी पाठ्यक्रम में बिहार प्रान्तक अन्यतम भाषा जकाँ सम्मिलित नहि कएल जाएत तावत् एकर समुचित उन्नति होएव असम्भव। कलकत्ता विश्वविद्यालय तँ पूर्वहिं सँ मैथिली कैं उचित स्थान देने छैक आव काशिओ हिन्दु विश्वविद्यालय एकर स्वीकृति दै देने छैक। तखन प्रान्तीय विश्वविद्यालय में मैथिलीक स्वीकृति सब कक्षा में नहिं हो, ई अन्धेर थिक। रमेश्वर मैथिली चेयरक प्रतिष्ठा सँ कोनो ने कोनो स्थान पटना विश्वविद्यालय में होएब अनिवार्ये अछि परंतु बिहारी लोकनिक मैथिली साहित्यिक अनभिज्ञता सँ अथवा भ्रमपुर्ण राष्ट्रीयता क दुर्भावना सँ अन्देशा अछि जे पूर्ण सफ्लता एहि विषय में नहिं हो। तैं हमरालोकनि क प्रथम कर्त्तव्य यैह अछि जे यावत् विश्वविद्यालय क सब कक्षा में मैथिली भाषा क स्वतंत्र रूपें स्वीकृति नहिं हो तावत् चैन नहिं ली।[82]

[If education is not provided to us in Maithili, if Maithili is not included in the curriculum, like other languages of the Government's education in the Bihar province, till then its real and appropriate growth is impossible. Maithili was recognized by Kolkata University a long time ago, now even Banaras Hindu University has also recognized Maithili. Still, it is not recognized as a subject of study in all the classes in the provincial University. This is a great injustice. With the establishment of the Rameshwar Maithili Chair in Patna University, it is most likely that some or the other place be granted to Maithili, but due to the ignorance of Bihari people about Maithili literature, it is possible that complete success may not be achieved. Hence, it is our primary duty not to sit idle until Maithili is recognized in the all the classes of Patna University as an independent language.]

In his opinion, besides fighting for the recognition of Maithili, Maithils should work together for publications of old and valuable Maithili works. A museum should be established to showcase Mithila art, photographs, manuscripts, *tamralekha* (bronze and copperplate inscriptions), *shilalekha* (rock/stone inscriptions), coins, and other historical artefacts. These should be preserved. The government was asked to recognize old and historical sites, monuments, and temples of Mithila by following the Old Monuments Act and preserve them accordingly. Finally, he demanded that the government must encourage the complete growth of Maithili literature, appropriate preservation of Maithili culture, and regard for Mithila.[83]

Vidyapati Jayanti was celebrated on 31 October and 1 November 1933 with Maharajadhiraja Kameshwar Singh as its chairman in Darbhanga Town Hall. He announced a cash prize of rupees 100 annually for five years for the best essay on Vidyapati.[84] In the same year a pamphlet, *The Case of Maithili before the Patna University*,[85] was published and distributed by the Parishad and a series of essay was published in *Indian Nation* and *Searchlight* for the recognition of Maithili in Patna University.[86]

In this booklet, it is said that the total number of Maithili speakers was two crores which also included Magadhi. Further, it claimed that the earliest Maithili literature was created in the eighth century. To substantiate their viewpoint, the recognition of Maithili by Calcutta and Banaras Universities and donation of rupees 1,20,000 by the Maharajadhiraja of Darbhanga to Patna University for the Rameshwar Maithili Chair, is mentioned on the front page of the booklet. The

The

Case of Maithili

before

THE

PATNA UNIVERSITY

Speaking population (*including Nepal*) 20000000

Literature

Recognised by   Dating from the 8th Century

Donation   Calcutta & Patna Universities

Rs. 120000

By present Maharajadhiraja of Darbhanga

for The *Rameshwar* Maithili Chair

Secretary

MAITHILI SAHITYA PARISHAD

Darbhanga

Image 3.6   *The Case of Maithili before the Patna University*

Source: British Library, United Kingdom (IOR MSS EUR E223/231).

booklet is divided into two parts. Part I presents a study of Maithili by modern philologists and an analysis of their opinions; Part II tries to prove the independence of Maithili by applying the criteria used for distinguishing language and dialects. This section also gives the details about Maithili's relations with Hindi and other dialects of Bihar.

This pamphlet explains that, among the European scholars, Maithili was for the first time mentioned in 1771 in the preface to *Alphabetum Brahmanicum*.[87] Colebrook and Aime Martin also referred to Maithili as a separate language. In 1874, Sir George Campbell classified Maithili as a dialect of Hindi in his *Specimens of Languages of India*. Campbell's classification was explained by the general belief of that time that 'Maithili was a corrupt form of Hindi'.[88] The study of this language, it was asserted, was biased and it remained more or less obscure until Sir George A. Grierson brought the rich and old literary traditions of Maithili to the English speaking world through his works.[89] The pamphlet regret the fact that despite so many authoritative studies on Maithili language that demonstrated its independence beyond any doubt, Maithili still continued to be regarded as a dialect of Hindi.[90] It asserted that Mithila remained an internally independent territory and there was uninterrupted literary production in Maithili. Although Hindustani had become the state language of nearly the whole of north India including Mithila, literary production in Maithili did not stop because of the continuing patronage of the rulers of Mithila and Nepal. And till the commencement of the British Raj, Maithili literature was as developed as any other modern vernaculars of India. Indeed, in comparison to some languages, its literature was more developed. But when the Court of Wards took over the administration of Darbhanga Raj, Maithili lost her state patronage.[91] Maithili was neglected even at home and Maithils could not adapt to modern education for a very long time. In the meantime, Mithila's towns were full of Muslim settlers, western traders, and outside officials who rarely took any interest in the language of the people, let alone attaching any importance to it. Hence, they reported wrongly that Hindustani was the language of the people and Maithili was a dialect of Hindi, as they were mostly living in town alone and rarely mixed with people of the *country*. (Emphasis mine)[92] Thus, Hindi got undue importance in the region due to official support. But despite officials 'indifference, neglect, ill-treatment, and even atrocities' towards Maithili it remained the living language of the region. The essay goes on to mention the texts available in Maithili.[93] In comparison to Bengali—the most advanced language of India—it is said that 'it had no better materials than Maithili a century before. On the contrary, it had to depend for its very existence and mode of living on the precious materials of Maithili. All Bengali scholars admit this great indebtedness of Bengali to Maithili. Assami [sic] and Oriya also had to do the same…. '[94] But whereas these languages developed with due recognition in proper time, Maithili lagged behind for want of such recognition. Hence, for the proper growth of the language, demand for education through one's own mother tongue was put forward.

In the second part of the booklet, it mentions that Maithili suffers not because of its inherent weakness but because of the lack of adequate knowledge about it. It was widely understood as a dialect of Hindi without its own separate existence. To remove such misconceptions, it asserted that Maithili's claim as an independent language in India 'is as strong as that of Hindi, Bengali, Oriya, or Assamese'.[95] These were all considered to have descended from an earlier Indo-Aryan language and to bear a natural affinity with them. With slight modifications of Suniti Kumar Chatterjee's classification of modern Indian vernaculars in his *Origin and Development of the Bengali Language* (Part–I, p. 6), a chart of modern Indian language is provided.

Through this chart, the independence of Maithili from Hindi was established. In the booklet, it is explained that they differ from each other not just in vocabulary but also in grammar, idiom, and phonetics. It explained that Maithili represented a culture and civilization too which was distinct from Hindi. Therefore, it demanded that Maithili's classification as a dialect of Hindi must be stopped and it should be treated as an independent language.[96] It is interesting to mention that in this booklet, Maithili and Magadhi is claimed to be one and the same language. Hence, it was opined in the booklet that with the recognition of Maithili there would be no need to recognize Magadhi separately.[97] These arguments explain not only the growing antagonism between Maithili and Hindi but also the expansionist ideas of the Maithili

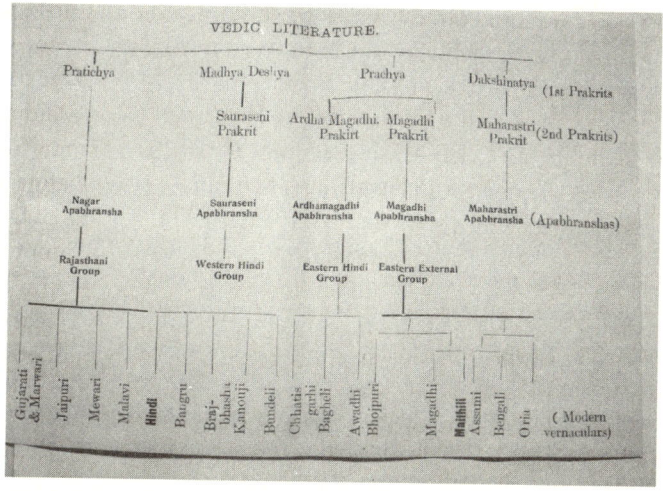

Image 3.7   A Chart of the Modern Indian Vernaculars

Source: British Library, United Kingdom (IOR MSS EUR E223/231).

activists and leaders. Bhojpuri in the pamphlet is regarded as different from Maithili as it was believed to be more influenced by Hindi. It
claims that Bhojpuri speakers, by then, were not so conscious about their
mother tongue and they did not bother much to cultivate it. Similarly,
Sadari (Santhali?) which was spoken in certain parts of Chhotanagpur,
was considered a corrupt form of Magadhi and Bhojpuri. It was not even
considered as a distinct 'dialect'.[98] Hence, in comparison to the other
'dialects' of Bihar, the richness of Maithili was shown in the pamphlet
and a demand for its recognition in the curriculum of Patna University
was put forward, particularly when the Calcutta and Banaras Hindu
Universities had already recognized Maithili as a subject of study.[99] Its
recognition was in no way considered as suppression and boycott of
Hindi.[100] Hindi's claim for Maithili being its dialect was rebuffed by
Pandit Rambhadra Jha.[101] He argues that if this claim was based on similarity of some of the vocabulary between Hindi and Maithili then why
was this not applicable to other languages like Marathi, Gujarati, and
Bengali, which also shared some vocabulary with Hindi? He illustrated
the difference between Hindi and Maithili based on grammar and phonology as well.[102] He questioned the census for not showing the number
of Maithili speakers separately. He wondered if this was done by the
biased supporters of Hindi and was surprised as educated Maithils did
not seriously notice it. He suggested that if it was difficult for them to
oppose this openly, then why did not they approach the Maharaja to
intervene on their behalf.[103] He reasserted the stand of Maithili supporters regarding Hindi that they were not against the status of Hindi
as the 'national' language, but it could not be accepted at the cost of
other provincial languages.[104] The mood of Maithils is reflected in this
statement which he made:

न्यायालय क कोन कथा प्रान्तीय शिक्षा विभागहु में मैथिली कें स्थान नहिं, विश्वविद्यालहु
में मैथिली कें स्थान नहिं। मिथिला क ई अवज्ञा, ई तिरस्कार, मैथिली क ई अवहेलना हमरा
लोकनि कें असह्य अछि।[105]

[Forget the courts, Maithili has no place even in the provincial education
department, not even in the University. This dishonour, this disrespect,
and disregard for Maithili is intolerable for us.]

A copy of the recommendation of the Parishad to recognize Maithili
in Patna University was sent to the university in 1933. Maharaja

Kameshwar Singh also wrote a letter to the Vice Chancellor of Patna University. The Vice Chancellor replied with some objections. The Maharaja informed the Parishad about those objections. In response, the Parishad published a memorandum in English (possibly the above-mentioned booklet) and through the Maharaja, sent it to Patna University. A meeting of the Hindi Boards of Studies was convened on 21 November 1933 for this purpose. Bal Mukund Mishra B. A. B. L. Jyotish Teertha (Madhubani), Narendranath Das Vidyalankar and the Mantri of Maithili Sahitya Parishad (Babu Bhola Lal Das) went to Patna to represent the case of Maithili. In the Hindi Board of Studies, except for Professor Hari Govind Chaudhary, no one knew Maithili. So, despite his opposition, it was recommended that the study of Maithili should be permitted only in MA. The next day on 22 November in the meeting of Faculty of Arts, the recommendation was brought for the discussion. The representatives of Maithili tried to convince the members of the Boards and the Faculty about the status of Maithili without success. Many members of the faculty known for their anti-Maithili stand made every effort to obstruct the recognition of Maithili. But due to the stand of many Bengali members of the faculty, particularly Niranjan Niyogi (he was in favour of the study of Maithili in all the classes), the recommendation of the Board was not only rejected but a subcommittee was formed to investigate and report to the faculty about the claim of Maithili.[106] The subcommittee rejected the demands of Maithili on the following grounds:

1. There was no loss to Maithili-speaking students, due to non-recognition of Maithili.
2. The teaching of different languages would create apprehension among the speakers of different languages in Bihar like Bhojpuri and Magadhi. It would block the growth of any one language in Bihar.
3. Recognition of Maithili would have negative impact upon Maithili students. Their prospects would be compromised.
4. Increase of classrooms in the schools would cause extra expenditure.

This decision of the subcommittee was considered biased, one-sided, and unjust by the Maithili leaders. Against these objections, they argued that:

1. The non-recognition of Maithili would be a great loss to the Maithili students. This could be proved through the investigation of schools, *pathshalas, tolas* (Sanskrit schools), and colleges in Mithila.
2. The recognition of Maithili would not hamper the growth of a common language in the province nor would it give rise to competition among the speakers of the different languages in Bihar. The demand to treat Maithili as an independent language was not new. This demand had been put forward before Patna University for 15–16 years, but no such demand had been made by the speakers of the other languages. This demand was accepted by the Calcutta and Kashi (Banaras) Universities but no such demand was presented by the Bhojpuri and Magadhi speakers there. Recognition of Maithili did not cause loss to the common language of those provinces.
3. The reasoning that the study of Maithili might have a negative impact upon the future of Maithili students reflects the unawareness of the committee. The truth was that precisely because of the lack of recognition of Maithili, expansion of education was very limited in Mithila.
4. The fear of expenditure was unrealistic. Maithili-knowing teachers were available in almost every school in appropriate numbers. Even if there was a need for some extra expenditure, the Faculty of Arts should not mind it considering the interest of the large number of Maithili students.
5. In the colleges, provision for the study of Maithili could be made without expenditure because of the donation of the Darbhanga Maharaja. It was also seen that even the accepted languages like Hindi, Bengali, and Urdu were not taught, yet the students had the liberty to opt for and give examinations for papers in those subjects.[107]

In this regard the sixth session of the Maithili Sahitya Parishad at Muzaffarpur in 1936 was very important. It brought a new life to the Parishad. Rai Bahadur Jayanand Kumar was the President and Bhuwaneshwar Singh 'Bhuwan' was the Chairman of the Reception Committee. In this session of the Parishad, for the first time, members of many castes participated as their name suggests.[108] But the internal differences within the elites were also visible. In the *Parishad Samachar* column of *Bharti*[109] Babu Bhola Lal Das writes that Bhuwaneshwar Singh

'Bhuwan' was campaigning in *Sotipura*[110] for sending a representative to the vice chancellor of Patna University for the recognition of Maithili and also for seeking subscribers for *Vibhuti* (a journal published by Bhuwaneshwar Singh 'Bhuwan' from Muzaffarpur). Babu Bhola Lal Das was critical of this approach of Bhuwan's, as he felt the Maithili Sahitya Parishad should have been informed before any campaign had been undertaken. According to him, the effort should have been collective and not individual. In the editorial column of the *Bharati*, he informs the reader about the decision of Mohammad Yunus (1884–1952), premier of Bihar province at that time, in which he had introduced the Urdu script in the law courts. This decision was to be implemented from 1 June 1937 and court papers were to be published in Urdu along with Hindi. Criticizing this decision, he states that there were virtually no demands by the people of Bihar to introduce Urdu in the court. He writes that there was strong opposition to the use of Urdu in the court by the people of Bihar, except for some literate Muslims. According to Das, despite all these difficulties and the huge expenditure that it might lead to, the minister ordered the use of Urdu. Similarly, at Patna University, Santhali was recognized by Blare because of his sympathy with that 'language'. He then asked why Maithili was not recognized. Would it cost more than the cost involved in the introduction of Urdu in the courts? Was the recognition of Maithili any less important for the people of Bihar? Babu Bhola Lal Das was of the view that, with the support of people in authority, Maithili would get its due recognition. He expected the vice chancellor of Patna University (Sachidanand Sinha) to take a decision in favour of Maithili.[111] And finally Maithili was recognized by the Patna University when the Maharaja of Darbhanga, one of the Patrons of the university, went into its senate meeting. Later on, the Tribhuvan University of Nepal also recognized Maithili as a major language. Other Universities of Bihar, like Bihar University, Bhagalpur University, Ranchi University, and Magadh University recognized Maithili as a subject of study at the highest level after their inception.

The Maithil Rashtra Sabha

Thakur Suryanarayan Singh wrote an article on *Maithil Rashtra Sabha O Mithilak Sangathan*[112] in which he explained the political aspirations of the Maithils. He defended those Maithils who believed that the Maithil

Rashtra Sabha[113] should only work for the political organization of the Maithils. In their opinion, Maithili should not be made the language of the Sabha. They believed that the Maithili movement-related work could be done by the Maithili Sahitya Parishad. Against this, he asserted that Maithili alone was suitable for the Sabha. Although he agreed that those representatives of Maithil unable to speak in Maithili could use any other language, the proceedings and deliberations of the Rashtra Sabha should be held in Maithili alone. He mentioned the growing formation of various caste-based and communal organizations in Mithila like the Rajput Sabha, Kushvaha (Koiri) Sabha, Yadav (Gop) Sabha, Bhumihar Sabha, Gohlot (Dusadh) Sabha, Nagavansi (Tamoli) Sabha, Jaiswal (Kalwar) Sabha, Hindu Sabha, Sanatan Dharma Sabha, and Kurmavanshi (Kurmi) Sabha. These local Sabhas were linked to national Jatiya Mahasabhas. Their meetings used to take place from time to time in Mithila, but because of their links with national Mahasabhas, they used Hindi for their deliberations. It was only the Maithil Mahasabha which used Maithili in its deliberations. Does it not show that only the upper-caste Brahmins and Kayasthas looked upon Maithili as their mother tongue and struggled for its recognition? An effort was made to include the other castes as well. But these castes either adopted Hindi in their separate caste associations or remained indifferent to Maithili. They were not sufficiently mobilized by the Maithili organizations despite their tremendous efforts to that purpose. What could be the possible reasons for that? Was it because of the Maithil Mahasabha as some scholars have argued? Or was it because of the high level of caste consciousness among the masses, which was quite usual for almost all parts of the country? Did they adopt Hindi to oppose the upper-caste challenges? Or was it because of their lack of awareness about the struggle for Maithili, though they were the speakers of the language? Or was it because they found standardized Maithili as difficult as Hindi and less lucrative than the later? The formation of these caste associations shows their political awareness but why did they not actively participate in the Maithili movement? Was this a strategic move or a deliberate attempt?

The Maithil Rashtra Sabha believed that besides social reforms, education, and village upliftment, it could also accommodate the different caste associations[114] and represent the voice of all Maithils. It was hoped that gradually all public association could be recognized by the Rashtra Sabha and in its meetings, common subjects would be discussed collectively. Caste-specific issues would be discussed by the concerned department on which experts could give their opinions. This kind of deliberation would gradually reduce the internal divisions in society and develop a new sense of fraternity among them with the slogan of Mithila, Maithil, and Maithili.[115] It was expected that the Maithil Rashtra Sabha should be formed independently of competitive political parties. Later, if it were to become a political organization and serve the interest of Maithils, there should not be a problem.[116] However, there is no report as to what extent the Sabha was successful in its endeavours; nonetheless, it is clear that efforts in that direction were already being undertaken.

The Ambivalent Maithil Elite and the Hindi–Maithili Debate

Dr Amarnath Jha was a strong supporter of Hindi as the 'national' language of India. Although he supported the promotion of Urdu as an important language of India, but when it comes to the national language of India, he wholeheartedly supported Hindi against Urdu or Hindustani. When there were attempts by the nationalist leaders like Rajendra Prasad and others to promote Hindustani as the national language of India—to ease the language tensions in the country—Amarnath Jha categorically opposed such moves.[117] He was a great supporter of his own mother tongue, Maithili, too. This he boldly emphasized in his Presidential address at the Abohar, 30th session of the Akhil Bharatvarshiya Hindi-Sahitya-Sammelan in December 1941. There, he clearly stated that Hindi was not his mother tongue. He also expressed his displeasure on how his proposal to provide primary education to the Maithil children in their mother tongue Maithili—with its rich and valuable literature, in its script that was distinct from Devanagari—was objected to by the member of the Education Committee formed by the Bihar government. Although all the members agreed on the point that primary education should be imparted in the mother tongue, Hindustani was imposed upon Maithili children.[118] Amarnath Jha's expression of these sentiments as the president of the Akhil Bharatiya Hindi Sahitya Sammelan shows his deep attachment to and regard for Maithili. He expressed these beliefs on other occasions as well. The dual support for Hindi and Maithili was common to other members of the Maithili literati as well, with a very few exceptions. Their support

for Maithili did not make them anti-Hindi in any way. These sentiments among the Maithili speakers developed when the very existence
of Maithili as an independent language was challenged. In one of his
essays, 'Maithili evam Hindi' published in *Mithilank*, Dr Amarnath
Jha argued that it was the duty of all Maithils to serve the interest of
Maithili. But it was important for the Maithils and for their progress
that they must also learn Hindi and English as well.[119] Similarly, in
his presidential address to the Maithili Sahitya Parishad at Darbhanga
in 1943, he rebuked the fear and anxieties of Hindi's supporters that
the progress of Maithili would obfuscate the growth of Hindi as the
'national' language. He said:

...हमर ई इच्छा नहि जे मैथिली हिन्दीक स्थान लेअय। हिन्दीकैं हम राष्ट्रभाषा मानैत छी,
हिन्दीक हम यथासाध्य सेवा करब, हिन्दीक समस्त देशमे प्रचार हो, तकर हम उपाय करब।
परंतु, हमरा इहो कहैत संकोच नहि जे हिन्दी हमर मातृभाषा नहि थिक। हिन्दी हमर मातृभाषाक
स्थान नहि ल सकैत अछि। हिन्दीक व्यवहार हम अपन नेना सभमे, अपन स्त्रीवर्गमे, अपन
घरक काजमे नहि क सकैत छी। राष्ट्रभाषाक प्रचारक अर्थ ई नहि जे प्रान्तीय भाषा सभक हानि
हो अथवा ओकर लोप हो।[120]

[It is not my intention that Maithili should replace Hindi. I adore Hindi
as the national language; I will serve it according to my capacity and I
shall also try to promote it in the whole country. But I have no hesita-
tion in saying that Hindi is not my mother tongue. Hindi cannot take
the place of our mother tongue. We cannot use Hindi amongst our children, amongst women, and in our household work. The promotion of
the national language does not mean that provincial languages should
be at a loss or vanish.]

He then went on to compare Maithili with Bangla and Hindi. According
to him, sixty or seventy years ago the status of Bangla and Hindi was
no better than that of Maithili. But these languages have achieved
remarkable success. A similar development could have been achieved
by Maithili too, had it been promoted as the medium of instruction
at the primary level and printing and publishing in Maithili were
encouraged.[121]

But this unequivocal support for Maithili was not true in the case of
all the sections of Maithil elites. Their approach towards Maithili was
somewhat compromised. It is reflected in the many issues of *Mithila*. It
was said that:

आई काल्हि अनेको बी ए और एम ए भेटताह जनिका षुद्ध मिथिला भाषा क परिज्ञानो नहिं होएतैन्हि और ने ओलोकनि एहि हेतु किच्छु चेष्टा करै छथि ।[122]

[Nowadays one may find a great many number of B.As. and M.As. who might not have a knowledge of correct Mithilabhasha, and they do not even make an effort to learn it.]

There was a growing contempt for the 'English'-educated Maithils who did not bother to use Maithili. A couplet by Kaviavar Sitaram Jha expresses it thus:

पढि लीखि कऽ जे नहि बजैछ हा मातृभाषा मैथिली।
मेन हैछ एहिना कपूतक, कान दुहु खेंचि ली।।
छाउड़ लेपि झट दऽ झिटुकि सँ जीह ओकर खेंचि ली।
पर हाय ई अधिकार हमरा ने देलनि "मैथिली"।।

[Those literates who do not speak their mother tongue Maithili,
I feel like pulling both the ears of such a worthless son,
And pulling his tongue through a potsherd by applying ashes,
Alas! Such a right to me is not given by 'Maithili'.]

This reveals the internal tensions among the Maithili speakers and their elites. Although harbouring contempt against those literate Maithils who did not bother to speak Maithili, Maithili activists suffered from a sense of helplessness. They were unable to do anything about that. Does this helplessness not suggest a lack of opportunities in Maithili? What if opportunities were made available in Maithili too? Would not their attachment with Maithili have been different?

The fourteenth All India Oriental Conference (15–18 October 1948) was organized at Darbhanga. The event was not only a great success but brought all the scholars of Oriental studies, particularly the scholars and pandits of Mithila together on a common platform where the history, culture, tradition, and language of Mithila, Maithili, were deliberated. The event had a tremendous effect on the consciousness of many Maithils and many other institutions such as the Rameshwarlata Sanskrit University and the Lakshmishwar Public Library also organized their events on the sidelines of the conference. This included meetings for the creation of a separate Mithila University. The members of the Proposed Mithila University Committee also observed 'University Day'. In the meeting, many distinguished scholars were present like

P.V. Kane, Vice Chancellor of the Bombay University; R.C. Majumdar; Amarnath Jha; the minister of education of Bihar, Badrinatha Varma; the minister of Local Self Government of Bihar, Vinodanand Jha; and others. It is interesting to note that in the name of the place of the event, instead of Bihar, Mithila (as a territorial unit) was mentioned after Darbhanga. During the conference, a symposium was also organized on the problem of Maithili. This emphasized the need to give the Maithili language its due place amongst the modern Indian languages and in the administrative and educational fields in Bihar'.[123] In the Symposium on the 'Problem of Maithili', the participants included Suniti Kumar Chatterjee, Subhadra Jha, Tantranath Jha, and Rajpandit Baldeva Mishra. According to Suniti Kumar Chatterjee, Maithili fulfilled all the criteria to be classified as an independent and competent language. These were: grammatically, on several factors, Maithili was considered different from the other north Indian languages; secondly, referring to the work of Jayakant Mishra, he said that it had a sufficiently rich and independent literary heritage. Regarding the question as to whether the language was desired by those who spoke it, he suggested that Maithils alone could testify to this and advised them to not to be shy in speaking out and using their mother tongue. Finally, he mentioned the difficulties experienced by Maithili speakers in learning Hindi.[124] Subhadra Jha supported these points and talked about the difficulties experienced by Maithili speakers in being forced to adapt to Hindi as their mother tongue. He also regretted that Patna University and the Bihar Government were not helping Maithili. Tantranath Jha demanded the inclusion of Maithili as a medium of instruction from the primary to the postgraduate levels of education. Rajpandit Baldeva Mishra called for the support of all the Maithils, irrespective of their caste and creed in the development of Maithili. It was envisaged that early acceptance of Maithili should be given in administrative and educational fields of the province.[125] Although all the proceedings in this symposium were conducted in Maithili[126] Chatterjee's third and fourth criteria indicate the prevalent mentality among the Maithili speakers, particularly among the modern English-educated Maithils. Why should a speaker of a rich language shy away from using it in public places? Why was learning Hindi made compulsory? The competence of their own language was supposed to be judged based on their difficulties while learning Hindi. So, in other words, for the supporter of Maithili, the problem was not just to contest the claims of Hindi supporters for whom Maithili was a dialect of Hindi. More importantly, there was a need to develop confidence among the Maithils, particularly educated ones, to use their own mother tongue, Maithili, in public. This was perhaps the greater struggle for the supporters of Maithili, and despite the many achievements of the movement, it could not be achieved unless Maithili was used and promoted as a medium of instruction in primary education.

Away from Orthodoxy: *Swadeshi–Vilayati* Movement

This *Swadeshi–Vilayati* movement of the 1930s was the culmination of all the internal contestations through which Maithili society was undergoing for four to five decades. However, this movement was confined to Maithil Brahmins, particularly the Shrotriya, and other caste groups had not much to do about it. But it was mainly through these Brahmins that new ideas—modern English education, women's education, and social reforms—perceived for a long time as irreligious, began to make its inroads in Mithila. As I have discussed in the previous chapter, all these ideas were deeply contested and most of the Maithils followed the traditional pattern of living and were averse to any kind of change. It deeply disturbed these 'reformers', who again and again termed Maithil Samaj as *'sutal samaj'* (sleeping/rigid society). But they themselves were in two minds about these changes and reforms. Until the 1930s, it was the followers of *Parampara* (traditions) who were strongly critical of and opposed to any changes in Maithil society.

The hold of orthodoxy can be understood from an incident that occurred in the last decade of the nineteenth century. According to the Maithili Pandits, Hindu shastras forbade them from crossing the oceans. It was a commonly accepted norm among the Pandits controlling their movement (journey) overseas. On the grounds of health, Maharaja Lakshmishwar Singh was advised to visit England, for which he had made all the arrangements. But he could not go because he feared that it might hurt the religious sentiments of his uncle. Four decades later, in 1931 a trip by his nephew, Maharajadhiraja Kameshwar Singh, to England for participating in the Round Table Conference, divided the Maithil Shrotriya Samaj into two groups, popularly known as

Swadeshi and *Vilayati*. Those who accepted and welcomed this visit by the Maharaja were called *Vilayati* and they were in a minority but had the full support of the Maharajadhiraja. But those who opposed this visit were called *Swadeshi*. They were in large numbers and migrated from Mithila, fearing that they would be *polluted* by staying in his Raj (Darbhanga). Their resistance to this visit was so strong that they excommunicated the Maharaja and called him a *Patit* (irreligious). The Maharaja organized a feast to win the support of this large section of his own community. This infuriated many of the orthodox Shrotriyas and they opposed the feast and even picketed at the Manigachhi Railway Station to protest against those who wanted to participate in it.[127] Some magazines, such as the *Mithila Mitra*, were not so critical of this journey. It criticized those Shrotriyas for daring to take *rajshakti* (power of the state) in their hands. At the same time, the same magazine, adhering to *Sanatana* principle, emphasized the need of launching a movement that could respond to Mahatma Gandhi's criticism of untouchability and Shastras and Smritis be protected.[128] Although such opposition died down gradually, this move of the Maharajadhiraja was successful in opening up a new path for the Maithils. Later, many Maithils were able to visit different parts of Europe and other countries.

Maithili as a Medium of Primary Education

The demand for the use of Maithili as a medium of primary education had been raised since the beginning of the twentieth century. The Bihar Education Reorganization Committee was formed by the government of Bihar to make recommendations about school education in Bihar, particularly about the use of the mother tongue as a medium of instruction at the primary level. Amarnath Jha, Rajendra Prasad, Sachidanand Sinha, and others were members of this committee. The committee accepted in principle the use of the mother tongue in primary education. But when it came to the use of Maithili in primary education in north Bihar, it dramatically reversed the earlier decision of the committee in which Maithili's use was accepted. About the meeting, Amarnath Jha writes:

> I regret that owing to a last-minute change in the dates of the meeting from February to March 1940, I was not able to attend it. I regret it all the

more as I find that a decision arrived at a general meeting of the full com-
mittee on 7 March 1939, is now being reversed. The decision to allow
Bengalis and Maithilas to use their mother tongues as media of Basic
Instruction was made when I was present.[129]

Rajendra Prasad wrote to him about dropping the claim of Maithili
as he believed it was 'opposed to public opinion'.[130] Sinha feared
that if such a position was granted to Maithili, then Bhojpuri speakers could also demand that their children should be taught in their
mother tongue and not in Hindustani.[131] Jha was of the opinion that
the mother tongue should be the medium of instruction at the primary
level while at the secondary and higher stages, the student should be
taught in Hindi or English. Ultimately he was permitted to 'append a
Minute of Dissent', which he did, but not without regret. Thus, through
deliberate political interference, promotion of Maithili as the medium
of instruction in primary schools was denied. Later, in 1949 when the
Government of Bihar recognized Maithili as the medium of instruction
from class one to seven, it was too late and too little attention was paid
for its proper implementation. Many Maithili leaders and activists argue
that this merely amounted to tokenism and nothing was actually done
to implement that decision. Textbooks were not available, either due
to lack of publication or poor distribution. The biased approach of the
government of Bihar towards Maithili can be understood from the following report of the Commissioner of Linguistic minorities. According
to the 17th Report of the Commissioner of Linguistic Minorities of
India in pursuance of the provisions given in the article 350 A of the
Indian Constitution, there were 358 separate classes or sections (as
against 283 for Bengali, 317 schools and 78 sections for Santhali, nil
for Oriya and 2,471 for Urdu) where instruction was imparted through
Maithili. About 358 teachers were employed (as against 915 for Bengali,
398 for Santhali, and 6,466 for Urdu) for teaching Maithili in the primary sections for 2, 937 students opted for the Maithili medium. At
the secondary level of education, there were 186 sections with 2,888
students taught by 186 teachers as in 1975–6.[132] Further, the fact that
it was not recognized in the eighth schedule of the Indian Constitution
already diminished its status, while the non-cooperative attitude by the
Hindi book sellers and administrative apathy towards Maithili ensured
its failure.

Mithila: The Demand for a Separate State

The history of Mithila, its legends, language, and culture gave rise to a sense of distinctiveness among the Maithils when the province of Bihar and Orissa was carved out of Bengal (1912). This sentiment was expressed in some magazines and journals like *Mithila Moda*. For the first time this demand was formally made by the Maharaja Rameshwar Singh of Darbhanga in 1921. In this connection he submitted a memorandum[133] to the then governor of Bihar and Orissa, Baron Sinha of Raipur. This memorandum was based on the principle of Montague which he expressed in the House of Commons on 10 July 1917. He stated the following principle of 'not one great Home Rule Country but a series of self-governing provinces and principalities federated by one central government'.[134] This proclamation was made in the context when the demand for Home Rule was raised by the Indian nationalists and the colonial government was seriously contemplating the viability of local self-government in India. Maharajadhiraja Rameshwar Singh went on to give extensive reasons for justifying his claim of being the ruling chief by citing almost all the *Sanads* in which the Maharajas of Darbhanga were called independent rulers. However, the government did not take this proposal seriously. The government was aware of the opposition of the peasants to the Maharaja. This claim was considered to be the personal ambition of the Maharaja. But such feeling for distinctness was expressed by the growing middle class of Maithil society as well. Their feelings got an impetus after the creation of Orissa on 1 April 1936 on linguistic basis.[135] In the 1940s again demands for a separate state of Mithila were made. The Maithil Mahasabha passed a resolution for the creation of separate statehood for Mithila[136] and a memorandum was also prepared. When Maharajadhiraja Kameshwar Singh was elected as a member of the Constituent Assembly of India, efforts for the creation of Mithila state increased. The Mithila Mandal Central Committee was formed for such purpose with Kumar Ganganand Singh as its president. He wrote to the secretary of the Constituent Assembly of India that the 'Indian nation has gained political power and in accordance with its repeated resolutions is going to constitute provinces on linguistic basis. We place our claim for a separate province on those accepted principles and earnestly request the members of the sub-Committee and the Constituent

Assembly to examine our claim ....'[137] In this regard several letters were exchanged between Ganganand Singh and Pandit Girindra Mohan Mishra, Assistant Manager, Raj Darbhanga.[138] Later on, apprehending the difficulties in the viability of such a demand, they pressed for a subprovince of Mithila within Bihar. The Maharajadhiraja himself proposed the creation of three sub-provinces within Bihar—Mithila, Magadh and Bhojpur, and Jharkhand.[139] In this regard, he also made a speech in the Constituent Assembly and pressed for the creation of the 'subprovince of Mithila with autonomous administrative powers'.[140] An effort was made for the next one or two years but then eventually it had to be dropped. The movement was sadly seen as an attempt of the Darbhanga Raj to save its zamindari. There is no evidence of their support for the separate statehood demand of Mithila launched by Janaki Nandan Singh and others in the 1950s during the linguistic reorganization of the Indian states (discussed in the next chapter).

In this period of the Maithili movement, we find increasing focus on the following aspects—The Maithili versus Hindi debate; setting up organizations to propagate and popularize the Maithili language, whilst expanding the concept of Maithils; the beginnings of writing, printing and publishing in Maithili; and the celebration of Vidyapati Smriti Parva and the other cultural aspects of Mithila. The Maithili movement was pitted against not just the Hindi supporters who wanted to subsume Maithili within Hindi's fold. A more intricate battle was being fought within, where a great many individuals and professionals adapted to Hindi. Although they were aware of the richness of Maithili, many of them shied away from using it publicly. Even hardline supporters, barring one or two of the Maithili activists, did not completely oppose Hindi.

This period was remarkable in the history of the Maithili community in other ways as well. The major events, which deeply affected and influenced Maithili community were the Sharda Act and the Swadeshi–Vilayati movement. It also helped in various ways to organize the society on modern lines, a trend which was facing stiff opposition from the traditional orthodoxy. On the other hand, beginning the celebration of Vidyapati Parva and Janaki Mahotsava, establishing the Maithili Sahitya Parishad and gaining recognition of Maithili in Patna University and later on official recognition of Maithili as a medium for primary education in Mithila helped in the progress of the Maithili movement. After

1940 there were attempts for the creation of a separate Mithila state. One of the drawbacks of the movement was that the small middle class of the society that was emerging were not completely independent in their social and political outlook. A major section of Maithili speakers was indifferent towards the Maithili movement. It appears that they were speaking the language without realizing any threat to its existence as the Maithili writers and literary elite wanted them to believe. So, there was a huge gap between the protagonists of the Maithili movement and the common speakers of the language. However, efforts to mobilize the masses through cultural celebrations like Vidyapati Parva and Janaki Mahotsava had enormous influence on the growth of Maithili movement. In many ways, some of the foundations for the Maithili movement were laid down in this period on the basis of which many new demands were made and most of them achieved in later decades, which is discussed in the next chapter.

Notes and References

1. Many Bengali students used to visit Mithila to study Hinduism and philosophy when Bengal came under direct Muslim rule and Mithila remained somewhat 'secluded' from direct Muslim interferences.

2. Like the role played by Sir Ashutosh Mukherjee, Dr Suniti Kumar Chatterjee, Sukumar Sen, Narendra Nath Gupta, Mathura Prasad Dikshit, and others in the promotion of Maithili language and literature.

3. This meeting was held in 1944 or 1945 (?). The statement of Chatterjee is quoted in the Welcome Speech by Dr Vishwambhar Jha, Chairman of the Reception Committee of the Seventeenth Session of the Akhil Bhartiya Maithili Sahitya Parishad at Sarisab in 1968; see *Smarika, Akhil Bhartiya Maithili Sahitya Parishad*, Lakshmiwati Nagar (Sarisab Pahi) Session, chief ed., Sadan Mishra, Darbhanga, Nav Bharat Press Laheria Sarai (1968), p. 3.

4. Quoted in the Presidential speech of Rambhadra Jha, at the third session of the Maithili Sahitya Parishad, 3–4 June 1934, Laheria Sarai, Maithili Sahitya Parishad (1934).

5. Mathura Prasad Dikshit, *Govind–Geetavali*, Ramlochan Sharan ed., (Laheria Sarai, Pustak Bhandar, n.d.), p. 2, particularly see footnotes no. 1 and 2 on page 2 about the books published in Bangla, and footnote no. 1 on page 3 about his imaginary biography. Its publication must be after 1932 as this year is mentioned in the *avedan* written by Sir Ganganath

Jha. In this work Dikshit does acknowledge the independent status of Maithili but finds its close affiliation with Awadhi and not with Magadhi. And he considered Bhojpuri also as a variety of Awadhi. Was this classification meant to strengthen the claims of Hindi against these vernacular languages? Awadhi, Magadhi, Shoursheni, and almost all the languages of India were considered to have originated from Prakrit. See pp. 17–18.

6. This refers to 'avedan' written by Sir Ganganath Jha as a preface to Mathura Prasad Dikshit's *Govind—Geetavali*, Ramlochan Sharan ed., Laheriasarai, Pustak Bhandar, n.d. For details, see footnote 5.

7. 'Rajan', Rajaram Prasad, 'Maithili Bhasha Andolan me Vidyapati Parvak Prasangikata', in *Vaidehi* (February 1989): 267–9.

8. Dhanishadhari Das, 'Janaki Mahotsava', in *Mithilank*, Darbhanga, Mithila Mihir (1936): 61–2.

9. Jayakant Mishra, *A History of Maithili Literature*, p. 18; cited in 'Amar', Chandranath Mishra, *Maithili Andolan*, p. 396.

10. *Mithila*, year 1, issue 1, Vaisakh, sal 1336, p. 1.

11. It is interesting that even in the 1930s, a term like Mithila Bhasha for Maithili was used.

12. *Mithila*, year 1, issue 1, Vaisakh, sal 1336, pp. 2–7.

13. Murlidhar Jha, 'Mithila Bhasha', in *Mithila*, year 1, issue 1, Vaisakh, sal 1336, pp. 11–14.

14. Jha, 'Mithila Bhasha'.

15. Possibly he was Janardan Mishra of Munger who opposed the promotion of Maithili while accepting Hindi and was enthusiastically working for its promotion in Bihar.

16. Cited in Bhuwaneshwar Jha and Ramanath Jha, 'Bihar mei Mithila Bhashak Stathan', in *Mithila*, year 1, issue 1, Vaisakh, sal 1336, p. 18.

17. Ganganath Jha was a great scholar of Sanskrit, vice chancellor of Allahabad University, and also a champion of the Maithili language. For details about him see the appendix on the short biography of Maithil intellectuals.

18. Bhuwaneshwar Jha and Ramanath Jha, sal 1336, pp. 18–19.

19. There was a practice of reading *Kanyadan* in Maithili-speaking areas where a literate person used to read it out for a group of illiterate persons. The interest in the work shown by the masses was unprecedented in the world of Maithili literature. Later, a film was also made on this novel by the same name in the 1970s.

20. Those who wanted the membership of this committee were asked to send their application to the Mantri of the committee at the following address 208, Harish Mukherjee Road, Kalighat, Kolkata. It was also advertised that Maithils could give financial assistance to the committee through

Gopi Raman Jha of Mangarauni. For details see *Mithila*, year 1, issue 1, Vaisaksh, sal 1336, p. 38.

21. *Mithila*, year 1, issue 1, Vaisaksh, sal 1336, p. 40.

22. *Mithila*, year 1, issue 2, Jyestha, sal 1336, p. 42.

23. *Mithila*, year 1, issue 2, Jyestha, sal 1336, p. 43.

24. *Mithila*, year 1, issue 2, Jyestha, sal 1336, p. 44.

25. *Mithila*, year 1, issue 1, Ashadh, sal 1336, p. 130, the following names were included in the beginning—Saheb Ramdas, Maharajadhiraja Mithilesh, prof. Radhakrishna Jha, Raja Kamlanand Singh, Babu Gopeshwar Singh, Dr Ganganath Jha, Babu Laliteshwar Singh, Munshi Lal Das, Vishwanath Jha, Adyadatt Thakur, Pt. Jagadish Jha 'Bimal', Kumar Ganganand Singh, Pandit Jayanand Kumar, Pandit Janardan Jha 'Janseedan', Pandit Harshanath Jha.

26. Harimohan Jha, '*Kanyadan*', in *Mithila*, year 1, issue 2, p. 76.

27. Jha, '*Kanyadan*', p. 60.

28. Jha, '*Kanyadan*', p. 70.

29. *Mithila*, year 1, issue 3, p. 86; here the opinion of George Grierson is also cited where he said 'Magadhi, indeed might very easily be classed as a sub-dialect of Maithili, rather than as a separate dialect'.

30. *Mithila*, year 1, issue 3, pp. 84–9; 'now there is growing demand by the speakers of these "dialects" to be considered as a separate language'.

31. *Mithila*, year 1, issue 3, p. 88.

32. *Mithila*, year 1, issue 3, p. 87.

33. *Mithila*, year 1, issue 4, Shrawan, sal 1337, p. 1.

34. *Mithila*, year 1, issue 4, Shrawan, sal 1337, p. 138.

35. *Mithila*, year 1, issue 4, Shrawan, sal 1337, p. 158.

36. *Mithila*, year 1, issue 4, Shrawan, sal 1337, p. 226.

37. *Mithila*, year 1, issue 6, Ashwin, sal 1337, pp. 230–7.

38. Ramanath Jha, 'Maithil o Maithili', in *Mithila*, year 1, issue 6, Ashwin, sal 1337, p. 247.

39. Ramanath Jha, 'Maithil o Maithili', in *Mithila*, year 1, issue 6, Ashwin, sal 1337, p. 248.

40. *Mithila*, year 1, issue 8, Agahan, sal 1337, pp. 314–18.

41. *Mithila*, year 1, issue 9, Paush, sal 1337, p. 392.

42. 'Madhur' Pulkit Lal Das, 'Maithili Sahityonnatik Upaya', in *Mithila Mitra*, uday 1, kiran 12 (December 1931): 301–04.

43. 'Madhur' Pulkit Lal Das, 'Maithili Sahityonnatik Upaya'.

44. Chandranath Mishra, 'Amar' (1962): 411.

45. In the first part of the essay, he explains the linguistic context and status of Hindi and Maithili under different subheadings, such as 'Vartamana Vikshobha', 'Virodhak Ashanka Byartha', 'Hindi O Maithili', 'Vartaman

Shiksha Pranali O Maithilik Anivaryata', 'Magahi-Bhojpuri-Maithili', 'Maithilik Sanrakshan O Prachar', 'Ayojan', etc. Mishra, 'Amar'.

46. Babu Bhola Lal Das (ed.), *Bharati* (Darbhanga: Maithili Sahitya Parishad, 1937), p. 435; cited in Mishra, 'Amar', p. 414.

47. *Bharati*, p. 138; cited in Mishra, 'Amar', p. 415.

48. *Mithila*, year 1, issue 12, Chaitra, sal 1337, pp. 413–14.

49. On 16 November 1937 with Kumar Ganganand Singh, Priyanath Mitra, Nageshwar Mishra, Jeevanath Rai, Baldeva Mishra, Surendra Jha 'Suman', Sukhadeva Das, and Bhola Lal Das, *Bharati*; cited in Mishra, 'Amar', 1962, p. 415.

50. Mishra Cited in 'Amar' (1981): 87.

51. *Mithila Moda*, new edition, Udgar–6, p. 24; cited in Mishra, 'Amar'.

52. *Mithila Moda*, new edition, Udgar–19, pp. 15–16; cited in Mishra, 'Amar', pp. 87–8.

53. *Vibhuti* (March 1937), varsha–1, ank–1, pp. 27–9.

54. *Vibhuti*, p. 27.

55. *Vibhuti*, p. 24.

56. *Vibhuti*, p. 25.

57. Mishra 'Amar' (1962): 410.

58. Such as—*Udayan Katha, Wakefieldak Padari, Chinik Laddu, Shakuntala, Shringar Bhajan, Ekawali Parinaya, Keechak Vadha*, Mishra 'Amar' (1962): 410.

59. Its chief editor was Surendra Jha 'Suman' and the members of the Editorial Board were Dharmapriya Lal, Shrikrishna Mishra, Suryakant Thakur, Kanchinath Jha 'Kiran', Mishra 'Amar' (1962): 423.

60. Mishra 'Amar' (1962): 424.

61. *Rag Tarangani*, widely regarded as lost by then, was being published by the Maharaja from the Raj Press, Darbhanga. There was also a handwritten manuscript by Chanda Jha—*Govind Geetavali*. It too was considered as lost but a copy of it was later found with Amarnath Jha and he was requested to publish it, though an edition of *Govind Geetavali* was published by Mathura Prasad Dikshit from Vidyapati Press. But it was considered as a Bengali edition and it was believed that the cause of Maithili would not be served unless a Maithili edition of the book was published. Mukund Jha 'Bakshi' was to publish the history of Mithila in *Padya*. Sitaram Jha published *Alankar Darpan*. Dr Sri Umesh Mishra edited and published *Krishna Janma* of Manbodh. He had also published a history of Maithili in Hindi. Suniti Kumar Chatterjee was involved in the edition and publication of *Varnaratnakar*. Chandra Dhari Singh of Madhubani's Chandranagar Dyaudhi was supposed to have written many texts in Maithili, which it was expected that he would publish soon. Mithila

Press at Sultan Ganj published the *Krishnawatar* of Gunvant Lal Das. Vidyapati Press published *Kanyadan*, the famous novel by Harimohan Jha. The Maithili Sahitya Samiti of Kashi also published some books in Maithili; see *Triteeya Maithili Sahitya Parishadak Karya Vivaran* (Laheria Sarai: Vidyapati Press, 1933), pp. 9–11.

62. *Triteeya Maithili Sahitya Parishadak Karya Vivaran*, p. 13.

63. Naresh Kumar Vikal, *Bhuwaneshwar Singh 'Bhuwan'* (Delhi: Sahitya Akademi, 2007), p. 74.

64. Like Suniti Kumar Chatterjee, Ganganath Jha, Amaranth Jha, Umesh Mishra, Mukund Jha 'Bakshi', Harimohan Jha, Sudhakar Jha, Sharda Charan Sen, Kavishekhar Badrinath Jha, Maithili Sharan Gupta, Shivapujan Sahai, Rahul Sankrityayan, Achyutanand Datt, Ramdhari Singh 'Dinkar', Baldeva Mishra, Narendranath Das, Kumar Ganganand Singh, Mathura Prasad Dixit, Rambriksha 'Benipuri', Arsi Prasad Singh, Girindra Mohan Mishra, Bholalal Das, Bhuwaneshwar Singh 'Bhuwan' and others; see *Mithilank* (ed.), Surendra Jha 'Suman', (Darbhanga, Mithila Mihir, 1936).

65. Suniti Kumar Chatterjee, 'Maithili Bhasha aur Sanskriti', in *Mithilank* (Darbhanga: Mithila Mihir, 1936), pp. 3–6.

66. 'Benipuri', Rambriksha, 'Vidyapati aur Hamara Kartabya', in *Mithilank*, pp. 84–5.

67. Gonu Jha, 'Gonu Jhaki Nasdani', in *Mithilank*, pp. 165–7; possibly it might be a pen name, Gonu Jha was a Maithili Brahmin and known for his wit and humour.

68. Umesh Mishra, 'Mithila-Maithil-Maithili', in *Mithilank*, pp. 9–15.

69. Babu Bhola Lal Das, 'Maithili Bhashak Rup me', in *Mithilank*, pp. 90–4.

70. *Mithila*, year 1, issue 1, p. 40.

71. *Mithila*, issue 3, p. 132.

72. *Mithila*, year 1, issue 10, Magh, sal 1337, p. 444.

73. *Mithila*, year 1, issue 11, Falgun, sal 1337.

74. *Mithila*, year 1, issue 12, Chaitra, sal 1337.

75. Mishra, 'Amar', *Maithili Sahitya Parishadak Samkshipta Itihas*, p. 2.

76. Mishra, 'Amar', p. 4.

77. Though there is confusion about when the session was held. Many like Chandranath Mishra 'Amar' believes that it was the third session of the Parishad, but I have the third annual *Karya Vivaran* of the Parishad in which it is clearly mentioned that the previous second session of the Parishad was held along with the Maithil Mahasabha at Ghonghardia and Mahamahopadhya Umesh Mishra delivered his speech on 16 April 1933. See *Maithili Sahitya Parishadak Triteeya Karya Vivaran*, p. 1.

78. He was a Sanskrit scholar based at Banaras and later at Darbhanga. He was a staunch supporter of Maithili in Mithila against Hindi. He proactively participated in the activities concerning Maithils, Mithila, and Maithili. For details on him see the appendix on famous Maithili personalities.

79. *Maithili Sahitya Parishadak Triteeya Karya Vivaran*, pp. 1–2.

80. *Maithili Sahitya Parishadak Triteeya Karya Vivaran*, p. 4.

81. *Maithili Sahitya Parishadak Triteeya Karya Vivaran*, pp. 4–5.

82. Speech of the President of the Swagat Karini Samiti (Welcome Samiti) at the third annual session of the Maithili Sahitya Parishad at Laheria Sarai.

83. Speech of the president of the *Swagat Karini Samiti* (Welcome Samiti) at the third annual session of the Maithili Sahitya Parishad at Laheria Sarai.

84. *Maithili Sahitya Parishadak Triteeya Karya Vivaran*, pp. 5–6.

85. The Secretary, Maithili Sahitya Parishad, *The Case of Maithili before the Patna University* (Darbhanga: Raj Press, 1933).

86. The Secretary, Maithili Sahitya Parishad, *The Case of Maithili before the Patna University*, p. 12.

87. Johannes Christophorous Amadutias's, *Preface* in Cassiano Beligetti *Alphabeticum Brahmanicum* (Rome: Italy, 1771). In this volume Maithili was referred to as Taurutiana (Tihutiya) and it was considered as one of the eighth languages of India. See also, Radhakrishna Chaudhary, *A Survey of Maithili Literature* (Ramvilas Sahu, 1976), p. 14. He refers to the term used for the language in the volume as Tourtiana.

88. The Secretary, Maithili Sahitya Parishad, p. 1.

89. Grierson examined the language thoroughly in his *Linguistic Survey of India [LSI]*. By the time the report of the *LSI* on Bihari languages was out, he wrote another book with Hoarnly, namely, *A Grammar of the Eastern Hindi compared with other Gaudian Languages*. In this book, the independence and distinctiveness of Maithili from Hindi was clearly mentioned. Other Europeans who took an interest in the language were: S.H. Fallon Kellog, Engelling Beames, and others. Besides many Indologists—Dr S.K. Chatterjee, Rai Bahadur Dinesh Chandra Sen, Nagendra Nath Gupta, Nalini Mohan Sanyal, Har Prasad Shastri, Mahavir Prasad Dwivedi, and Dr Umesh Mishra—took a keen interest in Maithili language and literature. The Secretary, Maithili Sahitya Parishad, pp. 1–3.

90. The Secretary, Maithili Sahitya Parishad, p. 3.

91. The Secretary, Maithili Sahitya Parishad, p. 3.

92. The Secretary, Maithili Sahitya Parishad, p. 4.

93. These were: 14 prose compositions, 43 poetic compositions some of which were lengthy epic works, 20 songs and prayers, 46 plays, 9 books of grammar and dictionaries, 8 on rhetoric and prosody besides 35 on

sundry subjects. In all, a list of 187 books was prepared, though the list was considered incomplete, The Secretary, Maithili Sahitya Parishad, p. 5.

94. The Secretary, Maithili Sahitya Parishad, p. 7.

95. The Secretary, Maithili Sahitya Parishad, p. 10.

96. The Secretary, Maithili Sahitya Parishad, p. 14.

97. The Secretary, Maithili Sahitya Parishad, p. 14.

98. The Secretary, Maithili Sahitya Parishad, pp. 15–16.

99. The Secretary, Maithili Sahitya Parishad, p. 17.

100. The Secretary, Maithili Sahitya Parishad, pp. 17–18.

101. Presidential speech of Rambhadra Jha, 3 and 4 June 1934.

102. Presidential speech of Rambhadra Jha, pp. 5–10.

103. Presidential speech of Rambhadra Jha, pp. 5–6.

104. Presidential speech of Rambhadra Jha, p. 10.

105. Presidential speech of Rambhadra Jha, p. 10.

106. *Maithili Sahitya Parishadak Triteeya Karya Vivaran*, pp. 6–7.

107. Ganga Nand Singh, Presidential Speech at the second session of the Patna College Maithili Sahitya Parishad's branch on 17 April 1937, quoted in Bhola Lal Das, 'Sansmaran', cmpld and ed., Phoolchandra Jha 'Praveen', *Babu Bhola Lal Das Rachnavali*, vol. I, Darbhanga, Mithilendu Prakashan (2008): pp. 161–3.

108. Babu Umashankar Prasad, Rai Bahadur Shyamnandan Sahai, Babu Rajeshwar Prasad Singh (Narahan), Sir Chandeshwar Prasad Narayan Singh, Rai Bahadur Shri Narayan Mahatha, Shri Maheshwar Prasad Narayan Singh, Pandit Dharma Rah Ojha, Pandit Yamuna Prasad Tripathi, Pandit Parmeshwar Tripathi, Kedarnath Mahatha, Gauridatta Jalan, Ramdeva Ojha, Lakshmi Narayan Gupta, Gaya Prasad, Ramacharan, Vindeshwari Prasad Verma, Janakdhari Prasad, Sharda Prasad, Madan Prasad, L.N. Goswami, Lakshmi Narayan Singh, Tarkeshwar Prasad, Shri Arsi Prasad Singh, Revati Raman Shriwastava, Shrimati Bhawani Mehrotra, Pandit Ramnandan Mishra, Surya Narayan Singh, Yogesh Chandra Mukherjee, etc. see Mishra 'Amar' (1969): pp. 11–12.

109. Babu Bhola Lal Das, *Bharati*, pp. 107–8.

110. Basically, this refers to the Darbhanga and Madhubani region of Mithila, where *Shrotriya* Brahmins live.

111. Babu Bhola Lal Das, *Bharati*, pp. 109–10.

112. Babu Bhola Lal Das, *Bharati*, pp. 85–9.

113. Whether such an organization was formed or not is not yet clear. But it was very much part of their discourse.

114. Babu Bhola Lal Das, *Bharati*, p. 87.

115. It appears this slogan of Mithila-Maithil-Maithili was increasingly being used from the 1930s onwards, and it gave the agitators a new and in

some senses a *secular* way of being and belonging to develop a common fraternity.

116. Babu Bhola Lal Das, *Bharati*, year 1, p. 89.

117. Presidential address of Amarnath Jha, 'Hindi Bhasha aur Sahitya', at the Abohar, 30th session of the Akhil Bharatvarshiya Hindi-Sahitya-Sammelan, 27–30 December 1941. In this connection, his other speeches are also important; 'Hindi aur Hindustani', a Presidential speech at the Suhrid Sangh at Muzaffarpur, 14, 15 March 1943 and 'Hindustani', published in *Bharat* (Prayag) (11 May 1937), These are published in his *Vichardhara* (Allahabad: Kitab Mahal, 1948), pp. 24–77.

118. Jha, *Vichardhara*, p. 54.

119. Amarnath Jha, 'Maithili evam Hindi', in *Mithilank* (Darbhanga: *Mithila Mihir*, 1936), p. 8.

120. Amarnath Jha, 'Maithili Sahitya', *Tilkor Bhag–1* (Patna: Bihar State Textbook Publishing Corporation Limited, 2007), p. 2.

121. Jha, 'Maithili Sahitya', *Tilkor Bhag–1*, p. 4.

122. *Mithila*, year 1, issue 7, Kartik, sal 1337, p. 300.

123. Umesh Mishra, 'Foreword', in *Proceedings of the Fourteenth All India Oriental Conference Darbhanga* (Mithila), vol. 1, Mahamahopadhyaya Dr Umesh Mishra, Local Secretary, XIV All India Oriental Conference, University of Allahabad (1949): pp. 7–8.

124. Umesh Mishra, 'Foreword', p. 136.

125. Umesh Mishra, 'Foreword', pp. 136–7.

126. Umesh Mishra, 'Foreword', p.137.

127. Govind Jha, *Janam Abadhi Ham* (Patna; Navarambha, 2010), pp. 35–6.

128. Editorial notes, *Mithila Mitra*, year 1, issue 10 (October 1931).

129. Amarnath Jha wrote a long note of dissent. Jayakant Mishra quoted the entire text of this 'note' in his lecture delivered at the All-India Maithili Sammelan held at Bombay in 1969; cited in Hetukar Jha, *Amarnath Jha* (New Delhi: Sahitya Akademi, 1997), p. 60.

130. Hetukar Jha, *Amarnath Jha*.

131. Hetukar Jha, *Amarnath Jha*, p. 62.

132. Uday Narayan Singh, 'Crises of Maithili Litterateurs', *Muse India*, issue 12 (2007), accessed on http://www.museindia.com/viewarticle.asp?myr=2007&issid=12&id=585 Tuesday, accessed on 12 March 2013, 1 a.m.

133. Memorial to His Excellency the Right Honourable Baron Sinha of Raipur, K.C., K.C. S.I., Governor of Bihar and Orissa from Maharajadhiraja of Darbhanga (Allahabad: The Pioneer Press, 1921).

134. Cited in Memorial to His Excellency the Right Honourable Baron Sinha of Raipur, K.C., K.C. S.I., Governor of Bihar and Orissa From Maharajadhiraja of Darbhanga, p. 2.

135. Pareshwar Sahoo, 'Formation of Orissa as a Separate State', *Orissa Review* (April 2006): 67–9, available at http://orissa.gov.in/e-magazine/Orissareview/April2006/engpdf/formation_of_orissa_as_separate.pdf; accessed on 15 March 2013.

136. Deep Narain Mishra (2005), *Emerging Pattern of Regionalism and National Integration: A Case Study of Mithila Raj Movement*, Final Report (2002–05) U.G.C. Supported Major Research Project in Political Science.

137. The telegram sent by Ganganand Singh to the Secretary, Constituent Assembly of India, New Delhi on 12 July 1947 from Darbhanga and confirmed by post on 29 July 1947 from Delhi. See Hetukar Jha (ed.), *Courage and Benevolence: Maharajadhiraja Kameshwar Singh 1907–1947* (Darbhanga: Maharajadhiraja Kameshwar Singh Kalyani Foundation, 2007), p. 136.

138. Jha (ed.), *Courage and Benevolence*, pp. 136–47.

139. The Notice of Amendment given by the Maharajadhiraja of Darbhanga on 24 August 1947 and repeated on 25 August 1947, Jha (ed.), *Courage and Benevolence*, p. 140.

140. The speech of the Maharajadhiraja of Darbhanga in the Constituent Assembly, Jha (ed.), *Courage and Benevolence*, pp. 141–2.

4 Maithili Language and the Movement, Part–II

The Maithili movement entered a phase of increasing politicization in post-Independent India. It was no longer led by the literary elite alone. Many political leaders and activists also joined and worked for the progress of Mithila and Maithili. Recurrent mass mobilizations, agitations, protests, and demonstrations for the rightful status of Mithila and Maithili were the major features of the Maithili movement. The political parties and leaders of Mithila began to use the issue of Maithili and Mithila strategically. Although they never rallied behind these issues in the same way as the literary and cultural elite of the region used to do, they could not ignore the concerns of Maithili any more.

One can divide the Maithili movement in this period into four phases. In the first phase, the separate statehood demand for Mithila became the central mobilizing factor immediately after Independence of India in 1950s. The demand for separate statehood extended further to claim Mithila as a union republic. The second phase of the movement was highlighted by the issues regarding recognition of Maithili as a modern Indian language in the Sahitya Akademi and the correct enumeration of Maithili speakers in the census. It also includes other demands, such as the opening of a Mithila University, and a radio station at Darbhanga. The third phase was about the demand for inclusion of Maithili in the eighth schedule of the Indian Constitution. This phase also witnessed many protests and demonstrations due to removal of Maithili from the Bihar Public Service Commission (BPSC) and for its re-inclusion; for the inclusion of Maithili in secondary school examinations; for implementation of the decision regarding the use of Maithili as a medium of instruction at the primary level; for publication of textbooks in Maithili and recruitment of Maithili teachers; for the recognition of Maithili as an administrative language in the state of Bihar, especially when Urdu was made the second official language in the state under a Maithili-speaking chief minister, Jagannath Mishra. The fourth and contemporary phase of the Maithili movement has witnessed the reassertion of separate statehood demand particularly after the recognition of Maithili in the eighth schedule of the Indian Constitution in 2003. In this contemporary phase, this demand for separate statehood is not based on distinct language and culture alone but on poor economic development. However, language and culture continues to form the very basis of the Maithili movement and the support base of the movement has been slowly but continuously expanding within Mithila and outside.

The Maithili movement, despite various challenges and shortcomings, can be considered as a successful movement. It has accomplished most of its demands except the demand for separate statehood and use of Maithili as a medium of instruction at the primary level of education. Although the government of Bihar formally recognizes Maithili as the medium of instruction at the primary and secondary level of school education, it has never been properly implemented.

This chapter examines the shifts and directions of the Maithili movement since India's political independence from colonial rule until the recognition of Maithili in the eighth schedule of the Indian Constitution in 2003. The following questions are discussed in this chapter: What were the major agendas and issues of the Maithili movements? What was the nature of its leadership? What kind of institutions and organizations were involved in the movement? How did political parties—national or regional—perceive the Maithili movement? Why and how did the political and literary elite of the region co-operate with and contest against each other? What were their contributions in the development and recognition of Maithili?

State Reorganization Commission: Separate Statehood Demand for Mithila

Demand for the separate statehood of Mithila received considerable support in the first decade after India's independence from colonial rule. A great many number of Maithils were discontented with the constitution of India as their language, Maithili, did not find a place in the eighth schedule. Secondly, when deliberate attempts were made to reduce the actual number of Maithili speakers and they were included as Hindi speakers in the 1951 census, they became far more infuriated. And one congress M.L.A. of the Bihar Legislative Assembly from the University constituency, Pandit Awadh Bihari Jha made it a subject of an adjournment motion in the assembly.[1] For them, Maithili was not just independent of Hindi but much older than it. And finally, when the State Reorganization Commission (SRC) was formed to consider the demands for the formation of new states in India on linguistic lines, they demanded the creation of separate Mithila State. Maithils were discontented with the government of Bihar. They claimed that under the government of Bihar the socio-economic condition of Mithila had deteriorated and its potential economic progress would be impossible to achieve unless it manages its own affairs. Under the leadership of Janaki Nandan Singh, an influential Congress leader and other Congress workers from the region, they worked vigorously for the creation of Mithila State.

In a conference of the Maithili Sahitya Parishad at Darbhanga on 24 December 1953, which was inaugurated by the then Chief Minister of Bihar, S.K. Sinha and presided over by the many ministers of Bihar, including Pandit Harinath Mishra, a resolution was unanimously adopted in which demand for the early formation of Mithila state was made.[2] In this connection, a meeting was presided over by Janaki Nandan Singh on 9 January 1954 at Darbhanga. In this meeting, many leading Congressmen, legislators, the members of local bodies, the members of the Provincial Congress Committee and District Congress Committee participated. They passed a resolution which says, 'In order to save the Congress organization and its workers from losing popular support it is urgent that a separate Mithila State be formed, so that the long-cherished aspirations of the people of this area be fulfilled'. However, S.K. Sinha was sceptical of the creation of separate state-hood for Mithila and his anticipated co-operation with SRC against such a demand led to another meeting presided over by Janaki Nandan Singh at Darbhanga on 17 January 1954. This meeting was attended by more than one thousand Congressmen from different districts of Mithila.[3] By this time, the government had made its stand clear and opposed a claim. However, in this meeting, demand for separate statehood for Mithila was reiterated on the ground of 'its glorious history, great traditions of culture, language, literature, script, way of life and philosophy', and demand was made for the formation of a Mithila Pradesh Congress Committee (MPCC). The Bihar Pradesh Congress Committee (BPCC) was requested to cooperate in such a formation. It was decided that a representation in this connection should be made to the All India Congress Committee (AICC) and its president Pandit Jawaharlal Nehru.[4] Many Congressmen including Janaki Nandan Singh proceeded to Kolkata on 22 January 1954, to attend a conference and to present to Nehru, who was the Congress chief at its Kalyani Session, a memorandum for the creation of MPCC for the impending Mithila state. But, before they could reach Kolkata, fifty-six of them were arbitrarily arrested at the Asansol station.[5] As soon as the news of their arrest reached Mithila there was a wave of public resentment against the government of Bihar. Shortly afterwards, they were released after the intervention of Nehru and the Chief Minister of Bengal, B.C. Roy. It is also claimed that the BPCC had made every effort to stop Nehru from having firsthand experience of these demands and in its meeting on 11 January 1954 called for the postponement of the work of SRC in Bihar. Meanwhile, in a meeting at Kolkata under the presidentship of Nageshwar Mishra, a huge number of Maithils reiterated the demand for separate statehood of Mithila and condemned the arrest of Janaki Nandan Singh and others at Asansol station. Although Janaki Nandan Singh could not reach Kalyani Congress to present the case of Mithila, he held a public meeting at Girish Park, Kolkata, on 26 January 1954 to mobilize the support for Mithila State. However, there was some opposition to this demand. In this meeting, a group, namely, the Maithil Yuvak Sangh, raised slogans against Janaki Nandan Singh and opposed the demand for separate statehood. Later, leaflets in which name of the person or organization was not mentioned, were printed and circulated in which a personal attack was made against Janaki Nandan Singh.[6]

Despite such challenges, the Maithils enthusiastically supported the creation of Mithila state by participating in demonstrations. Many rallies and demonstrations were organized in Patna, Darbhanga, Madhubani, and the other parts of Mithila. Janaki Nandan Singh proposed to set up a Mithila Rajya Kosha and within six months it was supposed to raise Rs 2 crore through which a university and an academy of music in Mithila was to be set up, independently of the government.[7] But it failed to build pressure on the authorities and the SRC did not even mention any such demand.[8] Later, when Janaki Nandan Singh was reinstated in the Congress, he also stopped leading any agitation for Mithila state. Paul Brass and others, who believed that the politicians have used the issue of Mithila for their personal political benefit, are correct but there is no reason to dismiss the fact that such mobilizations and agitations helped in developing consciousness among the masses about the issue of Maithili and Mithila. The next phase of the movement was led by the literary elite again and the establishment of Mithila University, recognition of Maithili by the Sahitya Akademi, and finally the inclusion into the eighth schedule of the Constitution became the major demands for the Maithili movement. However, in the last decade of the twentieth century, demands for separate statehood for Mithila resurfaced again.

Kolkata: 'Mini Mithila' and the Maithili Movement

In the context of the Maithili movement, it is often said that enthusiasm for the development and promotion of Maithili language and literature in modern times emerged mostly outside Mithila—in Jaipur, Banaras, Allahabad, Kolkata, and so on. However, Kolkata's contributions[9] to the Maithili movement have been far more influential and foundational in shaping the future course and nature of the Maithili movement, particularly after India's independence in 1947. It was Kolkata University which first recognized Maithili as a subject of study at the MA level in 1917. Ramanath Jha, the first representative of Maithili in Sahitya Akademi, had called Kolkata as 'Mithilak teerthasthali' (Sacred place of Mithila).

Lakshman Jha, a visionary thinker of Mithila and a socialist who fought unsuccessfully in the first general election, realized that poverty, illiteracy, floods, famines, and other socio-economic and cultural problems of Mithila could not be resolved by the present government of Bihar. So, he demanded separate statehood for Mithila. He even went to the extent of calling Mithila a sovereign Union Republic. To garner the support for this, he formed Mithila Mandal in Patna and received active support from Kolkata. Prabodh Narayan Singh, Babu Saheb Chaudhary, Devnarayan Jha, and others actively supported his demand. Lakshman

Jha also presented the case and problems of Maithili before the first prime minister of India, Jawaharlal Nehru at a meeting of the All-India Writers Association at Kolkata. Braj Kishore Verma 'Manipadma' and Harimohan Jha were also invited in this meeting. Babu Saheb Chaudhary played an active role in managing the invitation for these Maithils in Writers Association. He desired a legitimate place for the Maithili language and its writers as well.[10]

Girish Park of Kolkata is also called 'Mini Mithila' for many decades. Many Maithili speakers from every caste and class of Mithila used to congregate here. It has been a central place for many events, activities, meetings, public speeches, and mobilizations for Maithili, Maithils, and Mithila. It has been a congregation place for Maithils every Sunday. It

Image 4.1   Kolkata Mei Maithili: *Purvottar Maithil Samaj*

Source: Purvottar Maithil Samaj, October–December 2011, Issue–05, Image Courtesy, Vidyapati Chetna Samiti Guwahati.

was from this park that Babu Janaki Nandan Singh tried to mobilize the supporters in Kolkata for the creation of separate statehood for Mithila.

Many organizations[11] have been formed in Kolkata for the promotion and development of Maithili and Mithila. These organizations have played significant roles in shaping the all-round development of the Maithili language. Their contributions are in the field of research, book publication, and the organization of cultural and literary activities, dramas, and the political movement for a separate Mithila state. Many of these organizations were short-lived and were the outcome of internal factions within existing organizations. There were many organizations, which contributed in almost all the aspects of Maithili and Mithila movement. However, based on their functional specialties, these organizations can be classified into three broad categories: social and cultural, political and economic, and Maithili *natak* and drama.

One of the remarkable achievements of the Maithili movement in Kolkata was the publication *Mithila Darshan* by Prabodh Narayan Singh. Its main purpose was the development of Mithila and Maithili; and secondly, to encourage a movement for political rights.[12] The first issue of *Mithila Darshan* was published in January 1953 as a quarterly magazine from the Singh Press, Kolkata. From the very beginning, this magazine was fearless and confrontational. It attacked the political establishment in Patna in its April 1953 issue. In its editorial the census enumeration of Maithili speakers was criticized and the Government of Bihar was accused of conspiring against the interests of the Maithil:

जनगणनाक समय जनता केँ धोखा देल गेल जाहि मे पटनिया सरकारक निस्संदेह अप्रत्यक्ष हाथ छलैक। अशिक्षित तथा सरल स्वभावक जनता अपन मातृभाषा मैथिली लिखने छल किन्तु लिखनिहार सभ अपन प्रभुक आदेशानुसार हिंदी लिख लैत छलाह....अत: ई ललकार पूर्ण चुनौति निर्विकार रूपेँ देल जाय सकैछ जे गत जनगणनाक आधार पर केओ मैथिली के दवा नहि सकैत अछि...[13]

[At the time of the census enumeration, the masses were cheated. This is something in which the Patna Government certainly had an indirect hand. The illiterate and simple-minded people had mentioned Maithili as their mother tongue but the enumerators complying with the order of their superiors wrote Hindi...therefore, one can definitely challenge this move and assert that, on the basis of the previous census, no one can suppress Maithili.]

Prabodh Narayan Singh asserted through the editorials of *Mithila Darshan* that wherever the geographical, political, historical, cultural, economic, and linguistic factors like Mithila existed; and although deserved their own separate states but were neglected, exploited and marginalized; and if their population were determined, new states had to be created.[14] Similarly, criticizing the biased approach of Akashwani in Patna towards Maithili, he wrote that if its policies were not modified immediately then the officials would be compelled to do so through observing Radio Boycott Day in all parts of Mithila.[15] He was equally critical of Maithils and the Maithili society. In his opinion, until and unless Maithils freed themselves from the domination of Magadh through peaceful and nonviolent means, till then he could not remain silent. In this connection, he observed:

सम्प्रति हमरा चाही राघवाचार्यक उद्घोष, डा. लक्ष्मण झा तथा डा. लक्ष्मी नारायण सिंहक लगन, बाबू जानकी नन्दन सिंहक निर्भिकता[16]

[At present, we need the pronouncements of Raghavacharya, the dedication of Dr Lakshman Jha and Dr Lakshmi Narayan Singh, and the fearlessness of Babu Janaki Nandan Singh.]

It is important to note that Raghwacharya was a great supporter of Mithila state and he was assaulted by the Bihar Police of Magadh at Mahendra Ghat, Patna for his support of Mithila State. In one of his poems, he incited the Maithils—बीझ लागि गेल छौ, कृपाण के पिजा। [There have been rust, sharpen your sword]. Other figures like Dr Lakshman Jha went as far as demanding the creation of separate sovereign Republic of Mithila.[17]

Mithila Darshan was very radical and active in its support for the Maithili movement. From 1958, a provocative couplet by Kavivar Sitaram Jha was used in the magazine, which says:

अछि सलाइ मे आगि बड़त की बिना रगड़ने।
पायब निज अधिकार कतहु कि बिना झगड़ने।।

[There is fire in the matchbox, but will it burn without rubbing (with a matchstick)?
Similarly, could we get our rights anywhere without fighting?]

In 1963, Mithila Darshan Private Limited was created for the economic viability of the magazine and many people became its shareholders. Prabodh Narayan Singh became the chairman and Udit Narayan Jha (Basauli) its managing director. Rajnandan Lal Das was made its secretary. But due to the differences between the chairman and managing director, the publication of *Mithila Darshan* soon stopped. Then, Babu Saheb Chaudhary, a committed activist of the Maithili movement, published it from his own Mithila Art Press from 1971 to 1974. But the proprietorship of the magazine was with Prabodh Narayan Singh, so he took the publication rights from Babu Saheb Chaudhary and published it again from his Singh Press. And he managed to publish it until 1978. However, Babu Saheb Chaudhary continued the publication by changing the name of the magazine, *Maithili Darshan*, from July 1974. His editorials were radical and revolutionary. He writes in the issue of January 1981:

मैथिली प्रेमी सँ हमर अनुरोध अछि जे सरकार जाहि भाषा केँ बुझए, ताहि भाषा मे हमरा सभ केँ बात करबाक हेतु तैयार रहबाक चाही। जुलूस, सत्याग्रह, विधायक एवं सांसद लोकनिक घेराव, आमरण अन्नसन, आत्मदाह, सभ लेल तैयार रहबाक चाही। एहि पंक्तिक लेखक सभ किछु लेल तैयार छथि। मैथिली संग खाली भाषाक प्रश्न नहि छैक, मैथिली तँ एकटा साधन थिक, साध्य अछि मिथिलाक सर्वांगीन विकास।[18]

[I request the Maithili lovers that we should be prepared to talk in a language which the Government understands. We should be ready for everything—processions, Satyagraha, blocking the MLAs and MPs, hunger strike until death, self-immolation. The writer of this sentence is ready for everything. With Maithili, the question of language is not the only issue, *Maithili is only a means, but the end is all-round development of Mithila.* (Emphasis added)]

The last sentence in the above paragraph symbolizes a shift towards politicization in the Maithili movement, where the struggle was no longer for the recognition of the Maithili language alone. But it had become a tool for the all-round development of the language and the region both. However, this magazine also proved to be very irregular and it could not be published after March–April 1981. Its publication was restarted by some activists of the Akhil Bhartiya Mithila Sangh in 2004. Its editor was Sri Ramlochan Thakur. But only nine issues could be published. *Mithila Darshan* was again restarted by Uday Narayan Singh from May-June 2009. Since then, it has been published regularly as a bimonthly. Its executive editor is Ramlochan Thakur. In its new form, this magazine has been well-managed, published, and distributed with an estimated circulation of more than four thousand. The establishment of the Swasti Foundation in 2000 in Kolkata and the institution of the Prabodh Sahitya Samman[19] contributed immensely to the promotion of Maithili language and literature.

One of the oldest and the most active organizations in Kolkata, the Akhil Bhartiya Mithila Sangha was formed in 1957 after the persuasion of Harimohan Jha, Braj Kishore Verma 'Manipadma', and Lakshman Jha with the merger of the Akhil Bhartiya Maithil Sangh (ABMS) and the Maithil Lok Sangha (MLS). Its contributions to Maithili publications and journalism have been enormous. It published more than 50 books and orchestrated 13 Maithili dramas. The publication of the *Mithila Darshan* was the greatest achievement of the Sangha. But soon, due to internal differences and groupings, a new organization was formed in January 1959, known as the Mithila Sanskritik Parishad (MSP). It was formed exclusively for social, cultural, and literary developments. MSP has, since then contributed in many ways in the progress and development of Maithili language and literature. It celebrated its Golden Jubilee year in 2009. In its *Smarika*, published on the occasion, the purpose of the organization is described as the all-round development of Mithila, discussions on Maithili language and literature, Maithili culture, and the economic development of Mithila, preservation and propagation of Mithilakshar, preservation of manuscripts written in the Tirhuta script, publications of books and magazines, providing help to schools, colleges, libraries, and poor children, and so on.[20] There have been many achievements of the MSP, significant among them are: the commissioning of an oil portrait of Vidyapati (1960, the portrait was painted by Ramanand Singh of Munger District in Bihar); the release of a postal stamp on Vidyapati by the Department of Posts, Government of India on 17 November 1965;[21] and the publication of more than 30 Maithili books of which many have been included in the syllabus of universities. *Lorik Vijaya* by Manipadma was included in the UPSC's Maithili syllabus in 2005, and his *Naika Banijara* was given the Sahitya Akademi award in 1973. MSP also contributed in the recognition of Maithili by the Sahitya Akademi, Delhi and to achieve this purpose it constantly wrote to the Sahitya Akademi since 1964.[22] MSP has been a recognized literary association of the Sahitya Akademi since 1965. Similarly, it had played an important role in the establishment of Akashwani in Darbhanga and the recognition of Maithili as a subject of study at IGNOU, Delhi. Mahendra Narayan Jha was a founding member of the Parishad but, due to internal differences, he was excluded from the Parishad.[23] He formed a new organization, the Maithili Prakashan Samiti (MPS). Its only purpose, as the name suggests, was the publication of books. It published around ten books.[24] Another important contribution of the MPS was the publication of a research journal, *Maithili Prakash*. It was an irregular journal and its publication was completely stopped by 1988.[25] But some of its issues, such as issue 17 of January 1975 were important in many ways. In it, two major issues concerning Maithili were highlighted: first, Maithili should not be used just for poetry, stories, dramas, or novels but it must be used for writing texts on history, geography, commerce, economics, philosophy, physics, chemistry, biology, mathematics, and engineering as well; second, due to the lack of uniformity of standards in Maithili, the writing styles of Jeevanath Rai, Umesh Mishra, Ramanath Jha, Mahavaiyakaran Deenbandhu Jha, and Kanchinath Jha 'Kiran' should be followed. This issue of '*Maithili Prakash*' had a collection of eleven research articles[26] analysing different aspects of Maithili and Mithila.

There were many important magazines published from Kolkata that contributed in the growth of Maithili literature.[27] Although many of these magazines were short-lived, remained irregular, and had very limited circulation, one major achievement of these efforts was that such magazines were published continuously one after the other since the 1950s in almost all the branches of literature. The other major achievement in Kolkata for the Maithili movement was the publication of *Dainik Mithila Samad* in Maithili by Rajendra Narayan Vajpayee. Its editor was Tarakant Jha. Although this paper is no longer in circulation, its contribution has been significant in arousing the consciousness of Maithils about their language.[28] Although these magazines and dailies were short-lived and had very limited circulation, yet there was an unbroken continuity in such publications.

In Kolkata, there were many organizations formed for the political mobilization of Maithils. One such organization was Mithila Sangharsha Samiti (MSS). MSS was formed in 1974[29] to politically strengthen the Maithili movement. There were internal tensions within the Maithili movement. There were groups like MSS, which wanted to make the Maithili movement more and more political whereas other groups like MSP wanted to focus more on the cultural and literary development of Maithili. This resulted in a fierce rivalry between these two groups. Once MSS planned to protest before the governor of Bengal against the decision of the Karpoori Thakur Government in Bihar to do away with Maithili from the syllabus of matriculations and expected that in a function of MSP at Vishudhanand School an announcement to this effect would be made. But many activists of the MSP were against such an announcement and that resulted in a major scuffle between the members of the MSP and MSS. However, on 3 September 1978, a protest march was organized by the MSS. This protest march began from Rajendra Chhatravas (hostel), and from Grace Cinema turned towards Mahatma Gandhi Road and from Chitaranjan Avenue roundabout gathered at Girish Park in Kolkata. There were apprehensions that some member of MSP would try to misguide the protesters as well. However, according to Kamlesh Jha, the protest was successful. From Girish Park, some of the protesters went to Raj Bhawan (Esplanade East) under the leadership of Mithlendu, Sharat Chandra Mishra, Srimati Prabha Mishra, Kamlesh Jha, and others. They gave the memorandum to the Secretary of the Governor and were assured by him that he would write to the central government for this mistake of the government of Bihar. The slogans of the protest were—'बिहार सरकार मुर्दाबाद, संघर्ष समिति जिंदाबाद, मैथिलीक मान्यता देबय पड़तै।'[30]

[Down with the Government of Bihar; long live Sangharsha Samiti; they will be compelled to give recognition to Maithili].'

Then a delegation, consisting of Sharad Chandra Mishra, Kamlesh Jha, Shrideva Jha, and Javed Athar went to Patna to meet the Chief Minister of Bihar, Karpoori Thakur, and to present before him the grievances of Maithili speakers. They presented a memorandum to the CM of Bihar. It is possible that this might be one of the reasons for Karpoori Thakur to write a letter to the then Law Minister of India, Shanti Bhushan. In this letter, Karpoori Thakur recommended the inclusion of Maithili in the eighth schedule of the constitution.[31] In his memoirs, Kamlesh Jha also mentioned that in Patna they did not get the desired support from the Chetna Samiti, Patna. It reflects the lack of coordination and cooperation among the Maithili organizations even when they were all fighting for the cause of Mithila and Maithili.

In 1980, Jagannath Mishra became the Chief Minister of Bihar. Although he was a Maithili speaker and well aware about the demands to recognize Maithili as the second official language in the state of Bihar, he recognized Urdu as the second language in the state. It created a big uproar among the Maithili speakers. All India Maithil Sangh (AIMS), ABMS, MSP, and MSS came together and formed a new organization Maithili Mukti Morcha. Its co-ordinator was Ramlochan Thakur and the deputy co-ordinators were Kamlesh Jha and Ashok; Kishori Kant was treasurer.[32] It was a new shift in the Maithili movement where so many organizations came together on a common platform and participated in a huge rally at Patna on 9 December 1980. Police resorted to a lathi charge and many Maithils, like Sushil Jha and Vijay Kumar, were seriously injured. The major achievement of the protest was that the issue of Maithili and Mithila became politically very charged. Many political parties, particularly the Bharatiya Janata Party (BJP) took a very keen interest in the issue. Similarly, the Communist Party of India (CPI) under Bhogendra Jha and to a certain extent even the Indian National Congress took interest in Mithila and the Maithili issue. It is discussed in a later part of this chapter. Although Maithili and Mithila had always been a political issue, but after the 1980s, it acquired a strength of a different kind. Some parties were formed solely for the purpose of Mithila and Maithili. For instance, during the 1980 general election, MSS supported Vishnu Deva Jha 'Vikal' of Mithila Congress, as a candidate for the Bihar Legislative Assembly from the Ghanshyampur region of the Darbhanga district in Bihar. In this election, MSS published 'Ghoshnapatra' (declarations) for the candidate and workers of the MSS under the leadership of Sharad Chandra Mishra and campaigned for the candidate.[33] Another political party formed for the sole purpose of promoting the cause of Mithila and Maithili is the Akhil Bharatiya Mithila Party (ABMP).

Another shift in the movement since the 1980s is to mobilize the masses on the agendas and issues concerning them. In this connection rail roko, rasta roko, sansad gherao, Bihar bandh, Mithila bandh, and many such methods have been used. One of the most important protests and mobilizations in this period concerned the provision of better and standard rail facilities for Mithila. On 6 December 1981 a huge protest was registered at Howrah station.[34] In 1986, under the leadership of Jayakant Mishra, a public awareness campaign was launched to persuade the teachers of Mithila to implement the policy of using Maithili as a medium of instruction in the primary schools in Mithila.[35]

A Maithil Mahasangh was also constituted at Patna in 1983 on the initiative of Mritunjaya Narayan Mishra with the active participation of Pitambar Pathak and many Maithili activists and organizations from Kolkata. Its chairman was Mritunjaya Narayan Mishra, and pro-chairmen were Acharya Surendra Jha 'Suman', Babu Saheb Chaudhary, and Jayakant Mishra. From Kolkata, four organizations registered with the Mahasangh—ABMS, AIMS, MSS, and Navajagaran Maithil Sangh.[36] The very constitution of the Mahasangh reflected the willingness among the Maithili organizations to work together. It was able to organize a protest in Patna. It also published a magazine—*Koshi–Kusum*—for a brief period. However, this was a short lived organization and became completely inactive after 1985.[37]

It was also a period when Mithila Vikash Parishad (MVP) was formed by Ashok Jha in 1983. It has been a very active organization since then. It has played an important role in the recognition of Maithili in the eighth schedule of the Indian Constitution. It was due to the persuasion of this organization that the Trinamool Congress MP Sudip Bandopadhyaya first raised the question regarding the inclusion of Maithili in the eighth schedule, in the Indian parliament; after this, other MPs like C.P. Thakur and others from Mithila took up the issue. In this connection, the role of the Vidyapati Seva Sansthan (VSS) and Baidyanath Chaudhary Baiju was remarkable. The role of VSS is discussed in the latter part of this chapter. Another important achievement of the MVP is the installation of Vidyapati and Nagarjuna statues in the public parks of Kolkata.

Other major achievements of Kolkata's organizations was to present a memorandum to the then Prime Minister of India, V. P. Singh, for the inclusion of Maithili in the eighth schedule of the Indian Constitution. Bhogendra Jha took the initiative and invited Babu Saheb Chaudhary, leader of the ABMS, to present the memorandum. A delegation led by Babu Saheb Chaudhary visited Delhi.[38] Under the leadership of the MPs Bhogendra Jha, Hukumdeva Narayan Yadav, and Devendra Yadav the representatives of ABMS, Delhi, Vijay Chandra Jha and Ashutosh Kumar Jha a memorandum was presented to the then Prime Minister of India, V.P. Singh.[39]

The unique feature of the Maithili movement in Kolkata was that it could cut across the caste and class hierarchy. Although the organizations and leaderships were dominated by the upper-caste Brahmins and

Kayasthas, but in the events and the celebrations, all the Maithili speaking castes and classes participated. University professors, journalists, bus conductors, and taxi drivers all participated in the Maithili movement. It is possible that, away from the Maithili speech area, Kolkata provided the space for the Maithili speakers to not observe the social division based on caste and class in the same form as they used to observe in their homeland. Maithili might have become the only basis for their social interaction. It is also possible that observing the social and cultural activities of the Bengalis, Maithili speakers had realized the importance of Maithili literature, culture, and language, which they would not have otherwise acknowledged in Mithila. The major achievements of Kolkata's Maithili organizations were not only many literary publications and cultural celebrations but also their attempts to mobilize the Maithili-speaking masses politically. For many decades and, more actively since Indian independence, Kolkata became the centre of activities propagating pro-Maithili language and pro-Mithila statehood ideals.

Census and the Enumeration of the Maithili Speakers: The Contributions of Akhil Bhartiya Maithili Sahitya Parishad

The census has played a critical role in the classification of languages and 'dialects' in India. It seriously affected the prospect of a language or 'dialect'. The language and 'dialect' distinction has always been contentious. Since the first Census in 1872, language was a matter of great interest, not as a phenomenon , but rather as an index of nationality and a measure of population change. In the case of Maithili, though both Grierson and the then census commissioner agreed that Maithili was a regional 'dialect', they differed, however, in what it was a dialect of. For Grierson, Maithili was a 'dialect' of Bihari, but for the census commissioner it was a 'dialect' of Hindi. The issue of language was important for the colonial administrators to classify the communities in India according to the number of the speakers of a language. About the 1881 census, Richard Burghart writes that it 'retains a keen interest in nationalities, but more for the control of the populations than for glorification of the Raj. Language and birthplace were taken as the key indicators by which nationality might be determined'.[40] The issue of language and 'dialect' has been far from settled in census enumerations. As Burghart puts it, in the 1911 census Maithili was Hindi in its wider sense because it was not Bengali; from 1951 Maithili is Hindi in its wider sense because it is important that national language be the main language in as many areas as possible. According to Burghart 'the institutional continuity of the census and language policy in the colonial and the postcolonial India, including the unchanging classification of Maithili as dialect, implies that census has to do with the way in which modern states construct society as they monitor and control it'.[41] 'The 1951 census' writes Burghart:

> is of interest as it was the first census of independent India. The ruling Congress Party found itself, however, in a linguistic dilemma. Although the Indian National Congress had committed itself in 1921 to the idea of linguistic provinces in the belief that this was the only way to reach the mass of people in such a culturally diverse land, by the time the Congress Party had assumed power in 1949 the need for a common language to strengthen national unity was also recognized. The language of the former imperial rulers was an inappropriate symbol of national unity and Hindi was the most obvious candidate for elevation of that role. Thus, there was little reason for the state to recognize Maithili, for such recognition would exacerbate claims for regional autonomy and diminish the officially uncontroversial area where the 'main language' and the national language were one and the same. Yet the non-recognition of regional languages by Congress would betray the trust of those people who had fought to free the country of imperial rule. (See Government of India, 1956.)

Then, to solve this dilemma it was decided that 'if Hindi was to function as the national language it would have to be the subsidiary language of those region where it was not the main language'.[42] According to Burghart, the 1951 census returns marked the nadir of the Maithili language movement. It deeply enraged the Maithili speakers. They promoted an unsuccessful attempt to have the residents of Darbhanga and Bhagalpur districts entered *ipso facto* as Maithili speakers. Does not it show how Maithili language and its speakers were taken for granted and assimilated within the Hindi fold, both by British administrative policy in colonial era and after that the postcolonial government in India?

However, these attempts of the government could not discourage Maithili speakers. They gradually organized themselves to get their language recognized as an independent language of India. A

Table 4.1   Census Figures for Maithili (1971–2001)

Census Year	1971	1981	1991	2001
Maithili Speakers	6,130,026	7,522,265	7,766,921	
12,179,122				

Source: Census of India 2001, Paper 1 of 2007 Language India, States and Union Territories, Table C-16, Office of the Registrar General, India, p. 13, It is to be noted that Census figure of 1971–91 for Maithili was extracted from Hindi within which Maithili was enumerated as a mother tongue.

delegation of the Chetna Samiti, which was comprised of Shrikant Thakur 'Vidyalankar' (MLC), Dr Chetkar Jha (MLC), and Amresh Pathak (Organizing Secretary, Chetna Samiti) met Mr B.L. Das on 15 January 1971 to request him to get the speakers of the Maithili language correctly enumerated in the census of 1971. They complained that Maithili speakers could be 50 lakhs only due to the false enumeration of the 1961 census, in which most of the Maithili speakers were enumerated as Hindi speakers by the officials.[43]

The seventeenth session[44] of the Akhil Bhartiya Maithili Sahitya Parishad (ABMSP) of Darbhanga was imperative in various ways. Nature and the directions of the Maithili movement were thoroughly discussed in this session and the uneasy relationship in the Maithili movement between political leaders and the literary elites of the region resurfaced. In his welcome address, Vishwambhar Jha stated that had Maithili and Mithilakshar been used as the language of administration in the Darbhanga Raj, the consciousness about the language among the masses would have been developed much earlier. He lamented that the Maithil Mahasabha had not passed even a single resolution for that purpose. Although he believed that language consciousness was developing more and more, he expected it to be duly channellized and organized. He thought of language as a public property that requires the contribution of every group and class of the population. He also felt the threat from the caste- and class-based struggles and hoped that ABMSP would be spared from those divisive politics.[45] He also regretted that sessions of the ABMSP were not held for nine years and even more so for ABMSP's inactivity regarding the inclusion of Maithili in the eighth schedule of the Indian Constitution; the political conspiracy in Bihar whereby Urdu, and not Maithili, was recognized as the state's second administrative language; and the imaginary naming of the language of Bhagalpur as Angika.[46] The Maithili Sahitya Parishad (MSP) used to conduct examinations in Maithili literature. It was first started by Parmakant Chaudhary, and Subhadra Jha used to be its examiner. Then Shrikrishna Mishra shouldered that responsibility when Subhadra Jha went to Paris for his research on the *Formation of Maithili language*. This examination was conducted till the premiership (the main office bearer of the Parishad were called *Pradhanmantri*) of Kanchinath Jha 'Kiran'. Mahavaiyakaran Pt. Deenbandhu Jha was its *Pariksha Mantri* (Minister of examination). Thereafter, this examination was stopped. Shrikrishna Mishra believed that it was important for Maithili to become a medium for the subjects like history, geography, politics, economics, philosophy, and science. For this purpose the Maithili Vidyapeeth was established and the examination was restarted. He claims that despite the lack of funds, without even a single permanent employee, without a proper office, without the recognition of government or of any university, in 1963 and in 1965 twice examination were held successfully at 15 and 19 centres respectively. In 1965 for *Prathma* 290, for *Madhyama* 88, and for *Uttma* 6 students appeared for the examination.[47] The Principal of Chandradhari Mithila College, Lakshmikant Mishra and Prabodhnarayan Singh of Kolkata University actively supported this initiative. It was believed that the Maithili Vidyapeeth would play a critical role in the acceptance of Maithili as a medium of education in Mithila.[48]

In terms of making representations to the government on behalf of MSP, in February 1960, a delegation of Minister and MLA Ramakant Mishra and Bachha Thakur met the visiting commissioner of minority languages in Patna and informed him that the government of Bihar was not providing the facilities available for a minority language to Maithili, a language of most speakers in Bihar. The language commissioner merely assured help but nothing came out of it.[49] Similarly, during the census of 1961, MSP played an important role in convincing the masses to get Maithili written in the column for mother tongue. A delegation which included Ramanath Jha and Shri Surendra Jha 'Suman' met the commissioner of Indian Census at Laheria Sarai Circuit House and presented before him the anguish of Maithils because Maithili had not been enumerated accurately in the census. They were assured by the commissioner that the census staff would be instructed to not fill the mother tongue column on their own volition. In this regard, many letters were written to the government of Bihar as well.[50] In February 1961, Nalin Vilochan Sharma, Chairman of Bihar Hindi Sahitya Sammelan (BHSS) made some statements which infuriated many Maithili speakers. Similarly, Seth Govind Das and the chairman of BHSS, Ramdayal Pandey, in a meeting of the Hindi Prachar Sabha in Darbhanga on 31 January 1968 made a statement about Bihar being a Hindi-speaking province and Maithili as a sub-language (*Uppabhasha*) of Bihar. It was challenged by the Maithili supporters and they asserted that such an imposition of Hindi would make Maithils, otherwise supporters of Hindi, anti-Hindi. Surprisingly Seth Govind Das did not oppose Maithili being the medium of education at the proposed Mithila University, but he was opposed to the demand that Maithili be included in the eighth schedule of the constitution.[51]

Protagonists of the Maithili movement were unhappy with the conduct of the Bihar Rashtra Bhasha Parishad (BRP). Its project of conducting a linguistic survey in Bihar was opposed by them. They wanted it to be conducted by impartial scholars. They also objected to the policies of BRP, which was not only propagating Maithili as a 'dialect' of Hindi, but was trying to divide Maithili speakers by classifying the language spoken in Bhagalpur and Muzaffarpur as Angika and Bajjika respectively.[52] In the Sarisab session of the ABMSP, a discussion was organized on *Maithili Andolanak Ruprekha*[53] (An Outline of the Maithili Movement). The main theme of the discussion was whether the Maithili movement should become political or not? Many scholars—Jayadhari Singh, Braj Kishore Verma, Harinath Mishra, Kanchinath Jha 'Kiran', Madhava Narayan Jha, Ugranarayan Mishra 'Kanak', and Pradeep 'Maithili Putra'—believed that, for the Maithili movement to grow, political support was essential. There were others like Ramanath Jha, who believed that politics and literature, being two separate domains, should not be mixed. He urged that the platform of MSP should not be used for politics. There were others—Narendranath Das 'Vidyalankar', Devnarayan Jha, and Chetkar Jha—who focused on the need for the publication of one or two daily newspapers in Maithili and arrangements made by the government and parents/guardians in the Mithila region to successfully implement the use of Maithili as a medium of education in primary schools. They also reminded Maithils to use Maithili in public confidently and with passion.[54]

Sahitya Akademi and Recognition of Maithili as an Independent Modern Indian Language

Recognition of Maithili by the Sahitya Akademi in 1965 was a major achievement in the history of the Maithili movement. The fear among the Maithili speakers of being appropriated within Hindi disappeared somewhat and there have been recurrent agitations for the other demands based on Maithili and Mithila. The central demand, however, was the inclusion of Maithili in the eighth schedule of the Indian Constitution. Maithils were disappointed by not finding Maithili listed in the eighth schedule of the Indian Constitution. It was far more disappointing for them when even the Sahitya Akademi did not recognize Maithili as an independent modern Indian language. In the Sahitya Akademi, confusion prevailed over a long time regarding the status of Maithili. In its Annual Report 1961, some classics of Maithili are regarded as Hindi and Bengali simultaneously.[55] In a meeting of its executive board in 1957, a decision was taken in which it was said that 'languages like Maithili and Rajasthani did not need a separate programme as they could be well covered by the Akademi's programme in Hindi'.[56] Jayakant Mishra was of the opinion that if a Maithili representative were present in the board, such an erroneous decision could have been rectified. It was due to sheer confusion and vagueness about Maithili that the Sahitya Akademi undermined its independent existence, which has a literary tradition of over 700 years. However, the Akademi tried to promote Maithili within the Hindi programme and translations of some Maithili classics were included in its translation programmes. Similarly, a small prize of Rs 500 was awarded to the renowned Maithili poet Kavichudamani Kashikant Mishra 'Madhup' for his poem *Kobar-gita*.[57] But the Sahitya Akademi could not do much to promote Maithili as an independent modern Indian language on par with Bengali, Marathi, Oriya, Hindi, Gujarati, and Assamese. Its argument was that unless it was included in the eighth schedule of the Indian Constitution, it could not be treated as a separate language. But, according to Jayakant Mishra, that was an unfortunate mistake which could be rectified politically through political mobilizations and consensus However, the Sahitya Akademi being a literary body could recognize it as it had done in the case of Sindhi and English.[58] Jayakant Mishra, when elected to the General Council of the Sahitya Akademi in 1963, moved the following resolution for the recognition of Maithili:

> Resolved that, like English and Sindhi, Maithili be recognized as an independent regional modern Indian language of the state of Bihar on a par with Gujarati, Assamese, Oriya, etc., and not mixed up with Bengali and Hindi as at present (vide: 'Sahitya Akademi Report' for 1961 Hindi version pp. 4–5 and programme of translations form Hindi including Vidyapati p. 109 and that of translations from Bengali including selections from Vidyapati p. 113).[59]

Then he went on to quote Grierson's and Suniti Kumar Chatterjee's writings on Maithili to support its claim as an independent language. For Grierson: 'Maithili is a language and not a dialect…It differs from Hindi and Bengali both in vocabulary and in grammar, and is as much a distinct language from either of them as Marathi or Uriya'.[60] Similarly for Suniti Kumar Chatterjee:

> Maithili is a language by itself, with its own special characteristics. It is a language which has got a character of its own…. *By any stretch of imagination, it cannot be described as a dialect of Hindi.* It has a literature which goes back to at least the beginning of the fourteenth century and down through these centuries it has never ceased to be cultivated by its speakers.[61] (Italic in original)

Jayakant Mishra challenged those for whom recognition of languages like Maithili may weaken the unity and integrity of India. In this connection, he quotes the presidential address of the Non-Local Language Section of the All India Oriental Conference, 1941 Babu Ram Saxena,

> I believe that it is very much more convenient to have a neighbouring literary form of language as the medium rather than give the position to an international language, 6000 miles away from our land. With this belief, I put forward the suggestion in all humility that the people of Bihar should consider the plea for Hindi to replace English and the people of Assam should consider the advisability of having Bengali. I know the strength of sentiment in Mithila and Assam in favour of the mother tongue, but whether Assam with 20 lacs of speakers of Assamese and Mithila with a small proportion of speakers of Maithili in comparison with the numerous speakers of the other two dialects, Bhojpuri and Magadhi, in the

province of Bihar, could press their claims with any practical advantage is for them to consider.[62]

Jayakant Mishra considered such an argument as unfortunate and, citing the recognition of Assamese by the Sahitya Akademi, asserted that such an argument could not be held. For him, it was the absence of recognition that might weaken the unity of the nation and not the other way around. Although he rejected the 'violent and agitational approach' and Maithils were very much against such a move, he believed that a 'reasonable and equitious attitude' was always better, though he warned that it would be a mistake to underestimate the feelings of Maithili speakers because of their peaceful approach for the recognition of their language.[63]

Two other important events that helped in the recognition of Maithili by the Sahitya Akademi were the postcard movement and New Delhi Book Exhibition of Maithili Books and Manuscripts. The New Delhi Book Exhibition, which was held at Indraprastha Estate's Azad Bhawan from 9–11 December 1963 for three days, was organized by Jayakant Mishra and was inaugurated by the Prime Minister Jawaharlal Nehru. It was an exceptionally successful exhibition and Nehru was personally impressed by the sweetness of the Maithili language and its rich literary tradition. In the visitor book he wrote:

> I was happy to inaugurate yesterday the Maithili Book exhibition and to see the large collection of books and manuscripts in Maithili. This demonstrates that Maithili has been for a long time and is today a living language among the people of this area. The language deserves encouragement and this can best be done by good books being written in it.
> Dec. 10, 1963
>   Sd/- Jawaharlal Nehru[64]

This paved the way for the recognition of Maithili by the Sahitya Akademi as one of the modern Indian languages in 1965. The role of Jayakant Mishra was significant in the recognition of Maithili by the Sahitya Akademi, though other individuals and organizations were also pressing this demand for a long time. One such organization was MSP, Kolkata. Mahendra Narayan Jha, the Secretary of MSP had written a series of letters to the Sahitya Akademi since 8 May 1964. Its contributions were recognized by the Akademi as a Maithili-language literary body.[65] Internal rivalry also came at the fore once again and it is believed that, due to personal reason Subhadra Jha, whose work *Formation of Maithili Language* is considered a foundational work on the study of Maithili language and grammar, was not very supportive of Maithili's recognition by the Sahitya Akademi. However, due to persuasion and request Subhadra Jha did not object and Maithili was finally recognized by the Akademi (1965). This was a major victory for the Maithili protagonists. Now they were no longer as anxious about the independent status of Maithili as they used to be a decade before. In the next phase of the movement, emphasis was shifted towards more and more space for Maithili: its inclusion in the eighth schedule of the Indian Constitution, its use as a medium of instruction at the primary level, and finally there was a revival of the demand for separate statehood for Mithila.

A Deeper Struggle Within: Political Leaderships and Demands for the Inclusion of Maithili in the Eighth Schedule

Maithili organizations and its leaderships were fighting not just anti-Maithili forces in Bihar and other parts of India, but a more intricate battle was to tackle the internal challenges within the Maithili movement. One such challenge was the assertion of Angika and Bajjika as a separate language, although it was earlier considered as a part of southern Maithili. A number of Maithili supporters and scholars still believe that Angika and Bajjika are 'dialects' of Maithili. According to them, these two were promoted to weaken the social base of the Maithili movement. In a meeting of TNB College MSP, Bhagalpur on 11 February 1966 in his presidential address Kumar Taranand Sinha said, 'that B(r)ajika a regional language of Muzaffarpur and Angika of Bhagalpur have been the part of Maithili and as such it required progress and development'.[66] Although for the Maithili protagonists the issue of Angika and Bajjika have been supported and promoted by the government of Bihar and Bihar Rashtrabhasha Parishad to weaken the Maithili movement, one can only understand the niceties of such developments historically. In the beginning, people of the region where Angika and Bajjika are spoken, were in favour of Hindi as a medium of education. They did not support the Maithili leaders when the demand for the use of Maithili as the medium of instruction in primary education was raised in the early twentieth century in Bihar.[67] Besides the geographical division of Mithila into *Pubairpar* and *Pachhabairpar*, with cultural and social division attached to it, the people of these two regions were already suspicious of each other. And when attempts were made to standardize Maithili with a consideration to make the speech form of one particular region *Panchkoshi*[68] as standard and undermining the speech forms of other regions, it further disconnected them from the Maithili movement. Now with the direct or indirect support of the government of Bihar, the speakers of Angika and Bajjika demanded recognition of their 'language' as an independent language.

However, the recognition of Maithili by the Sahitya Akademi gave momentum to the Maithili movement. A number of political parties and leaders began to take interest in the Maithili issue. Laying the foundation for the Maithili Writers Conference Building under the auspices of the Vaidehi Samiti, Satyanarain Sinha, former Union Minister for Communication and Parliamentary Affairs and the leader of the Lok Sabha, commended the decision of the Sahitya Akademi to recognize Maithili as an independent language. According to him, the Maithili Book Exhibition, Delhi in 1963 and its inauguration by Jawaharlal Nehru and the release of the Vidyapati postal stamp by the government of India played a critical role in the recognition of Maithili. He pointed out the step-motherly treatment of Maithili by All India Radio in Patna and exclaimed that a new radio station at Darbhanga alone could solve the problem. He also demanded that textbooks should be published for primary classes and requested the Education Minister of the Government of Bihar to take necessary steps for the same.[69] A delegation of students on 19 March 1967 met the then education Minister of Bihar, Karpoori Thakur, and pressed the demand for the inclusion of Maithili as an optional paper in the competitive examinations of the Bihar Public Service Commission (BPSC). They also told him that delay in the inclusion of Maithili recommended by an expert group constituted by former Chief Minister of Bihar, Shri Krishna Sinha, 'caused resentment among many Maithili graduates'.[70]

There were interesting developments taking place among the political parties in Bihar regarding the language issue. When a non-congress coalition government was formed for the first time in Bihar, there were near unanimous consensus among all the political parties in Bihar including Congress, except Jan Sangh, to recognize Urdu as the second language of the state. This move was opposed by many individuals and groups in Bihar. They believed that politics based on language may damage the secular framework of society and would be a step further in communalizing the language. They asserted that language belongs to everyone inhabiting the region and it did not divide them on the basis of religion or caste. They cited the example of Bengali spoken by Bengali Hindus and Muslims alike. They also asserted that Muslims living in the villages, away from urban areas, speak the same language as other villagers do. Those languages in Bihar are Maithili, Magadhi, Bhojpuri, Santhali, and other tribal languages. Second opposition was that it would led to the same kind of demand by the Maithils, Bengalis, Bhojpuris, Magadhis, and other people of Bihar. So, if Urdu was to be recognized as the second language of the state, then these other languages should be granted the same status too. Madan Prasad Srivastava, Secretary of the Nagar Vidyarthi Parishad, Darbhanga:

> vehemently opposed the coalition Government's proposal to recognize Urdu as second official language, and pleaded that only that language should be allowed that honour which was spoken by majority of the people of the state. He claimed that Maithili was the language of more than half of the total population of the state of Bihar and as such Maithili alone deserve to occupy the place of second official language.[71]

The demand for the recognition of Maithili as the second official language in the state of Bihar was also put forward by the All India Maithil Mahasabha (AIMM) in its meeting on 19 March 1967 at Laheria Sarai. This meeting was presided over by Krishnanandan Singh of Raghopur Deorhi and most of the participants were lawyers, University teachers, and professors.[72] Meanwhile, a new organization was formed at Darbhanga by the name of Mithila Maha Parishad with a broader outlook. This meeting was presided over by Shailendra Mohan Jha and many university teachers and advocates besides others also presented their views. They believed that a broader outlook was needed in the movement as it was limited to the issue of Maithili alone and this kept a large section of the population in the region indifferent to the development of Mithila and Maithili.[73] Many new proposals also came in during this period like the newly constituted AIMM in a meeting under the chairmanship of Rajkumar Subheshwar Singh proposed to establish a *Maithili Anusandhan Samiti* (Maithili

Research Committee).[74] Similarly, on the occasion of the annual Vidyapati festival at Bisafi on 15 June 1967 the Commissioner of the Tirhut Division, N.P. Sinha urged for the construction of a research institute on Vidyapati.[75]

In this context, a statement by the then Education Minister of Bihar, Karpoori Thakur, himself a Maithili speaker, in the Bihar Assembly on 10 July 1967 caused an uproar among the Maithili speakers and supporters. During the question hour session replying to the question put up by Nagendra Jha, the minister said 'there were practical difficulties and complications in making Maithili as second language as the Government would have to concede to the demands and claims of other dialects'. He further said that the government was considering the demand of Urdu for other reason to fulfil the constitutional obligations to protect the language and culture of the minority. More than his rationale it was the facts and figures about the Maithili speakers that he presented in the Vidhan Sabha that infuriated Maithili speakers. According to him, 'In Bihar there were 78 lakh Bhojpuri speaking people, 28 lakh Magahi speaking, 49 lakh Maithili speaking, 41 lakh Urdu speaking, 11 lakh Bangla speaking and 2.5 crore Hindi speaking people'.[76] This stand of Karpoori Thakur was ridiculed by scholars like Ramanath Jha, Member of the Sahitya Akademi[77] and Upendra Thakur, of Magadh University, Gaya,[78] A group of eleven scholars[79] and a separate essay in protest was published by Purushottam Jha, General Secretary, All India Maithili Mahasabha, Darbhanga.[80] It reflects the unanimous protest by the scholars across the disciplines against the anti-Maithili stand of the government of Bihar. Similarly, a memorandum was submitted by the Maithili Sangram Samiti, Kolkata to the members of Parliament through the speaker explaining the biased approach and the conspiracy of the government against Maithili.[81] Purushottam Jha, Secretary, All India Maithil Mahasabha, complained regarding the discriminatory practices of the state government regarding the Maithili-speaking people of north Bihar.[82]

Similarly with regards to road and rail communication, north Bihar was lagging. 'It was not possible for a person to travel by road from Purnea to Champaran ... while the whole of south Bihar was linked with broad gauge railway line in north Bihar ... cover only a length of 60 kilometres....'[83] So, now mobilizations and agitations were not limited to the issue of Maithili language alone.

Table 4.2   Regional Disparities between North and South Bihar

	North Bihar	South Bihar
Radio Station	Nil	3
Universities	2	4
Medical College	1	3
Engineering Colleges	1	5
Veterinary Colleges	Nil	2
Agricultural Colleges	1	2

Source: Indian Nation, 5 May 1967, Courtesy, University of Washington Libraries, Special Collections.

The move of the government to recognize Urdu as the second language of the state of Bihar was opposed in a public meeting organized at the Town Hall at Munger. Describing the complication of having two official languages, principal Kapil of R.D. College, Munger said that recognition of Urdu would not even benefit all the Muslims. He asserted that Muslims living in Mithila and Bhojpur speak Maithili and Bhojpuri and not Urdu. Hence the move of the government to yield to the communal threat would result in stiff opposition from the Maithili and Bhojpuri speakers.[84] Similarly in a meeting at Rajendra Bhawan, Darbhanga, organized under the auspices of the Maithili Pracharak Sangh, the demand was repeated to grant the status of the second language of the state to Maithili. The meeting also demanded the inclusion of Maithili as an optional subject by the BPSC, the establishment of a radio station and a university at Darbhanga and the facilities of teaching up to middle school in Maithili medium.[85]

The Mithila Chhatra Sangh, Muzaffarpur, organized Maithili Bhasha Vikas Sammelan on 13 August 1967 at the Theosophical Hall in Muzaffarpur. The Sammelan was chaired by Kumar Ratneshwari Nandan Sinha. He stressed the importance of the Maithili language and demanded its inclusion in the eighth schedule of the Indian Constitution. The Secretary of the Mithila Chhatra Sangh said that 'non-recognition of Maithili by the Government would cause upheaval among the youths of this part of the country and it must be placed on the 8th Schedule of the Indian Constitution'.[86] Speaking on the occasion Braj Kishore Verma 'deprecated the mentality of the Hindi protagonists to super-impose Hindi on the people of Mithila residing in the vast region extending from the Himalayas to the Gangetic belt and Purnea to Motihari'.[87] Binodanand Jha was also present on the occasion and in his speech 'declared that Maithili had been the source of inspiration to Gurudev Rabindranath Tagore and poet Sankardeo of Assam.[88] Demand for the inclusion of Maithili in the eighth schedule of the Indian Constitution was also supported by about 100 legislators of the Maithili- speaking area in a conference at Patna on 27 July 1967 organized by the Chetna Samiti. The conference was chaired by the speaker of the Bihar Assembly, Dhanik Lal Mandal. 'By another resolution the conference urged the government to make Maithili an optional subject in Bihar Public Service Commission examinations. It also urged the Government to implement its earlier decision without further delay to make Maithili compulsory subject of study at primary stages'.[89] According to Dhanik Lal Mandal, Maithili would be able to get its due on its own merits, as it was spoken by more than two crore people of Bihar. Harinath Mishra, the former minister for cooperatives of the government of Bihar, regretted that Dogri, spoken by not more than forty to fifty lakh people, was being included in the eighth schedule but Maithili, spoken by more than two crores people in Bihar, had been left out. Raj Kumar Purbe of the CPI demanded that Maithili should be compulsorily taught in the primary stages in Maithili-speaking areas.[90] In another attempt in a meeting of over 400 Maithili-speaking students in Patna, Bihar Prantiya Maithili Bhashi Chhatra Sangharsha Samiti was formed on 22 July 1967. It urged its members to be prepared for the sacrifices for the due recognition of their mother tongue Maithili. They believed that then non-congress government of Bihar, like the previous Congress government, was apathetic to the demands of Maithili. Their twofold demands were recognition of Maithili as an optional subject by the BPSC and recognition of Maithili as the second official language of the state.[91]

Considering the linguistic complexity of the state and dubious enumeration by the census officers, the government of Bihar undertook the task of *a fresh* linguistic survey of Bihar. The Board of Control of the Bihar Rashtrabhasha Parishad, in its meeting on 28 July 1967 'decided to conduct a systematic and scientific survey of all the languages and dialects of Bihar ... A subcommittee under the chairmanship of L.N. Sudhanshu was set up to guide the survey work.'[92] There was opposition to the conduct of this survey by Purushottam Jha, General Secretary; All India Maithil Mahasabha. He stated that instead of promoting the languages of Bihar by opening up academies for them 'the state government has taken up the impossible task of linguistic survey and dividing the people into various groups which will not contribute anything either to the unity or to the general well-being of the state'.[93] Similarly Bhagya Narayan Jha, Joint Secretary, Chetna Samiti opposed the appointment of Lakshmi Narayan Sudhanshu, former speaker of the Bihar Legislative Assembly, as the chairman of the subcommittee. He stated that Sudhanshu, a Maithili speaker himself, was famous for his anti-Maithili stand and was a strong protagonist of Hindi. Further he asserted that Sudhanshu was a controversial figure on the language issues and was not a recognized linguist but a politician and known protagonist of Angika. Bhagya Narayan Jha asserted that it 'arouses suspicion and confusion among the Maithili-speaking people of the state' and went on to say that 'we Maithili-speaking people do not know what is Angika or Bajjika. This is definitely an attempt to damage the cause of Maithili, which is spoken in Purnea, Saharsa, Muzaffarpur, north Munger, north Bhagalpur, Darbhanga, and Santhal Pargana districts with slight variations in the accent'.[94] He wanted linguists of repute either from West Bengal or from south India to be entrusted with the responsibility of such a linguistic survey. He demanded that until such persons were appointed, the Linguistic Survey in Bihar should be stopped.[95]

There was also a growing belief among the Maithili speakers that agitation alone would force the government to include Maithili in the eighth schedule of the constitution and not merely the promises by the politicians.[96] Nagarjun, a well-known Hindi poet demanded on the occasion of Vidyapati Parva at Bhagalpur in February 1968 that Maithili needed all the help and cooperation from the government and the people to develop. He also said that Hindi cannot flourish so long as regional languages were not developed.[97] During the third All India Maithili Writers Conference in Darbhanga they apprehended that anti-Maithili agitations were still active in Bihar. Inaugurating the Conference, Kumar Ganganand Singh, then the V.C. of Kameshwar Singh Sanskrit University, Darbhanga 'stressed the need for combined effort to produce standard books in Maithili for the proper growth and development of Maithili language'.[98] Jayakant Mishra, President of the

All India Maithili Sahitya Samiti, Allahabad urged the Maithili speakers 'to face the anti-Maithili agitations boldly'.[99] Deva Narain Jha of the All India Maithili Lok Sangha, Kolkata similarly urged the people 'to fight for the rightful existence and development of Maithili language and literature'.[100] Ramanath Jha lamented the non-implementation of Maithili medium at the primary stage by the Bihar government. There was stress on the revival of Maithili script by Krishnanandan Singh, who presided over the conference.[101]

In another meeting organized by the Mithila Seva Sangh, at Rajendra Bhawan, Darbhanga under the chairmanship of Bhola Nath Mishra, the need for strong agitation was reasserted. They warned the government that if the long standing demands like inclusion of Maithili in the eighth schedule of the constitution, Maithili as a subject in BPSC and imparting of education at the primary stage through the medium of Maithili were not met 'a strong mass agitation had to be organized for the purpose throughout the Maithili speaking region…'.[102] Demand for the inclusion of Maithili in the eighth schedule to the constitution was reiterated by Ramanath Jha, Representative of Maithili in the Sahitya Akademi. He was agitated by the decision of then Minister of Education, Government of India, Sher Singh, to not give Maithili representation in the Bharatiya Bhasha Samiti, a committee constituted for the development of Indian languages, as Maithili was not included in the eighth schedule of the Indian Constitution. Although Ramanath Jha presented a memorandum in this regard which was 'backed by the thirteen legislators of Bihar and recommended by Sahitya Akademi',[103] still the memorandum was not accepted. He stated in the memorandum that it may further agitate Maithili speakers to launch a mass movement for their legitimate demands. He declared that 'recognition by Sahitya Akademi has turned out to be without any substance, only a sop to satisfy and quieten us for the time being'.[104] In a rally on 9 August 1968 organized by the Akhil Bharatiya Maithili Mahasangh in Patna, they decided to present signatures of one lakh Maithili speakers to the state government in support of its eleven-point demands.[105] However, it is reported that ABMM submitted a memorandum to the governor of Bihar on 10 August 1968 in support of their eleven demands.[106] The other demands were: Maithili as one of the state languages, along with Hindi, as its speakers were more than fifty per cent of the population in the state of Bihar; scrapping the linguistic survey under the auspices of Bihar

Rashtrabhasha Parishad; and the acceptance of government documents in Maithili. They also 'described the appointment of Language Survey Commission headed by Dr. L. N. Sudhanshu as "political conspiracy" against Maithili'. They demanded that, if the government was honest about the linguistic survey, then such a task should be allotted to 'an eminent and impartial linguist and philologist'. It lamented the government apathy towards the publication of Maithili-medium books.[107]

The language controversy again erupted in Bihar when a Language Seminar was organized in Patna by the Bihar Citizens Council on Education, Patna. In the seminar, it was alleged that sufficient representation was not given to the minority languages—Maithili, Urdu, Bengali, Bhojpuri, Magadhi, Oraon, and Oriya. Against these moves, Abdul Moghni of the department of English, Patna University proposed that an immediate meeting should be organized by these minority languages in Bihar to counter the threat that such a language seminar had posed to their language and culture. He also alleged that the language issue became for these 'selfish secterians' to enter the public life of Bihar through the 'back door'. He also proposed that, as a matter of policy, 'mother tongue as the one and only medium of all the public activities and educational pursuits' should be accepted.[108] Babu Bhola Lal Das as the chief guest of the two-day Vidyapati Parva celebration of the Chetna Samiti demanded that the need of the hour was the establishment of a Maithili Akademi, as well as a modern University and a branch of AIR in Darbhanga. He asserted that 'mass awareness' was needed 'to secure rightful place to Maithili in the family of languages of the Indian Union'.[109]

There was one interesting episode during this period about the language controversy in Bihar. Seth Govind Das, then M.P. and the President of the All India Hindi Sahitya Sammelan, opined that except Punjab there was no other state in the country which could claim to have a second language. He said that for such a claim, it was necessary that the speakers of such a language should be more than 40 per cent of the total population in that state. Thus, regarding the declaration of Urdu as the second language of the state, he opined that though the language deserved all encouragement but its recognition as the second language of the state 'did not fulfil the criteria laid down in the constitution'. He further said that Maithili and other dialects of Hindi should be encouraged from the literature point of view but it should not be included in the eighth schedule of the constitution.[110] Nagarjun was very critical of these statements of Seth Govind Das, particularly his stand against the demand of Maithili to be included in the eighth schedule of the Indian Constitution. Nagarjun stated that 'it was a pity that Seth Govind Das is ignorant about a rich and developed language like Maithili'. He urged Das 'to become acquainted with the views of the former (elected) President of the Akhil Bharatiya Hindi Sahitya Sammelan, the late Dr Amarnath Jha, about Maithili'.[111]

There was also an attempt to link the growth and spread of the language and literature to the economic prosperity of the region. Bihar Congress leader Lokesh Nath Jha on 2 November 1968 on the occasion of Vidyapati Parva at Vidyapati Nagar said that 'unless economic dynamism was generated in the Maithili-speaking areas in North Bihar, the traditional, intellectual, and moral values were bound to disappear in this region. Comprehensive economic activities and financial spurt were essential to retain and promote language and culture in the Maithili region'.[112] Inaugurating a Ramavatar Munideo Hostel of D.B. College, Jayanagar, Union Minister of State for Education, Bhagwat Jha Azad stressed the need for education through mother tongue.[113]

However, the anti-Maithili stand of the Bihar Government once again caused a lot of tension among the Maithili speakers. Revenue Minister Indradeep Sinha made a statement in the Bihar Legislative Council on 11 June 1968 that 'Maithili could not be a regional language in this state as the Maithili-speaking people constituted only 10.7 per cent of the population. He also said that government was unable to make Maithili a medium of examination in the Public Service Commission.'[114]

> With a view to carry out an intense campaign for the use of Maithili language in day to day work by the Maithili speaking population of Darbhanga, Saharsa, Madhubani, Purnea, and parts of Muzaffarpur and Munger districts, an organization named as Maithili Prachar Sena has been formed.... with Mr A. C. Deepak as its convenor. The organization has already enrolled 200 members....[115]

The leader of the organization still believed that region's development was dependent on the development of a regional language, Maithili. He regretted that very little had been done in this direction and asserted that the Prachar Sena was formed for this purpose 'with a militant spirit to take direct action if needed'.[116] He also criticized the government for not publishing any textbooks in Maithili despite the provision of the government to impart primary and middle school education in Maithili-speaking areas in Maithili. 'He appealed to all sections of people living in Mithila, irrespective of caste and creed, to help the movement started by the Mithila Prachar Sena as Maithili language did not belong only to Maithil Brahmins but to all sections of the people living in the area.'[117]

Lalit Narayan Mishra, former Union Minister of State for Defence Production, at Kalidas Samaroh at the Saurath Sabha on 7 June 1969 surprisingly put forward the demand for a separate Mithila state. He said,

> When states have been created and are being created on the basis of language, there is no reason why there should not be a separate state for Mithila. Mithila has its own language with its own script and rich literature. If such a state is created it would be economically viable unit and geographically compact unit both (with) a population of more than two and a half crores.[118]

He also stated that Maithili language was not given due recognition by the framers of Indian Constitution and demanded that it was high time that it should be now included in the eighth schedule of the Indian Constitution.[119] Shiva Chandra Jha of SSP even introduced a Constitutional (Amendment) Bill in Lok Sabha seeking recognition of Maithili in the eighth schedule of the constitution.[120]

The government of Bihar had a dubious stand with regard to its language policy. Hindi being the official language of the state they took every step to promote it. However, they could not completely ignore the regional languages—Maithili, Magadhi, Bhojpuri, Santhali, and Santhali. Therefore, they promised to plan for promoting these languages. But such promises were not implemented properly. Regarding Maithili, replying to a question of Raj Kumar Purbe (CPI), the then Chief Minister of Bihar, Sardar Harihar Singh, told the Vidhan Sabha on 24 March 1969 that the question of including Maithili in the schedule of languages as a medium for public service commission examination, and the question of recommending to the Union Government for the inclusion of Maithili in the eighth schedule of the Indian Constitution was under consideration of the government.[121]

There was an attempt to Sanskritize Maithili for its proper development. The Lieutenant Governor of Delhi, Aditya Nath Jha, inaugurating a literary journal *Sahitya Patra*[122] in Darbhanga said that, without Sanskrit, the glory of Maithili would be lost. He said 'Maithili has a glorious record of literary achievement not less important than any of the languages of the country only because Maithili has followed the traditions of Sanskrit literature since the days of Jyotirishwara'.[123] He also said that a liberal stand should be taken in reconsidering the regional dialects so that every dialect might feel proud of Maithili.[124] Similarly, Ramanath Jha in his presidential address at the Pavas Parva Samaroha organized by the Mithila Sanskritik Parishad, Sitamarhi, explained 'that though Maithili was spoken differently in this region, it was Maithili all the same. He said marks of great persons like Haldar Das and Mangani Jha who belonged to Muzaffarpur district were slowly finding place in Maithili literature'.[125] He urged the Parishad to collect more such works written by the people of that region. Jayadhari Singh in his speech exhorted the organizers of the Parishad and people of that subdivision to think in terms of developing Maithili language.

Quoting from Subhadra Jha's 'Dialects of Maithili Language', he said that it was not a fact that people of Muzaffarpur district spoke a distorted form of Maithili. In fact, they spoke Maithili like the people of Madhubani, and the only difference was that the dialect of Madhubani was considered and regarded as the standard form of Rashtra Maithili. He deprecated the move of the Bihar Rashtrabhasha Parishad and other such institutions to separate Muzaffarpur in the name of so called Bajjika language.[126]

The protagonists of the Maithili movement made various attempts to take along the varieties of Maithili speakers, but such attempts were met with little success.

However, there had been untiring efforts to mobilize and educate the masses about the Maithili language and the movement. The Mithila Sahitya Sansthan of Patna came out with a quarterly research journal of Maithili which was formally inaugurated by Sudhakar Jha Shastri, Research Professor at Patna University.[127] The Mithila Mandali, Bombay organized an All-India Maithili Writers Conference for three days—18, 19, and 20 October 1969.[128] The Conference demanded the inclusion of Maithili in the eighth schedule of the Indian Constitution. In another resolution, it urged the census authorities to not to mark Hindi as the mother tongue for Maithili speakers. Other demands that it put forward were: establishment of an All India Radio station at Darbhanga;

introduction of Maithili as a compulsory medium of instruction at the primary stage in Maithili-speaking areas; and emancipation of Maithili-speaking womenfolk. Speaking at the conference, Lalit Narayan Mishra, former Minister of State for Defence Production, Government of India urged that for Maithili to flourish as a living language, efforts should be made to mobilize public opinion. For such efforts, he said, a fund should be raised in which he promised to contribute Rs 50,000.[129] Umesh Mishra said that there was no clash between Hindi and Maithili and the former 'had its own role to play in the emotional integration of the country'.[130]

In other developments, the central executive committee of the Akhil Bhartiya Mithila Maithili Pracharak Sangh decided to go on a hunger strike to press the demand for the inclusion of Maithili in the eighth schedule and a place for Maithili in the examinations of the Union and State Public Service Commissions.[131] In the two-day annual session of the All India Maithil Mahasangh at the Town Hall, Darbhanga on 30 November 1969, it was demanded that the 'government should treat Maithili at par with other major languages of the country'.[132] It warned the government if such a place was not accorded to Maithili, the Mahasangh would launch a mass agitation. Bibhuti Bhushan Mukhopadhyaya, an eminent Bengali novelist, who was inaugurating the session said that 'all of us living in the Mithila region, irrespective of caste and creed, were Maithils'.[133] Similarly, Radha Krishna Kejriwal, President of the Mithila Chamber of Commerce, who was the chief guest of the session said 'that people living in Mithila, whether they were Hindus or Muslims, Marwaris or Bengalis, were Maithils and their language was definitely Maithili, which they used at home and outside'.[134] S.N. Chaudhary, president of the Maithili Mahasangh, said that there were twenty one organizations affiliated to the Mahasangh working in different parts of the country to serve the cause of Maithili. Speaking at the session Bhola Lal Das appealed to the masses to respond to the call of the Mahasangh for a mass movement. A number of resolutions were passed, demanding: 'inclusion of Maithili in the eighth schedule of the Indian constitution; provision for teaching in primary and secondary schools through the medium of Maithili; publication of textbooks in Maithili; provision of Maithili in the Union and State Public Service Commission competitive examinations, etc'.[135] A delegation on behalf of the Mahasangh met the district magistrate of Darbhanga and submitted a memorandum demanding various measures to raise the status of Maithili, after successfully organizing a big demonstration and a public meeting at the polo ground.[136]

The Maithili movement in this period also witnessed the involvement of villages and leaders of the panchayats. In a meeting of mukhiyas of gram panchayats of Madhubani subdivision organized by the Akhil Bhartiya Maithili Vikas Sangha on Tuesday, 17 March 1970 a demand was made for the inclusion of Maithili in the eighth schedule of the Indian Constitution. This meeting was inaugurated by Ramakar and presided over by educationist Chandradhari Singh. C.S. Jha, a former representative of India at the United Nations sent a message supporting the endeavour of the conference.[137] Similarly addressing the Vidyapati Jayanti at Sidgora, the renowned Maithili and Hindi poet 'Yatri' or 'Nagarjun' threatened to go on hunger strike for the recognition of the Maithili language. 'He demanded immediate inclusion of Maithili in the eighth schedule of the constitution; its proper place in the public service commission; Maithili news broadcasts from All India Radio; primary education in Maithili in Maithili-speaking areas; and establishment of a Sahitya Akademi for the development of Maithili'.[138] All the speakers on this occasion, which included Babu Saheb Chaudhary, Rajkumar Jha, Madhab Mishra, Rameshwar Sharma, Akhileshwar Jha, Laxmi Nidhi, and Dinraj, 'favoured direct action for the recognition of Maithili as they felt that it was only the language of agitation that could draw the attention of the authorities towards the long standing legitimate demands of the Maithili speaking people'.[139] The former Chief Minister of Bihar, Daroga Prasad Rai, replying to a question of Rajkumar Purbe (CPI) said in the Bihar Assembly that the 'government was actively considering the proposal for opening Mithila University at Darbhanga'.[140] He said that 'it is a long-cherished desire of lakhs of sweet-tongued Maithili-speaking people whose culture, civilization, and sentiments had their own place'.[141] Interestingly 'replying to another question of Rajkumar Purbe, Niteshwar Prasad Singh, Minister of State for Education said that Maithili was a part of Hindi and therefore it did not deserve special favour of the government'.[142] He also said that the Government of Bihar had written to the Union Government for the recognition of Maithili in the eighth schedule of the Constitution.[143] 'Karpoori Thakur took a serious view of the state minister's version that the Maithili was not different from

Hindi. He assured him that Maithili was an independent language and it should be given due recognition'.[144] Chetkar Jha, professor of Political Science at Patna University also objected to this observation of Niteshwar Prasad Singh.[145] Similar views against the minister were expressed by many Maithili speakers like Bhaskara Jha,[146] Vidyapati Samiti, Ranchi.[147] The Vidyapati Samiti went on to consider the statement of the minister Niteshwar Prasad Singh 'deliberately mischievous, provocative, and politically motivated' and it also criticized those Maithili-speaking legislators who did not protest against such a statement in the house.[148]

Subhadra Jha, presiding over the concluding session of the two day Vidyapati Jayanti at Ranchi, in January 1970 urged the Maithili-speaking people to wage a relentless war against the government for neglecting Maithili.[149] Pandit Harinath Mishra, former Bihar Minister, inaugurating the conference on minority languages of Bihar at the two-day twelfth Bihar State Bengali Conference, asserted that 'our national language Hindi was not the mother tongue of any considerable section of the people of Bihar'.[150] He also said that a conspiracy to enroll people speaking different languages as speakers of Hindi was the real cause for the increased number of Hindi speakers in Bihar. He also suggested that an Institute of Minority Languages should be immediately established for the proper development of these languages.[151] Harinath Mishra was also of the view that it was due to the under-developed state of their mother tongues that speakers of some languages of the state continued to have the tendency to get enumerated as the Hindi speakers. He stated that while Bengali and Oriya enjoy the patronage of their native state and Urdu has the support of at least two Universities—Aligarh and Hyderabad—Maithili alone was the native language of Bihar and thus had special claim on the state government.[152] Meanwhile a private member's bill was moved by an MP, Yamuna Mandal, for the inclusion of Maithili in the eighth schedule of the Indian Constitution. It was supposed to come up for the discussion on 27 February 1970. AIMM, MSP, Maithili Sahitya Samiti, Writers Conference, Vaidehi Samiti and Navaratna Goshthi pressed for such a demand. Dozens of telegrams, resolutions, and memoranda were sent to the president, the prime minister, the speaker of Parliament, union ministers, and others requesting them to fulfil the demand of about three crores of Maithili speakers in the country.[153]

In another development in the language debate in Bihar, Hindi supporters began to accept Maithili as an independent language. One such acceptance came from the eminent Hindi scholar Hazari Prasad Dwivedi. While inaugurating the first All-India Maithili Conference in Varanasi in April 1971 he said that Maithili was an independent language and deserved patronage. He also urged the Maithili literati to produce quality and standard books in Maithili. In this conference some important resolutions with regard to women, such as education of Maithili girls, no dowry in marriage, were passed by the women delegates—Vidya Jha and Harmaya Devi of Kanpur and Haripur respectively.[154]

In his address to the 35th annual session of the Maithili Sahitya Parishad, Patna University on 9 May 1970 Subhash Chandra Sarkar, editor of the *Searchlight*, highlighted the need for the increased use of Maithili by its speakers themselves even for formal communications. He said that despite the large number of population:

> the state of contemporary Maithili literature and Maithili journalism is extremely weak for lack of readership support. The total circulation of Maithili periodicals in Bihar in 1968 was 2,674 only. There were two newspapers published from Kolkata with a combined circulation of 981 copies. In other words, the combined circulation of all the Maithili newspapers in India was only 3,655.[155]

Then he connected this state of readership crisis to the low literacy rate among the men and women in Bihar, particularly in the Maithili-speaking area where this was even worse than other parts of Bihar. Similarly, in the annual meeting of the Maithili Sahitya Sansthan on the premises of the Bihar Research Society in Patna on 15 May 1970, R.C. Haldar, describing the connections between Mithila and Bengal, lamented that during the last fifty years Maithils have forgotten Maithili scripts. Other blunder committed by sections of the Indian population was the belief that Maithili as a 'dialect' was spoken by Maithil Brahmins alone.[156]

A delegation comprised of Gunanand Thakur, Jamuna Prasad Mandal, Shiva Chandra Jha (all MPs.), Kameshwar Singh, Bhabesh Mishra, Tulmohan Ram, and Babu Saheb Chaudhary met the Prime Minister Indira Gandhi for the inclusion of Maithili in the eighth schedule of the Indian Constitution. It was claimed that they were assured by the Prime Minister about the inclusion. 'A meeting in this connection was held at the residence of Mr Lalit Narayan Mishra, Minister for Forests and Trade when a committee was formed to facilitate inclusion of Maithili in the eighth schedule during the budget session of the Parliament'.[157]

It was certainly a new development in the Maithili movement. The issue of Maithili was no longer a concern for the Maithili writers and scholars alone. Even the politicians of almost all the parties, administrators, social leaders, and students were increasingly participating in the Maithili movement. The Vidyapati Parva Samaroha became a tool for the mobilization of Maithils and for pressing the political demands for Maithili and Mithila.

The Maithili Movement in 1970s

The Maithili movement and the challenges it faced during the 1970s are very well described in a play, *Santo*, by a prominent Maithili activist Rajanandan Lal Das.[158] The play begins with the problems that students in Maithili-speaking regions had to face in the beginning of their school education in the comprehension of Hindi terminologies. When the students were forced to speak in Hindi, they mixed Maithili words in their sentences. It is quite clear in this conversation:

[Rama is a student and had been asked by her teacher to write an essay on the cow which she had not written.]

"शिक्षक – इतना भी नही जानती ? क्या तुमने कभी गाय नहीं देखी है ?

[Teacher: Don't you even know this? Have you not seen a cow?]

रमा – जी हाँ।

[Rama: Yes, I have seen one.]

शिक्षक – तो बोलो ! एक गाय का वर्णन करो।

[Teacher: Okay then speak! Describe a cow.]

रमा – गाय एक जानवर है। उसको चारिटा टाँग होता है। एकटा नाँगरि होता है।

[Rama: The cow is an animal. It has four legs (in the sentence the word that is used for this is not Hindi). It has one tail (again the word that is used is Maithili).]

शिक्षक - (तमसा कए) तुम्हारे पास लेख की किताब है न ?

[Teacher: (with anger) You do have an essay book, don't you?]

रमा - जी हाँ।

[Rama: Yes, I do.]

शिक्षक - पढ़ो तो!

[Teacher: Read it.]

रमा - (गाय पर लेख पढ़ैत अछि) गाय एक पषु है गाय को चार टाँगें तथा एक लम्बी पूँछ होती है।
(प्रष्न करैत) मास्टर साहेब पूँछ ककरा कहैत छै ?

[Rama: (reading an essay on the cow) The cow is an animal. The cow has four legs and one long tail. (Asking) Teacher what is tail? (here the word that is used is not Maithili which is used by the child earlier but Hindi).]

शिक्षक - पूँछ नहीं समझती हो ?

[Teacher: Don't you know tail?]

रमा - जी नहिं।

[Rama: No sir.]

शिक्षक - अरे, दुम समझती हो, दुम!

[Teacher: Arre, do you know tail, tail (using other similar word for tail).]

रमा - जी नहिं।

[Rama: No Sir.]

शिक्षक - तुम लोगों को समझाना बड़ा कठिन है।"[159]

[Teacher: It is very difficult to make you people understand.]

This extract demonstrates the inevitable use of Maithili words in Hindi by the student and their difficulties in comprehending Hindi. It also illustrates the teacher's difficulties to make the student comprehend Hindi words. Later, in this play, the teacher has understood that they have been instructed to teach in Hindi alone. So even if it is difficult for the students to comprehend in Hindi, teachers had to teach them in Hindi alone. It indicates the violation of the three-language formula and violates the rights of the Maithil children to be taught in their mother tongue. Another irony with Maithili is that it is not used in primary schools. Only in high schools it is used and that too as an optional. But there are several students who undertake Maithili as an honours subject in BA and MA. There are many scholars pursuing PhDs in Maithili. They find it very difficult to get a job after completion of their studies. So gradually there is lack of enthusiasm among the students to undertake Maithili as a subject of study at the higher level.

The main character of this play Santo Mahto—rightly the title of play is based on this character—is one such student who has a first class first in BA in Maithili. He was ill=treated everywhere for his subject of study. He could not sit for even the state public commission's (BPSC) exam as till then Maithili was not recognized as a subject. It is important to note here that the main character of the play is a non-Brahmin and non-Kayastha person. It shows, at least symbolically, that non-Brahmins and non-Kayasthas have also turned to the study of Maithili. Santo went on to organize the movement in different villages of Mithila. He was inspired by Rekha—another character in the play who was studying English literature in Kolkata but was committed to the cause of Maithili. She had vowed to carry forward the work done by her late father under Mithila Sangh. The play also shows the attitude of different sections towards Maithili. It portrays the sad state of Maithils and their detachment from their language, particularly of the educated, who abandoned Maithili as they moved out of Mithila. They hesitated to use it even with their fellow Maithils. So, Maithili was facing the indifference of not only the government but also of the businessmen, traders, professionals, learned teachers, and professors who were Maithili speakers themselves. So, for Santo and Rekha the only hope were the masses and students' groups. They tried to work together with members of different political parties as well. After initial objections from the masses, (as they thought that it may give rise to a language problem in the nation and it will be detrimental to Hindi) all agreed to fight together under the leadership of Rekha and Santo. Together they launched a strong political movement but faced a government crackdown. Santo was arrested and sent to jail for a year, as a first-rate political prisoner. The play end with the hope—"जा धरि एकोटा मैथिल संतान जीबैत रहत, मातृभाषाक रक्षाक लेल लड़ैत रहत।" (as long as even a single

Maithil child is alive fight for the protection of the mother tongue shall be continued).

The significance of this play is that it shows for the first time that the leadership of the movement can be provided by non-Brahmins and women as well. Another important indication in the play is the focus on the necessity of the political movement for the development of the Maithili and Mithila. The next phase of the Maithili movement witnessed increased political participation. There were an increasing number of public processions, protests, and demonstrations.

There was another serious examination of the Maithili movement and its challenges in a report, *Nation Building in a North Indian Region* (*The case of Mithila*).[160] In this report, Hetukar Jha has critically investi-gated the sociologically limitations, constrains, and possibilities of the nation building exercise in Mithila. He has looked at the construction of nation building in terms of togetherness between elite and masses and, following Paul Brass, observed that in Mithila the elites have failed in 'transmitting their sense of regional identity to the mass of the Maithili-speaking people'.

Hetukar Jha states that 'the nation building of a society has to be understood in the light of the nature of elites, the mass of people, and the relationship in terms of togetherness and separation between them'.[161] In his study, he finds that there have been at least three objective bases for the identity—what is Mithila? These are common language, com-mon territory, and finally common cultural heritage. According to Jha, 'before 1960 "territory" seems to be most emphasized base of Maithil identity. But after that "language" takes the lead'.[162] He also finds that the there is greater stress on Mithila after 1960, and language becomes the crucial component in it. Hence, he believes that the elites were becoming more conscious of their regional identity. But they cared very little about the socio-economic condition of the people. That was the reason, according to Hetukar Jha, that masses did not participate vigorously in the Maithili language movement. Further, he classified the elites into three groups:

1. Political elites—MLAs, MPs, and MLCs.
2. Organizational elites—'those who occupy or once occupied the key positions such as President or Secretary of the organizations working for the cause of Mithila'.

3. Cultural elites—'those who are journalists and intellectuals (authors of important books on Mithila which have had an influence on some)'.

The masses of Mithila, mostly landless agricultural labourers and poor peasants, largely reside in the rural areas. They remained somewhat indifferent to the whole issue of Mithila and Maithili. And the situations had not changed by then. The elites had done very little to mobilize the rural masses. The alliance of political elites 'with the non-Maithil Bihari elites and their neglect of the Maithils causes are held as important factors, working against the interest of Mithila'.[163] With regard to the cultural elites, which he studied indirectly through Maithili magazines, he concludes that for the cultural elites the issue of Maithili literature, art, and culture remained more significant than the socio-economic condition of the masses. Organizations and organizational elites from Darbhanga, Patna, and Kolkata were studied and Hetukar Jha concluded that these leaders and organizations were engaged much more in occasional activities and were mostly urban-centred. Almost all the organizations were overwhelmingly dominated by the Brahmins and they gave a higher priority to language, art, and culture than the socio-economic condition of the masses. They didn't have cordial relations among themselves. In these organizations, decisions were taken by a few influential persons and even by a single person. According to Hetukar Jha, these organizational elites and their involvement in any activities were driven more by their personal interest and ego instead of the common cause of Mithila and Maithili. The political elites seem to have largely neglected the issue of Mithila. Even among them it was Brahmins who have shown some concern with Maithili and its problems. The non-Brahmin political elites have shown very little or no concern at all with the issue of the Maithili language and culture. Almost all the elites had a very weak orientation towards the actions and mobilization of masses. There prevails a very strong sense of separateness between the elites and the masses. Lack of co-operation, and the presence of hostility even among these elites made the situation even worse. Their actions were oriented more towards the central and state governments than the concerns of the masses. This did not allow the spread of the consciousness of Maithili identity among the masses of Mithila. This certainly shows the indisputable dominance of Brahmins in the Maithili movement and their indifferent attitude towards the socio-economic ills afflicting the masses.

Although, in this report, there has been a thorough attempt to study the organizations, their leadership, their base and membership, demands and decision-making processes and empirical study of some of the villages to assess the nature and condition of the masses but most of the conclusions that he draws reaffirm the assertion of Paul Brass's study of the Maithili movement in north Bihar. He did not analyse the different phases of the Maithili movement comprehensively in his study. In the phase of the 1970s, which he undertook for the study, the Maithili movement was taking a shift towards inclusion of Maithili in the eighth schedule of Indian Constitution. In the previous phases of the movement under the leadership of Janaki Nandan Singh and Lakshman Jha, the demand was more political in terms of separate statehood to an extent of forming *Mithila as a union republic*. He completely missed these aspects of the movement. More fundamentally, the main constraints in his studies, like Brass, is an ahistorical approach towards the movement. The awakening in Mithila about its language, culture, and identity had arisen in a context when Hindi, and along with that, Indian nationalism, were making strong inroads into Mithila. So, any understanding of the limitations or weaknesses of the Maithili movement is incomplete, unless it is studied historically in its social and political context.

Another important reason for the weakness of the movement was the internal hierarchy among the Brahmins themselves, the most vocal castes in the Maithili movement. Rabindra Ray[164] in his report on *The Indianization of the Maithils*, states that Maithils, of course by which he means Maithil Brahmins alone, superior *Shrotriyas* to lesser respectable *Yogya* and *Panjibadha* and their genealogical history is recorded in the Panjis. Then below them were the *Jaibar* Brahmins, who were much inferior in rank and respect among the Brahmins. Brahmins were further divided into two groups within Mithila, *Pubairpar* and *Pachhvairpar*. As a rule, Brahmins who reside in *Pubairpar* or the Mithila heartland of Darbhanga and Madhubani were considered superior to *Pachhvairpar* Brahmins living outside the Mithila heartland (that is, in Bhagalpur). This division of society into different castes and hierarchies within a caste remained the single greatest obstacle in the development of any consciousness in the region whether it is based on language, that is, Maithili, or region, that is, Mithila or nation. So, it seems a common selfhood based on any of these *symbolic* identities did not develop sufficiently in Mithila. According to Ray 'nationalism has never been politically significant or a popular politics in Mithila. Maithils who associated with the Congress party in the heyday of nationalist agitation dissociated themselves from the mainstream of Maithil culture and indeed practiced their politics outside Mithila'.[165] So Mithila has a peculiar condition in terms of its self-awakening. Here national consciousness first emerged among the elites and they willingly adored and propagated Hindi at the cost of Maithili. Although since the beginning there were individuals like Chanda Jha, Raghunandan Das, and Babu Bhola Lal Das who championed the cause of Maithili and worked for the preservation and promotion of Maithili culture. But their voices were weak and marginal even in Mithila. For large numbers of Maithili speakers, initially these issues were non-existent and they had an indifferent attitude towards the issue of language. But through school education, newspapers, and magazines Hindi gradually became the language of public space with a certain degree of social prestige. And Maithili was labelled as a *Gawanru Bhasha* (language of the illiterates) driving it more inwards even in a household, also called as *Janana Bhasha* (feminine language). Thus, there were enormous challenges that the Maithili movement was facing in this period. Throughout its struggle, the Maithili movement had gone through different phases. And gradually but undeniably it had expanded its social and political base both among the elites and among the masses.

Struggles for Maithili as a Medium of Primary Education

Looking at the functioning of the government of Bihar with regard to making provisions for the implementation of Maithili as the medium of instruction at primary schools in the Maithili-speaking areas, Jayakant Mishra observed that despite

> in 1949 (vide D.P.I's Circular No. 3189/400–49 dated 22 March 1950) the Chairman of District Boards in the Maithili speaking areas (Districts of Darbhanga, Saharsa, Purnea, Muzaffarpur, etc.) issued letters to Chairmen Local Boards, Chairmen Town Committees and the Presidents Union Boards and the Headmasters of all Middle Schools asking them to

adopt 'Maithili as medium of instruction in the schools under them'....
syllabus for the primary classes was also got translated into Maithili by
the D.P.I. But no steps were taken to implement these circulars or print
the Maithili version of the syllabus.[166]

Again in 1953 (vide Government of Bihar's Resolution No. 645 Ranchi,
10 August 1963 (or is it 1953?) the Government of Bihar decided
regarding mother tongue to be adopted as a medium of instruction up
to the eighth class. But when it came to the publication of textbooks,
no such books were printed. Thus, while on paper the government now
recognized the rights of Maithili children to get an education in their
mother tongue, nothing was done to let them exercise such a right.
Reprimanding the claim of the government that textbooks could not
be published because of the shortage of demand, Mishra argues that:

> the facts are that again and again the inspector of schools and head-
> masters and guardians have been demanding for printing at least 2
> lakh text books of all varieties and for all classes but the Government
> is consistently refusing to do anything about the matter. In 1966, the
> state Government made it known that they propose to publish some text
> books on an experimental basis whose number might be raised with the
> increase in demand. But this is 1969 and not a single text book properly
> speaking has come in the market of the Maithili-speaking areas.[167]

He also exposed the government biases regarding the Maithili language. He alleged that the Bihar Text Book Publishing Corporation Ltd.
(BTBPCL) has been printing textbooks in Bengali, Urdu, Oriya, Oraon,
and other languages with a fewer number of speakers than Maithili.

Table 4.3   Speakers of Different Languages in Bihar, 1970

Languages	Number of Their Speakers
Maithili	4,982,615
Urdu	4,149,245
Bengali	1,164,047
Oriya	302,951
Oraon	32,725
Santhali	1,659,225

Source: Indian Nation, 7 February 1970, Courtesy, University of Washington
Libraries, Special Collections.

Even based on the Census of 1961, according to him, the number of the Maithili speakers of the different languages in Bihar was more than 49 lakhs (see Table 4.3).

Jayakant Mishra alleged that though some languages were not spoken in Bihar yet texts were published in these languages, while Maithili was not even given the position of a minority language even in its home districts. B.N. Chaudhary, Superintendent of Education, Saharsa, issued a circular for all primary and middle schools of the district to impart education through the mother tongue, namely, Maithili.[168]

There was a revival of the demand for the primary education in Maithili. In his letter of 13 September 1973, Kailash Bihari Sharma, Director of Education (Primary Education) and Deputy Secretary to the District Education Officers of Darbhanga, Saharsa, and Purnea passed an order to implement on priority basis the government of Bihar decision to impart primary education in Maithili. He also stated in the letter that this was due to the indifference of the teacher that the decision could not be implemented properly, even when books were prescribed in the syllabus for classes one to seven. He ordered

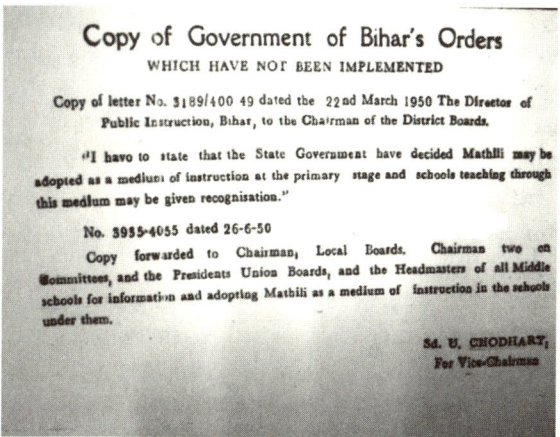

Image 4.2   Order of the Government of Bihar Regarding the Use of Maithili as the Medium of Instruction in Primary Education

Source: *Miathili Samachar*, year 27, Jan–Dec, 1990, Image Courtesy, All India Maithili Sahitya Samiti, Allahabad.

the officials to ensure that the required Maithili books were available and teachers should teach those books. He wanted those teachers to be punished who did not comply with the order.[169] But nothing could be done with regard to the implementation of Maithili as the medium of instruction at the primary level. On the contrary, the government of Bihar, under a Maithili-speaking chief minister, Karpoori Thakur, removed Maithili as a subject of study from the matriculation examination. It infuriated Maithili-speakers, particularly the students at Patna University. Interestingly this happened after the JP movement and students were already agitated. Maithili-speaking students at Patna University had already formed a Maithili Bhashi Chhatra Sangh to press their demands. When the decision for the removal of Maithili from the matriculation examination was taken by the Karpoori Thakur Government, the Sangh was transformed into the Nikhil Bharatiya Maithili Bhashi Chhatra Sangh. It played a crucial role in the protest movement and a two-day hunger strike was held at the Dak Bangla *Chauraha* in Patna. It also participated in the huge protest march in Patna from Gandhi Maidan to R Block *Chauraha* in which around 15,000 people participated.[170] These protests were successful and the government restored the status of Maithili in the matriculation examination.

This clearly reflects the increasingly agitative modes of protest in the Maithili movement. There was a persistent demand for the implementation of Maithili as the medium of primary education. In this regard, again in a letter to Sangam Lal, Managing Officer, Bihar State Textbooks Publication Ltd. Patna, Bhaskar Banerjee, Secretary to the Government, Department of Education, Government of Bihar asked him to immediately publish textbooks in Maithili for class three to ten.[171]

Committees were formed and textbooks were published.[172] Even the District Education Officer of Saharsa, B.S. Vaishyak ordered all the education officers at the Block (*Prakhand*) level and the inspector of schools of Saharsa to ensure that from 1987 education was to be imparted through Maithili medium at the primary and middle level.[173] But it is surprising that nothing could be done to implement this order, despite the repeated demands for the same by the protagonists of the Maithili movement. By now there developed an unenthusiastic attitude towards Maithili among the parents, besides the status-quoist attitude of the teachers. Parents, when incapable of sending their children to English medium schools, preferred Hindi medium schools over Maithili.[174] How can we understand this attitude of Maithils? Why did this feeling germinate about their own language? Would conditions have been the same had employment opportunities been made available in Maithili? Or if Maithili as a medium of education been implemented when modern school education began in Mithila? It appears that this attitude towards their mother tongue developed in a particular historical and political context of nationalism in India. In such a context, one language was preferred over many other independent languages and the growth of any other languages was considered as an impediment for the progress and social expansion of the 'national' language Hindi. But such a design of Hindi supporters was challenged by the Maithili speakers, although at the same time they accepted Hindi as the 'national' language of India. This threat from the Hindi supporters was felt by the Maithili speakers through different mechanisms of the state as late as the census of 1991. The Chetna Samiti, Patna had urged the Maithils to be aware of the anti-Maithili stands of the census officials. It requested them to ensure that Maithili was written in the census of 1991 as their mother tongue.[175]

Political Attitude towards the Maithili Movement

Using Article 347 of the Indian Constitution, a delegation of MPs led by Bhogendra Jha, Hukumdeva Narayan Yadav, Rajendra Prasad Yadav, and Ziaur Rahman gave a memorandum to the President demanding the declaration of Maithili as the state language of Bihar.[176] Although nothing came out of this, it proved that now political representatives of the region could no longer ignore the demands of the Maithili speakers. In other words, more and more political parties and their leaderships were aligning themselves with the Maithili movement. However, there were contradictory views as well, such as Chaturanand Mishra, an MP, for whom recognition of Maithili would not be of much use except getting a place on currency notes. He went on to say that:

हमर निश्चित विचार अछि जे वर्त्तमान राजनीतिक संदर्भ मे मिथिलाक खासकय उच्च जाति क बच्चा सबकएँ मैथिली मे समय नहिं विता विज्ञान, तकनोलोजी, संस्कृत, हिन्दी, अंग्रेजी दिस जेबाक चाही कारण मैथिली आब हुनकर भविष्य मे कोनो सहायता आब नहिं

दय सकतीन्ह। लाख लाख पिछड़ल लोक जकरा मैथिली' क अनिवार्यता पछिला दशक तक छलैक से दिल्ली, पंजाब, हरियाणा, उत्तर यू.पी आदि विकासवान क्षेत्र सँ मिथिला मे जोरदार रूपे हिन्दी कए लऽ जा रहल अछि जाहि सँ मैथिली-हिन्दी क विलयन दिस झुकाव किछू दशाब्दी मे जायत।[177]

[It is my definite view that, in the present political context, the children of Mithila, particularly of upper castes, instead of spending time in the study of Maithili should go for the study of science, technology, Sanskrit, Hindi, English because Maithili can no longer help them in their future. Lakhs and lakhs of the people for whom Maithili was a compulsion until the last decade are taking Hindi on a large scale in Mithila as a result of their migration to Delhi, Punjab, Haryana, U.P., and other such developing regions and due to this there will be shift in Hindi-Maithili assimilation in some decades.]

It clearly shows that Mishra was more interested in the use of a language than the preservation and growth of Maithili. But it also indicates the use of Maithili or Hindi by different castes of Mithila. He suggested that Maithili may not be helpful for the upper caste students in the future. But for those for whom Maithili's use was compulsory were now carrying Hindi un-proportionately from their work-places in Delhi, Punjab, Haryana, and North U.P. However, Chaturanand Mishra demanded that the language, recognized by the Sahitya Akademi, should be included in the UPSC examination. And while supporting the bill for the recognition of Manipuri, Konkani, and Nepali in the eighth schedule of the constitution, he meekly stated that such an inclusion should be based on the criteria of the Sahitya Akademi, so that no scope should be left for any accusations.[178]

Maithili protagonists had to constantly fight against the government of Bihar's biased and disconcerting attitude towards Maithili. In an order of 12 August 1988, the government replaced Maithili as the mother tongue in the proposed syllabus for the middle and secondary schools. This created misconceptions among the Maithili speakers as Nageshwar Jha was then the education minister of Bihar then and it was believed that such an order was passed in consultation with him, but later on it was discovered that such a decision was taken at the level of officials.[179] Similarly, when Maithili was excluded from the BPSC by the Rashtriya Janata Dal government in Bihar, Maithili speakers were shocked and agitated.[180] There was a huge protest march and demonstration in Patna.

Another important development in the Maithili movement of this period was the support they received from Maithili speakers in the United States of America, particularly Manikant Thakur and Amarnath Jha 'Bakshi'. They remained firm supporters of the Maithili movement, and they suggested that, for the development of the region, it was important that the focus of the movement should be Mithila in place of Maithili. They believed that the protection and promotion of Maithili was not possible within the province of Bihar. So, they supported the demand for the separate statehood of Mithila.[181]

Maithils were demanding the inclusion of Maithili in the Indian Constitution since its inception. They thought that exclusion of Maithili from the eighth schedule was a mistake on the part of the members of the Constituent Assembly and it should be immediately rectified. Devnarayan Yadav presented a recommendation in the Bihar Assembly in which he requested the government of Bihar to recommend to the central government to include Maithili in the eighth schedule of the Indian Constitution.[182] A relentless demand for the same had been made since the recognition of Maithili by the Sahitya Akademi in 1965. Maithili supporters were still suspicious of the motives of the protagonists of 'Hindi imperialism'. Jayadhari Sinha representing the case for Maithili for the inclusion in the eighth schedule said that 'Maithili-speaking people are not very conscious of politics; it may be submitted with apologies that our sense of respect towards Hindi, and the pious motive behind, are very tragically misunderstood and exploited by some diehard protagonists of Hindi imperialism'.[183] Looking at the details about the structural independence, literary history of past and present, popular recognition by cultural and academic institutions, and finally the census position of Maithili, Sinha made a strong plea to Indira Gandhi's government to include Maithili in the eighth schedule of the Indian Constitution.[184] Yamuna Prasad Mandal, MP, Congress (I), brought a private member's Bill in the parliament to include Maithili in the eighth schedule of the Indian Constitution along with Sindhi in 1967.[185] Thereafter, Karpoori Thakur, then Chief Minister of Bihar made a formal representation to the central government for the recognition of Maithili.[186] There was a formal discussion on the issue of Maithili in Bihar Legislative Council on 21 December 1978 and a resolution was passed and sent to the central government.[187]

27 March 1992 is a memorable day in the history of the Maithili movement. Once again, Maithili speakers had to protest against the unfair attempts of the government of Bihar to undermine the independent existence of the Maithili language. Laloo Prasad Yadav's Rashtriya Janata Dal government in Bihar excluded Maithili from the BPSC examination. His argument was that Maithili was the language of Brahmins only and it was not even recognized by the Indian Constitution. Second, in his opinions it unduly favoured the Maithili-speaking people in the competitive examinations. He believed that it was against the social justice programme of the government of Bihar. Around twenty-five thousand Maithili speakers cutting across caste, class, gender, and region protested against this policy of the government in a big rally in Patna on 27 March 1992. Women and young people participated in great numbers in this protest.[188] Maithili leaders asserted that a language does not belong to a particular caste but to a region and the people inhabiting it. Second, they argued that Santhali and Nepali were also not included in the eighth schedule of the Indian Constitution but Santhali was recognized as a subject of examination by BPSC, and Nepali was recognized in Bengal. Thirdly, they asked that BPSC recognized Bengali, Oriya, Santhali, and Urdu. If these languages were not against the social justice programmes, then why were such accusations levelled against Maithili?[189] They believed that it was just a baseless and biased stand of the Government of Bihar to diminish Maithili.

Communist Party of India, Bhogendra Jha, and the Maithili Movement

Bhogendra Jha was an active member of the CPI and MP from the Madhubani constituency for many times since the independence of India. He always raised the issue of the social and economic deprivations of the toiling masses of the Mithila region in parliament. He was also aware of the Maithili language movement and its various demands. Time and again, he supported these demands, like the setting up of a modern university in Mithila, a branch of AIR in Darbhanga, and a broad-gauge line between Darbhanga and Samastipur. Indeed, it was he and the CPI in the Mithila region that used Maithili in its official proceedings. Their cadres in the region used Maithili in their speeches and discussions.[190] Bhogendra Jha made a difference between a spoken language and an understandable language in any region, particularly in Uttar Pradesh, Bihar, and Madhya Pradesh except its tribal areas and Rajasthan. According to him, in these regions, Hindi is understood but not spoken. Hindi is not the mother tongue of the masses in these regions. He says:

.... बोलने वाली भाषा नहीं, समझने वाली भाषा। यह जो द्वंद है, यह द्वंद आज तक हिन्दी के बहुत से विद्वान समझ नहीं पा रहे हैं। कहते हैं यह हिन्दी भाषी राज्य है। लेकिन ये हिन्दी भाषी नहीं हैं, ये हिन्दी समझने वाले राज्य है। पूरा उत्तर प्रदेश, कुछ आदिवासी इलाकों को छोड़ कर पूरा मध्य प्रदेश, पूरा बिहार, राजस्थान, ये सब हिन्दी समझते हैं, हिन्दी बोल नहीं सकते। आम लोगों की मातृभाषा हिन्दी नहीं है।[191]

[... not the language of speech, but the language in which one understands. This dialectic has not been understood by the many scholars of Hindi. They say it is a Hindi-speaking state. But these are not Hindi-speaking states, but states where Hindi is understood. All of Uttar Pradesh, excluding some Tribal areas, all of Madhya Pradesh, all of Bihar, Rajasthan, these all understand Hindi, but cannot speak Hindi. Hindi is not the mother tongue of the common man.]

Bhogendra Jha was aware of the compulsions of using the mother tongue, Maithili, by the illiterate and marginalized agricultural labourers, who may understand Hindi but could not speak in it. So, he stressed the need for using Maithili in the official proceedings of the CPI.[192] He also described the internal divisions within the Congress about the use of Hindi or Hindustani as the national language of India. For Gandhi, Hindustani should be the national language, and for this purpose he supported Rajendra Prasad as his candidate in the presidential election of the Hindi Sahitya Sammelan. In this election, besides Gandhi, Jawaharlal Nehru, the Communists, such as Bhogendra Jha, and Congress Socialists such as Jayaprakash Narayan supported Rajendra Prasad. But Rajendra Prasad was defeated by Purushottam Das Tandon and with that Gandhiji's projection of Hindustani as the national language of India was also defeated. However, in Bihar, attempts were made to promote Hindustani. One such incident was the publication of textbooks during the Congress ministry in 1937. Saiyad Mahmood was the education minister; following Gandhiji's formula he published the textbooks in both scripts, in which Ram and Sita were mentioned as *Badshah* Ram and *Begum* Sita. It gave rise to huge social tensions and particularly the Hindu

Mahasabha strongly objected to such publications and people were not ready to read such texts.[193]

Bhogendra Jha believed formation of states based on languages in India was not yet complete. He was in support of formation of smaller states on the basis of language for economic development.[194] He consistently raised the issue of Maithili and the economic development of the Mithila region of north Bihar in the parliament of India. He also introduced a private member's Bill in the Parliament to include Maithili, Bhojpuri, and Rajasthani in the eighth schedule of the constitution on 23 July 1971. The bill was debated in the parliament and many MPs supported the Bill too. But the debate was adjourned by a motion introduced by S.M. Banerjee seeking a reply on the matter by the government and the government was of the opinion that schedule eight of the constitution was meant to promote Hindi and not the languages listed in it, so the development of a language would not be affected by its inclusion or non-inclusion in the eighth schedule and urged Bhogendra Jha to withdraw the Bill as government was contemplating a comprehensive Bill to deal with the recognition or non-recognition of the languages.[195] In the 1980s and 1990s, he became very vocal for the rightful claims of the Maithils. To draw his attention to the neglect of Maithili, the ABMS and its Secretary Pitambar Pathak played a critical role.[196] ABMS wrote a letter to Mufti Mohammed Sayeed, Minister of Home Affairs, Government of India, demanding constitutional recognition of Maithili. In this letter it was also mentioned that the then PM of India, V.P. Singh, also met a Maithili delegation on 7 September 1990 and assured them about the 'sympathetic consideration and suitable decision at the earliest'.[197] ABMS wrote a letter to P.V. Narsimha Rao as well for the recognition of Maithili in the eighth schedule of the constitution.[198] Bhogendra Jha in his letter to the Secretary General, Lok Sabha on 31 May 1990 wrote about the neglect of and discrimination against the Mithila region of north Bihar. He said that:

> even the existing industries like the Ashoka Paper Mills, Thakur Paper Mills, fruit processing factories of Madhubani and Darbhanga and OCM are languishing and the old sugar mills of Raiyam, Lohat, and Sakari are not being modernized. The completion of Western Koshi canal is being delayed ... per capita power consumption is less than one-fifth of that of Bihar, which itself is less.[199]

Bhogendra Jha was also contemplating an 'All-Party Conference to discuss and demand solutions of problems like the flood, drought, and electricity crisis of this region'.[200] Even the union government of India continued to believe that the major language of the Mithila region was Hindi. This is reflected in a reply to Bhogendra Jha's question about the news broadcast in Maithili from the Darbhanga Akashwani Station, when Minister of state for Information and Broadcasting K.P. Singh Deo stated that 'a news summary in Maithili of five minutes' duration is broadcast from AIR Darbhanga thrice a week. There is no proposal either to increase the duration or frequency of this news summary as adequate number of news bulletins are being broadcast by the station in *the principal language of the station which is Hindi* (Emphasis mine).'[201] Bhogendra Jha raised the issue of upgradation of the capacity of the television centre at Madhubani;[202] enhancing the transmitting capacity of the Darbhanga Station of AIR;[203] broadcasting of the Vidyapati serial produced by Tridip Kumar Films from Doordarshan;[204] news bulletins in Maithili language at Mithila (Darbhanga Station of AIR);[205] and correct enumeration of the number of Maithili speakers in the census report[206] to the concerned authorities. In a letter to Ajit Panja, then Minister for Information and Broadcasting, Bhogendra Jha described the peaceful demonstration of the thousands of Maithili speakers for the inclusion of Maithili in the eighth schedule of the Indian Constitution on 21 July 1992 and hunger strike since 29 July 1992. He complained about the non-coverage of these protests by AIR or Doordarshan and urged the minister to 'ensure that AIR and Doordarshan adequately cover hereafter particularly the demonstration rally of 6 August 1992'.[207] It was a massive demonstration and rally by the Maithili speakers. Bhogendra Jha wrote a letter to the then Prime Minister of India, P.V. Narsimha Rao, and the Minister of Home Affairs S.B. Chavan for the inclusion of Maithili in the eighth schedule of the Indian Constitution.[208]

In his other letter to S.B. Chavan, Bhogendra Jha proposed that all the remaining six languages recognized by the Sahitya Akademi, that is, Maithili, Manipuri, Nepali, Konkani, Rajasthani, and Dogri should be included in the eighth schedule of the Indian Constitution. He also stated that exclusion of Maithili might be 'mistaken as a punishment for the Maithili-speaking people because of their remaining peaceful in their demands and agitations'.[209] He also demanded that immediate steps should be taken to 'provide the use of Maithili language for all or some of the official purposes in the Maithili speaking area of Bihar under Article 347 of the constitution of India'.[210] He also provided a report on the Maithili language, which was made available in the Lok Sabha for the perusal of Members of Parliament about the case of Maithili language for inclusion in the eighth schedule of the Indian Constitution. Here, he elaborated on various constitutional provisions–Articles 210 (1), 341(1), 345, 347, 351 and institutional support for the promotion of regional languages.[211]

In his reply to a question raised by Bhogendra Jha about the plan of the government regarding inclusion of Maithili and other languages recognized by the Sahitya Akademi in the eighth schedule of the constitution, M.M. Jacob, Minister of state for Home Affairs in Lok Sabha replied that 'the Government are of the view that inclusion of more languages in the eighth schedule to the constitution would create other repercussions and reactions. However, it will continue to be the endeavour of the Government to develop cultural and literary heritage of all the languages irrespective of their being included in the eighth schedule or not'.[212]

A memorandum for the recognition of Maithili in the eighth schedule was presented to the Prime Minister and a copy was made available to members of both the houses of the Indian Parliament by Amresh Pathak as a representative of the Maithili Sangharsha Samiti, Patna, Bihar on 16 May 1992.[213] In this memorandum Pathak also supported the demand of Manipuri, Nepali, Rajasthani, Dogri, and Konkani along with Maithili. He asserted that once a language fulfils the criteria of the Sahitya Akademi, then such a language should also be included in the eighth schedule of the constitution. He also stated that the recommendation for the inclusion of Maithili in the eighth schedule of the Indian Constitution was first made in 1977 by the then chief minister of Bihar, Karpoori Thakur, to Shanti Bhushan, the former law minister, Government of India. Similar recommendations were also made during the chief ministership of Jagannath Mishra and Bhagwat Jha Azad.[214] A combined memorandum was also submitted to the prime minister of India for the inclusion of Maithili in the eighth schedule. It was signed by the Vidyapati Seva Sansthan, Darbhanga, Akhil Bharatiya Maithili Sahitya Parishad, Darbhanga, Mithilanchal Vikas Parishad, Laheria Sarai, and Akhil Bharatiya Mithila Sangh, Delhi.[215]

Bhogendra Jha raised the demand for the inclusion of Maithili in the Parliament again on 6 August1992 and proposed its inclusion along with five other languages—Rajasthani, Nepali, Manipuri, Konkani, and Dogri—recognized by the Sahitya Akademi in the eighth schedule of the Indian Constitution.[216] The stand of the government of Bihar was exposed again when it did not respond to the repeated reminders of the Ministry of Home Affairs regarding its view on the matter of Maithili's inclusion in the eighth schedule of the Indian Constitution. In a comment the Ministry of Home Affairs, on the representation of Bhogendra Jha, pointed out that 'the Bihar State Government was requested to give their comments on the points raised in the representation as they were primarily concerned with this matter. However, the State Government has not furnished any views on this matter, despite reminders. Home minister has also written a letter to Chief Minister, Bihar in the matter'.[217] The comment further elaborated on Article 345 of the Indian Constitution, which empowers the state to make any language of the state for partial or full official purpose. It also stated that inclusion in the eighth schedule of a language does 'not by itself confer a constitutional duty on the state Government to direct its use for a particular purpose'.[218] Finally the Government of India through the 78th Constitutional Amendment included Manipuri, Nepali, and Konkani in the eighth schedule of the constitution and Maithili was left out.

Support for Maithili was widening in this period as many MPs across the party lines supported the claim of Maithili. Describing Maithili as having a rich classical and modern literature Syed Shahabuddin also supported the demand for the inclusion of Maithili in the eighth schedule.[219] Political demand for separate statehood for Mithila was also being re-asserted and the Mithila Rajya Sangharsha Samiti was formed with Jayakant Mishra as its Chairman. Jayakant Mishra was also thinking of forming a new party altogether for this purpose with Bhogendra Jha as its leader.[220] Laloo Prasad by now had become critical of Bhogendra Jha. This was due to Bhogendra Jha's open support for Maithili. It distressed the Maithils even more.[221] Dhanakar Thakur, being himself, a supporter of BJP acknowledged the role of Bhogendra Jha (CPI MP) in the Maithili movement. For Thakur, without the creation of a separate state of Mithila, Maithili could not survive.[222]

1992 was a crucial year in the Maithili movement as ABMS systematically protested, demonstrated, and launched a hunger strike at the boat club before the parliament of India from March 1992 to 8 December 1992. Shri Jagannath Mishra courted arrest for the inclusion of Maithili in the eighth schedule (see Image 4.8).[223] Similarly a dozen students participated in a cycle procession from Darbhanga to Delhi in support of the demand for Maithili under the leadership of Ranabir Kumar Chaudhary. They started from Darbhanga on 25 November 1994 and reached Delhi on 6 December 1994. They also presented the memorandum in support of Maithili to the Prime Minister, Home Minister, many Cabinet Ministers, and Members of Parliament.[224]

Despite his staunch support for Maithili's demand Bhogendra Jha was aware of the different problems of the movement. He considered that the Treaty of Sugauli by the British politically divided Maithili-speaking people; river Koshi geographically divided the region; the social divisions of Mithila do not allow all the castes and communities of Mithila to come together on a single platform; and finally the Maithili movement was divided organizationally; supporters of the Maithili movement very often form new associations, refusing to come together to form and strengthen one organization for the purpose.[225]

Vidyapati Seva Sansthan and Antarrashtriya Maithili Parishad

The Vidyapati Seva Sansthan[226] is one of the most vocal and active organizations in the contemporary phase of the Maithili movement along with the Mithila Vikas Parishad and Antarrashtriya Maithili Parishad. Its main objective is to awaken the masses through movements, protests, demonstrations, and memorandums. This organization is politically oriented and has played a critical role in bringing Mithila and the Maithili-speaking region of India and Nepal together. It came into being on 7 October 1980. Braj Kishor Verma 'Manipadma' was the main motivator besides Kumar Subheshwar Singh, Baidyanath Chaudhary 'Baiju', Dayanand Jha, and Umakant Jha.[227] Presently this organization works under the leadership of Baidyanath Chaudhary 'Baiju'. Every year it organizes the Mithila Vibhuti Parva and on this occasion, it commemorates and celebrates Maithili-speaking personalities and their contributions. Its contributions are duly recognized in the implementation of Maithili as a medium in primary education in some parts of Darbhanga, Madhubani, Saharsa, and Purnea. It has fought for the broadcasting of all the programmes at Akashwani (All India Radio) Darbhanga, and Bhagalpur in Maithili. It launched a persistent movement since 1984 for the all-round development of Mithila. Among its activities were: the *Rail Roku Aandolan* (Stop Railway Movement) on 16 December 1985; throughout Mithilanchal the same movement was launched on 7, 8, and 9 January 1986 in which more than five thousand people were arrested; on 18 January 1986, Darbhanga Samahartak Gherao (Encirclement of the collector of Darbhanga) in which women also participated; on 27 January 1986 throughout Mithilanchal a bandh (closure) was observed; on 24 February *Baat Chhek Aandolan* (Obstruct the Road Movement). On 13 August 1986 a big mass procession was organized in Delhi where the Janata Party leader of the parliament Madhu Dandawate, MP Vijay Kumar Mishra, former MP Hukumdeva Narayan Yadav, and then Chairmen Vidyapati Seva Sansthan and former MP, Surendra Jha 'Suman', Babu Saheb Chaudhary, Dev Narayan Jha, Pitambar Pathak, and others were part of the rally. These are the following *thirteen demands* of the Sansthan for the all-round development of Mithila:

1. Immediate construction of big gauge railway line from Samastipur via Darbhanga to Jayanagar, Nirmalli, and Narkatiyaganj, along with the beginning of work for the small gauge line between Sakari–Hasanpur.

2. Solutions for distresses, such as floods, *raudi* (drought), and lack of electricity.

3. All the ailing mills of Mithilanchal must be modernized and there should be industrialization of the region. There should be immediate beginning and production work of Ashok Paper Mills; Samastipur Paper Mills; Baijnathpur Kagaj Mill; Thakur Paper Mill, Samastipur; Jute Mill, Katihar; and Jute Mill, Forbesganj. Also, the Glucose Mill of Pandaul, Raiyam- Lohat-Sakari Sugar Mill, and Samastipur Railway Coach Factory must be expanded.

4. There must be an establishment of a university in Saharsa, a medical college in Purnea, and petro-chemicals in Begusarai, along with the establishment of a graphite factory in Samastipur.

5. Keeping in mind cultural and linguistic unity, there should be a direct connection between Darbhanga and Saharsa through rail and road; and immediate completion of the National Highway lateral road, which is of strategic importance.

6. Strengthening and expansion of rail and road transportation throughout Mithilanchal—(a) Sakari–Hasanpur, (b) Nirmali–Bhatiyahi, (c) Big Gauge Railway line between Samastipur–Udaipur–Nepal, (d) Muzaffarpur–Sitamarhi, (e) Simari–Bakhtiyarpur–Bihariganj, (f) Madhepura–Triveneeganj–Veerpur, (g) Forbesganj–Thakurganj, (h) Nirmalli–Jaiyanagar.

7. Throughout Mithilanchal Maithili should be used as a medium of education till high school.

8. Maithili be recognized in the state as an official language.

9. Immediate inclusion of Maithili in the eighth schedule of the Indian Constitution.

10. A Doordarshan centre in Darbhanga.

11. Provision for the broadcasting of all the programmes of *Akashwani* Darbhanga and Bhagalpur in Maithili.

12. Repeal of the decision about the transferring of Sanjay Gandhi Diary Technology—temporarily coordinated by Rajendra Prasad Agricultural University. It should be established in Darbhanga.

13. One-third of the property of the Raj Darbhanga be set aside for public welfare.

Image 4.3   Protest for the Constitutional Recognition of Maithili—1

Source: Vidyapati Chetna Samiti, Patna.

Image 4.4   Protest for the Constitutional Recognition of Maithili—2

Source: Vidyapati Chetna Samiti, Patna.

Image 4.5   Protest for the Constitutional Recognition of Maithili—3

[Members of the *Maithili Sangharsha Samiti* holding a demonstration in New Delhi on 21 July 1992 in support of their demand for inclusion of Maithili language in the eighth schedule of the Constitution, Image courtesy, *Indian Express* Archive/Arun Jetlie]

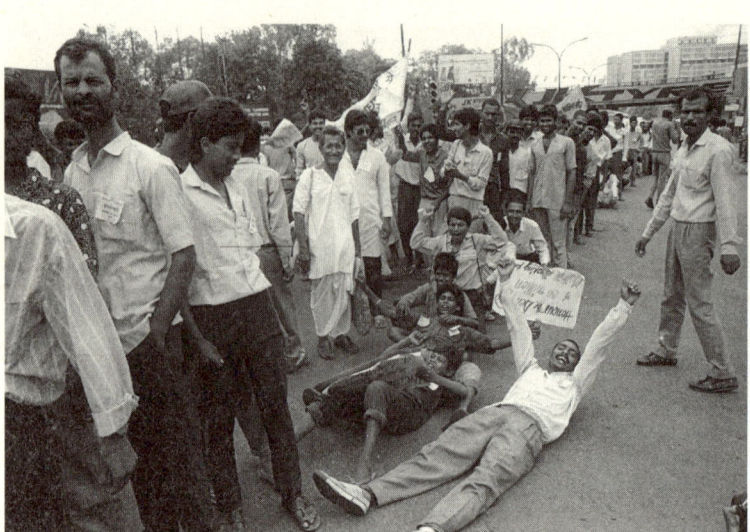

Image 4.6   Protest for the Constitutional Recognition of Maithili—4

[Members of the Maithili Sangharsha Samiti holding a demonstration in New Delhi on 21 July 1992 in support of their demand for inclusion of Maithili language in the eighth schedule of the Constitution, Image courtesy, *Indian Express* Archive/Arun Jetlie]

The Vidyapati Seva Sansthan is also trying to coordinate between different organizations of Mithila and Maithili throughout India to chart out the strategy of the movement and to work together for the cause of Mithila. It also celebrates Janaki Navami as Maithili Diwas. Till 1986 it had thirty-two branches in the different villages of Darbhanga, Samastipur, Muzaffarpur, Saharsa, and Purnea.

19 and 20 June 1993 proved to be a milestone in the history of the Maithili movement with the organization of the first International Maithili Conference in Ranchi. It received support from India, Nepal, and the US. The conference was inaugurated by Jayakant Mishra and Babu Saheb Chaudhary of Kolkata and Amresh Narayan Chaudhary, chairman of Nepal Maithili Samaj, was the chief guest. Subhadra Jha suggested that if Maithili was to develop it was necessary for all the people inhabiting Mithila to declare themselves as Maithil, as they were all the children of Mithila and their language was Maithili and

Image 4.7 Protest for the Constitutional Recognition of Maithili—5

[Activists of the All India Mithila Sangh taking out a rally on the Bahadur Shah Zafar Marg in the Capital. Image Credit, *The Pioneer*/Manish Swarup]

not Hindi or English. He also considered the condition of Maithili would have been different had Maithili and its script Tirhuta been respected in the courts of the Darbhanga Raj, Betiya Raj, Banaili Raj, and in the King of Nepal's court. It was also stressed that Maithili's biggest enemy were Maithils themselves; combined with the political divide of the region based on caste, the very existence of Maithili had been threatened. In the conference, it was declared that Maithili was an international language and the purpose of the AMP was the development of Maithili. Besides the demand for social and economic development of Mithila, AMP demanded that, based on population, Maithili must be declared the second language of the state in Bihar under Article 347 of the Indian Constitution. Second, a Bill should be

Image 4.8   Protest for the Constitutional Recognition of Maithili—6

[The former Chief Minister of Bihar, Dr Jagannath Mishra, and activists belonging to the Akhil Bhartiya Mithila Sangh (ABMS) and Vidyapati Seva Sansthan (VSS) courting arrest for the inclusion of Maithili in the eighth schedule of the Indian Constitution, Boat Club, New Delhi on 19 August 1992, Image courtesy, *Indian Express* Archive/Virender Singh]

introduced in the parliament for the inclusion of Maithili in the eighth schedule of the constitution.[228] The AMP is organizing conferences and various training camps at regular intervals to prepare Maithili volunteers in different parts of Mithila. It is important to remember that this conference was organized when Laloo Prasad Yadav's government in Bihar excluded Maithili from the BPSC. And there was discourse at the centre about the expansion of eighth schedule of the Constitution of India. So, the conference was organized in a politically charged atmosphere.

The Bharatiya Janata Party and Inclusion of Maithili in the Eighth Schedule of the Indian Constitution

The Bharatiya Janata Party (BJP) supported the Maithili movement particularly when Tarakant Jha, a renowned advocate at Patna High Court and a long-term associate of BJP since the days of *Jana Sangh*, was the President of Bihar State BJP in 1990s. Tarakant Jha was associated with the Rashtriya Swayamsevak Sangh (RSS) since the very beginning. He was its *pracharak* for fifteen years. Thereafter, he pursued the legal profession at the Patna High Court with distinction and went on to become the Advocate General in 1976. Later, he joined the BJP after its formation in 1980. He was a very close observer of the Maithili movement and shaped the growth of the Chetna Samiti. He actively participated in its activities and events. He also played a key role in the establishment of the Maithili Akademi in 1976 in Patna. In the later years of his life, he provided leadership to Mithila and the Maithili movement and after the creation of Jharkhand in 2000, launched an extensive campaign for the separate statehood of Mithila.

He was elected as a Member of the Legislative Council (MLC) of Bihar on 22 July 1992. When the Government of Bihar, led by Laloo Prasad Yadav, removed Maithili from the BPSC on 27 February 1992, the Bihar BJP organized a *bandh* on 1 March 1992 throughout Mithilanchal, which was supported by NSUI's President Premshankar Mishra as well.[229] Tarakant Jha also led a protest march in Patna.[230] It is important to note here that Maithili was recognized by the Government of Bihar in 1972 as an optional paper in the BPSC examination, conceding to the long standing demand of the Maithili speakers.[231] When Laloo Yadav's Government refused to restore the previous status of Maithili in the BPSC, many cases were filed in the Patna High Court[232] and Tarakant Jha played an instrumental role in that. The High court in its judgement lamented the Government of Bihar for excluding Maithili on the pretext of a case pending in the High Court,[233] and stated that 'merely because a matter was pending at the High Court could not offer ready excuse to the state to withdraw Maithili language as a subject in the examinations conducted by the Bihar Public Service Commission. This was an exercise in politics'.[234] The court further added that,

> [l]inguistic identities are not quirks of history. As heritage, a language lives with a civilisation and passes out with it. A language flourishes with patronage and recedes into disuse with lack of it. State hostility to language will be its death knell. [A] *hostility to a language is hostility to the people who use it.* Even a dominant language, thus, recedes into the background.[235] (Emphasis added)

Thus, the High Court quashed the order of the government dated 29 February 1992 and directed the government 'to insert Maithili language in the syllabi of the Bihar Public Service Commission as it was before … if the state may like to take any other decision on the inclusion of other languages, it may, but it will have to be within the framework of law and the constitution of India'.[236] Here the court was referring to Bhojpuri particularly. Against this judgement, the RJD government of Bihar took the case to the Supreme Court but when the case was still pending in the Supreme Court, Tarakant Jha could successfully persuade the Nitish Kumar government to restore the status of Maithili in the BPSC examination in 2006.[237] He was so much involved in the issue of Maithili and Mithila that some leaders within the BJP started to criticize his move. This was the context when he organized Mithilanchal Jagaran Yatra in 1995. He had also got a resolution passed in the executive meeting of Bihar BJP at Madhubani on 8, 9, and 10 July 1994 regarding Maithili to be included in the eighth schedule of the Indian Constitution. In the election manifesto of BJP for the 1995 Assembly election in Bihar, it was stated that if voted to power, the BJP would restore the previous status of Maithili in the BPSC and pressurize the central government to include Maithili in the eighth schedule of the constitution.[238] It was a historic incident in the history of the Maithili movement as, for the first time, a political party included the demand for Maithili in its election manifesto. When the news of these moves was making the rounds in Mithila and people came out in its support, Tarakant Jha was expelled from the BJP for six years on 20 November 1998.[239] He continued his work for the recognition of Maithili and development of Mithila. On 12 May 2000, he submitted a memorandum to the President of India for the recognition of Maithili in the eighth schedule of the Indian Constitution signed by twenty-seven lakh people.[240] When a Bill for the creation of Jharkhand, Uttaranchal (now Uttarakhand), and Chhattisgarh was passed in the Parliament on 3 August 2000, the very next day on 4 August 2000 he organized a press conference and put forth the demand for separate statehood of Mithila. However, he rejoined the BJP by the end of 2003.

There was an overwhelming support for the inclusion of Maithili, Bodo, Santhali, and Dogri in the eighth schedule of the Indian Constitution. Regarding Maithili's inclusion in the constitution, a question was raised in the parliament by the All-India Trinamool Congress MP

Sudip Bandopadhyaya on 3 December 2002.[241] After that almost all the MPs of Mithila supported that demand across caste and party lines. Ramchandra Paswan, MP from Rosara, during the zero-hour session of the Lok Sabha on 15 December 2003, criticized the government for their lukewarm attitude towards Maithili despite repeated assurances. He even cautioned the government that the issue of Maithili was related to four and half crore of the people, and they were eagerly waiting for the government to introduce a Bill for the inclusion of Maithili in the parliament at the earliest.[242] And on 22–3 December 2003, the Parliament passed the constitutional amendment Bill including Maithili in the eighth schedule of the Indian Constitution. Tarakant Jha was present among the audience on both days in the parliament.[243] And Maithili along with Bodo, Dogri, and Santhali was included in the eighth schedule of the Indian Constitution by the ninety second constitutional amendment to the constitution.[244]

Mithila: Revival of Separate Statehood Demand

One very important shift taking place in the Maithili movement was its focus from the issue of Maithili language to economic backwardness and poverty of the region. It has now become the central agenda for political mobilization. In a two-day conference in Muzaffarpur, when a group of concerned citizens tried to pass the resolution for making Maithili the medium of education, Tarakant Jha according to Kamlesh Jha had said that the Mithila Rajya Abhiyan[245] would discuss the issue of poverty and development.[246] Ayodhyanath Jha, in his support for Mithila statehood demand, did not even mention the name of Maithili:

विदेहसुता जानकीक ई क्षेत्र अपन उपेक्षा आ अपमानसँ मुक्तिक लेल, दरिद्रता एवं विपन्नता दूर करबाक लेल, विकासक गति के तीव्र करबाक लेल, देशक सुरक्षा आ अखंडता के अक्षुण्ण रखबाक लेल, रौदि-दाही सँ त्राण पएबाक लेल आ अपन प्राचीन गरिमा के प्राप्त करबाक लेल पृथक मिथिला प्रान्तक संघर्षक आह्वान करैत अछि।[247]

[This is the region of the daughter of Videha—Janaki; we call for a struggle for a separate Mithila state, to free itself from neglect and contempt, to eradicate absolute poverty and vulnerability, to increase the pace of development, to keep the security and integrity of the country intact, to protect itself from drought and floods and regain its past glory.]

To discuss the viability of a separate Mithila, a two-day meeting was held on 21 and 22 October 2000 at J.N. College, Madhubani in which 181 people participated of the 250 invited. In this meeting, leaders like Devendra Prasad Yadav, MP (JDU), Jhanjharpur; Ramashish Yadav, MLA, Benipatti; and Rajkumar Yadav, MLA, Phulparas were present.[248] Inaugurating the central headquarters of Mithila Rajya Abhiyan on 11 November 2000 at Gauri Niwas, Raham Ganj, Laheria Sarai, Chetkar Jha, renowned political scientist and former Vice Chancellor of Lalit Narayan Mithila University, Darbhanga stated that earlier he was opposed to the Mithila movement based on Maithili language but he now supported the demand for Mithila state as it was based on demand for development.[249]

In February, Janaki Rath and Ganga Gandak Rath Yatra was organized to mobilize the masses across the length and breadth of Mithila.[250] In these yatras, a slogan coined by Mohamad Hazi Iliyas became quite popular and also reflected the growing discontent among all the caste and religious groups of Mithila—आगां आगां टीकीवाला तकर पाछा टोपीवाला, तखन बनते मिथिला राज्य[251] [in front line tikiwala (referring to Hindu), behind them topiwala (referring to Muslims), Only then Mithila state can be created].

In a two-day programme at Saharsa on 25–6 May 2001, representatives of all the districts of Mithila associated with Mithila Rajya Abhiyan participated. In the meeting, it was decided to launch Koshi Rath Yatra to mobilize the masses of Saharsa, Madhepura, Supaul, and Purnea. But it could not be organized.[252] However, it shows the growing interest among the Maithils for the demand of separate statehood. Similar events were held in Samastipur, Devghar, Khagariya, Patna, and other places in Mithila as well.[253] They had also started the publication of Jai Mithila—the mouthpiece of Mithila Rajya Abhiyan. Its editor was Sureshwar Jha.[254] The Mithila Seva Trust was also registered in 2001 to raise funds for the separate statehood movement for Mithila. A successful *nakabandi* in the support of their demand was organized for four hours on 22 June 2002.

In the meanwhile a judgement of Patna High court on 26 September 2002 in which the Bihar government was reminded that it was the duty of the state government to provide education at primary level in the mother tongue Maithili in Mithila, gave considerable encouragement to the Mithila movement.[255] In a two-day programme at Darbhanga on

28–9 February 2004 to celebrate the inclusion of Maithili in the Indian Constitution Tarakant Jha reiterated that his priority was Mithila and Maithili even after joining the BJP and he would fight for the realization of Mithila state.[256]

One of the interesting developments of the movement in this period was an increasing belief among the people of the region that without the political mobilization and mass agitations, the region could not be developed economically and separate statehood was vital for that. And only through separate and independent statehood of Mithila, the Maithili culture and language could be protected and promoted. Another interesting development in the movement is the growing assertion of the non-Brahmins and non-Kayastha castes and their opposition to the Brahminical domination over the language and culture of Mithila. And these contestations will shape the future course of the Maithili movement.

Leaders of all the political parties of Mithila had raised the issue of Maithili and Mithila at one point or the other. They are doing so even more actively since the 1980s. It is alleged that they use the issue of Maithili and Mithila for their own personal progress within their respective political parties. But it had certainly led to the development of tacit consensus among all the political leaders of Mithila that issue of Maithili and Mithila could not be undermined. Now there are formations of political parties like ABMP with the sole purpose of development of Mithila and Maithili. In other words, the issue of Mithila and Maithili has become a powerful political issue in the region.

Another remarkable development of the period is greater willingness among the organizations and the individuals to work together for the cause of Maithili. Internal factions and social division of Maithili organizations were one of the biggest reasons for the slow development of the Maithili movement. Although it is true that it had worked against extremely odd conditions and fought against Hindi, which was supported by emerging nationalism in India, the Maithili language movement has been successful in meeting almost all its demands but failed in many ways to connect and sufficiently mobilize the masses on the issue of Maithili, despite a century of the history of the movement. It is still its biggest challenge.

The social base of the movement has certainly increased, perhaps because of the growing number of middle class among the Maithils.

The participation of non-Brahmin and non-Kayastha castes are increasing. And the issue of Mithila after recognition of Maithili in the eighth schedule of the Indian Constitution is bound to become the political issue in the region. However, the characteristic of the movement itself remains far from a mass movement, perhaps the biggest contradiction of the Maithili movement.

Notes and References

1. Raj Chandra Jha, 'Mithila Movement', in Sureshwar Jha (ed.), *Mithila—Tradition and Change: Essays in Honour of Pt. Tarakant Jha* (Darbhanga: Tarakant Jha Felicitation Committee, 2008), p. 101.
2. Raj Chandra Jha, 'Mithila Movement', in Sureshwar Jha (ed.), *Mithila Tradition and Change Essays in Honour of Pt. Tarakant Jha*, p. 103.
3. Raj Chandra Jha, 'Mithila Movement', in Sureshwar Jha (ed.), *Mithila Tradition and Change Essays in Honour of Pt. Tarakant Jha*, p. 103.
4. Raj Chandra Jha, 'Mithila Movement', in Sureshwar Jha (ed.), *Mithila Tradition and Change Essays in Honour of Pt. Tarakant Jha*, p. 104.
5. It was widely believed that these arrests were made by the Bengal Police on the instigation of the government of Bihar. However, the government of Bihar denied its role in such arrests, though it accepted the fact that the Criminal Investigation Department (CID) had informed the Bengal police that Janaki Nandan Singh with many other Maithils were proceeding towards Kalyani to demonstrate at the residence of the Bihar Chief Minister there, for the creation of separate Mithila State and present to Pt. Nehru a memorandum for the creation of a separate Mithila Pradesh Congress Committee. The Bengal government also made its position clear on the issue through a press release of 29 January 1954 in which it said that the police authorities felt that to allow this group to reach Kalyani led by ex-Congressmen Janaki Nandan Singh might create disturbances and message of the C.I.D. of Bihar was for the purpose of warning the Bengal Police about the disturbances that this group might create; see Raj Chandra Jha, 'Mithila Movement', in Sureshwar Jha (ed.), *Mithila Tradition and Change Essays in Honour of Pt. Tarakant Jha*, pp. 101–22.
6. This group was supposed to be the result of political rivalry and was working at the behest of the Bihar Government; for such a purpose, an influential minister of Bihar visited Kolkata; see Raj Chandra Jha, 'Mithila Movement', in Sureshwar Jha (ed.), *Mithila Tradition and Change Essays in Honour of Pt. Tarakant Jha*, p. 108.

7. Raj Chandra Jha, 'Mithila Movement', in Sureshwar Jha (ed.), *Mithila Tradition and Change Essays in Honour of Pt. Tarakant Jha*, p. 115.

8. See 'State Reorganization Commission Report', 1955.

9. For the details on the contributions of Kolkata in all the spheres of the Maithili movement–literary, cultural, or political, see a special issue, 'Kolkata mei Maithili', *Purvottar Maithil Samaj*, quarterly, issue–5, October–December, Guwahati, Vidyapati Chetna Samiti (2011).

10. Narendra Jha, 'Babu Saheb Chaudhary: Mithila–Maithilik Amar O Nirbhik Senani', *Karnamrit* (April–June 2002): 17.

11. Maithili Shikshit Samaj (1919), Maithili Yuvak Sangh (1937), Mithila Sevak Sangh, Akhil Bhartiya Maithil Sangh (1945), Mithila Lok Sangh (1952), Akhil Bhartiya Mithila Sangh (1957), Mithila Sanskritik Parishad (1959), Vidyapati Vidya Mandir (1960), All India Maithil Sangh, Mithila Kala Kendra (1959), Mithi Yatrik (1973), Jhankar, Kokil Manch (1990), Mithila Vikas Parishad (1983), Kurmi–Kshatriya Chhatraviti Kosha, Karngoshthi, Maithili Prakashan Samiti, Maithil Mitra Sangh, Tirhut Vaidehi Seva Sansthan, Vidyapati Smarak Manch, Vaidehi Seva Manch (1990), Mithila Chamber of Commerce and Industries, Mithila Udaya Sangh, Vaidehi Parishad, Maithil Swajan Sangh, Mithilodaya Prakashan, Bhumija Sanskritik Kendra, Maithili Mukti Morcha (9 December 1980), Mithila Chetna, Sampark (1985), Mithila Sangharsha Samiti, Mithila Seva Samiti, Mithila Navachetna Samiti.

12. Rajnandan Lal Das, 'Kolkata O Maithili Patrakarita', *Purvottar Maithil Samaj*, quarterly, issue–5, October–December, Guwahati, Vidyapati Chetna Samiti (2011): 33.

13. Cited in Das, 'Kolkata O Maithili Patrakarita'.

14. *Mithila Darshan* (February 1955); cited in Das, 'Kolkata O Maithili Patrakarita'.

15. *Mithila Darshan* (March 1955); cited in Das, 'Kolkata O Maithili Patrakarita'.

16. *Mithila Darshan* (May 1955); citied in Das, 'Kolkata O Maithili Patrakarita'.

17. See Lakshman Jha, *Mithila a Union Republic* (Darbhanga: Mithila Mandal, 1952). He even prepared the draft constitution for the Union Republic of Mithila, pp. 161–85.

18. Cited in Das, 'Kolkata O Maithili Patrakarita', p. 34.

19. In 2013 this prize was given to Subhash Chandra Yadav.

20. Kishori Kant Mishra, 'Mithila Sanskritik Parishad, Kolakatak Karmamay Pachas Varsha', in Mithilesh Kumar Jha (ed.), *Parishad Varta Swarna Jayanti Visheshank (1959–2009)* (Kolkata: Mithila Sanskritik Parishad, 2009), p. 118.

21. See the exchange of letters between the Mithila Sanskritik Parishad and the Government of India, Mishra, 'Mithila Sanskritik Parishad, Kolakatak Karmamay Pachas Varsha', Jha (ed.), *Parishad Varta Swarna Jayanti Visheshank (1959–2009)*, pp. 89–96.

22. Mishra, 'Mithila Sanskritik Parishad, Kolakatak Karmamay Pachas Varsha', 97–101.

23. Das, 'Kolkata O Maithili Patrakarita', p. 38

24. Govind Jha, *Maithilik Udgam O Vikas;* 'Shrutdhar', Jayakant Jha, *Vidyapati Saurabh;* Radha Krishna Chaudhary, *Dhammapad;* 'Manipadma' *Raja Salhes* and *Lavahari–Kushahari;* Arsi Prasad Singh, trs., *Meghdoot.* See Das, 'Kolkata O Maithili Patrakarita'.

25. Das, 'Kolkata O Maithili Patrakarita', p. 38.

26. These are—(a) 'Lalit', Lakshman Chaudhari, *Vidyapati Padawali O Puran;* (b) 'Shrees', Durganath Jha, *Sukavi Kamalnayan O Hunak Chari Got Pad;* (c) 'Kiran' Kanchinath Jha, *Maithili Bhashak Vyakaran Par Ek Drishti;* (d) Amarnath Jha, *Mithila me Ram Kathak Parampara;* (e) Radhakrishna Chaudhary, *Vichar–Vimarsha;* (f) 'Manipadma', Braj Kishore Verma, *Maithili Lokgathak Itihas;* (g) Jeevakant, *Maithilik Adhunik Katha Sahitya;* (h) Ranjana Jha, *Patrahin Nagna Gachhak Kavya Vaibhav;* (i) Rajeshwar Jha, *Gam Saun Sambadh Pratyant Shabdak Vivechana;* (j) Vishwanath Thakur, *Darshanik Shiromani Vachaspati;* (k) Jayakant Mishra, *Katok Maithili Shabda Sabhak Rochak Byutpata*, see Das, 'Kolkata O Maithili Patrakarita'.

27. Like *Akhar* (1967); *Maithili Kavita* (April 1968); *Lok Manch* (September–October 1969); *Mi* (1970, mini Maithili magazine its total shape was 10/6 cm); *Agni Patra* (February 1973); *Rangamanch* (1974); *Shikha* (May, 1974); *Shulfa* (Handwritten, May 1975); *Deskosha* (1 May 1981); *Karnamrit* (1981); *Desil Bayna* (October 1981); *Pravasak Bhent; Maithili Sangya* (April 1994); *Mithila Samad* (September 1994); *Mithila Chetna* (April 1997); *Mithila Chamber Sanes* (2000); *Shri Mithila* (2002); *Bhorukba* (Vaisakh, 2058); *Dainik Mithila Samad* (31 August 2008); For details about how these magazines contributed to Maithili literature, see Das, 'Kolkata O Maithili Patrakarita', pp. 32–44.

28. Another daily Maithili newspaper was published from Darbhanga by the name of *Mithila Awaz* (December 2012). Although, the circulation of this newspaper is limited, however it ends the need for a daily newspaper in Maithili.

29. Its main activists were Sharad Chandra Mishra, Kamlesh Jha, Amarnath Chaudhary, Awadhesh Kumar Mishra, Nirmal Kumar Jha, R.P. Sinha and Pt. Harischandra Mishra 'Mithlendu'. Some of them also participated in the JP movement in Bihar. Kamlesh Jha spent around twenty days in Jail with Arvind Kumar Akku. His other jail mates were Abdul Bari

Siddaqi and Ramdev Mahto. Kamlesh Jha, 'Kolkata Mahanagar aa Hum', *Purvottar Maithil Samaj*, quarterly, issue-5, October–December, Guwahati, Vidyapati Chetna Samiti (2011): 24.

30. Jha, 'Kolkata Mahanagar aa Hum', p. 27.
31. Jha, 'Kolkata Mahanagar aa Hum', p. 27.
32. Jha, 'Kolkata Mahanagar aa Hum', p. 28.
33. Jha, 'Kolkata Mahanagar aa Hum', p. 28.
34. Jha, 'Kolkata Mahanagar aa Hum', p. 28.
35. Jha, 'Kolkata Mahanagar aa Hum', p. 30.
36. Jha, 'Kolkata Mahanagar aa Hum', p. 29.
37. Jha, 'Kolkata Mahanagar aa Hum', p. 29.
38. Other members of the delegation were Pitambar Pathak, Kamlesh Jha, Mithilesh Kumar Jha, Lokeshnath Jha, Vijay, and some representatives of the Mithila Udaya Sangh, see Jha, 'Kolkata Mahanagar aa Hum', p. 30.
39. Jha, 'Kolkata Mahanagar aa Hum', p. 30.
40. Richard Burghart, 'A Quarrel in the Language Family: Agency and Representation of Speech in Mithila', *Modern Asian Studies*, vol. 27, no. 4 (October 1993): 783.
41. Burghart, 'A Quarrel in the Language Family: Agency and Representation of Speech in Mithila', p. 801.
42. Burghart, 'A Quarrel in the Language Family: Agency and Representation of Speech in Mithila', p. 787.
43. *Indian Nation*, 1 January 1971.
44. Though it is also considered as the thirty-seventh session of the Parishad, as it was the thirty-seventh year of its existence and it was supposed to hold a session annually. But many annual sessions were not held at all. See Mishra 'Amar', *Maithili Sahitya Parishadak Sankshipta Itihas*, and *Smarika*, Akhil Bhartiya Maithili Sahitya Parishad, Lakshmiwati Nagar (Sarisab Pahi) session, chief ed., Sadan Mishra (Laheria Sarai: Nav Bharat Press, 1968).
45. *Smarika*, Akhil Bhartiya Maithili Sahitya Parishad. Welcome Speech of Dr Vishwambhar Jha, pp. 2–7.
46. *Smarika*, Akhil Bhartiya Maithili Sahitya Parishad, p. 7, it is a well-established fact by the many philologists including Grierson, Subhadra Jha, and others that the language spoken in Bhagalpur and its adjoining areas are dialects of Maithili. Now it is a recognized subject of study at Tilaka Manjhi Bhagalpur University from 10 June 2002.
47. *Smarika*, Akhil Bhartiya Maithili Sahitya Parishad, pp. 21–3.
48. *Smarika*, Akhil Bhartiya Maithili Sahitya Parishad, pp. 23–4.
49. *Smarika*, Akhil Bhartiya Maithili Sahitya Parishad, p. 25.
50. *Smarika*, Akhil Bhartiya Maithili Sahitya Parishad, pp. 25–6.

51. *Smarika*, Akhil Bhartiya Maithili Sahitya Parishad, pp. 26–8.
52. *Smarika*, Akhil Bhartiya Maithili Sahitya Parishad, p. 27.
53. *Smarika*, Akhil Bhartiya Maithili Sahitya Parishad, pp. 69–87.
54. *Smarika*, Akhil Bhartiya Maithili Sahitya Parishad.
55. Pages 109 and 113 respectively of Sahitya Akademi's Annual Report 1961, cited in Jayakant Mishra, *The Case of Maithili before the Sahitya Akademi*, p. 4.
56. Quoted in Mishra, *The Case of Maithili before the Sahitya Akademi*, p. 18.
57. Mishra, *The Case of Maithili before the Sahitya Akademi*, p. 3.
58. Mishra, *The Case of Maithili before the Sahitya Akademi*, p. 3.
59. Cited in Mishra, *The Case of Maithili before the Sahitya Akademi*, p. 2.
60. George A. Grierson, *Maithili Grammar*, p. 2; cited in Mishra, *The Case of Maithili before the Sahitya Akademi*, p. 5.
61. Cited in Mishra, *The Case of Maithili before the Sahitya Akademi*, p. 6.
62. Mishra, *The Case of Maithili before the Sahitya Akademi*, p. 10.
63. Mishra, *The Case of Maithili before the Sahitya Akademi*..
64. Cited as Appendix 1, in Govind Jha (ed.), *Jayakant Jayantika* (Patna: Shekhar Prakashan, 2010).
65. See Mithilesh Kumar Jha (ed.), *Parishad Varta Swarna Jayanti Visheshank* (Kolkata: Mithila Sanskritik Parishad, 2009 [1959]).
66. *Searchlight*, 16 February 1966.
67. For details, see Chapter 3.
68. The region of Darbhanga and Madhubani are generally considered as part of *Panchkoshi*.
69. *Searchlight*, 13 July 1966.
70. *Indian Nation*, 20 March 1967.
71. *Indian Nation*, 4 May 1967.
72. *Searchlight*, 24 March 1967.
73. *Indian Nation*, 22 June 1967.
74. *Indian Nation*, 5 May 1967.
75. *Indian Nation*, 22 June 1967.
76. *Searchlight*, 11 July 1967.
77. *Indian Nation*, 20 July 1967.
78. *Indian Nation*, 21 July 1967.
79. Chetkar Jha, Patna University, Braj Kishor Jha, Lecturer, Political Science, Patna College, Patna, Kashikant Mishra, Deptt. of Sanskrit, Patna College, Amaresh Pathak, Deptt. Of Maithili, Patna College, Ashutosh Singh Thakur, Deptt. of History, Patna College, S. Jha Shastri, Deptt. of Maithili P. U., Lekhanath Mishra, Deptt. of Maithili, Patna College, Patna, Dinesh Kumar Jha, Lecturer in Maithili, Patna University, Patna, Indra Kant Jha, Junior Research Fellow (U.G.C.) Deptt. of Maithili, Patna University,

Patna, Mitra Nandan Jha, Lecturer Deptt. of Political Science, Patna
College, Patna, Baleshwar Thakur, Deptt. of Geography, Patna University,
see *Indian Nation*, 29 July 1967.

80. See *Indian Nation*, 29 July 1967.
81. *Indian Nation*, 21 July 1967.
82. *Indian Nation*, 5 May 1967.
83. *Indian Nation*, 5 May 1967.
84. *Searchlight*, 17 August 1967.
85. *Searchlight*, 12 August 1967
86. *Searchlight*, (unclear 15 August 1967; but Paul Brass has written 18 August
    1967).
87. *Searchlight*, (unclear 15 August 1967; but Paul Brass has written 18 August
    1967).
88. *Searchlight*, (unclear 15 August 1967; but Paul Brass has written 18 August
    1967).
89. *Indian Nation*, 28 July 1967.
90. *Indian Nation*, 28 July 1967. Some important figures who supported
    the demand of Maithili were: M.P. Sinha, then leader of Opposition
    in Bihar Assembly; Tej Narayan Jha (Communist Party); Dumar Lal
    Baitha, Ramesh Jha, Shrimati Kishori Devi, Brinda Pd, Rai Birendra,
    Mahabir Prasad Yadav, Sami Nadis, Chandreshwar, Narayan Prasad
    Singh, Basistha Narayan Singh, Rama Kant Jha, Shafiqullah Ansari, Kedar
    Pandey, Badri Mehra, Pramod Kumar Mishra, Ram Krishna Mahto, Prof.
    Anirudh Jha, and others. This clearly signifies that Maithili was gaining
    its ground among the political leaders of all the parties and all the castes
    of Maithili-speaking area.
91. Its office-bearers were–President–Dinesh Chandra Mishra, Vice-
    President–Indranath Thakur, Secretary–Shyama Nand Mishra, Joint-
    Secretary–Kamla Kant Mishra, Publicity Secretary–Maithili Saran Prasad
    Karn, Treasurer–Prabodh Jha and Jayanand Jha; see *Indian Nation*, 24 July
    1967.
92. *Indian Nation*, 29 July 1967.
93. *Searchlight*, 16 January 1968.
94. *Searchlight*, 11 January 1968.
95. *Searchlight*, 11 January 1968.
96. *Searchlight*, 23 January 1968.
97. *Searchlight*, 22 January 1968.
98. *Searchlight*, 20 May 1968.
99. *Searchlight*, 20 May 1968.
100. *Searchlight*, 20 May 1968.
101. *Searchlight*, 20 May 1968.

102. *Searchlight*, 9 June 1968.

103. *Indian Nation*, 1 July 1968.

104. *Indian Nation*, 1 July 1968.

105. Which 'includes—inclusion of Maithili in the eighth schedule of the constitution; recognition of Maithili as one of the subjects for BPSC examinations; immediate implementation of government policy to impart education from primary to the higher standard through the medium of Maithili language in Mithilanchal; recognition of Maithili as a medium of examination up to the University level for non-language subjects as it was permissible in respect of Bengali, Oriya, and Urdu; establishment of a modern University in Mithila; opening of a radio station in Mithila; opening of a rural University in Saharsa; etc'; see *Indian Nation*, 4 August 1968.

106. The delegation was comprised of Prof. S.N. Chaudhary, President; Pt. Dev Narain Jha, Vice-President; Babu Saheb Chaudhary, General Secretary of the ABMM; and Bindeshwar Mandal; see *Indian Nation*, 11 August 1968.

107. *Indian Nation*, 11 August 1968.

108. *Indian Nation*, 5 August 1968; for further details on the allegations and counter-allegations on the issue see *Indian Nation*, 9 August 1968; 14 August 1968.

109. *Indian Nation*, 4 November 1968, During the Parva, there was a consensus on the demand for a Maithili Akademi on the lines of the Bihar Rashtrabhasha Parishad. Baidyanath Mishra 'Yatri', i.e., Baba Nagarjun also supported such a demand; see *Indian Nation* 3 November 1968.

110. *Indian Nation*, 7 November 1968.

111. *Indian Nation*, 13 November 1968.

112. *Searchlight*, 8 November 1968.

113. *Indian Nation*, 1 December 1968.

114. *Searchlight*, 12 June 1968.

115. *Searchlight*, 10 July 1969.

116. *Searchlight*, 10 July 1969.

117. *Searchlight*, 10 July 1969.

118. *Searchlight*, 10 June 1969.

119. *Searchlight*, 10 June 1969.

120. *Searchlight*, 5 April 1969; *Indian Nation*, 5 April 1969.

121. *Indian Nation*, 25 March 1969.

122. A journal first published by Ramanath Jha in 1930s now being restarted by the Ramanath Jha Abhinandan Grantha Samiti, with the remaining funds of the Samiti.

123. *Indian Nation*, 23 February 1969.

124. *Indian Nation*, 23 February 1969.

125. *Indian Nation*, 3 August 1969.

126. *Indian Nation*, 3 August 1969.

127. *Indian Nation*, 18 August 1969.

128. *Searchlight*, 18 September 1969.

129. *Indian Nation*, 30 December 1969.

130. *Indian Nation*, 30 December 1969.; *Searchlight*, 29 December 1969.

131. *Searchlight*, 15 November 1969.

132. *Indian Nation*, 4 December 1969.

133. *Indian Nation*, 4 December 1969.

134. *Indian Nation*, 4 December 1969.

135. *Indian Nation*, 4 December 1969.

136. *Indian Nation*, 3 December 1969.

137. *Searchlight*, 23 March 1970.

138. *Indian Nation*, 3 March 1970.

139. *Indian Nation*, 3 March 1970.

140. *Indian Nation*, 18 March 1970.

141. *Indian Nation*, 18 March 1970.

142. *Indian Nation*, 18 March 1970.

143. *Indian Nation*, 18 March 1970.

144. *Indian Nation*, 18 March 1970.

145. *Indian Nation*, (Brass has marked on it 29 March 1970; but it should be 19 March 1970?).

146. *Indian Nation*, 2 April 1970.

147. *Indian Nation*, 6 April 1970.

148. *Indian Nation*, 6 April 1970.

149. *Indian Nation*, 15 January 1970.

150. *Indian Nation*, 17 February 1970.

151. *Indian Nation*, 17 February 1970.

152. Harinath Mishra, 'Minority Language of Bihar', in *Indian Nation*, 22 February 1970.

153. *Indian Nation*, 27 February 1970.

154. *Indian Nation*, 23 May 1971.

155. *Searchlight*, 14 May 1970.

156. *Searchlight*, 19 May 1970.

157. *Indian Nation*, 24 December 1970.

158. It was later published by *Karnagoshthi*, Kolkata in 2009.

159. Rajnandan Lal Das, *Santo* (Kolkata; Akhil Bhartiya Mithila Sangh, 1990) (later reprinted by Kolkata, Karnagoshthi, 2009), pp. 4–5. This play was written in the 1970s and was staged at various places before publication.

160. This unpublished report of Hetukar Jha, then a Lecturer in Sociology at Patna University was conducted under the supervision of Sachidananda

and it was a project on the study of some aspects of micro civilization in Mithila, which was submitted to the A.N. Sinha Institute of Social Studies, Patna in 1976.

161. See Hetukar Jha. *Nation Building in a North Indian Region: The Case of Mithila*. (Patna: A.N. Sinha Research Institute of Social Studies, 1976), p. 5.

162. Jha, *Nation Building in a North Indian Region*, p. 25.

163. Jha, *Nation Building in a North Indian Region*, p. 35.

164. Rabindra Ray, *The Indianization of The Maithils* (Allahabad: Govind Ballabh Pant Social Science Institute, 1987), unpublished project report.

165. Ray, *The Indianization of The Maithils*, p. 31.

166. *Indian Nation*, 7 February 1970.

167. *Indian Nation*, 7 February 1970.

168. *Indian Nation*, 14 February 1970.

169. Letter No. 7/M7-0147/70 Edu. 5720, Government of Bihar, Department of Education; cited in *Maithili Samachar*, mouthpiece of Akhil Bhartiya Maithili Sahitya Samiti, Prayag, year 27 (January–December 1990), p. 14.

170. Personal Interview with one of the participants and an active member of Nikhil Bharatiya Maithili Bhashi Chhatra Sangh, Bibhuti Anand, Darbhanga, 29 June 2011.

171. Letter No. 10-P2-02-86, Edu., Government of Bihar, Department of Education, dated 17 October 1986; cited in *Maithili Samachar*, p. 15.

172. Personal Interview with Prof. Amresh Pathak, Patna, 17 July 2011. He was also a member of the textbook committee; see also *Maithili Samachar*, p. 16, which says that Maithili textbooks were published by the Government of Bihar and were ready for sale.

173. Letter No. 3678-25, 24 December 1986; cited in *Maithili Samachar*, p. 20.

174. Jeevakant Letter to Jayakant Mishra, Date not mentioned; cited in *Maithili Samachar*, p. 11.

175. Jeevakant Letter to Jayakant Mishra, date not mentioned; cited in *Maithili Samachar*, p. 12.

176. Panchanan Mishra, 'Samvidhan aa Maithili Battis Barakhak Upabandha Kahiya Dhari Mook Rahat?' *Mithila Mihir* (30 January 1983): 7.

177. Letter to Prof. Amresh Pathak, date mentioned as 13 August (possibly 13 August 1992?)

178. Letter to Prof. Amresh Pathak, date mentioned as 13 August (possibly 13 August 1992?)

179. Amresh Pathak letter to The Commissioner of Education, Government of Bihar, 24 July 1989. This letter of Prof. Pathak was signed by the sixteen MLAs of Mithila region. Prof. Pathak also wrote a letter to K.P. Unnikrishnan, Minister for Surface Transport and Communication,

Government of India on 5 September 1990 reminding him about his sympathetic view on Maithili and requesting him to 'put legitimate pressure on the central government for the inclusion of Maithili in the eighth schedule of the constitution of Indian'. His letter to Dr. Shakilur Rahman, M. (Janata Dal) on 14 July 1990 was also to request him to work for the inclusion of Maithili in the eighth schedule of the constitution. Also see Dr Shakilur Rahman's letter to Prof. Pathak on 20 January 1990, in which he said that he wrote a letter to the Prime Minister regarding the inclusion of Maithili in the eighth schedule and it was directed to the Ministry of Home Affairs 'to examine the matter'. Interestingly, in this letter he mentioned that there was a proposal from S. Ganguly to the Human Resource Development Minister, Government of India, regarding creation of a permanent Vidyapati Chair in Delhi University. This proposal was referred to the MHRD and UGC 'for action and consideration vide Government of India, Ministry of Human Resource Development, (Department of Education) F. No. N–2/5/88-Desk (U) New Delhi, dated 29 January 1988'; see Prof. Pathak's letter to Shri L.P. Shahi, MSHRD, GOI, and Secretary UGC on 29 March 1988. This clearly expresses the increasing collaboration between the Maithili protagonists and the political leadership of the Maithili-speaking region.

180. Prof. Pathak's letter to the then Chief Minister of Bihar, 27 March 1992; this letter was signed by Prof. Pathak as the Co-ordinator of the Maithili Sangharsha Samiti and counter signed by Jatashankar Das, Secretary, Chetna Samiti, Patna and Narayan Jha, Chairman, Maithili Bhashi Chhatra Sangh, Patna.

181. Amarnath Jha's letter to Prof. Pathak, n. d.

182. *Mithila Darshan*, Sampadkiya, year 4, no. 3, March 1956.

183. Jayadhari Sinha, *Claims of Maithili for Indian Constitution* (Darbhanga: Maithil Mahasabha, 1967?)

184. Sinha, *Claims of Maithili for Indian Constitution*, pp. 8–24.

185. *Mithila Darshan*, 1–3 May–July 1967, p. 20 cited in *The Maithili Language Movement in North Bihar: A Sociolinguistic Investigation*, an unpublished project report undertaken by Udaya Narayana Singh, Pradip Kumar Bose, and N. Rajaram, Department of Linguistics, South Gujarat University, Surat (April 1985): 38.

186. Karpoori Thakur's letter No. 3/R-1-1914/78 to Shanti Bhushan, Minister of Law dated 22 December 1977(?).

187. Bihar Vidhan Parishad, Satra (Session)–73, *Vadvreet*, No. 4, Friday, dated 29 December 1978, pp. 61–3 (attached in memorandum 7 May 2003)

188. Rajnandan Lal Das, 'Maithilik Hetu Andolan', *Karnamrit*, year 12, Kolkata (January–March 1992): 2.

189. Das, 'Maithilik Hetu Andolan'.

190. Interview with Mohan Jha (MP, CPI) by Usha Prasad on 6 June 1996, Nehru Memorial Museum and Library Oral History Transcripts, Acc. No. 775, Shri Mohan Jha, pp. 69–70.
191. Interview with Bhogendra Jha (MP, CPI) by Shyam Lal Manchanda on 22 April 1989, Nehru Memorial Museum and Library Oral History Transcripts, Acc No. 766, Shri Bhogendra Jha, Part–II, p. 317.
192. Interview with Bhogendra Jha (MP, CPI) by Shyam Lal Manchanda on 22 April 1989, Nehru Memorial Museum and Library Oral History Transcripts, Acc No. 766, Shri Bhogendra Jha, Part–II, p. 319.
193. Interview with Bhogendra Jha (MP, CPI) by Shyam Lal Manchanda on 22 April 1989, Nehru Memorial Museum and Library Oral History Transcripts, Acc No. 766, Shri Bhogendra Jha, Part–II, p. 322.
194. Interview with Bhogendra Jha (MP, CPI) by Shyam Lal Manchanda on 22 April 1989, Nehru Memorial Museum and Library Oral History Transcripts, Acc No. 766, Shri Bhogendra Jha, Part–II, p. 334.
195. Gazette of India, Extra Ordinary, Part III, Section 2, dated 5 August 1971; there are other pages also attached with this which seem to be the Gazette papers but its date and the place of publication is not comprehendible. Copies are attached in the memorandum 7 May 2003.
196. Pitambar Pathak's letter to Bhogendra Jha, 2 June 1990.
197. Pitambar Pathak's letter to Mr Mufti Mohammed Sayeed, Minister of Home Affairs, Government of India, dated 12 October 1990; the letter was forwarded to Bhogendra Jha as well for his consideration;
198. Pitambar Pathak, General Secretary, ABMS, to P.V. Narsimha Rao, Prime Minister of India, dated 24 December 1991.
199. Bhogendra Jha to the Secretary General, Lok Sabha, New Delhi, 31 May 1990.
200. Dhanik Lal Mandal, Governor, Haryana Letter No. 2-HRB-SSG-90, dated 12 June 1990 to Prof. K. K. Mishra, Secretary, All India Maithili Writers Conference (Darbhanga, Vaidehi Samiti).
201. Lok Sabha, Unstarred Question No. 1770 Bhogendra Jha (to be answered on 7 March 1994), Bhogendra Jha private files.
202. Bhogendra Jha's letter 255/90 to P. Upendra, Minister of Information and Broadcasting, Government of India, 20 September 1990; Bhogendra Jha's letter 438/91 to Ajit Kumar Panja, Minister of Information and Broadcasting, Government of India, 4 December 4, 1991.
203. Bhogendra Jha's letter 201/90 to P. Upendra, Minister of Information and Broadcasting, Government of India, 27 August 1990.
204. P. Upendra's letter D.N. No. 1607/90-VIP/1055 to Bhogendra Jha, 26 June 1990.
205. Bhogendra Jha's letter 201/90 to P. Upendra, Minister of Information and Broadcasting, Government of India, 27 August 1990; Bhogendra

Jha letter 439/91 to Ajit Kumar Panja, Minister of Information and Broadcasting, Government of India, 4 December 1991 and 3 August 1992; Bhogendra Jha letter 162/93 to K.P. Singh Deo, Minister of Information and Broadcasting, Government of India, 13 May 1993; no. 281/93, 23 August 1993; no. 371/93, 11 October 1993; K.P. Singh Deo letter 2822/VIP/93 to Bhogendra Jha, 4 December 1993; Ajit Kumar Panja letter 13/105/92-VIP/1900 to Bhogendra Jha, 27 August 1992; Bhogendra Jha, Unstarred Question No. 77, Lok Sabha, regarding the Upgradation of Darbhanga AIR Stattion (to be answered on 26 July 1993); Bhogendra Jha's letter to Subodh Kant Sahay, Minister of State for Home Affairs, Government of India, 12 March 1991; Bhogendra Jha's letter 568/90-91 to Chandrashekhar, Prime Minister of India, 1 April 1991.

206. Shri Bhogendra Jha, Lok Sabha Unstarred question No. 2142 to be answered on 8 August 1991); Bhogendra Jha letter to M.M. Jacob, dated 6 December 1991; S.B. Chavan, Minister of Home Affairs, Government of India, letter D. O. NO: H.11013/13/91-Parl.(Pt.), 25 October 1991; letter no. V-293/92-HMP, 21 February 1992; no. V–1586/94-HMP, 5 September 1994; Bhogendra Jha's letter 537/91–92 to S.B. Chavan, Minister of Home Affairs, Government of India, 5 February 1992; no. 307/94, 11 August 94.

207. Bhogendra Jha letter 196/92 to Ajit Panja, Minister of Information and Broadcasting, Government of India, 4 August 1992.

208. Bhogendra Jha letter 170/92 to P.V. Narsimha Rao, the Prime Minister of India, 2 July 1992; P.V. Narsimha Rao letter to Bhogendra Jha, 9 July 1992; Bhogendra Jha letter 171/92 to S.B. Chavan, Minister of Home Affairs, Government of India, 2 July 1992; S.B. Chavan letter V-1841/92-HMP, 13 July 1992; P.M. Sayeed, Minister of State for Home Affairs, Government of India, letter 1-14014/5/92-NID-1 to Bhogendra Jha 10 January 1994.

209. Bhogendra Jha letter 203/92 to S.B. Chavan, Minister of Home Affairs, Government of India, 11 August 1992.

210. Bhogendra Jha letter 308/94 to S.B. Chavan, Minister of Home Affairs, Government of India, 11 August 1994.

211. Lok Sabha Secretariat, Member's Reference Service, Ref. No. 3438/Ref/90, 16 August 1990.

212. Bhogendra Jha, Unstarred Question No. 3923, Lok Sabha (to be answered on the 16 December 1991).

213. Memorandum to Honourable Prime Minister, Government of India, for Inclusion of Maithili and other languages recognized by Sahitya Akademi, in the eighth schedule of Indian Constitution, Maithili Sangharsha Samiti, Patna, Bihar. Similarly, one memorandum was

submitted by Vidyapati Seva Sansthan, Darbhanga to the President of India on 6 August 1992.

214. Memorandum to Honourable Prime Minister, Government of India, for Inclusion of MAITHILI and other languages recognized by Sahitya Akademi, in the eighth schedule of the Indian Constitution, Maithili Sangharsha Samiti, Patna, Bihar; Similarly one memorandum was submitted by Vidyapati Seva Sansthan, Darbhanga to the President of India on 6 August 1992. Though he attaches the letter of Karpoori Thakur along with the memorandum but do not attach anything in support of these other Chief Ministers of Bihar recommendation for the same.

215. A memorandum for inclusion of Maithili in the eighth schedule of the Indian Constitution submitted to the honourable Prime Minister, Government of India, new delhi, date and year not mentioned; Another such memorandum was submitted to the Prime Minister P.V. Narsimha Rao collectively by Pitambar Chaudhary, Mahamantri, Maithili Bhashi Chhatra Sangharsha Samiti, Ranchi, Ram Ikbal Singh, President, Maithili Vikash Parishad, Ranchi and Vindeshwar Jha date not mentioned; one more memorandum was submitted to the Government of India, by Mithilanchal Bhasha Sangharsha Samiti, Darbhanga; Mithila Dal, Darbhanga; Mithila Chhatra Sangh, Darbhanga; Mithila Sanskritik Parishad and Vaidehi Kala Manch, Kolkata; and Mithila Sangharsh Samiti, Darbhanga. All these memoranda are contained in Bhogendra Jha's private files.

216. KSP/S-3/6.8.'92/Nishi, (Perhaps Lok Sabha Proceedings, Uncorrected not for publication, Bhogendra Jha (IV to VI), Subject File No. 13 Part II.

217. Comments dated 8 April 1994 furnished by the Ministry of Home Affairs on the Representation of Shri Bhogendra Jha, MP, regarding inclusion of Maithili language in eighth schedule to the constitution, etc. and also a letter no. 53/C1/92/R-46, dated 4 August 1994 from S.P. Jain, Under Secretary, Lok Sabha to Bhogendra Jha.

218. Comments dated 8 April 1994 furnished by the Ministry of Home Affairs on the Representation of Shri Bhogendra Jha, MP, regarding inclusion of Maithili language in the eighth schedule to the constitution, etc. and also a letter no. 53/C1/92/R-46, dated 4 August 1994 from S.P. Jain, Under Secretary, Lok Sabha to Bhogendra Jha. .

219. Syed Shahabuddin, MP letter to M.M. Jacob, Minister of State for Home Affairs, dated 10 August 1992.

220. Jayakant Mishra's letter to Bhogendra Jha, dated 9 May 1996.

221. Jayakant Mishra's letter to Bhogendra Jha, dated 9 May 1996.

222. Dhanakar Thakur's letter to Bhogendra Jha, 8 May 1996.

223. *Akhil Bhartiya Mithila Sangh, Ek Samkshipta Parichaya*, Mahasachiva, ABMS, *Smarika*, Rajat Jayanti Samaroha Evam Mithila Vibhuti Smriti Parva, 1995.

224. Dr Jayakant Mishra's letter to Bhogendra Jha, dated 9 May 1996.

225. Bhogendra Jha's letter to Premkant, 9 November 1993.

226. Dr Bhimnath Jha, *Darbhanga me Maithil–Sanstha* (Darbhanga: Vidyapati Seva Sansthan, 1987) (3 November Vidyapati-Smriti-Parva), pp. 34–40.

228. *Antarrashtriya Maithili Parishad*, Maithili, Year 10, Issue 2 (1993) (Published from California, US). Some of the organizers of the conference were—N.K. Gami, Bharati, MECKON-SAIL Pariwar; Ram Iqbal Singh 'Vinit', *Maithili Vikash Parishad*, Ranchi; I.N. Jha, Videh, CCL *Pariwar*; Lakshman Rawat, *Vidyapati Samaroha Samiti*, H.E.C. Pariwar; Shankar Jha, Vidyapati Samarak Samiti, Ranchi; Lakshmi Narayan Singh 'Suman'; Murlidhar Jha; Purnanand Pathak; Rajkumar Mishra; Rani Jha; Vindeshwar Jha; Dr Dhanakar Thakur, The conference also proposed the celebration of Janaki Navami as Maithili Divas; Its organizing members were—Nepal Maithili Samaj; Maithili, California, USA; Akhil Bharatiya Mithila Sangha, Delhi and Kolkata; Mithila Seva Samiti, Kanpur; Chetna Samiti, Patna; Vidyapati Seva Sansthan, Darbhanga; Mithila Sanskritik Parishad, Bokaro; Bharati, MECKON-SAIL, Ranchi; and three more organization was supposed to be added two from Nepal and one from west/south India; see *Pamphlets Pratham Antarrashtriya Sammelan*, Ranchi, Ashadhi Amawashya, Saal 1400 (19–20 June 1993), by Dhanakar Thakur.

229. Uday Shankar Mishra, 'Mithila Putra Pt. Tarakant Jha', *Mithila Tradition and Change Essays in Honour of Pt. Tarakant Jha* (ed.), Sureshwar Jha, Darbhanga, Tarakant Jha Felicitation Committee (2008): 58, A letter to the effect of removal of Maithili from the BPSC was written by Harsha Bardhan, Joint Secretary of the Government to the Secretary of the BPSC dated 29 February 1992, in which it was claimed that a case against Maithili was filed in the Patna High Court by Rakesh Kumar and others in which it was claimed that in the census of 1990–1 the speakers of Maithili were fewer in number than the speakers of Bhojpuri, tribal, and Magadhi languages, therefore it was not proper to include Maithili as an optional paper in the BPSC examination. Hence the government of Bihar took the decision to remove Maithili from the BPSC. The letter was included in the Memorandum 7 May 2003.

230. Ratish Chandra Jha, 'Pandit Tarakant Jhak Jeevangatha', *Mithila Tradition and Change Essays in Honour of Pt. Tarakant Jha* (ed.), Sureshwar Jha, Darbhanga, Tarakant Jha Felicitation Committee (2008): 6

231. The Bihar Gazette, Patna, Wednesday, 9 August 1972, p. 723. In a meeting of Ministers chaired by the Chief Minister on 13 June 1972, the proposal regarding inclusion of Maithili in the BPSC examination was accepted.

232. C.W. J.C. No. 2263 of 1992, Binay Kumar Mishra Versus State of Bihar and others; C.W. J.C. No. 3379 of 1992, Praveen Kumar Jha and others Versus The state of Bihar and others; C.W. J.C. No. 3624 of 1992 Indra Kumar Thakur Versus the state of Bihar and others; C.W. J.C. No. 3669 of 1992 Chetana Samiti Versus the state of Bihar and others; C.W. J.C. No. 5160 of 1994, Narayan Jha and others Versus the state of Bihar and others; C.W. J.C. No. Navchetna through its secretary Satish Chandra Jha Versus the state of Bihar and others, Patna High Court Judgement dated 30 October 2000.

233. C.W. J.C. No. 6582 of 1991 Rakesh Kumar Versus the state of Bihar and others, Patna High Court Judgement dated 30 October 2000.

234. Patna High Court Judgement dated 30 October 2000. Present were the Hon'ble Chief Justice Sri Ravi S. Dhavan and The Hon'ble Mr Justice Aftab Alam, p. 3.

235. Patna High Court Judgement dated 30 October 2000. Present were the Hon'ble Chief Justice Sri Ravi S. Dhavan and The Hon'ble Mr Justice Aftab Alam, p. 5.

236. Patna High Court Judgement dated 30 October 2000. Present were the Hon'ble Chief Justice Sri Ravi S. Dhavan and The Hon'ble Mr Justice Aftab Alam, p. 8.

237. Uday Shankar Mishra, 'Mithilak Putra Pt. Tarakant Jha', p. 58.

238. Excerpts and translated into Hindi from the resolution of Executive Committee Meeting of Bihar BJP at Madhubani, 8, 9, 10 July 1994 originally in Maithili; see the Memorandum 7 May 2003.

239. Ratish Chandra Jha, 'Pandit Tarakant Jhak Jeevangatha', p. 6.

240. Jha, 'Pandit Tarakant Jhak Jeevangatha', p. 6.

241. Lok Sabha, Matter Under Rule 377, Sudip Bandopadhyaya, 3 December 2002, (A copy of it was compiled in the memorandum submitted to the Prime Minister of India on 7 May 2003 by Vidyapati Seva Sansthan, Darbhanga, Akhil Bhartiya Mithila Sangh, Delhi and Mithila Vikas Parishad, Kolkata) other memorandum for the same purpose was submitted by Antarrashtriya Maithili Parishad, on 20 April 2000; Vidyapati Seva Sansthan, Darbhanga in March 2001.

242. A copy of the proceeding is attached in the Memorandum of 7 May 2003. It is also to be noted that Ramchandra Paswan also provided leadership to the protesters marching towards the Parliament on 19 December 2002 and courted arrest along with hundreds of other Maithili supporters for the recognition of Maithili in the constitution.

243. Jha, 'Pandit Tarakant Jhak Jeevangatha', p. 6.

244. The Gazette of India, Extraordinary, Part II Section I, Ministry of Law and Justice (Legislative Department), No. 8, New Delhi, 8 January 2004. The role of C.P. Thakur Minister of North East Development and Small Industry in National Democratic Alliance government and some central government's Maithili-speaking officials acknowledged by the Maithili leaderships besides acknowledging the role of the Vajpayee-led NDA government. In this Bill, it was also mentioned that there were 33 other languages for which demands were made for the recognition in the eighth schedule of the constitution, important among them were–Rajasthani, Brij Bhasha (spoken in Rajasthan, K. Natwar Singh's area) Bhojpuri, Bundeli, Khasi, Kok, Barak, Tulu, Rajbanshi, Pahadi, Nicobari Tribal languages, Koran, Malbani, etc. (papers related to these are attached in the Memorandum, 7 May 2003).

245. It was established in November 2000 at Madhubani, which claims to have its unit in twenty districts out of the proposed twenty-two districts of Mithila; see Mishra Uday Shankar (2008), p. 59.

246. Kamlesh Jha, 'Tara Babu–Mithila Maithilik Antarmukhi Sadhak', Mithila Tradition and Change, p. 56.

247. Ayodhyanath Jha, 'Pt. Tarakant Jha O Mithila Rajya Abhiyan', Mithila Tradition and Change, p. 73.

248. Jha, 'Pt. Tarakant Jha O Mithila Rajya Abhiyan', pp. 74–6.

249. Jha, 'Pt. Tarakant Jha O Mithila Rajya Abhiyan', p. 77.

250. Jha, 'Pt. Tarakant Jha O Mithila Rajya Abhiyan', p. 77.

251. Jha, 'Pt. Tarakant Jha O Mithila Rajya Abhiyan', p. 78.

252. Jha, 'Pt. Tarakant Jha O Mithila Rajya Abhiyan', p. 78.

253. For details see Jha, 'Pt. Tarakant Jha O Mithila Rajya Abhiyan', pp. 73–87.

254. Jha, 'Pt. Tarakant Jha O Mithila Rajya Abhiyan', p. 79.

255. Jha, 'Pt. Tarakant Jha O Mithila Rajya Abhiyan', p. 81.

256. Jha, 'Pt. Tarakant Jha O Mithila Rajya Abhiyan', p. 86.

Conclusion

Language as a Conceptual Category and Inner Contradictions of the Maithili Movement

Language can be used in three senses. First, as a means of communication, its role is vital in the growth of a civilization. Second, as a marker of group identity, it has infinite power to form a new identity and to appropriate other rival identities. And finally, it can be used as a conceptual category to understand the rise, growth, and evolution of a linguistic community. Here, by using language in the third sense—as a conceptual category—I do not intend to take a philosophical stand on the issue of language. Instead, I wish to use it as a conceptual tool to understand the making, remaking, or unmaking of a linguistic community through critically examining the language politics in India as it has evolved since the nineteenth century. In the present study, I have used language mostly in the second sense, that is, language as a marker of group identity and sociopolitical mobilizations in the context of the 'Hindi heartland'. However, I have also tried to use language in the third sense—as a conceptual category—to understand the social and political development of the Maithili linguistic community and the movement. Using language as a conceptual category allows us, in my opinion, to explore the varied experiences of different linguistic communities with our 'colonial modernity'. Besides, it also allows us to revisit some of the important concepts like nation, nationalism, tradition, modernity, and how these terms were used and understood by different linguistic communities particularly in the vernacular spheres. The study of a language is not merely the study of a speech form, but it also involves a whole web of interconnected themes, ideas, and activities, which together constitute the totality of human existence. Language as a conceptual category provides a valuable link to approach that reality in all such complexities. And this is what makes the studies of language so fascinating and the reason why it has caught the attention of scholars throughout the ages.

The study of the language movements in the Hindi heartland, like the Maithili language movement, would be incomplete unless it also considers the social-political and historical context in which such movements have emerged. Movements like these evolved without popular political support and patronage, with the indifferent attitude, even apathy, from their own speakers. For a long time, these movements had been sustained by the tireless activities of the leaders involved, even at the cost of their personal loss. The Maithili language and the movement have not only evolved in such a context but have also been successful in competing against the all-pervasive expansionist agenda of Hindi and its combined forces of nationalism and Hinduism. The Maithili language movement faced not only the political apathy of the provincial government in Bihar but even from the Maithili speakers as well. And yet it has been successful in its fight against the imperialist agendas of Hindi supporters, though the relationship between the two is not that of total opposition. In fact, Maithili speakers actively supported Hindi's claim as the 'national' language of India. But when they felt that there were systematic attempts made by the Hindi zealots to classify Maithili as a 'dialect' of Hindi, they started to mobilize public opinion and began to assert the independent status of Maithili. This misconception about Maithili being part of Hindi was the biggest challenge for the Maithili movement in the twentieth century to overcome. Although official and institutional recognition to Maithili as an independent language had been granted, but in public discourse the same misconception is being repeated time and again. Another factor that makes the Maithili movement a successful movement is that all its demands have been met with the notable exception of the separate statehood demand. In support of such a demand, public and political mobilizations, demonstrations, and protests are still going on with greater zeal. There are various internal tensions within this movement too. This requires serious and careful investigations, but undermining the movement's worth just because of these internal tensions would end the possibility of exploring the other, often obscure, aspects of the language-based politics in India particularly as it was played out in the context of the national movement in the 'Hindi heartland'.

With the beginning of philological studies in the eighteenth and nineteenth centuries, a link is established between language and race. It took a different shape when the nation state emerged as the most desirable form of political community. One of the essential features for these political communities has been standardization of a language as the national language, in such a way that connects the heterogeneous masses emotionally and psychologically together. This formation of a national language is often contested by the speakers of heterogeneous languages within a nation. This contestation is far more complex in a multilingual and heterogeneous country like India. In the present study, I have explored the discrepancies and inherent contestations of this kind of formation in the context of the 'Hindi heartland' while exploring the Maithili movement as a case study. In India, with the classification of language and its standardization through grammars and dictionaries, a new kind of identity—a form of linguistic communities—was being formed from the beginning of the nineteenth century. This process was even more consolidated with the beginning of modern education and particularly, of vernacular education. These practices developed a new sense of attachment among the people to their languages. Now language no longer belongs to the region, it belongs to the people.[1] In the beginning, such formulations were based on regional or provincial languages, like Bengali, Marathi, Gujarati, Punjabi, Assamese, Oriya, Maithili, and so on. This process of linguistic identity formations simultaneously carries the process of linguistic appropriation, domination, and marginalization over the 'minor' and *not-so-developed* languages often categorized as 'dialects'. And what makes this kind of classification more problematic is that it has been done not on linguistic criteria alone, but also because of intense sociopolitical mobilizations. Such classifications entered a troubled zone when a link language—other than Sanskrit and English—was being developed consciously with remarkable success but not without prolonged and consistent opposition. The expectations and impositions from the nationalist leadership that provincial languages should make the way for the 'national' language has created an unresolved tension between national and regional/provincial languages in India.

In the present study I have tried to understand such processes in the context of Hindi and Maithili. I have also tried to understand and analyse the evolution of Maithili as a linguistic community, its organizations, problems, successes and failures, its internal dynamics, and external antagonisms. Throughout the history of the Maithili movement, what one finds is not just an opposition to Hindi's claim of Maithili being its 'dialect' or the ambivalent relationship between the two. More appropriately, we can see a double movement. The authority and power of Hindi was strengthening with the adoption and promotion of Hindi in the Maithili speaking region at the same time as the Maithili assertion was becoming more powerful with the making of a separate Maithili linguistic community.

The Maithili language movement can be categorized as a cultural movement led mostly by the middle class. But in the beginning, this class was socially and economically too weak to fight independently or for too long. It was dependent upon the patronage of the rich landlords and the Maharajas. However, the Maharajas and landlords were not unambiguously supporting Maithili, while the masses were largely indifferent to the issue of language. Meanwhile Hindi was already introduced in school education and was being increasingly used in public places and in the administration of the court. Clearly the Maithili middle class professionals were working for the growth of Maithili in enormously unfavourable circumstances. It is to their credit that Maithili after many years is recognized as an independent language in India.

The indifferent attitude of the masses towards the Maithili language movement can be explained through the idea of Ashis Nandi about the non-participation of the masses in the modernizing process.[2] All the problems that these modernizing elites were facing could not be categorized as the problem of the masses too. In the case of the Maithili movement, we find that the masses were still using the language as they were using it before, without perceiving any threat to its existence from outside. It was the elite, particularly Sanskrit scholars, who first realized this threat and gradually mobilized opinion in support of Maithili. But for a considerable period, such mobilizations remained confined to the literary elite.

However, there has been continuous social and political expansions of the Maithili language movement over the decades, more so since the 1980s. Started as a movement for the recognition of Maithili as one of the independent languages of modern India, the Maithili movement remained a 'non-political', cultural and linguistic movement. Although, the politics and demand for separate statehood for Mithila was there, the struggle for the recognition of Maithili as an independent language was the focal point of the movement. And for many decades the Maithili movement was organized and led by Maithili writers, journalists, and scholars. Their major forms of activism were the publication of more and more journals, magazines, and books in Maithili to check the growing misconception about Maithili as a 'dialect' of Hindi. But there was a gradual shift in the agendas and methods of the Maithili movement. During the 1950s, the political demand of separate statehood for Mithila was the most emphasized agenda and there were considerable political agitations for it by the common/ordinary Maithili speakers as well. The main ideologues of such demands were Lakshman Jha and Janaki Nandan Singh besides many others. Since then political leaders of the region also raised the issue of Mithila and Maithili time to time, and agitations, mass protests, and demonstrations became the medium of the expression for their demands and discontents.

Although the social base of the Maithili movement has increased considerably, it is yet to acquire the form of a mass movement. There are many reasons for this: the lack of employment opportunities in Maithili, and the non-implementation of Maithili as the medium of education at the primary level in the beginning of modern education in Mithila. It is surprising that Maithili was recognized as a subject of study at the university level since 1917, but at the primary and secondary level, it is still not taught. At the secondary level, students may opt for Maithili and that too as an optional. It is not compulsory; that makes a mockery of the government decision to make the mother tongue the medium of instruction for the Maithili-speaking child. In the beginning, Maithili needed promotion and patronage by the state government, which was not only denied but when sufficient pressure was put on the government, the latter conceded this demand. But they did so in a way that the progress of Maithili was always hindered. Besides, due to lack of employment opportunities in Maithili, parents who could not send their children for English-medium education preferred Hindi over Maithili, as there were/are more opportunities available in Hindi as compared to Maithili. Their commitment to the study of Maithili can be understood from the fact that millions of students still opt for Maithili at secondary, intermediate, and graduation levels. However, when the children do not have to study Maithili at the primary level, it is less likely that they would opt for Maithili at the university level. Hence, all the university departments of Maithili in Bihar are not unaffected by this ironical situation of Maithili.

Since the 1990s, there have been major shifts in the Maithili movement. Maithili remains the dominant issue for mobilization, but the issue of the economic development of the Mithila region, along with the separate statehood demand for Mithila, has become an important agenda for social and political mobilizations. Many organizations came together to launch a combined struggle. One such umbrella organization is the Antarrashtriya Maithili Parishad. Their claim is that the proper growth of the language and the proper development of the Maithili-speaking region are not possible within the existing state of Bihar.

However, the greatest challenge of the Maithili movement is that, despite more than a century of struggle, it has failed to sufficiently connect with the masses and to mobilize them systematically in a sustained manner. There have been instances of popular support to the movement but these have not been properly harnessed. The large number of people remained indifferent and even suspicious of the objectives of the Maithili movement. The suspicion of the Maithili movement among the non-Brahmins and the non-Kayasthas in Mithila remains very high. Caste consciousness is dominant in the thinking of even the leaders of the Maithili movement. They are internally divided based on caste. In the beginning, it was between the Brahmins and the Kayasthas; even among the Brahmins, there were divisions based on region, that is, *Pubairpar* and *Pachhbairpar* and *Panji Vyavstha*.

The Maithili movement in the contemporary phase is struggling with two major internal issues—one is the two voices within the movement where one speaks of the Maithili language movement, whereas the other speaks about the Mithila state movement. The other issue is the challenge to the Brahminical domination of the Maithili movement and its leaderships. Now, increasingly non-Brahmins and non-Kayasthas in Mithila interrogate this domination. Another challenge is how to connect with the masses. In the contemporary phase of the movement, it is increasingly perceived by the protagonists of the Maithili movement that, to connect to the masses, language alone is not a sufficient ground. Unless the social and economic issues affecting the people of Mithila are included in the agendas, channelizing mass support would be an arduous task. The future course of the Maithili movement will be determined by the outcome of these internal tensions and external support to the movement.

Based on my study I have drawn the following conclusions:

1. The relationships between a language and 'dialects' are not static but contingent. And this relationship depends upon the social political and historical conditions as well as the consciousness of the speakers about their language.

2. Language, as a tool for social and political mobilization, connected with nationalism and religion, proved to be a powerful concept to explain the social, political, and historical evolution of a linguistic community, precisely because of its emotional and cultural roots among the speakers.

3. The challenges to the Maithili movement has been its failure to diminish the social divisions based on caste, combined with emerging nationalism and expansion of Hindi as the 'national' language; its assertion and development as an independent Indian language had not only been discouraged but also suspected.

4. The major contradictory element in the Maithili movement is its increasing politicization—from Hindi-Maithili antagonism to territorial consciousness and political demand for the separate statehood of Mithila has gone hand in hand with the persistent indifferent attitude of the masses.

Notes and References

1. Lisa Mitchell, *Language Emotions and Politics in South India* (Ranikhet: Permanent Black, 2010).
2. Ashis Nandi, *The Intimate Enemy: Loss and Recovery of Self under Colonialism* (Delhi: Oxford University Press, sixth impression, 1992 [1983]).

Appendix

Short Biographies of Maithili Writers and Activists

These short biographies of Maithili writers and activists are meant to provide brief information about the literary works composed in Maithili. I have also tried to give a brief account of their family background, education, literary works, and their contributions, if any, in the Maithili language movement. For the information, I have relied mostly on Bhimnath Jha's *Parichayika*, but I have also consulted *Mithila Darshan*, *Karnamrit*, and a variety of other sources. These sources are all quoted in the Bibliography. This list of Maithili writers should not be considered as complete or even representative. It has not been possible to include all the names and I am aware of the omissions of some of the great Maithili writers. However, my purpose here is to give an account of the expanding literary world of Maithili particularly from the middle of the nineteenth century onwards.

Jyotirishwar (1294–1348)

So far, the earliest prose text available in Maithili or any other north Indian languages is *Varnaratnakar*, written by Jyotirishwar in the fourteenth century. He was a *Pali Moolak* Maithili Brahmin. His father's name was Dhireshwar and his grand-father was Rameshwar. His period was considered to be the reign of the last Karnat ruler in Mithila—Maharaja Harisingh Dev. According to Dr Jayakant Mishra, his lifespan is 1280–1340.

Jyotirishwar's *Varnaratnakar* is one of his best-known works in Maithili. There have been two authentic publication of this work, so far. The first was published by the Royal Society of Bengal in 1940 under the editorship of Suniti Kumar Chatterjee and Babuaji Mishra. And the second was published by the Maithili Akademi, Patna in 1980 under the editorship of Anand Mishra and Govind Jha. Harprasad Shastri visited Nepal twice during 1895–1900. During these visits, his disciples—Rakhalchandra Kabyateerth and Vinod Bihari Kabyateerth researched this book in Mithila. There were two manuscripts of this book but now there is only one copy that is available. This manuscript of *Varnratnakar* is kept in the library of the Bengal Royal Asiatic Society. It is written in Tirhuta. This manuscript originally had 77 leaves, but by the time it was recovered, 17 leaves were lost. The work is divided into eight chapters, which is called *Kallol*. It is a nuanced description of medieval Mithila, its society, cities, lifestyle, music, beauty, palaces, forest, mountains, seasons, saints, poets, rivers, pilgrimage places, marriage rituals, thieves, weapons, fortress, state, and so on. According to Suniti Kumar Chatterjee, its greatness lies in the profusion of its details, and in the fact that it includes description of almost all things worth describing in human life. This work is of great value to understand the society, economy, culture, and politics of medieval Mithila.

His other works are *Dhurtsamagam* and *Panchayak*. According to Jayakant Mishra, it is obvious from the maturity of style and composition of Jyotirishwara's vernacular (Maithili) works that in his literary use of the vernacular, Jyotirishvar was neither the first nor the only one. But so long as other older Maithili specimens are not discovered, his works will be considered as the earliest literature in Maithili.

Vidyapati (1350–1448)

Vidyapati is considered not just as the pillar of the Maithili language and major source of inspiration for the Maithili movement and Maithili identity too. The Vidyapati Parva Samaroha has played a critical role in shaping linguistic consciousness among the Maithils. It is Vidyapati—the poet, and Maithili—the language, which have been instrumental in bringing different caste and class groups in Mithila together. It is widely acknowledged that it was because of Vidyapati that Maithili was revived and gradually flourished as a modern Indian language.

Vidyapati was born at village Bisafi in Madhubani district. He was a *Darbari* (royal court) poet, and worked in the court of Raja Shiv Singh. There is a difference of opinion regarding the period of his birth and death. Despite being a prolific poet and writer, he has left no traces of his birth and death. Many scholars like Chanda Jha, Subhadra Jha, Ramanath Jha, and Shashi Nath Jha considered AD 1350 as his year of birth. However, for Umesh Mishra and Jayakant Mishra, he was born in AD 1360.

There is a legend widely narrated in Mithila that Mahadev (God Shiva) himself worked in his household as a servant, Ugana. It is also believed that Ganga (a river, also called mother Ganga) changed its course to take him in her lap at the time of his death. That place is known today as Bajitpur, Vidyapati Nagar.

Vidyapati wrote in Sanskrit, Avahatta, and Maithili. However, his popularity is based on his vernacular writings in Maithili. Besides, Vidyapati's own creativity and sweetness of his *Padas*, it is the women folk of Mithila who kept these *Padas* alive almost for six centuries through oral transmission. His *padas* and songs are rooted in the cultural milieu of Mithila, which is their real strength.

His famous works are: *Bhuparikrama, Vibhasagar, Dan-vakyawali, Purush-Pariksha, Durgabhakti-Tarangani, Mani-Manjari, Likhanawali, Kirtilata, Kirtipataka,* and *Goraksha-Vijaya*. His Maithili *padas* are popular in Mithila, Bengal, and the Terai region of Nepal—these have been compiled and published by the Bihar Rashtrabhasha Parishad, Patna in three volumes.

Bihari Lal 'Fitrat' (1829–?)

Bihari Lal was one of the main contributors in the modern historiography of Mithila. He wrote *Aina–i–Tirhut* in Urdu. It was published in 1883 from Lucknow. The book is recently reprinted by the Kalyani Foundation, Darbhanga in a Hindi translation (not Maithili) under the editorship of Hetukar Jha in 2001. This book is considered the first serious attempt at history writing in Mithila. It gives a vivid account of the polity, society, economy, and history of Mithila in the late nineteenth century.

Bihari Lal was born into an elite family of Darbhanga. He passed the examination for becoming a lawyer in 1856 and he was made an honorary Magistrate in 1877. The next year, he was made a government lawyer in the court of the Munsif at Darbhanga. He was also made a member of the district school committee in 1878 and a municipal commissioner in 1879. During his time, Arabic or Persian and later, Urdu was the language of administration. Knowledge of Persian, Arabic, or Urdu was considered necessary to enter into the administration of revenue and judicial transactions in the region. The spread of English education was very limited. He and his family were closely associated with the Darbhanga Raj and his own position as a lawyer and government servant gave him an important position in the cultural and intellectual life of Darbhanga.

Chanda Jha (1831–1907)

Chanda Jha has been a major source of inspiration for modern Maithili writers, poets, and authors. He was the first in modern times who made sincere efforts to restore the lost pride in the mother tongue, Maithili. During a period when Sanskrit was the only language considered worthy of serious study and Maithili was regarded as a language of the commoners and unworthy of higher studies, it was Chanda Jha who took the trouble to show the literary capacity of Maithili. His love for the mother tongue was so firm that he never deterred from writings in Maithili. Although he was called *Bhat kavi* (a derogatory term used to make fun of literary figures whose works were considered less important, lacks literary finesse) by his contemporaries, yet he successfully established Maithili as the language of literature. And in the later years of his life, he was admired and was called *Kavishwar* (the greatest poet). His *Mithila Bhasha Ramayan* transformed the pundit's perception about Maithili. He was the first to set Maithili free from the clutches of *Shringar* (love) and *Bhajan* (prayer) songs. He made the language relevant to the changing social and political context. Though, most of his own writings are in these two genres, yet he also wrote on socially, culturally, and politically relevant issues.

His full name was Chandrakant Jha. His father's name was Bhola Jha. Chanda Jha was born in his maternal village, Badagaon in Saharsa district, where he spent most of his early life until the age of seventeen. Because of the troubles with the local landlords at his paternal village, Pindaruch in Darbhanga, he left his village and settled in his in-laws' village, Thadhi in Madhubani. He served in the courts of Maharaja Lakshmishwar Singh and Maharaja Rameshwar Singh and was well respected among the Pundits of the court.

Chanda Jha was a prolific writer. His original works include *Lakshmishwar Vilas, Mithila Bhasha Ramayan, Geet-Sudha, Padyavali,* and *Ahalyacharit Natak.* His translation of Vidyapati's *Purush Pariksha* led to further research and studies on Vidyapati. He also edited *Saheb Ramdas Geetavali* which was published in 1901. There are other works like *Gitasaptsati, Mula-Grama-Vichar, Chanda Vichar, Vathvana,* and *Raskaumudi* which are attributed to Chanda Jha by many scholars but these works are not available today.

His greatest contribution was the establishment of Maithili as a literary language on par with any other modern Indian language. It is said that what Vidyapati did for Maithili in the fourteenth century has been done by Chanda Jha in the nineteenth century; perhaps his contributions are more profound than that of Vidyapati.

Harshanath Jha (1845–1899)

Harshanath Jha was the last poet who followed the Vidyapati tradition and the literary style of the middle ages. He was a Sanskrit scholar working as a *Sabha* Pandit in the court of Maharaja Lakshmishwar Singh. In Maithili, he is famous as a poet and as a playwright. He is regarded as the last playwright in the *Kirtaniya Natak Parampara* of Mithila.

He was born in Shardapur of village Ujan in Darbhanga. In Maithili, his famous plays are *Ushaharan* and *Madhavanand.* He wrote many Sanskrit plays in which Maithili is used for the songs. He wrote different varieties of Maithili songs: devotional, *Sohar, Uchiti,* and *Tirhuti.* These are quite famous among the masses. A complete collection of his Maithili compositions is compiled and edited by Ridhinath Jha and Amarnath Jha, entitled *Harshanath-Kavya-Granthavali.* His main contribution in Maithili literature is that he kept the literary tradition of Vidyapati alive.

Jeevan Jha (1848–1912)

Jeevan Jha's main contribution in Maithili literature is in the field of modern Maithili plays. In Mithila, traditionally plays were written in a mixture of Sanskrit and Prakrit; most of the dialogues were written in

Sanskrit but the songs and dialogues of 'second-rate characters' used to be in Prakrit or in Maithili. Jeevan Jha was the first to write complete plays in Maithili.

He was born in village Haripurba in Samastipur. His full name was Jeev Nath Jha. He worked as head of charity at the palace of the King of Kashi, Prabhu Narayan Singh.

Jeevan Jha also wrote Maithili *padas* on traditional line, but he is more popular because of his Maithili plays. These include *Sundar Sanyog* (1904), *Narmada Sagar Sattak* (1906), *Maithili Sattak* (Not published in book form but partially published serially in *Mithila Moda* and *Maithil Hit Sadhana* in 1906), and *Samvati Punarjanma* (1908). In all his plays, he depicts Mithila's social life and its evil practices. In 1980, all his writings were compiled and edited by Chandranath Mishra 'Amar' and Ramdeo Jha, entitled *Kavivar Jeevan Jha Rachnavali*. It was published by the Maithili Akademi, Patna.

Lal Das (1856–1911)

He was a great poet in the Ram Kavya tradition in Mithila after Chanda Jha. He was born into a prestigious Kayastha family of village Kharaua in Madhubani. He worked in the court of Maharaja Rameshwar Singh. His most admired work in Maithili is his *Rameshwar Charit Mithila Ramayan*. Rameshwar in the title of his Ramayana is believed to be his tribute to Maharaja Rameshwar Singh. His work played an important role in the recognition of Maithili as an independent language in modern India. He also wrote many books in Maithili and one in Hindi, *Mithila Mahatmya*. These are *Saang Saptashati Durgak Teeka, Chandicharit Arthat Saptashati Durga, Ganeshkhand, Maheshwar-Vinod Athva Gaurishambhu Vinod, Haritali Vrat Katha, Vaidhavya-Bhanjani Arthat Somvari Vrat Katha, Virudawali, Ganga-Mahatmya, Janaki Ramayan, Shrimad Bhagwat Geeta, Brahmottar Khand, Radha Kand, Lakshmi Kand, Savitri Satyavan*(Play), and *Streedharma Shiksha* (Prose).

His *Rameshwar Charit Mithila Ramayan* was published in 1954. The Maithili Akademi, Patna had published *Savitri–Satyawan* and *Janaki Ramayan* in the years 1979 and 1980 respectively. Other works by him were published but are found rarely nowadays. His use of language is neither too standard to be inaccessible for the masses nor too colloquial.

Parmeshwar Jha (1856–1924)

Parmeshwar Jha is the celebrated author of *Mithila Tatvavimarsha*—the first work in Maithili on the history of Mithila. He was born in village Tarauni in Darbhanga. He studied Sanskrit grammar in Kashi and then went to Rajputana and taught Sanskrit there in a school for four years. In 1880, he worked with the ruler of Purnea, Raja Padmanand Singh, as a Rajpandit. He worked for twelve years in Gandhwari Dyaudhi in Madhubani. Thereafter, he joined the court of the Darbhanga Maharaja, Rameshwar Singh, and was appointed as a Rajpandit on 1 July 1899. He also worked as the principal of the Rameshwar Lata Sanskrit college of Darbhanga. He established the Parmeshwar Library in village Tarauni in 1916. He guided K.P. Jaiswal and S.N. Singh, respectively, on their research on Mithila.

He wrote around forty books in Sanskrit. In Maithili, he wrote *Simantini Aakhyahika* and *Mithila Tatvavimarsha*. One can understand the condition of publishing books in Maithili during those days when such a book as *Mithila Tattvavimarsha* was not published till 1949, twenty-five years after the death of its author.

Despite being a traditional Sanskrit scholar, he had unconventional views on many of the prevailing social conditions and practices in Mithila. He was against the institution of *Panji*. For him, it created a hierarchy and divided society. It hampered the growth of fellow feelings among the Maithili speakers. When English education in Mithila was looked down upon with contempt, he saw progress in the study of English. He himself studied the language and used many English words in his *Mithila Tattvavimarsha*. He was against the practice of excommunication of the Maithils on minor ritualistic pretexts. He believed that it obstructed the growth of unity among the Maithils.

When Kolkata University recognized Maithili, it was Parmeshwar Jha who was asked to teach the subject in the university. He refused because Maharaja Rameshwar Singh was so impressed with his scholarship and work that he wanted him to stay in Darbhanga. So, he could not accept the offer. However, he continued to work for Maithili. He established the competency of Maithili even for the serious work like history writing.

Raghunandan Das (1860–1945)

Munshi Raghunandan Das was an expert on medieval Maithili literature. Initially, he began to write in *Braj-bhasha* before he started working for the growth and development of Maithili literature. His contribution to Maithili literature, besides inspiring many of his contemporaries to write in Maithili, is well acknowledged. He was the main motivator to persuade Babu Bhola Lal Das to work for Maithili.

He was born in village Sakhbar in Madhubani. He received his primary education in his maternal village. He worked with Raj Darbhanga as an accountant. There, he met Sir Ganganath Jha, Mukund Jha 'Bakshi', and Pt. Chetnath Jha. It is believed that, with their inspiration and encouragement, he started to write in Maithili. His famous works are *Mithila Natak*, *Sudarshan Natak*, *Dutangadavyayog*, *Vrat Katha*, *Veer Balak*, and *Subhadra-Haran*. His *Subhadra-Haran* and *Mithila Natak* was very popular. Two of his works—*Mithila Natak* and *Dutangadavyayog*—were published by the Maithili Akademi, Patna in 1984. His *Mithila Natak* is influenced by the *Bharat-Durdasa* of Bhartendu Harischandra. But the major difference between these two *Nataks*, according to Lekhnath Mishra, is that in *Bharat-Durdasha*, *Des-Prem* is highly emphasized; whereas in *Mithila Natak*, the contemporary degraded state of Maithil society was shown with their possible solutions, and with an aim for the growth of Mithila, Maithils, and Maithili. In other words, the stress on *Desha* is obscure in *Mithila Natak*. For his contribution to Maithili literature, the Maithili Sahitya Parishad awarded him the title of '*Sahitya Ratnakar*'. A mixture of Sanskritized, Farsi-Urdu words with a clear taste of chaste Maithili is a distinctive characterisitc of his writings.

Mukund Jha 'Bakshi' (1860–1938)

Mukund Jha 'Bakshi' was a famous scholar of Sanskrit literature, particularly *Karmakanda*. He studied in Kashi and then taught *Karmakanda* in Dharmasamaj Sanskrit College, Muzaffarpur from 1919 to 1938. He also worked for some time as Dwar-Pandit of the king of Patiala. He lived in Kashi in the last years of his life.

In Maithili, he wrote a short grammar and a *Teeka* on Amarkosha. His historical work in Maithili is *Mithilabhashamaya Itihaas*. In this work, he narrates the history of the last ruling dynasty of Mithila, the Khandawala Kula, from its first ruler, Mahesh Thakur to the then ruling Maharajadhiraja Rameshwar Singh. According to Jayakant Mishra 'it is a valuable work because it contains a very detailed history of the entire Khandavalakula Dynasty up to the present day. Numerous sidelights are given on various events and episodes in the palace and in the realm during the four hundred years it professes to cover.' This work of Mukund Jha 'Bakshi', though he used esoteric Sanskritized words, is considered as a representative text on the history of Mithila in the last four centuries

Murlidhar Jha (1869–1929)

Murlidhar Jha is regarded as the promoter of modern prose in Maithili. Though he was a great scholar of *Jyotish*, through the publication of *Mithila Moda*, he created a new space for Maithili writers and provided a distinct direction to the Maithili movement.

His paternal village was Bharam in Madhubani but he was settled in Shyamshidhap. He studied at Queens College at Kashi (now Banaras) and later became the professor of Jyotish at the same college.

His works include *Arjun Tapashya* (novel), *Hitopadesh*, and *Maithili Vyakaran*. But his popularity in the Maithili literary world rests on his publication and editing of *Mithila Moda*. This magazine had an influence on Mithila and created for the first time a limited but steady Maithili reading public. It is said that the publication of *Mithila Moda* ushered a new era in Maithili writing. Many famous writers like Sitaram Jha, Jyotish Baldeva Mishra, Umesh Mishra, Trilochan Jha, Ramchandra Mishra, Anoop Mishra, and Kusheshwar Kumar, and many others, were first introduced to the Maithili world by *Mithila Moda*. This journal was published from 1907 to 1927 and again after his death from 1936 to 1941. The publication of *Mithila Moda* is a milestone in Maithili language and the movement. He was also successful in arousing the conscience of Maithils through his fierce and critical statements.

It is believed that he played a critical role in the recognition of Maithili in Kolkata University. He established Kashi-Vidvatjan-Samiti. He was also in favour of one standard format for Maithili writing. He was a fierce supporter of Maithili against Hindi and openly regarded Hindi as an obstruction for the proper growth of Maithili.

Sir Ganganath Jha (1871–1941)

Sir Ganganath Jha was one of the first students in Mithila who studied in English medium. He was a great scholar of Sanskrit, Mimansa, and Indology. Although he spent most of his life in Allahabad, his association with Mithila and Maithili culture was unfading. His contribution in shaping modern discourses and ideas among the highly conservative society of Mithila was remarkable. His time was very crucial and shows intense aversion to English education. Higher and credible studies were conceivable only in Sanskrit and English education was regarded as still an attack on the very soul of Maithili culture.

In this atmosphere, he was born at Sarisab Pahi village in Madhubani. As per the family custom, he started his early education in Sanskrit in his maternal village, Gandhavair. His family was closely associated with the Darbhanga Raj. When Maharaja Lakshmishwar Singh, himself, aware of the importance of modern education especially English, advised his family that the boys should be taught in English medium, the family of Sir Ganganath Jha gladly accepted it. Then he along with his brothers came to Darbhanga and studied in the Raj School under the patronage of Maharaja Lakshmishwar Singh. Thereafter, he went to Kashi and got admission in the prestigious Queens College. He was the first in the region to complete his post-graduation in 1892. For some years, he worked under Lakshmishwar Singh and thereafter Rameshwar Singh in the newly established Raj library, Darbhanga. Then he joined Queens College in 1902 as a Sanskrit teacher. He went on to become the Vice Chancellor of Allahabad University for three terms. Although he lived in Allahabad throughout his life, he remained deeply attached to Mithila and Maithili culture.

Most of Jha's works are in English and Sanskrit, yet he also wrote in Maithili. He, along with his son Amarnath Jha, edited *Chandrakavi Praneet Maheshwani Sangraha* in 1920, published from Indian Press, Allahabad. He was closely associated with the Maithili Sahitya Parishad—one of the earliest literary organizations which played a pioneering role in creating a literary culture in Maithili. He wrote *Vedant Deepak* in Maithili, which was published by the *Parishad* in 1936. In its session of 1937, in village Sarisab-Pahi, Jha's proposal that Maithili should be recognized by Patna University was passed unanimously. He also wrote a critical essay on *Mithilak Gati* in Maithili, which was published in *Mithila Mihir* (*Mithilank*, Vasant Panchami, 1936). When in the 1930s and 1940s, Mithila society (mainly the Shrotriya Samaj) was divided between *Swadeshi* and *Vilayati*, he took the side of the *Vilayati* group. This division was so intense that it is also called *Swadeshi* and *Vilayati* movement. Maharaja Kameshwar Singh was boycotted by the *Shrotriya samaj* for his travel to England to attend the Round Table Conference. Jha not only supported the Maharaja but permitted his son Amarnath Jha to visit Europe. This was the heaviest blow on the highly conservative and obstructive society of Maithili *Shrotriya* Brahmans.

For his translation of *Jaimini's Mimansa Sootra* in English, the Royal Asiatic Society, Bombay branch gave him the Campbell gold medal. He was also made an honorary member of the Royal Asiatic Society of Great Britain and Ireland. In 1941, the British Academy selected him as its distinguished member and in the same year the British government conferred a knighthood upon him.

Deenbandhu Jha (1878–1955)

Mahavaiyakaran Pandit Deenbandhu Jha was regarded as the Panini of the Maithili language, for he was the first to write a grammar of Maithili on the pattern of Panini's Sanskrit grammar. To establish and strengthen the status of Maithili as an independent language, his book *Mithilabhasha-Vidyotan*, which was published in 1945, played a critical role. His Maithili grammar is still considered as one of the finest grammars of Maithili.

He was born in the village of Ishahapur in Madhubani. His father's name was Vidyanath Jha. After his primary education, he went to Kashi for higher education in 1893 where he received regular training in learning from Mahamahopadhyaya Shivkumar Shastri. He passed *Dhautpariksha*[1] in 1908. He spent all his life in learning and teaching in his own village, Ishahapur, Devaghar, Lakshmipur, Darbhanga, and Sarisab. He was known for his devotion and equal respect for all kind of works—manual or intellectual.

He wrote mostly in Sanskrit: *Rameshwarpratapodayam*, *Samasa-shaktideepika*, *Bakarvivek*, and *Shradhadhikarinirnaya*. His four books in Maithili have been published: *Mithilabhasha-Vidyotan* (1945), *Dhatu path* (1949–50), *Mithilabhasha-Kosha* (1950), and *Alankar Sagar* (1967).

The last of his Maithili works, *Alankar Sagar,* was not completed during his life time and it was published after his death.

He was the first to provide a dictionary of the Maithili language: *Maithilibhasha-Kosha.* Together with *Dhatu path,* this work contains more than six thousand Maithili *Deshaj* (indigenous) words, many of them no longer in use. He had also worked for the standardization of Maithili but he did not enter any conflict over it, as his successors did. Though he did not write fiction, he did play an influential role in establishing the status of Maithili as a distinct and independent language. In 1941, the Maithili Sahitya Parishad, in its Madhubani Session, awarded him with the title of Mahavaiyakaran.

Shyam Narayan Singh (1883–1948)

History of Tirhut From the Earliest Times to the End of the Nineteenth Century, published by the Baptist Mission Press, Kolkata in 1922 is his greatest contribution to the history writing of the region. It is the first English book written on the history of Mithila. It is Shyam Narayan Singh who brought the culture, history, and society of Mithila to the notice of national and international Indologists and other intellectuals.

He was born at a village called Ahiyapur in Aurangabad. His father Narsingh Narayan Singh was a Zamindar related to the Tekari Raj of Gaya. After completing his early education in his village, he was admitted to Patna College. After obtaining a BA degree, he joined the Bengal Civil Service in 1906. He was appointed to several distinguished positions in the administration of Bihar. He was decorated with many awards and honours for his service such as a Member of British Empire (MBE) and Officer of the British Empire (OBE).

During his service, he came in the close contacts with Motilal Nehru, Sachidananda Sinha, and Rajendra Prasad. This might have inspired him to think more sympathetically towards his own society, its culture, and history. Prior to the publication of *History of Tirhut* he had also written *The Industries in Bihar and Orissa.* He also wrote a small booklet on Hindu-Muslim unity, which was based on the life experiences of both the communities.

Besides fulfilling his responsibility, he was also very conscious of the political and economic condition of the people, particularly of Tirhut. It is though surprising that he used the term 'Tirhut' and not 'Mithila'.

Was it because Mithila had not sufficiently caught the imagination of the masses to refer to their region? But it is in his account that we find the history of Vaishali and Champaran mentioned within the history of Tirhut. He also included the accounts of many dialects or languages, different traditions, and the economic condition of the masses in his history.

Raja Tankanath Chaudhary (1884–1928)

Raja Tankanath Chaudhary of Rajaura was a great admirer and patron of Maithili language and literature. He provided much-needed financial support for recognition of Maithili in the Kolkata University. Two Maithili chairs were established in Kolkata University with the help of Raja Kirtyanand Singh of Raj Banaili. Two professors were appointed for the teaching of Maithili and their salary was paid from the contributions of these two Rajas. Kumar Gaganand Singh, Babu Gangapati Singh, Brajmohan Thakur, and Bidyanand Thakur all played significant roles in the recognition of Maithili. This was the first time that Maithili was recognized as a modern Indian language, which laid the foundation for greater and greater recognition of Maithili.

Raja Tankanath Chaudhary was born at Durgaganj in Katihar. His father, Raja Budhinath Chaudhary, died in 1885. Since he was very young at that time, the Court of Wards took over the administration of his Zamindari. His primary education was imparted at Krishna Nagar of Navadvip district in Bengal. From the Presidency College, Kolkata he completed his BA with English and Philosophy as subjects. He took admission in MA, but in 1904, when the administration of the Court of Wards ended, he stopped his formal education and started to look after his Zamindari.

Raja Tankanath Chaudhary established a school in 1915 in the memory of his father at Ramnagar. In this school, Maithili students were given free education; tuitions, food, and free lodging were also provided to the poor students. There was also a Maithili Student Union, which used to meet regularly. In their meetings, Maithili essays and poetry were discussed. The famous Maithili writers like Kashinath Jha and Kanchinath Jha 'Kiran' received their education in this school.

He was the member of many public bodies as well, such as the Dinajpur Municipal Board for fifteen years and a member of the Bengal legislative council. He was a regular participant in the sessions of the Maithil Mahasabha. He established a huge library of rare books and manuscripts. His contributions to Maithili language is multifaceted. In *Mithila Moda*, he started an essay competition in Maithili on socially relevant issues, such as the appropriateness of foreign travel for Maithil Brahmins. We find many essays in *Mithila Moda* in favour of or against this topic. He was a very close friend of Maharajadhiraja Rameshwar Singh of Darbhanga and used to discuss all the important issues concerning Mithila and Maithili with him.

Braj Mohan Thakur (1889–1977)

His contribution to the recognition of Maithili by Kolkata University was an important achievement which laid the foundation for the struggle for the institutional recognition of Maithili in later years. It inspired many of his contemporaries to work more ardently for Maithili.

He was born at Araria Bairgachi, in Araria (then Purnea District). He started his primary education at Araria and passed the entrance examination from Araria High School. Thereafter, he went to Bhagalpur and passed the BA from TNJ College, Bhagalpur (now TNB College). Then, he went to Calcutta to study philosophy as a postgraduate with the financial help of Raja Kalikanand Singh of Srinagar Deorhi. He got an MA in 1918 with 'Sankhya and Vedanta' as his areas of specialization. He also received the BL Degree from Kolkata University by taking admission in the evening classes. While studying law, he met Rajendra Prasad, who was a year senior to him. They became very close friends and together they formed Vidvat Samiti, with Prasad as its President.

After the completion of his studies he was appointed as a translator by the Government of Bengal. Very soon, he was appointed as a professor of Hindi at the Kolkata University. He continued to be a member of the board of higher studies and a paper setter for Hindi (MA examinations) from 1921 to 1925.

When Kolkata University under the vice chancellorship of Sir Ashutosh Mukherjee started higher studies in fourteen modern Indian languages including Bengali, Marathi, and so forth, Maithili was left out. Brajmohan Thakur was surprised and disturbed by the omission of Maithili. He met Sir Ashutosh Mukherjee and told him about this mistake and pleaded for the inclusion of Maithili as a subject of higher studies. Sir Ashutosh himself was surprised and accepted the mistake but he told him that as the funds available for such studies had been already distributed, he could do nothing. But he promised that if the requisite sum of rupees 2,500 was made available within a few days, he could include Maithili as a subject of study at the post-graduation level. With the help of Raja Tankanath Chaudhary of Rajour and Raja Kirtyanand Singh Bahadur of Raj Banaili a total amount of Rs 10,000 (Rs 3,500 by Rajour Estate and Rs 7,500 by Raj Banaili) was deposited in the Kolkata University and the education committee in its meeting of 7 August 1919 and 8 August 1919 accepted Maithili as a subject of study at the postgraduate level. And a Rajour–Banaili chair for Maithili was established at the Kolkata University. It was a milestone for Maithili, as it is widely considered that, had the Kolkata University denied such recognition to Maithili, the further development of Maithili would have been obfuscated and perhaps Maithili would have been very well appropriated by the supporters of Hindi as its dialect.

The other contributions of Braj Mohan Thakur were to appoint two teachers for the teaching of Maithili and prepare its syllabus. For this purpose, he visited Raj Darbhanga and approached Parmeshwar Jha. Parmeshwar Jha accepted the proposal but thought it necessary to take the consent of the Maharajadhiraja of Darbhanga, Rameshwar Singh. Rameshwar Singh did not give his consent and instead increased his salary. The Maharjadhiraja wrote his displeasure to Sir Ashutosh about this act of Braj Mohan Thakur. Finally, Babuaji Mishra and Babu Gangapati Singh were appointed for the post.

Braj Mohan Thakur was, as the letter of the Kolkata University says, dated 19 August 1919 'on deputation from the Kolkata University for making a collection of books and manuscripts in Maithili'. He was given 23 days to make this collection, that is, from 19 August 1919 to 10 September 1919. He visited different parts of Mithila, Mathura, Kashi, and Alwar and collected published and unpublished books and manuscripts. It is believed that he was the first who prepared a comprehensive list of all the published and unpublished works in Maithili.

Besides Hindi he was a good scholar of English, Sanskrit, Bengali, Maithili, and Urdu also. He was the first MA, BL degree holder in the old Purnea district. On the request of Raja Kalikanand Singh Bahadur, he returned to Purnea and joined the Bar of the District Court, Purnea.

He was offered the post of Hon'ble Justice at the Indore High Court but he could not join it and practiced till 1965 at Purnea District Court. He took mostly civil cases. It is doubtful if he worked for the cause of Maithili during his long and distinguished public life in Purnea. He was felicitated with a *Tamrapatra* by the Chetna Samiti, Patna in the year 1972. Later, on 14 March 1983 Braj Mohan Thakur Law College was established at Purnea in his memory.

Sitaram Jha (1891–1975)

Sitaram Jha's contributions to modern Maithili poetry are compared with the contributions of Murlidhar Jha in Maithili prose. He was a Sanskrit scholar and had written more than seventy-five books in *Jyotish-Shastra*. But he was equally committed to the cause of the mother tongue, Maithili. He was a disciple of Murlidhar Jha and under his inspiration began to write in Maithili. He wrote mainly poetry. But there are also his acclaimed prose writings. He played an influential role from Varanasi (Kasi or Banaras), where he spent most of his life, in shaping the consciousness among the Maithils about their mother tongue. He also influenced Baidyanath Mishra 'Yatri'—one of the most influential writers in modern Maithili—to write in Maithili.

He was born at village Chaugama in Bahera Parishar of Darbhanga district. From 1921 to 1962, he was a renowned scholar of Sanskrit at Sanyasi Sanskrit College at Kasi and after that, he was appointed to teach in Banaras Sanskrit University.

His sixteen Maithili works have been published and include *Ambacharit* (*mahakavya*—long poem), *Alankar Darpan (2 vols)*, *Atichar-Nirnaya*, *Unta Basat*, *Updeshakshamala*, *Geetatatvasudha* (Translation of *Geeta*), *Padhua-Charitra Tatha Purvapar Vyavahar*, *Parva-Nirnaya*, *Parichaya-Darpan*, *Bhukamp-Varnan*, *Maithili Kabyashatras*, *Maithili Kavyopavan*, *Ratnasangraha*, *Loklakshan*, *Vyavahar-Vivek*, and *Sikshasudha*.

He was mainly a poet and even his prose writing is a testimony to his poetic expressions. He was influenced by the writings of Murlidhar Jha and Jeevan Jha. He co-edited *Mithila Moda* with Anoop Mishra from 1920 to 1927. He was a follower of the *Mithila Moda shaili* (a writing style in Maithili) but he was not totally against any other *shailis*. His writings reflect the complete cultural and social life of Mithila. His writings are also famous because of his use of Maithili's *deshaj (thenth)* words and proverbs (*lokoktis*). One can feel the scent of Maithili culture and society of his time in his writings. He wrote on almost all aspects of Mithila's culture.

His speech as a chairman at the sixth session of the Maithili Sahitya Parishad at Muzaffarpur was a call for duty to Maithils to struggle for Maithili and Mithila and it became the slogan of the Maithili movement in later years. He said:

पायव किछु अधिकार कतहु की बिना झगड़ने ?

अछि सलाइमे आगि, बरत की बिना रगड़ने ?

[There is fire in the matchbox, but will it burn without rubbing (with a matchstick)?
Similarly, could we get our rights anywhere without fighting?]

Badri Nath Jha (1893–1973)

Kavishekhar Badri Nath Jha was a great scholar of Sanskrit literature, in which he wrote more than twenty books. In Maithili, he has written only one *mahakavya*, *Ekavali-Parinaya*. Besides, he has also edited and compiled a *Maithili Geet Ratnavali*, which is a collection of Maithili songs from the age of Vidyapati to his times, written in the traditional style.

He was born in village Sarisab Pahi in Madhubani. For a very long time, he worked as a professor of literature in Dharmasamaj Sanskrit College at Muzaffarpur. Many poets of modern Maithili, like Suman, Madhup, and Mohan were his students.

His *Ekavali Parinay* is considered the first published *mahakavya* in Maithili. It was first published in a serialized form in *Sahitya Patra*, edited by Ramanath Jha. Later it was published in a book form in 1942 from the Raj Press, Darbhanga. The subject of this work is based on the sixth *skanda* of the *Devibhagwat*. His language is highly Sanskritized and almost inaccessible for common readers. But his use of words and poetic style touched the zenith of literary expressions.

Umesh Mishra (1895–1967)

Umesh Mishra's contribution to Maithili language and literature is enormous. He contributed in various ways to champion the cause of

Mithila and Maithili. He was the last in the line of Mahamahopadhyas in Mithila. He was a great scholar of Sanskrit, propagator of Maithili, and was good at English too.

He was born in village Gajahara in Madhubani. His father, Mahamahopadhyaya Jayadev Mishra, was also a great scholar of Sanskrit. He studied under the guidance of his father and Sir Ganganath Jha. He was a professor of Sanskrit at Allahabad University from 1923 to 1959. He also served as the Director of Mithila Research Institute, Darbhanga. He was the first Vice Chancellor of Kameshwar Singh Sanskrit University, Darbhanga between 1962 and 1965.

His famous works are *Kamala*, *Upakhyanmala*, *Tirhuta Aksharak Utpati aur Vikash*, and *Vidyapati Thakur* (its Hindi translation has also been published). He edited *Krisnajanma*, written by Manabodh. He also edited *Srikrisnajanma Rahasya Natak* of Srikant Ganak with his son and a great campaigner of the Maithili movement, Jayakant Mishra. He has also translated many Sanskrit works into Maithili.

Some of his speeches, such as those in the third and sixth sessions of the Maithili Sahitya Parishad at Ghonghradiya and Muzaffarpur respectively put him in the category of the finest essayists in Maithili. In both these speeches, he fiercely supported the claim of Maithili against Hindi and provided enough evidence for the assertion of Maithili as an independent language. He also provided solutions for developing a standard writing style for Maithili.

Amarnath Jha (1897–1955)

Amarnath Jha is renowned for his commitment to the growth of a healthy culture in educational institutions in India, particularly Allahabad University. His three-and-a-half decades of association with this university saw him in many roles; first as a student, then as a member of the English faculty at age twenty-two, and finally as the Vice Chancellor of the University at the age of forty one. He was the Vice Chancellor of the Allahabad University from 1938–47. For a brief period, he was appointed as the Vice Chancellor of the Banaras Hindu University in 1948. He was also the chairman of the U.P. Public Service Commission (1947) and the Bihar Public Service Commission (1953). He was elected as the President of the All India Hindi Sahitya Sammelan (1941), the Kashi Nagari Pracharani Sabha, and the U.P.

Sahitya Sammelan (1946). He took a very keen interest in the linguistic affairs of the country. But above all, he was a great educationist and wanted to keep educational institutions away from the undue interference of politics. He was quite disturbed by the growing political interference in the matter of education.

He was born to the great Indologist Sir Ganganath Jha and spent his initial years in Darbhanga before going to Allahabad in 1902. He passed his secondary examination in 1913 with a first class and with distinctions in English, Hindi, and Sanskrit. Then he was admitted to Muir Central College, from where he passed the intermediate examination in 1915. He passed his B.A. in 1917, standing first in first class. The same year, he joined the department of English as an assistant professor at the age of twenty, on the invitation of Ranford, Principal of the Muir Central College, while simultaneously attending lectures for the MA examinations. Later, he joined *Leader*, a well-known journal published by C.Y. Chintamani. He passed his M.A. in 1919 in English. Although his educational and most of his professional life, except for a brief period when he was appointed as the chairman of the BPS, were spent in the city of Allahabad, he remained committed to Mithila and Maithili.

Some of the important works of Amarnath Jha include *Dashkumaracharita*, *Hindi Sahitya Sangraha*, *Rasarnava of Shankara Mishra*, *Chandra Kavi Praneet Maheshwani Sangrah* (edited with Sir Ganganath Jha), *Tales from Indian Epics*, *An Anthology of Modern Poetry*, *Harshanath Granthawali*, *Shringar Bhajanavali*, *Vichardhara*, *The Educational System*, *Sarojini Naidu: A Personal Tribute*, *Urdu Poets and Poetry*, and *Literary Studies*.

Although he took very keen interest in the language problems in India and supported Hindi's claim to be the 'national' language against Hindustani, but according to him this whole issue of language is the construction of 'our leader' and for 'the masses for whom the leader speaks—the problem just does not exist'. He was also a great champion of mother tongues. He believed that the medium of primary education should be the mother tongues. Thus, he supported Maithili instead of Hindi as the medium of instruction at the primary level in the Mithila region; he eventually succeeded in persuading the concerned committee regarding this. For political reasons, the idea was later dropped by the committee in his absence, which he considered 'forced absent'. He opposed the idea of classifying Maithili as a 'dialect' of Hindi.

Babu Bhola Lal Das (1897–1977)

He is also known as *Maithilik Dadhichi* for his struggles and sacrifices for the cause of the Maithils, Mithila, and Maithili. He was a great social reformer. His role in Mithila is compared with Raja Ram Mohan Roy's in Bengal, but unlike Roy he never got such support from either the British or the Maharajas of Darbhanga. He was also a great organizer, institution builder, and committed leader with high ideals. He played a remarkable role and successfully led the struggles for the recognition of Maithili in the Patna University from the primary to the university level. He was a lawyer but left his profession and lived a simple life with unmatchable dedication and commitment for the development of the Maithils, Mithila, and Maithili; from the establishment of a press, to publication, distribution, and circulation of books. His contributions in Maithili's development are greatly admired with reverence by his contemporaries and younger generations alike.

He was born in 1897[2] in village Kasraur in Darbhanga. He received his elementary education in his maternal village, Mahishi. After graduating in 1917 from TNB Jubilee College, Bhagalpur and getting an LLB from Allahabad University, he took up the law as his profession. In the beginning, he championed the cause of Hindi as the national language, but after Raghunandan Das convinced him about the richness of the Maithili language and its literature, he took up the cause of Maithili as his life-long mission. He also participated in the national movement, led by Mahatma Gandhi, and taught in different colleges established by Gandhi and other nationalist leaders. According to Jatashankar Das, he was a staunch supporter of Maithili; being a nationalist, he never doubted the claim of Hindi as the national language in India. He was very critical of the imperialist agendas of *Hindiwallas*.

He was a first-ranked leader of the newly formed the Maithili Sahitya Parishad, Darbhanga and was its *pradhan mantri* (chairman) from 1939 to 1940. The Parishad played the role of a crusader to champion the cause of Maithili. He was basically an *andolani*,[3] so comparatively his literary contribution in Maithili is relatively less. But whatever he wrote proved to be a milestone in the further development of the Maithili language and its literature. His major works are *Vyakaran Prabodh*, *Subodh Vyakaran*, *Saral Vyakaran*, *Maithili Sahitya Lahiri* (*Balpothi Bhag* 4), and *Sansmaran*. He edited *Gadya Kusumanjali*. He also edited two monthly journals, which set the standards in Maithili journalism; *Mithila* and *Bharati*.

He was awarded the *Vidyaratna* on 29 October 1968 by the Mithila Sahitya Sanskriti Sansthan, Darbhanga. Patna's famous cultural organization, Chitragupta Sabha, awarded him the title of *Mithila Saroj* in 1941. In 1976, Bihar Rashtra Bhasha Parishad, Patna in recognition of his service for Hindi and Maithili, awarded him a *Tamrapatra* and offered to pay him Rs 300 per month for his lifetime from its Sahityakar-Kalyan-Kosha. Sankalp Lok, Laheria Sarai gave him the title of *Mithila Vibhuti* in 1977.

Babuaji Jha 'Agyat' (1904–1996)

He lived through almost the entire twentieth century, which is considered as full of constructive, destructive, and reconstructive events. His long life had seen many a great and disturbing occurrences in the world and his own region, Mithila. These happenings aroused his thinking deeply and these all are vividly reflected in his writings, particularly his poems.

During this period, the condition of Maithili and Mithila had worsened. The old systems and structures of life were falling apart but the new were still not in sight. Sanskrit education for the elite was still regarded as high learning at the cost of modern education and the mother tongue, Maithili. It is this narrow-mindedness and conservative attitude towards modern learning and life, combined with feudal structure, that restricted the growth of Mithila and Maithili. It is an irony that it is believed that Mithila and Bengal share a very close cultural and social affinity. But in the beginning of the twentieth century, while Bengal aspired for modern English education, in Mithila, the focus was still on the establishment of Sanskrit *tolas* and *pathshalas*. This intense focus on the preservation of traditional methods of learning produced a great many Sanskrit scholars but it isolated Mithila culturally, socially, economically, and educationally.

In such circumstances, Babuaji Jha 'Agyat' was born at village Bath in Madhubani, to Kantir Jha and Draupadi Devi. His father was an illiterate Maithil Brahman who did not like his aspirations for higher education. So, he had to struggle and work hard to get an education after primary. He passed *Prathma* with first class from the Sanskrit school,

Garatol. Then, he also passed the *Shastri* examination mostly through self-education with the help of Triloknath Mishra of Lohna Vidyapeeth. Only by dint of his sheer love for learning, he passed *kavyateerth* from Bengal, *Sahityacharya* from Bihar and *Sahityotma* examination from Baroda state. He also cleared the *Ayurvedacharya* examination from Bengal in 1942.

He worked in Vishudhanand Hospital in Kolkata but soon returned to his native village and started practicing Ayurveda. His interest in learning led to his joining the Sanskrit college in Forbesganj and then the Sanskrit High School in Balua Bazar, Saharsa. He worked there till 1968; only after his retirement, he devoted himself to literary pursuits. He got some poems and articles published in *Mithila Darshan, Mithila Moda*, and *Vaidehi*. His most important works are *Rukmani Parinaya* (1980) and *Partigya Pandav* (1995). Both works are based on stories from the *Mahabharata*. His other literary compositions are compiled in *Tarangani*, which is still unpublished.

He was facilitated by the Sanskritik Parishad, Madhepura, Vidyapati Seva Sansthan, Darbhanga, Sankalp-Lok, Laheriya Sarai, and Chetna Samiti, Patna. According to Sureshwar Jha, the poet 'Agyat' might be unknown earlier but now he is well-known. He is considered as a great poet of Maithili's ancient tradition though his assessment of modern life and its problem and their solutions in his *Muktak Kavitas* put him among the great Maithili modern poets.

Ramanath Jha (1906–1971)

Ramanath Jha was first among the Maithili writers who initiated the discussion about the proper scientific standard of prose writing in Maithili. His *Sahitya Patra* (published quarterly from 1937 to 1939) played a critical role in the formulation of a writing style of prose. In this *Patra*, a style had been followed so strictly and consistently that for a very long time this style of writing came to be known as the Ramanath School. Although it did not settle the controversy regarding the prose writing style, in the very beginning *Mithila Mihir* adopted a different form than that suggested by Jha. No doubt this is to his credit that Maithili writers started to work seriously in prose writing and maintaining some form of uniformity in their writings. However, this controversy is far from being settled even at present.

Ramanath Jha was very concerned about prose writings in Maithili. He understood that prose writing is necessary for the proper development of any modern language. So, he spent considerable time and energy to develop standard prose writings in Maithili. Jha also introduced and strengthened literary criticism and critical enquiry, which were then acutely lacking in modern Maithili literature. He was a dispassionate researcher. Through the serious study of *Panji Prabandha*, he could solve many controversies surrounding Vidyapati, Govind Das, Chanda Jha, and others.

He was born in village Ujan Dharampur in Darbhanga. He passed his MA in English from Patna University in 1930. He was the Headmaster of Madhepur High School from 1930–6. In 1936, he was appointed as the Head Librarian of the Darbhanga Raj Library. From 1952–62, he taught English in Chandradhari Mithila College. When in 1962, the study of Maithili began at the post-graduation level, he was appointed as the reader and the head of the department of Maithili. In 1965, he was elected as the representative of Maithili in the Sahitya Akademi and elected as a member of its executive council. He remained there till 9 December 1971, the day he died.

His main research works are *Nibandhmala*, *Prabandh Sangrah* (based on classical stories), and *Udyan Katha* and *Baruch Katha* are his literary works. He translated *Vidyapati's Purush Pariksha*. His compilation and edited works are *Maithili Padya Sangraha*, *Maithili Gadya Sangraha* (in three parts), *Kavita Kusum*, *Pracheen Geet*, *Katha Kavya*, and *Naveen Geet*. His famous edited works are Manbodh's *Krishnajanma* and Chanda Jha's *Mithila Bhasha Ramayana*. His monograph on Vidyapati published by the Sahitya Akademi is translated into more than seven Indian languages. His other famous creative works are *Mithila Bhasha Prakash*, *Alayi Kul Prakash*, *Maithilik Vartman Samasya*, *Maithili Gadyak Prasang*, *Maithili Brahmano Ki Panji Vyabastha*, and *Tales from Vidyapati*.

Kashikant Mishra 'Madhup' (1906–1987)

Kashikant Mishra 'Madhup' is a very popular modern Maithili writer. He is widely admired and respected for his literary fineness. He used simple *deshaj* words rooted in everyday lives of the people. And perhaps that is the reason his songs are widely sung by them in all kinds of congregations—be it ritual practices, *Kavi sammelans*, pilgrimages, marriage ceremonies, haat and bazars, or any form of sports. His songs can be heard everywhere. Perhaps he is unrivalled in modern Maithili literature for his popularity among the common people. His songs reached the lips of both old and young, boys and girls, men and women, lettered or unlettered alike. He wrote for every section of the Maihili society and touched every aspect of their lives.

He was born in village Koilakh in Madhubani. But he settled in his maternal village Korthu. He was a bright scholar of Sanskrit literature and became Vyakaran-sahityacharya and then Vedant-shastri. He was the headmaster of Bahera's Jayanand High School. It was while working at this school that he committed to literary pursuits and he inspired a generation of Maithili writers, such as Brajkishor Verma 'Manipadma', Ramchartira Pandey 'Anu', Radhakrishna Jha 'Baher', and Ramkrishna Jha 'Kishun'. He was very active in Maithili Kavi sammelans as well.

His important works are—*Apporva rasgoola* (1941); *Jhankar* (1942); *Shatadal* (1944); *Tatka jalebi* (1945); *Kobar geet* (1945); *Panchmer* (1949); *Triveni* (1955); *Tandav* (1959); *Geet manjari* (1963); *Chaunki chuppe* (1966); *Radha virah* (1969); *Vidageet* (1973); *Gangatarangawali* (1974); *Batsavitri* (1975); *Durgasaptasati Maithili sudha* (1978); *Dwadashi* (1979); *Prerana punj* (1980); *Bola-bam* (1981); *Madhup saptasati* (1982). He was given the Sahitya Akademi award in 1970 for the mahakavya *Radha virah*. Maithili Akademi, Patna, gave him the Vidyapati *puraskar* in 1983 for *Prerana punj*. His *Ghasal atthanni* became very popular where he describes the pathetic end of a poor labourer and her child due to the cruel, casteist, patriarchal, and exploitative social relations prevalent in Maithili society. He attacked the prevailing evils and cruelties of Mithila. He also translated many Sanskrit works into Maithili.

Kanchinath Jha 'Kiran' (1906–1988)

Kanchinath Jha 'Kiran' is regarded as 'a man of the earth who sees things from the common man's point of view'. He was actively engaged in the service of Maithili language through original creative writings as well as through his participation in the Maithili movement. He was an unrivalled organizer. He actively participated in the organization of the Vidyapati Parva. He made this Parva a means to develop *bhasha prem* among the Maithils. He was the prime minister of the Maithili Sahitya Parishad for six years (1947–53).

He was born in village Ujan Dharampur in Darbhanga. He went to Kashi for study. There he played a critical role in the Maithili language movement. His role in the recognition of Maithili as a course of study in the Kashi Hindu Vishwavidyalaya was commendable. For a very long time, he was a teacher in the Sarisab High School and later joined Lalit Narayan Mithila University as a reader in Maithili. Bhimnath Jha has pointed out that in the last fifty-five years of the Maithili language movement, 'Kiran' had always actively participated in every event.

His published works are *Chandragrahan* (1932), *Vijeta Vidyapati* (1972), *Dhruv, Abhimanyu,* and *Jai Janmabhumi* (1953). His other famous works are *Madhurmani* and *Parashar.* For *Parashar*, he was given the Sahitya Akademi Award in 1989.

He was a progressive writer. Going against the dominant belief system of Mithila society, he discarded the concept of divine authority and extensively wrote upon the social and economic inequality and vehemently opposed social stagnancy. He was a staunch supporter of educating women and quite apprehensive of the upper castes' idleness. The strong support for social reforms is quite visible in his writings.

Lakshmipati Singh (1907–1979)

Babu Lakshmipati Singh's contribution to Maithili literature has been in various roles—as a journalist, novelist, poet, critique, essayist, and children's writer. He edited many magazines which influenced many Maithili writers and developed children's literature in Maithili.

He was born in the Khandawala ruling dynasty of Mithila to Babu Himpati Singh in Madhepur Dyaudhi (Palace) in Madhubani. He graduated in 1929 and worked as a teacher in Madhepur High School for some years. He worked at newspapers and publications (Aryavart Press) at Patna. His wife Lakshmiwati Leela also used to write in Maithili.

His main works are *Chamunda* and *Panchavati* (novels), *Atitak Smriti Patal* (autobiography), *Hindi-Maithili Shikshak* (grammar), and *Maithili Kusumanjali* (edited). He edited three magazines—*Maithili Bandhu* (from Agra), *Mithila Jyoti* (from Patna), and *Chaupari* (from Patna). He used to write reviews of almost all the books published in Maithili from 1950 to 1977 in English, which used to be published in *Indian*

Nation. He also wrote memoirs of some of his contemporaries like Mahavaiyakaran Deenbandhu Jha, Kavishekhar Badrinath Jha, Acharya Ramanath Jha, and Sitaram Jha. All his life, he tried to contribute in different ways to develop and popularize Maithili literature and language. He worked closely with many organizations and individuals associated with Maithili language and the movement.

Bhuwaneshwar Singh 'Bhuwan' (1907–1944)

Bhuwaneshwar Singh Bhuwan's entry into the Maithili literary field brought about revolutionary changes in Maithili writing and journalism. It was he who persuaded a famous Hindi writer of that time, Arshi Prasad Singh, to write in Maithili. Bhuwan also freed Maithili from the clutches of medieval songs on gods and goddesses and brought it closer to the reality of modern life.

He was born in the Khandawala ruling dynasty of Mithila in Anandpur Dyaudhi (Palace) in Darbhanga. He dedicated all his property and life to the cause of Mithila and Maithili. It is said that due to his investments for the cause of Maithili, the last years of his life were extremely depressed. His workplace was mostly in Muzaffarpur. He was mainly a poet but he also wrote prose. His prose writing is unique in terms of the flow of the language, the clarity of thoughts, and the beauty of sentence constructions. He used to write in Hindi also.

His major works are *Asadh* (1936) and *Smritikan* (1945) collections of poems; an edition of Ramadasa's *Ananda Vijaya Nataka*; translation of Michael Madhusudan Dutt's Bangla novel *Virahani Brajangana* into Maithili, about which it is said that it was as pleasing as the original. Durgananth Jha 'Shreesh' has published the compilation of all his writings, including translations, by the name of *Bhuwan-Bharati* in 1958.

'Bhuwan' also edited one of the highly acclaimed but short-lived Maithili magazines, *Vibhuti* (1936–8). It gave a new direction to Maithili journalism. According to Jayakant Mishra,

> the *Vibhuti* began well. It was priced very low, considering that it is used to give very interesting, though at times provocative matter and that an established writer like 'Bhuvan' was associated with it. Its articles were revolutionary in spirit and envisaged a new line of work—that of ready wit and humour. It met with its end soon because its style of spelling was

new to Maithili readers, because it went too far in criticizing old institutions and because it gave an impression of malicious propaganda.

Although it is true that he did not refrain from discussing his personal issues, particularly with the Raj Darbhanga with whom he was fighting many legal cases, his contribution towards the development of Maithili language and literature are extremely important. He also gave many new and prominent writers to Maithili.

Harimohan Jha (1908–1984)

Harimohan Jha was the first modern Maithili writer who created a bigger readership for Maithili literature. He was very critical of Mithila's customs and traditions and through his writings like *Khattar Kakak Tarang*, *Kanyadan*, *Pranamya Devta*, and others he fiercely attacked these static customs and traditions of Mithila. He also depicted the uneasiness and contradictions in the interaction of modernity and traditions in the early twentieth century in Mithila and through his writing also tried to establish a possible harmonious relationship between the two. Although he wrote in all genres of literature, he is famous for his satirical prose writings in Maithili.

He was born in Kumar Bajitpur in Vaishali. His father, Janardan Jha 'Janseedan', was a great scholar of Maithili and also wrote in Hindi. Harimohan Jha was a bright student and after completing his MA in philosophy, joined B.N. College Patna as a lecturer, and then he joined Patna College and finally became the head of the postgraduate Department of Philosophy, Patna University. He was also the Research Professor at Patna University for five years. But throughout his academic career, he maintained his interest in Maithili and continuously wrote in it.

His major works are *Kanyadan* (1933), *Dwiragaman* (1943), *Pranamya Devta* (1945), *Khattar Kakak Tarang* (1949), *Rangshala* (1950), and *Charachari* (1960). He also wrote his autobiography entitled *Jeevan Yatra*, which was published after his death in 1984.

Subhadra Jha (1909–2000)

Dr Subhadra Jha was born in Nagdaha village in Madhubani. After graduating from Scottish Church College, Kolkata, he worked as a research scholar at the Patna University from 1936 to 1940. In 1941, he joined Chandradhari Mithila College, Darbhanga, as a professor. Patna University awarded him a D. Litt. in 1944. Thereafter, for further studies, he went to Paris in 1946. For a very long time, he worked as a librarian in Varanasi Sanskrit University. After that, he joined Yogda Satsang College, Ranchi, as a Principal. He then joined as research Professor for Mithilesh Rameshwar Singh Maithili Chair at the Patna University.

His contributions in Maithili literature are *Pravas-jeevan, Yatra-Prakaran-Shatak*, and *Natik Patrak Utter*. His most important contribution as a linguist is *Formation of Maithili Language*, for which he was awarded D. Litt. Jayakant Mishra complimented the book by saying that 'the study of the Maithili Language as language has been best done by Subhadra Jha'. His *Natik Patrak Utter* is written as a series of letters, where he depicts the social, literary, political, and personal issues concerning the Maithili language movement. For this work, he was given Sahitya Akademi Award in 1986. According to Bhimnath Jha, Subhadra Jha will be ever commemorated in Maithili for providing a scientific basis for the Maithili language, for providing a correct explanation of *Vidyapati-Padya* in English and bringing it to the world, for providing complete and authentic account of ancient Maithili treasure with his contemporary criticism, and for his unique literary style.

Surendra Jha 'Suman' (1910–2002)

Surendra Jha's contributions to the development of modern Maithili literature are enormous. Not only did he contribute to Maithili literature; he also inspired and promoted many talented poets to write in Maithili. Chief among them are Kashikant Mishra 'Madhup', Upendra Thakur 'Mohan', Chandrakant Mishra 'Amar', Bhimnath Jha, and others. He is considered as the greatest poet in modern Maithili, a popular editor, a great teacher, an essayist of high merit, and a successful critic. He translated many works of Bangla and Sanskrit into Maithili and composed poetry in Sanskrit and Hindi.

Besides literature there is a political part of his personality as well. He was a great orator. He represented Darbhanga in the Bihar legislative assembly and then in the Indian parliament. He was also a representative of Maithili in the Sahitya Akademi from 1983 to 1987 and a member of its executive board. He was also *Maha mantri* of the Maithili Sahitya Parishad and for many decades worked as its chairman.

He was born in village Ballipur in Samastipur. He was a meritorious student of Sanskrit literature and completed *Sahityacharya* from Dharmasamaj Sanskrit College, Muzaffarpur. He started his career as a teacher in a high school. In 1935, he joined *Mithila Mihir* as an editor. He remained at this post till 1953. In the year 1953, he joined Chandradhari Mithila College's Maithili department as a professor; then he joined the PG Maithili department of Lalit Narayan Mithila University and retired from there as the Head of the Department. After retirement, he completely devoted his time to politics and literature. He also started the publication of a Maithili daily, *Swadesh*,[4] from Darbhanga from 15 August 1982. The daily was short-lived for the want of readership but it shows his love and affection for the cause of Maithili and Mithila.

He has thirty publications to his credit besides many edited and translated works, which is around fifteen. Important among his works are *Pratipada, Archana, Savon-Bhado, Ankawali, Antarnad, Bharat-Vandana, Payaswani,* and *Uttara. Purush Pariksha, Anugitanjali, Ritushringar,* and *Badki-Dai* are his translated works. Among his edited works, the most important are *Varnaratnakar, Parijat-Haran, Krishna-Janma, Anand-Vijay,* and *Govind-Gitanjali.*

Among the critics of Maithili literature, he was regarded to be more a Sanskritist and conventional than modern. According to Ramanath Jha, 'he was more an ancient and less a modern'.

Aarsi Prasad Singh (1911–1996)

Aarsi Prasad Singh was basically a Hindi poet and writer. He had also worked as a producer in Akashwani in Lucknow and Allahabad. He resigned from the post for his anti-government stand on Hindi. Then he worked at Khagariya College as a Hindi teacher. Thereafter, he wrote as an independent creative writer. He started writing in Maithili much later when Bhuwaneshwar Singh 'Bhuwan' persuaded him to do so.

He was born in Arout village in Samastipur. He could not attend college for higher education. But by dint of self-education, he acquired a lot of knowledge and skills. In his time, he was considered one of the foremost writers of Hindi in the province.

He is regarded mainly as a lyricist. But he also wrote in prose and *Muktak Kavya*. His major works in Maithili are *Matik Deep* (1958), *Poojak Phool* (1967), and *Suryamukhi* (1981). For *Suryamukhi*, he was awarded a Sahitya Akademi Award in 1984. The Maithili Akademi also gave him the Vidyapati Puraskar for the same work in the year 1982. He also translated Kalidasa's *Meghdoot*, which was first serialized in *Mithila Mihir* (in 1973–4). Later, it was published as a book by the Maithili Prakashan Samiti, Kolkata. His short story on a bicycle, 'Hamr Jeevan Sangini', is quite famous. He also wrote *Sanshamaran* (memoirs) on Ramlochan Sharan and Harimohan Jha.

Baidyanath Mishra 'Yatri' (1911–1998)

'Yatri', widely known and appreciated as 'Nagarjun', was also a Maithili poet and novelist, who brought a true *Lokbhasha* (colloquial language) in Maithili literature. He composed in chaste Maithili. He was a wanderer, a revolutionary, a great and sympathetic observer of everyday life, and critical of tradition and orthodoxy. He wrote satirically about the misery and hypocritical lives of the bourgeoisie. He was a great visionary. He also wrote in Hindi and his immense contribution in Hindi literature is widely recognized. In Hindi, he is better known as Baba Nagarjun.

He is regarded as the first Maithili writer who rescued Maithili from the clutches of Sanskritized language and used chaste Maithili to bring it closer to *Lokbhasha*. His writings acquaint the reader more closely with Maithili culture and society, particularly that of *Sarvahara*. According to Ramanath Jha, his specialty was that he interpreted communist literature in chaste Maithili, in *Bandhanhin Chhanda*.

He was born in village Tarauni in Darbhanga district to a low-middleclass Maithili Brahman family. He did his education partly in his village and partly in his maternal village Satlakha. He also studied Sanskrit literature for some time in Kashi. Then, after becoming a *Baudh bhikshu* (Buddhist monk), he went to Sri Lanka.

His works include *Chitra* and *Patrahina Nagna Gachha* (collections of poems), as well as the novels *Paro*, *Navaturiya*, and *Balchanma*. All his works are quite famous and their uniqueness lies in his style and minute observations of the subject matter. Particularly *Balchanma* is considered a path-breaking novel in modern Maithili literature. Regarding his poetry Jayakant Mishra writes—'The change in the idiom of these poems is remarkable. The poet does not use Sanskritized words, and raises a colloquial style to the poetic level. Ingenious thoughts, an epigrammatic and terse style, colloquial diction, unparalleled speed and tempo, and pointed observation characterize these poems'. About his well-known poem *Anhar Jinagi*, where he describes the atheistic, unstable, and confused life in modernity, Jayakant Mishra writes 'the greatest lyric he has written—*Anhar Jinagi*—can very well claim to be the greatest single poem of modern Maithili'. For his poetry collection, *Patrhina Nagna Gachha*, he was awarded the Sahitya Akademi Award in 1968.

Upendra Thakur 'Mohan' (1913–1980)

Upendra Thakur 'Mohan' served the interest of Maithili language and literature for more than half a century. By profession, he was a journalist. This enabled him to study closely the major and minor social, cultural, political, and economic events of his time and this shaped his writings as well. He was a Sanskrit scholar too.

He was born in Chatariya village in Darbhanga. He passed the examination of *Sahityacharya* in the first division. He was awarded the 'Sahitya Ratna' after passing an examination conducted by the Baroda Raj. He worked in the research division of *Aryavart* from the beginning of its publication. Then, he joined *Mithila Mihir* in 1960 and worked for it as a sub-editor in the beginning and then as an assistant editor. He retired in 1977.

He wrote many essays under different pseudonyms, such as Vijayanand, Kunjranjan, Sudarshan, Pundarid, Baman Shastri, Baman, Kashyap, Shri Thakur, and so on in different issues of *Mithila Mihir* and other magazines and newspapers. These prose writings by him are not compiled in a book to judge their merit, although these are said to be of a very high standard. His three collections of poetry have been published; these are *Fuldali, Baji Uthal Murali* (1977), and *Itishree* (published in 1982 after his death). He also published a book in Sanskrit, *Ugravansha-Prashastih*. For *Baji Uthal Murali*, he was given the Sahitya Akademi Award in 1978.

Lakshman Jha (1916–2000)

Lakshman Jha was a staunch supporter of a separate Mithila State. He played a critical role in the Mithila movement in the 1950s. He was a great scholar. In 1949, he earned his PhD from the London University on Mithila and Magadh. He was, for some years, deputy director of the Kashi Prasad Research Institute, Patna. In 1952, he left that job and fought a parliamentary election on the Socialist Party's ticket, which he lost. Thereafter, he extensively wrote on the issues concerning Mithila and championed the struggle for a separate state of Mithila. He was also appointed as the Vice Chancellor of the Lalit Narayan Mithila University, Darbhanga (1977–1978). He accepted this job without payment and left it within ten months. In his personal life, he was inspired by Mahatma Gandhi to maintain the utmost austerity.

He was born to Smt. Kirti Devi and Kari Jha of Rashiyari village in Darbhanga. He completed his primary education in his village and, for middle and high school, he joined the Coronation High School, Madhepura. He passed the high school examinations in 1937. At that time, Dr Ramanath Jha was the Head Master of that School. Then, he joined T.N.J. College, Bhagalpur and passed his intermediate in 1939. In 1941, he graduated with a first class in Sanskrit from Patna College. In 1941, he got admission in MA but soon he left college and joined the Quit India Movement. He was arrested and sent to jail. After he was released from jail, he went to England on a Bihar government scholarship and was awarded an MA in 1947 and PhD in 1949 on the subject of *Mithila and Magadh*.

Since 1952–3, Lakshman Jha continuously fought for the upliftment of Mithila. When his endeavour for the creation of a separate Mithila state failed, he started to fight for the sovereign republic of Mithila. Firstly, under the Mithila Socialist Party, he launched a movement— *Gorkha Payak Virodh*—to protest the treaty of Sugauli (4 March 1816) by which five thousand square miles of land were handed over to the Gorkha King by the East India Company. The people of this region who speak Maithili have been always treated differently in Nepal. Jha wanted to reunite them by creating the republic of Mithila. He also worked for the revival and promotion of Mithilakshar or Tirhuta. He has created an institution—*Mithila Mandal*—for publications in Maithili. Through this, he awakened Maithils about the demands for a separate state of Mithila. He was the founder editor of a weekly journal *Mithila*.

His famous published works in English include *Mithila a Union Republic, Mithila in India, Mithila A Sovereign Republic, Mithila Will Rise,* and *The Northern Borders.* In Maithili, his published works include *Mithila Bhasha, Mithilak Uddhar,* and *Mithilak Mukti.* He also wrote one hundred and thirty columns in *Indian Nation,* Patna, from February 1963 to March 1972 as a regular columnist. Besides there are twenty-eight books in English, seven in Sanskrit, six in Maithili, and ten in Hindi which are still unpublished.

Babu Saheb Chaudhary (1916–1998)

He was a lifelong campaigner for Maithili. He supported the Maithili language movement and the separate statehood demand. It was due to his tireless activities that many non-Brahmin Maithili speakers also began to participate in the Maithili movement. He believed that all those who were born in Mithila were Maithils. Those who joined the movement because of his persuasions include Varahil Mandal, Mohamad Abdulla, Shrikant Mandal, and Vindheshwari Mandal. He also tried to expand the narrow definition of Maithili by the Maithil Mahasabha in its Maldah conference. He supported Lakshman Jha's demand for separate statehood for Mithila. He could garner the support of all the sections of Maithili speakers. In his endeavours, he was supported by Prabodh Narayan Singh, Devnarayan Jha, Pitambar Pathak, and Upendra Narayan Chaudhary. For a very long time, Babu Saheb Chaudhary became synonymous with the Maithili movement in Kolkata.

He was born into a Brahmin family of village Dularpur in Darbhanga. He was educated till class X and came to Kolkata immediately after World War II. Here, he worked in a transport company as a supervisor and helped many Maithils in getting jobs in the company. One such person was Devnarayan Jha, who was recruited as a time keeper. Later, he became a great organizer and supporter of Maithili and the Mithila movement. Throughout his life, he supported Babu Saheb Chaudhary. According to Rajnandan Lal Das, Chaudhary himself became a great supporter of Maithili, while listening to a speech in Maithili by Harischandra Mishra 'Mithlendu' in Kolkata's Kalighat Park on 31 December 1944. He joined his organization Maithil Sangh, when the demand for separate statehood for Mithila was being raised. Along with Devnarayan Jha and Prabodh Narayan Singh, he formed the Maithili Lok Sangha. Later, when the Akhil Bhartiya Mithila Sangh was formed in 1957, with the help of Harimohan Jha and Braj Kishore Verma 'Manipadma', he joined it and remained committed to it till the end of his life. But, later in his life, he tried to associate himself with all the organizations and individuals concerned with the Maithili movement.

Besides being an activist, he was also a writer and established the Maithili Art Press to promote publications in Maithili. He edited and published *Maithili Darshan* from his press from 1974 to 1977. On Vidyapati Parva, organized by the Chetna Samiti, Patna in 1974, when the former Prime Minister of Nepal, Matrika Prasad Koirala was invited, he spoke in Maithili. But in the presidential address Janardan Mishra began to speak in Hindi. Babu Saheb Chaudhary at once objected to it and when Mishra started his speech again in Hindi, he boycotted the whole event. He could not compromise on Maithili in any event connected to Maithili and Mithila. His contributions in developing co-operation among Maithili organizations through an organization like the Maithili Mahasangh (1982–3), protest marches in Patna, leading the delegations to Chief Ministers, Governors, Prime ministers, and other government functionaries to express the grievances of Mithila and Maithili, are well recognized by the institutions and the activists of the Maithili movement. He also openly criticized the focus of Maithili organizations on Vidyapati alone; he wanted Lori, Salhesh, Deena-Bhadri, Chanda Jha, Lal Das, Sitaram Jha, Kanchinath Jha 'Kiran', Kashikant Mishra 'Madhup', and Surendra Jha 'Suman' should be given their due place too. He believed that Vidyapati Parva was only the means and the end was all-round development of Maithili and Mithila.

His important works are *Kuhesh, Achhinjal,* and a transliteration of D.L. Roy's Bangla play, *Chanakya,* into Maithili. Although he remained committed to Mithila and Maithili all his life, in the last years of his life, his economic situation worsened; he had to sell his press and leave Kolkata.

Braj Kishor Verma 'Manipadma' (1918–1983)

Braj Kishor Verma, better known as 'Manipadma', was not only a literary writer, but also a courageous freedom fighter and a great orator. He was also a follower of Tantrism and a historian. He was also a homeopathic doctor and was interested in drawing and hunting. He wrote in almost every genre of literature but his contributions are more in Maithili novels. His novels are based on social, historical, and mythological stories. He, like many other Maithili literary figures, started his writings in Hindi and English too and later, he began to write in Maithili and committed himself to promote and propagate the cause of Maithili and Mithila.

He was born in his maternal village, Jagtapur. His father Jugal Kishor Das shifted his home from Baur to Bahera due to fear of floods. He worked there in the registry office. His mother, Gangavati Devi, was daughter of Sonelal Das, the Diwan of Ganhbariya Dyaudhi, of Jagtapur. He spent his childhood in his maternal village Jagtapur under the guidance of Krishna Ballabh Lal Das. For higher education, he went to Kolkata and studied in Santiniketan. He also obtained an MD degree in homeopathy, went back to his village, and practised as a doctor in village Kamad Bishanpur, gaining great respect in the neighbouring villages. It is here that he also devoted his time to literary pursuits. He joined the Quit India Movement in 1942, was arrested by the British government, and was jailed for four years. He spent one year there, studied socialism, and emerged from prison as a believer in the communist philosophy. After that, he settled in his village Bahera, practiced homeopathy, and pursued his literary interests together with looking after his agricultural duties. It is said that he used to follow an unusual routine. He used to get up early in the morning at 2 a.m., and, after an hour of *Yoga*, used to write till 6 a.m. Then after 8 a.m., he used to sleep again for an hour or two, and thereafter he used to look after his other household and professional works.

His best-known writings are *Vidyapati* (1960), *Cobragirl* (1970), *Lorik Vijaya* (1970), *Naika Banjara* (1972), *Raja Salhesh* (1972), *Labahari-Kushari* (1976), *Ram-Ranpal* (1976), *Footpath* (1978), *Dulara Dayal* and *Ardha-Narishwar* (1981), *Kantahar*, *Jhumaki* (1977), *Hunka Saun Bhent Chhal*, and *Ohi Tham Gel Rahi*. He has translated two works of Bangla into Maithili—Vibhuti Bhushan Mukhopadhyaya's *Kushi Pranganer Chitthi* (1979) and Sukumar Sen's *A History of Bangla Literature*. For *Naika Banijara*, he was given the Sahitya Akademi Award in 1973.

He was associated with many Maithili organizations, such as the Maithili Akademi, Patna, of which he was a founder member; the

Maithili Paramarsh Samiti; the Sahitya Akademi, Delhi; the Rashtra Bhasha Parishad, Patna; the Harinandan Smarak Trust (for the propagation of Maithili), the Darbhanga Nyasi (Trust), and the Vidyapati Seva Sansthan, Darbhanga—of these last three, he was founder chairman.

Sudhanshu Shekhar Chaudhary (1922–1990)

Sudhanshu Shekhar Chaudhary was the editor of the famous Maithili journal *Mithila Mihir*, published from Patna for twenty-two years (1960–82). Before that, he worked as an editor, along with Surendra Jha 'Suman' and Krishnakant Mishra, for *Vaidehi*, published from Darbhanga. His contributions to the Maithili movement were through the coverage of the issues and events, big and small, related to Mithila and Maithili in *Mithila Mihir*. He continuously tried to mobilize the opinion of the Maithil masses and inform the authorities about the concerns and demands of the Maithils.

He was born at the centre of Mithila-Maithili activities and movements, in Darbhanga in a locality called Mishratola. He worked in Kolkata and Jamshedpur, and as a high school teacher for some time, before entirely devoting his time and energy to the promotion of language and literature. He was actively involved in Maithili journalism and inspired a new generation of writers to write in Maithili. He also took interest in printing and publishing in Maithili.

He wrote in all the genres of literature but he considered himself mainly as a playwright. His plays include *Bhapait Chahak Jinagi* (1975), *Letait Anchar* (1976), and *Pahil Sanjh* (1982). His plays were performed successfully on the stage. His other works are *Tar Tatta Upar Patta*, *Ee Bataha Sansar*, *Daridrachhimari*, and *Nivedita* (all novels), and *Sandarbha* (1981, a collection of critical essays). For *Ee Bataha Sansar*, he was given the Sahitya Akademi Award in 1980. All his writings revolve around the contemporary social, political, and economic life of the people.

Jayakant Mishra (1922–2009)

He is credited with providing the first highly acclaimed history of Maithili language and literature in the English language. His work, *A History of Maithili Literature* in two volumes, first published from Tirbhukti Publications, Allahabad in 1949–50, according to Bhimnath

Jha, not only familiarized the scholars of other languages about the chronological history of the Maithili language but also provided to its own speakers the history of the language in one text, which was otherwise scattered at different places. For the first time, speakers of the Maithili language got a sense of the history of their own language. His work, since then, has become an indispensable reference book for any kind of research in the Maithili language and literature. He had spent all his life in researching and republishing texts that were almost lost, as well as facts and figures of Maithili language and literature. In short, his contribution to the development of modern Maithili language is immense and widely acclaimed.

He belonged to village Gajahara in Madhubani, but he was born in Kashi, where his father Umesh Mishra was a renowned scholar of Sanskrit and Oriental Studies. Although he did his masters in English literature from Allahabad University, he had a sound knowledge of Sanskrit and Maithili as well. He joined the same university as an assistant professor of English in 1944 and retired from there in 1983 after being appointed as the Head of the Department.

He formed the Akhil Bharat Maithili Sahitya Samiti, and established a press, Tirbhukti Publication, in Allahabad. These two organizations played a crucial role in the development of the modern Maithili language. He organized a book exhibition of Maithili books in Azad Bhawan, Indraprastha Estate, Delhi, from 9–11 December 1963, which was inaugurated by the then Prime Minister of India, Jawaharlal Nehru. This exhibition played a solid foundation for the demand that Maithili be included initially as one of the modern Indian languages in the Sahitya Akademi and then in the eighth schedule of the Indian Constitution. The Sahitya Akademi recognized Maithili in 1965, and after the death of first Maithili representative in Sahitya Akademi, Ramanath Jha, in 1972, Jayakant Mishra represented Maithili in Sahitya Akademi till 1982. He also demanded and fought for the use of the mother tongue in primary education in Mithila. He believed that it should be imparted through Maithili as a medium, and only then, would Maithili regain its lost glory. For this purpose, he organized a conference on primary education in Maithili, in the Bihar Chamber of Commerce Bhawan, Patna on 11 August 1973. He also supported the demand for a separate Mithila state and wrote a pamphlet for this purpose, 'Why Mithila a Separate State' which became very popular.

His other major works are: *The Folk Literature of Mithila, part–I, Kirtaniya Natak, Tirhuta Kakahara Pothi, Brihat Maithili Shabdakosha, Fascicule–I & II,* and *Maithili Samachar* (English and Maithili). He also published many other works in Maithili and English, and edited important works of Maithili. He wrote extensively on the issue of Mithila and Maithili.

He was awarded the *Bhasha Samman* by the Sahitya Akademi in 2000. For his immense contribution in championing the cause of Maithili, he was called the Field Marshal of the Mithila Movement by Dhanakar Thakur, and *Illahabadak Maithili–dhwaja* (Symbol of Maithili in Allahabad) by Jeevkant.

Ramkrishna Jha 'Kishun' (1923–1970)

Mainly a poet, Ramkrishna Jha 'Kishun' worked tirelessly to expand the base of Maithili literature and made it accessible to the common masses. He was a pillar in Saharsa and Supaul with regard to the activities of the Maithili movement. It is to his credit that people of this region became much more conscious of the Maithili language. Gradually this region started to play a significant role in the movement. He inspired many, including Mayanand Mishra, to write in Maithili. He himself came to the Maithili literary field due to the persuasion of Kavichudamani Kashikant Mishra 'Madhup'.

He was a brilliant student of Sanskrit literature. He taught Sanskrit in the high school of Supaul, for the rest of his life. In the beginning, he followed the traditional style of writing songs and poems. But soon he familiarized himself with the modern style.

Aatmanepad (1963) is a collection of thirty-one poems, which was published in his lifetime. He also edited *Maithili Navakavita*, a collection of sixteen new poems. It was published after his death. In this collection, he discusses the importance of modern poetry in Maithili. Not just the collection but also because of its deep analysis of modern poems it is still considered as a representative text in Maithili. He also wrote a play, *Ugana Re Mora Katay Gelah*, which was enacted in 1956 on the first session of the Akhil Bhartiya Maithili Lekhak Sammelan in Darbhanga. All his writings are compiled in three volumes, *Kramshaha, Swayamvar,* and *Vaicharik,* which was published in 1982 under the joint editorship of Mayanand Mishra and Kedar Kanan.

Rajeshwar Jha (1923–77)

Rajeshwar Jha was one of the few writers in Maithili who devoted his attention to develop all the genres of Maithili literature. His greatest contribution to Maithili literature is his research on the different aspects of Maithili and Mithilakshar. Besides that, he also wrote plays, stories, novels, and folk literature in Maithili.

He was born in Rasuar village in Saharsa. He could not continue his studies after passing matriculation. But, through his interest and hard work, he published many works in Maithili of immense value. He began his career by joining the service of the Raj Darbhanga. But after the abolition of zamindari, he worked in the office of *Indian Nation*. He soon moved to the Bihar Research Society, Patna and worked there as a clerk. Here, he devoted all his effort to enriching Maithili language and literature. It is stated that he had become an institution in himself with regard to the activities of Mithila and Maithili for a very long time.

His important works are *Maithili Sahityak Aadikal*, *Mithilaksharak Udbhava O Vikas*, *Madhyakalin Purvanchalak Vaishnav Sahitya*, *Vidyapati Sangeet me Varnit Nayak–Nayika Bhed evam Rag Raginik Vargikaran*, *Menka*, *Ekadashi*, *Vidyadharak Katha*, *Urvashi*, *Dharmabyadha Katha*, *Jata-Jatin Nrityageet*, *Shyama Chakeba Nrityageet*, *Dukhiya Babak Khatras*, and *Abhatta: Udbhava O Vikas*. He also published three books in Hindi, *Kalchakra Ki Utpatti Evam Utpanna Kramo Ki Samkshipta Vyakhya*, *Maharaja Lakshmishwar Singh*, and *Shakhya Shree Bhadra Ki Jivani*. His three plays in Maithili—*Mahakavi Vidyapati*, *Kandarpighat*, and *Shastrarth*—are of historical importance. For *Abhatta: Udbhava O Vikas*, he was given the Sahitya Akademi Award in 1977. He was a major inspiration underlying the establishment of the Maithili Sahitya Sansthan and edited its famous quarterly research journal *Mithila-Bharti*.

Pandit Govind Jha (1923–)

Pandit Govind Jha is a grammarian, lexicographer, translator, creative writer, poet, and a campaigner for the Maithili movement. He also writes in Sanskrit and Hindi. In his inclination towards Maithili, he was greatly influenced by his father, Mahavaiyakaran Pandit Deenbandhu Jha. He was born in village Ishahapur in Madhubani. In the beginning, he received his education from his father and under his able guidance he learned grammar, literature, and philosophy in Sanskrit. He also studied Bangla and English literature.

His famous published works are: Plays—*Basat* (1954), *Raja Shivsingh* (1972), and *Antim Pranam* (1982); Grammar: *Chhandshastra* (1960), *Laghuvidyotan* (1963), and *Uchchtar Maithili Vyakaran* (1979); Linguistic: *Maithilik Udgam O Vikas* (1968); Biography: *Umesh Mishra* (1984), Translations: *Malvikagnimitra* (1947) and *Chandidas* (1983); Edited—*Vibhasagar* (1975), *Varnaratnakar* (1980), *Vidyapati-Geetavali* (1981), *Govindadas-Bhajanawali* (1982), and *Smriti-Sandhya Bha-2* (1984).

Prabodh Narayan Singh (1924–2005)

Prabodh Narayan Singh was born in village Partapur in Saharsa. During the Quit India Movement, he joined the militant freedom struggle. He started his academic career initially with *Sahityalankar* (1945) and *Sahityratna* (1947) from the Hindi Sahitya Sammelan, Prayag. He worked in the editorial team of a Hindi journal, *Mel-Milap*. Then, he settled in Kolkata, first as an assistant editor of a Hindi daily, *Dainika Lokmanya*, and later as a professor in the University of Calcutta.

He was married to Anima Singh (Originally Anima Dhar from Mymensingh now in Bangladesh) on 28 July 1950. Anima Singh worked for various causes related to Maithili language development and later became a celebrated scholar in Maithili folklore studies. She also became a Professor of Hindi at Lady Brabourne College, Calcutta. Ila Rani Singh, daughter of Singh from his first wife Binda Devi, became an eminent poetess in Maithili as well as a scholar-teacher in Maithili and Hindi, having taught at Bhagalpur and University of Calcutta. She passed away in 1995.

Prabodh Babu edited a Maithili journal *Mithila Darshan* (since 1951), and a few anthologies like *Caryariksa* (1952) and *Tatka Gapp* (1968). Later, he participated in the theatre movement in Maithili. His translation of Qurratulain Haider's *Patjhar Kii Awaaz* (1997) from Urdu to Maithili got him a Sahitya Akademi award for translation in 2002. As a social organizer, he was always at the forefront of the Maithili movement. He worked hard to set up the Akhil Bhartiya Mithila Sangh in Kolkata, jointly with Babasaheb Chaudhary and Devnarayan Jha, and later he worked for the Akhil Bhartiya Mithila Mahasabha, which was an umbrella organization of numerous Maithili outfits.

His house at Kolkata always throbs with activities and many Maithili writers—Baidyanath Mishra 'Yatri' (Nagarjun), Subhadra Jha, and Jayakant Mishra—used to visit there. He was also associated with Maithili Rangmanch, an organization devoted to the performing arts and Lok Sahitya Parishad, devoted to the folklore studies of Mithila. He set up a printing press for Maithili publications. He was a member of the advisory board of the Sahitya Akademi (New Delhi) and associated with the organizations like Maithili Akademi (Patna), Rajendra Chhatra Bhawan (Kolkata), and Hanuman Mandir Sahitya Nyas (Kolkata). Now there has been a prize instituted on his name, Prabodh Sahitya Samman, since 2004.

Chandranath Mishra 'Amar' (1925–)

Chandranath Mishra 'Amar' has played many roles in the Mithila and Maithili movement. Since his entry in the movement in 1940, he has relentlessly taken up various responsibilities and continues to do so even today. Although he is renowned for his humorous poems and songs, he has written in almost all the genres–novels, stories, essays, dramas, one act plays, criticism, memoirs, surveys, and research in Maithili. He has also edited several Maithili journals and magazines and was a regular speaker at Maithili *Kavi Sammelans*. He has acted in many Maithili plays and in a Bollywood film, *Kanyadan*. He founded an organization for Maithili writers and activists, *Navartan Gosthi*, in Darbhanga in 1943.

He was born in village Khojpur in Madhubani. His father, Muktinath Mishra, was a Sanskritist and under his guidance, Chandranath Mishra learned Sanskrit and earned the degree of *Vyakarnacharya*. Thereafter, he joined M.L. Academy, Laheria Sarai as a Maithili teacher, from where he retired in 1983. He presently lives in Darbhanga and has been playing an active role in Mithila and Maithili activities. Since the very beginning, he has been deeply influenced and inspired by one of the great modern Maithili writers, Surendra Jha 'Suman'. Chandranath Mishra 'Amar' also played a key role in strengthening the Akhil Bhartiya Maithili Sahitya Parishad and was the Maithili representative in the Sahitya Akademi. He has been awarded with Akademi's Scholars in Residence award in 2010.

His important works are *Gudgudi* (1946), *Yugachakra* (1952), *Ritupriya* (1963), *Ahsa Disha* (1975), *Veer Kanya* (1950), *Bidagari* (1963), *Maithili Andolan: Ek Sarvekshan; Maithili Sahitya Parishadak Itihas* (1995), *Maithili Mahasabhak Itihas* (1995), and *Maithili Patrakaritak Itihas* (1981). He was given the Sahitya Akademi Award for *Maithili Patrakaritak Itihas* in 1983.

Lily Ray (1933–)

Lily Ray has brought about a new, particularly feminine perspective in Maithili prose writing. She has eloquently described the decaying feudal grandeur, degenerating traditional values, and the defiance of the new generation in her writings. Her flamboyant *Rangin Parda* (1956) was more like a shock to Maithili readers and many writers alike. She wrote this story under a pseudonym, Kalpana Sharan. This story was first published in *Vaidehi*, in which she published four more stories-*Rogini* (July 1955); *Thakpanj* (September 1955); *Kee Kahu?* (January 1956); and *Hummar Gapp* (February 1957). Thereafter, for the next twenty-two years, she did not write anything in Maithili and her identity remained hidden from many. It became known when she published her next long story entitled *Antaral* (22 January 1978) in *Mithila Mihir*, this time, using her original name. She is the recipient of a Sahitya Akademi award for *Marichika* in 1982 and the Prabodh Sahitya Samman in 2004.

She was born to a prosperous family in Madhubani. Her in-laws' home is in Durgaganj village of Katihar district and her parents' home is in village Ramanagar in Purnea district. However, as her father was in the Indian Police Service, she spent her childhood outside Mithila in many places. She was married to H.N. Ray, who later became a doctor and with whom she now lives in Darjeeling. Apart from her interest in Maithili folk songs, crafts, and traditions, Lily Ray is also an accomplished stage actress.

Her important works are *Patakshep* (First published in Mithila Mihir; 1 July–7 October 1971); *Marichika*-vols I and II (1981 and 1982); *Bihari Aibasaun Pahine; Chakra; Duvidha; Pahun; Gulab Jaan; Jeed; Chandramukhi;* and *Maya*. Her novel *Patakshep* has a special place in modern Maithili writings. It successfully depicts the activities of the Naxalite movement in very lively prose.

Mayanand Mishra (1934–2013)

Mayanand Mishra was mainly a poet and a lyricist but he also wrote stories, novels, and criticisms. Although he followed the traditional style of literary writings, he also composed several well thought-out poems following the modern style. He is famous for his satirical as well as psycho-analytical stories.

He was born in village Banainiya in Saharsa. He completed his MA in Hindi and Maithili respectively and joined the *Chaupal* programme of All India Radio in Patna. Thereafter, he joined Saharsa College, Saharsa as a lecturer of Maithili and worked there until his retirement. He was very active in *Kavi Sammelans* and stage performances. He was well acknowledged as the *mancha sanchalak* (stage manager).

His important works are *Bhangak Lota* (1951), *Aagi Mom aa Pathar* (1960), *Chandrabindu* (1983), *Bihari Paat Paathar* (1960), and *Dishantar*. He also wrote a serialized novel in *Mithila Mihir* from 1965 entitled *Khonta aa Chirai*. It has not been published as a book. He also edited a critically acclaimed Maithili journal *Abhivyanjana*. It is believed that he also gave birth to a new *ism* in Maithili literature: *Abhivyanjanavad*. He actively participated in the protests and demonstration for the demands of Maithili. He led the protest march in Patna in the 1990s and in Ranchi, Jharkhand.

Ramdeo Jha (1936–)

Ramdeo Jha, a scholar, writer, dramatist, and essayist has contributed significantly to the promotion of the Maithili language. He has been associated with the Maithili movement since his student days and has played a major role in the promotion and recognition of Maithili as an independent language in modern India. He served the Sahitya Akademi as a representative of Maithili and as a member of the Maithili Advisory Board of the Akademi (1988–97). He received the Sahitya Akademi Award in Maithili for his collection of dramas, *Pasijhaita Pathar*, in 1991. He also received the Akademi's translation award (1994) for his Maithili translation of Rajinder Singh Bedi's Urdu novel *Ek Chadar Maili Si* (entitled *Sagai* in Maithili). He was also selected for the Sahitya Akademi's Scholars in Residence programme in 2009.

He was born in village Kabilpur in Laheria Sarai, Darbhanga. He completed his primary and middle schooling in Laheria Sarai and Darbhanga. After completing his MA in Maithili from Patna University, he taught Maithili for many years in Dumka College, Dumka. He not only greatly influenced the teaching and research in Maithili, but when it was not easy for the students to find Maithili books in the library, he took personal interest and ensured that the college library had a sufficient number of Maithili books and magazines. Thereafter, he taught in CM College, Darbhanga. He also taught for many years in the post-graduate Maithili department, Lalit Narayan Mithila University, from where he retired in 1996. He was deeply interested in the promotion of Maithili language and literature and he sees the Maithili movement primarily as a language movement. He was also the joint secretary of the Akhil Bhartiya Maithili Sahitya Parishad (1957–9) and is presently associated with several Maithili literary organizations: Sankalp Lok, Laheria Sarai; Maithili Research Society. He completed his PhD on *Maithili Shaiv Sahitya* from Patna University in 1970.

His important published works are *Ek Kheera Teeh Phank* (1965); *Manuk Santan* (1966); *Dharti Mata* (1985); *Aaji Maa* (2009); *Pasijhaita Pathar* (1989); *Ijoti Rani* (1967); *Angareji Phoolak Chitthi* (2002); *Bahinak Virog* (2002); and *Ramjori Kagatak Pankhi Par* (2002). He also has several research works to his credit. These are: *Shakuntala Natak: Ek Adhyayan* (1959); *Maithili Shaiv Sahitya* (1979); *Umapati* (1980); and *Maithili Lok Sahitya: Swarup O Saundarya* (2002). He also wrote monographs on *Jagatprakashmall* (1990); *Jagjyotirmall* (1995); *Janardan Jha 'Janaseedan'* (1998); and *Subhadra Jha* (2010). He has also edited many valuable works in Maithili: *Hargauri Vivah Natak* (1970); *Kavivar Jeevan Jha Rachnawali* (1980); *Maithili Prachin Geet Manjari* (1991); *Vidyapati Geet Sanchay* (1999), and *Parmeshwar Jha Kreet Seemantani Aakhyayika* (2011). Besides, he has numerous essays, poems, stories, *nataks*, and articles published in leading Maithili journals and magazines.

Bhimnath Jha (1945–)

Bhimnath Jha is a writer, poet, critic, and an ardent supporter of Maithili movement. He is now retired as a professor of Maithili from Lalit Narayan Mithila University, Darbhanga. He has a matchless ability to balance between his poetic skills with his critiquing and satirical prose writings. He has inspired numerous researchers in Maithili. He has tirelessly fought for safeguarding the interests of Mithila and Maithili and is a recipient of the Sahitya Akademi award in 1993 for *Vividha*. His life and services to Mithila and Maithili are widely acknowledged and appreciated by the commoners and scholars alike.

He was born in village Koilakh in Madhubani. After completing his primary and middle education from Shyama Mandir and Harishchandra Collegiate School, Varanasi, he did his matriculation from the High School, Koilakh and Intermediate from R.K. College, Madhubani. Again, for Graduation he went to Darbhanga Chandradhari Mithila College and did an MA in Maithili from Magadh University, Bodhgaya. He also did a PhD on *'Kavichudamani Kashikant Mishra Madhupak Maithili Kritik Alochanatmak Adhyayan'* (A Critical Study of Maithili Writings of the Kavichudamani Kashi Kant Mishra Madhup) from Lalit Narayan Mithila University, Darbhanga in 1982. This moving from one place to another in search of better education did continue in his professional journey as well. He started his professional life with a book seller and distributer in Patna, Novelty and Company. He also worked as a clerk and a library assistant before joining the Indian Nation press as a deputy editor of its weekly journal, *Mithila Mihir*. Thereafter, he joined Chandradhari Mithila College as a lecturer and retired as a professor from the postgraduate Maithili Department of the Lalit Narayan Mithila University, Darbhanga. He was a member of the Maithili Advisory committee of the Sahitya Akademi from 1978 to 1987 and was also a member of the Akhil Bhartiya Maithili Sahitya Parishad from 1990 to 1994. Throughout his professional career and more so in his retirement, he remained an ardent supporter of Mithila and the Maithili movement. He presently lives in Darbhanga and is socially, culturally, and intellectually engaged with the issues related to Mithila and Maithili.

His important works are: *Parichayika* (two editions 1978 and 1985), *Darbhangamei Maithili Sanstha* (1987) *Vividha* (1989), *Kavichudamanik Kavyasadhana* (1989), *Vimarsha* (2004), *Tridhara* (1968), *Veena* (1971), and *Man-Aanganme-Thadh* (2000). He has also written two monographs on *Sitaram Jha* (1983) and *Upendra Thakur Mohan* (1995).

Notes

1. It was an examination conducted by the Raj Darbhanga to test the knowledge of different scholars in various branches of learning, primarily in Sanskrit. It was considered as the most prestigious testimony of one's learning. It was instituted by the founder of the Raj Darbhanga Mahamahopadhyaya Pandit Mahesh Thakur.

2. Some people like Fulchandra Mishra 'Raman' established his year of birth as 1894; though many still believe it was 1897.

3. Loosely translated as revolutionary, but not in the classical sense of the term. However, his contribution to the cause of Mithila and Maithili is not any less than a revolutionary.

4. This daily was published earlier also from 1948, initially as a monthly under his own editorship and later as a daily from 9 October 1955 to 27 December 1955.

Select Bibliography

Maithili

Journals/ Magazines/ Periodicals/ *Smarikas*

Bhuwan, Bhuwneshwar Singh (ed.), *Vibhuti*, Varsha-1, Ank-1, Muzaffarpur (March 1937).

Chaudhary, Shardindu (ed.), *'Samay Saal'*, *Maithili Bimonthly Magazine*, Patna, Shekhar Prakashan, February–March 2005; August–September 2007; October–November 2007; December 2007–January 2008; February–March 2008; April–May 2008; June–July 2008; August–September 2008; June–August 2009.

Das, Babu Bhola Lal (ed.), *Bharati*, Darbhanga, Maithili Sahitya Parishad (April 1937).

Das, Rajnandan Lal (ed.), *Karnamrit*, Kolkata, year–23, January–March, issue–89 (2003); year 26, January–March, issue–101 (2006); year 31, July–September. issue–123 (2011).

Ghar–Bahar, Chetna Samiti, Patna (April–June 2011; July–September 2011).

Jha, Jagdish Chandra, *Mithila Bharati*, issue–1, March–June, part–1 and 2, chief editor, Maithili Sahitya Sansthan, Patna (1969).

Jha, Murlidhar (ed.), *Mithila Moda*, vol. 2–59, Benares, Prabhakari Yantralaya (1906–20)

Jha, Surendra (ed.), *'Suman'*, *Mithilank*, Darbhanga, Mithila Mihir (1936).

Kumar, Kusheswar and Babu Bhola Lal Das (eds), *Mithila*, year–1, issue 1–12 Laheria Sarai (1930s).

Maithili Samachar, mouthpiece of Akhil Bhartiya Maithili Sahitya Samiti, Prayag, year–27 (January–December 1990).

Maithili Sandesh, issue–30, Jaya Nagar, Antarrashtriya Maithili Parishad (2010).

Mithila Darpan, Mumbai, year–6, issue–4 (March–April 2011).

Mithila Mihir, Maithili Daily, Darbhanga (5 November 1972); 2 July 1972; 30 April 1972; 21 June 1972; 21 May 1972; 28 May 1972.

Mithila Shodha Sansthan Shodh Patrika Mithila ki Lok Sanskriti Visheshank, vol. IX, part II (2007).

Mishra, Sadan (ed.), *Smarika*, Akhil Bhartiya Maithili Sahitya Parishad, Lakshmiwati Nagar (Sarisab Pahi) Session, Darbhanga, Nav Bharat Press Laheria Sarai (1968): 1–33, 69–91, 1–54, 83–138, 76–138, 1–19.

Parishad Vaarta Swarna Jayanti Visheshank, 1959–2009, Kolkata, Mithila Sanskritik Parishad (2009).

Purvottar Maithil Samaj, issue–5, October–December, Guwahati, Vidyapati Chetna Samiti (2011).

Pathak, Pankaj Kumar (ed.), *Samidha*, Jan Jagriti Manch, New Delhi, pp. 9–18, 21–5, 27–33, 39–41, 49–53, 55–8.

Rajat Jayanti Visheshank evam Baidyanath Mishra, 'Yatri-Nagarjun' Jeek Moorti Anavaran Samaroha, Kolkata, Mithila Vikas Parishad (2007).

Singh, Prabodh Narayan and Anima Singh, *Mithila Darshan*, Founder ed., vol. II, no. 8 (July–August 2010); vol. II, no. 11 (January–February 2011), vol. I, no. 2 (March–April 2011); vol. I, no. 3 (May–June 2011); vol. I, no. 4 (July–August 2011); vol. I, no. 5 (September–October 2011); vol. I, no. 6 (November–December 2011); vol. II, no. 1 (January–February 2012).

Smarika, Vidyapati Parva Samaroha, Patna, Chetna Samiti (1989).

Smarika, Vidyapati Smarak Manch, Kolkata, Ravindra Sarani (2004–6).

Smarika, Vidyapati Smriti Parva Samaroha, Patna, Chetna Samiti (2010).

Project Reports/Speeches/Memorandums/Private Papers and Pamphlets

Mishra, Chandranath, 'Amar', *Maithil Andolan: Ek Sarvekhsan*. Darbhanga: Vaidehi Samiti evam Akhil Bhartiya Maithili Sahitya Sammelan, 1962).

Chaudhary, Shardindu Kumar (ed.), *Abhimat Mithila Rajya Banam Mithilanchal ka Vikash* (Patna: Mithila Seva Trust, 2003).

Jha, Bhogendra, Private Papers, (IV–VI); acc no. 742, part–I; acc no. 766, part–II, (Oral History Transcript), New Delhi, Nehru Memorial Museum and Library [All the letters and other papers concerning Bhogendra Jha cited or quoted in Chapter 4 are part of this file.].

Jha, Kamla Kant, *Antarrashtriya Maithili Parishad: Vikash Yatra* (Jaya Nagar: Shri Ramesh Prakashan, 2009).

Jha, Kamla Kant, *Antarrashtriya Maithili Parishad O Mithila Maithili* (Jaya Nagar: Antarrashtriya Maithili Parishad, n.d).

Jha, Tarakant (ed.), *Chir Upeksha Saun Mukti Lel Kshetrak Vikas Lel* (Patna: Mithila Rajya Abhiyan, 2001).

Maithili Sahitya Parishadak Triteeya Karya Vivaran (Darbhanga: Vidyapati Press, 1933).

'Pamphlets', Akhil Bhartiya Mithila Party (2010).

Pathak, Amresh, *Private Papers* (personal collection, mostly letters of 1990s).

Presidential speech of Rambhadra Jha at the third session of the Maithili Sahitya Parishad, 3 and 4 June (Laheria Sarai: Maithili Sahitya Parishad, 1934).

Singh, Ganga Nand, Presidential Speech at the second session of the Patna College Maithili Sahitya Parishad's branch on 17 April 1937.

Speech of the president of the Swagat Karini Samiti at the third annual session of the Maithili Sahitya Parishad at Laheria Sarai.

Speeches, Articles, and Essays in Magazines and Periodicals

Chaudhary, Shashinath, *Maithili Sahitya Mala Mithila Darshan* (Darbhanga: Maithili Sahitya Parishad, 1931), pp. 1–30, 42–65.

Das, Bhola Lal, 'Maithili Bhashak Rup me', *Mithilank* (ed.), Surendra Jha 'Suman' (Darbhanga : *Mithila Mihir*, 1936), pp. 90–4.

Das, Bhola Lal, 'Sansmaran', cmpld and (ed.), Phoolchandra Jha 'Praveen', *Babu Bhola Lal Das Rachnavali*, vol. I (Darbhanga: Mithilendu Prakashan, 2008),

Das, Dhanushadhari, 'Janaki Mahotsava', *Mithilank* (ed.), Surendra Jha 'Suman' (Darbhanga; *Mithila Mihir*, 1936), pp. 61–2.

Das, Rajnandan Lal, 'Kolkata O Maithili Patrakarita', *Purvottar Maithil Samaj*, quarterly, issue–5, October–December (Guwahati: Vidyapati Chetna Samiti, 2011).

Das, Rajnandan Lal, 'Maithilik Hetu Andolan', *Karnamrit*, year 12, January–March, Kolkata (1992).

Jha, Amarnath, 'Maithili evam Hindi', *Mithilank* (ed.), Surendra Jha 'Suman' (Darbhanga: Mithila Mihir, 1936).

Jha, Amarnath, 'Maithili Sahitya', *Tilkor Bhag-1* (Patna: Bihar State Textbook Publishing Corporation Limited, 2007).

Jha, Bhuwaneshwara and Ramanath Jha, 'Bihar mei Mithila Bhashak Stathan', *Mithila*, year 1, issue 1, Vaisakh, sal 1336.

Jha, Gonu, 'Gonu Jhaki Nasdani', *Mithilank* (ed.), Surendra Jha 'Suman' (Darbhanga: Mithila Mihir, 1936), pp. 165–7.

Jha, Kamlesh, 'Tara Babu-Mithila Maithilik Antarmukhi Sadhak', *Mithila Tradition and Change Essays in Honour of Pt. Tarakant Jha* (ed.), Sureshwar Jha (Darbhanga: Tarakant Jha Felicitation Committee, 2008).

Jha, Kamlesh, 'Jayakant Babu ke Jena Ham Dekhaliyain', in Gobind Jha (ed.), *Jayakant Jayantika* (Patna: Shekhar Prakashan, 2010), pp. 143–52.

Jha, Kamlesh , 'Kolkata Mahanagar aa Hum', *Purvottar Maithil Samaj*, quarterly, issue 5, October –December (Guwahati: Vidyapati Chetna Samiti, 2011).

Jha, Murlidhar, 'Mithila Bhasha', *Mithila*, year 1, issue 1, Vaisakh, sal 1336, pp. 11–14.

Jha, Narendra, 'Babu Saheb Chaudhary: Mithila–Maithilik Amar O Nirbhik Senani', *Karnamrit* (April–June 2002).

Jha, Ramanath, 'Maithil o Maithili', *Mithila*, year 1, issue 6, Ashwin, sal 1337.

Jha, Ratish Chandra, 'Pandit Tarakant Jhak Jeevangatha', *Mithila Tradition and Change Essays in Honour of Pt. Tarakant Jha* (ed.), Sureshwar Jha (Darbhanga: Tarakant Jha Felicitation Committee, 2008).

Jha, Shashinath, *Dinbandhu Smritigranth*, Madhubani, Dinbandhu Jha Shatabdi Samaroha Samiti, Sake 1900, pp. 1–35, 41–7, 77–81, 106–13, 151–7.

Jha, Sushil Chandra, 'Bhamati', *Bhangima Natya Vishayak Aniyatkalin Patra*, year–10, issue–18 (4–5 August 1993): 1–42.

'Madhur' Pulikt Lal Das, 'Maithili Sahityonnatik Upaya', in *Mithila Mitra*, Uday 1, Kiran 12 (December 1931): 301–4.

Mishra, Kishori Kant, 'Mithila Sanskritik Parishad, Kolakatak Karmamay Pachas Varsha', in Mithilesh Kumar Jha (ed.), *Parishad Varta Swarna Jayanti Visheshank (1959–2009)* (Kolkata: Mithila Sanskritik Parishad, 26–7 December 2009).

Mishra, Panchanan, 'Rajneetik Dal O Maithili Natakak Patakshep Kahiya Dhari', in *Mithila Mihir* (31 May 1981).

Mishra, Panchanan, 'Samvidhan aa Maithili Battis Barakhak Upabandha Kahiya Dhari Mook Rahat?' in *Mithila Mihir* (30 January 1983).

Mishra, Uday Shankar, 'Mithila Putra Pt. Tarakant Jha', in Sureshwar Jha (ed.), *Mithila Tradition and Change Essays in Honour of Pt. Tarakant Jha* (Darbhanga: Tarakant Jha Felicitation Committee, 2008).

Mishra, Umesh, 'Mithila-Maithil-Maithili', in *Mithilank*, ed. Surendra Jha 'Suman' (Darbhanga: Mithila Mihir, 1936).

'Rajan', Rajaram Prasad, 'Maithili Bhasha Andolan me Vidyapati Parvak Prasangikata', in *Vaidehi* (February 1989): 267–9.

Jha Durganath, 'Shrish', *Maithili Sahityak Itihas*, Darbhanga, Bharati Pustak Kendra, Saal 1376, pp. 1–67.

Jha Surendra 'Suman', *Presidential Address of Akhil Bhartiya Maithili Sahitya Parishad on the Occasion of 55th Year* (Darbhanga: Maithili Diwas (Janaki Navami), 28–9 April 1985).

Jha Vidyanath 'Vidit', *Maithili O Santhali: Sampark Aa Samipya* (Patna: Maithili Akademi, 1977), pp. 21–39.

Autobiographies/Biographies, Felicitation Volumes, and Monographs

Mishra, Chandranath, 'Amar', *Kashikant Mishra 'Madhup'* (Delhi: Sahitya Akademi, 1994).

Mishra, Chandranath, *Ateet Manthan* (Darbhanga: Navratna Goshthi, 2010).

Anand, Vibhuti and Ashok Kumar Mehta (ed.), *Bhav Bhumi Raswant Bhimnath Jhak Samagra Mulyankan* (Darbhanga: Jakhan Takhan, 2011).

Bharadwaj, Mohan, *Ramkrishna Jha 'Kishun'* (Delhi: Sahitya Akademi, 2006).

Das, Jata Shankar, *Bhola Lal Das* (Delhi: Sahitya Akademi, 1999).

Hansraj, *Manipadma* (Delhi: Sahitya Akademi, 1996).

Jha, Bhimnath, *Upendra Thakur 'Mohan'* (Delhi: Sahitya Akademi, 1995).

Jha, Sureshwar, *Sanagharsha Aa Sehanta* (Darbhanga: Rambha Prakashan, 2009).

Jha, Khushilal, *Lakshminath Gosain* (Delhi: Sahitya Akademi, 2000).

Jha, Mahendra, *Shailendra Mohan Jha* (Delhi: Sahitya Akademi, 2000).

Jha, Govind, *Janam Abadhi Hum* (Patna: Navarambh, 2010).

Jha, Govind (ed.), *Jayakant Jayantika* (Patna: Shekhar Prakashan, 2010).

Jha, Purushottam (eds), *Ramanath Jha Abhinandan Granth* (Darbhanga: Shri Ramanath Jha Abhinandan Granth Samiti, 1968).

Jha, Ramanath, *Vidyapati* (Delhi: Sahitya Akademi, 1987).

Jha, Ramdeo, *Subhadra Jha* (Delhi: Sahitya Akademi, 2010).

Jha, Shailendra Mohan, *Harimohan Jha* (Delhi: Sahitya Akademi, 1994).

Jha, Sureshwar, *Babuaji Jha 'Agyat'* (Delhi: Sahitya Akademi, 1998).

Jha, Sureshwar, *Lakshman Jha* (Delhi: Sahitya Akademi, 2006).

Jha, Vednath, *Ishnath Jha* (Delhi: Sahitya Akademi, 1997).

'Kant', Shivshankar Jha, *Tantranath Jha* (Delhi: Sahitya Akademi, 1996).

Mishra, Jayamant, *Surendra Jha* (Delhi: Sahitya Akademi, 2005).

Mishra, Kulanand, *Kanchinath Jha 'Kiran'* (Delhi; Sahitya Akademi, 1998).

Mishra, Mayanand, *Akath Katha* (Supaul: Kisun Sankalplok, 2004).

Mishra, Girindra Mohan, *Kichhu Dekhal Kichhu Sunal* (Darbhanga: Pandit Madan Mohan Mishra, n.d).

Pathak, Amaresh, *Ramanath Jha* (Delhi: Sahitya Akademi, 1995).

Pathak, Amaresh (ed.), *Savyasanchi Dr. Ramdeo Jha: Samvet Sandarshan* (Darbhanga: Dr. Ramdeo Jha Abhinandan Grantha Samiti, 2011).

Vimal, Naresh Kumar, *Bhuvaneshwar Singh 'Bhuvan'* (Delhi: Sahitya Akademi, 2007).

Viyogi, Taranand, *Dhumketu* (Delhi: Sahitya Akademi, 2004).

Books

Ahmad, Humayun, *Nandit Narke*, orgnl. Bangla Maithili trs. Ramlochan Thakur (Ghaziabad: Antika Prakashan, 2011).

Mishra, Chandranath, 'Amar', *Maithili Sahitya Parishadak Sankshipta Itihas* (Darbhanga: Nav Bharat Press, 1969).

Mishra, Chandranath, 'Amar', *Maithili Patrakaritaak Itihaas* (Patna: Maithili Akademi, 1981).

Mishra, Chandranath, 'Amar', *Akhil Bhartiya Maithili Mahasabhak Sankshipta Itihas* (Darbhanga: Akhil Bhartiya Maithil Mahasabha, 1999).

Mishra, Chandranath (ed.), 'Amar', *Adhunik Maithili Rangmanch Atit Bartman O Bhavishya* (Delhi: Sahitya Akademi, 2008).

Bharadwaj, Mohan (ed.), *Maithili Patra Patrika* (Delhi; Sahitya Akademi, 2007).

Bharati, Om Prakash, *Maithilik Loknatya* (Sahibabad: Dharohar Kala, Sanskriti evam Sahitya Sansthan, 2009).

Chaudhary, Rajkamal, *Lalka Pag*, Shaharpura, Vidyapati Parishad, second edn, 2008 (1968).

Das, Rajnandan Lal, *Chitra–Vichitra*, colctn. and ed. Premshankar Singh (Kolkata: Karnagoshthi, 2006).

Das, Rajnandan Lal, *Munshi Raghunandan Das Vyaktitva O Krititva* (Kolkata: Karnagoshthi, 1983).

Das, Rajnandan Lal, *Swargiya Bholalal Das: Swargiya Rajeshwar Jha Vyaktitva and Krititva* (Kolkata: All India Maithil Sangha, 1978).

Das, Rajnandan Lal, *Santo* (Kolkata: Karnagoshthi, third reprint, 2009 [1968]).

Devi, Lalpari, *Nahi Kichhu Nahi* (Darbhanga: Abhilasha Prakashan, 2004).

Devi, Lalpari, *Kavishwarak Ramayanme Lokokti* (Darbhanga: Abhishek Prakashan, 2009).

Jha, Devkant, *A History of Modern Maithili Literature* (Delhi: Sahitya Akademi, reprint, 2007 [2004]).

Jha, Amarnath, *Kavishwar Chanda Jha O Hunak Mithila Bhasha Ramahyan* (Patna: Maithili Akademi, second edn, 2007 [1977]).

Jha, Bhimnath, *Parichayika* (Patna: Bhawani Prakashan, 1985).

Jha, Bhimnath, *Darbhangame Maithili-Sanstha* (Darbhanga: Vidyapati Seva Sansthan, 1987).

Jha, Bhimnath, *Vividha* (Darbhanga: Vidyapati Seva Sansthan, 1989).

Jha, Bhimnath, *Laghoottariya*, Dr Daman Kumar Jha (Darbhanga: Jakhan Takhan, 2003).

Jha, Bhimnath, *Vimarsha* (Darbhanga: Jakhan Takhan, 2003).

Jha, Indrakant, *Vidyapatikalin Mithila* (Patna: Maithili Akademi, 1986).

Jha, Indrakant, *Hathkari Baaji Uthal* (Patna: Indralaya Prakashan, third edn, 1989 [1980]).

Jha, Indrakant, *Vidyapati Kee Anupam Kathayen* (Patna: Indralaya Prakashan, 1989).

Jha, Indrakant (ed.), *Vidyapatikrit Likhnawali* (Patna: Indralaya Prakashan, 1990).

Jha, Indrakant, *Pahun Bilami Jau* (Patna: Navarambha, 2010).

Jha, Kamlakant, *Mithila Rajyak Punarsthapana* (Patna: Shekhar Prakashan, 2010).

Jha, Lakhman, *Vichar Chintamani*, colctd. and ed. Sureshwar Jha (Darbhanga: Mithila Mandal, 2002).

Jha, Raman, *Bhinna-Abhinna* (Madhubani: Suman Prakashan, 2008).

Jha, Shailendra Mohan, *Vidyapati* (Patna : Maithili Akademi, second edn, 1989 [1977]).

Jha, Sureshwar, *Swatantrata Andolan me Mithilak Yogdan* (Kolkata: Mithila Sanskritik Parishad, 1989).

Jha, Sureshwar (ed.), *Maithili Kavyak Vikash* (Delhi: Sahitya Akademi, reprint, 2009 [1998]).

Jha, Sureshwar, *Janak aaor Yagyavalkya* (Kolkata: Mithila Sanskritik Parishad, 1993).

Jha, Sureshwar, *Chintana O Archana* (Darbhanga: Rambha Prakashan, 2004).

Jha, Vasukinath (ed.), *Maithili Bhasha Sahitya Par Janjagaranak Prabhava* (Patna: Chetna Samiti, 2005).

Jha, Harimohan, *Khattar Kakak Tarang* (Vaishali: Janasidan Prakashan, third edn, 2009 [1999]).

Jha, Harimohan, *Pranamya Devta* (Vaishali: Janasidan Prakashan, 2001).

Jha, Lakshman and Lakshminarayan Singh, *Mithila Bhasha O Aarthik Sthiti* (Darbhanga: Mithila Mandal, n.d.).

Jha, Parmeshwar, *Mithila Tatva Vimarsha* (ed.), Govind Jha (Patna: Maithili Akademi, 1977).

Jha, Govind, *Maithilik Udgam O Vikas* (Kolkata: Maithili Prakashan Samiti, 1968).

Jha, Govind, *Maithili Parichayika* (Patna: Shekhar Prakashan, 2007).

Jha, Govind, *Maithili Parishilan* (Patna: Maithili Akademi, 2007).

Jha, Govind, *Anuchintan* (Patna: Navarambha, 2010).

Jha, Ramdeo, *Bahinak Virog* (Darbhanga: Mithila Research Society, 2002).

Jha, Ramdeo, *Ramjodi Kagatak Pankhipar* (Darbhanga: Mithila Research Society, 2002).

Jha, Ramdeo, *Aaji Maa* (Darbhanga: Mithila Research Society, 2009).

Jha, Ramdeo, *Angrejeephulak Chithee* (Darbhanga: Mithila Research Society, 2002).

Jha, Shankardev, *Amarjeek Parichaya-Sansar O Patrachar* (Darbhanga: Navaratna Gosthi, 2001).

Lalit, *Prithviputra*, (Patna: Maithili Akademi, third edn, 2002 [1984]).

Malangiya, Mahendra (ed.), *Maithili Ekanki Sangraha* (Delhi: Sahitya Akademi, 2003).

Mallick, Virendra, *Agni–Shikha* (Kolkata; Karnagoshthi, 2006).

Mallick, Rajkumar, *Kathopanishad (Maithili Vyakhya)* (Kolkata: Mithila Sanskritik Parishad, 1993).

'Manipadma', Brajkishor Verma, *Dulara Dayal* (Kolkata: Mithila Sanskritik Parishad, 1984).

'Manipadma', Brajkishor Verma, *Sahityakarak Din*, colct. and edn, Prem Shankar Singh (Kolkata: Mithila Sanskritik Parishad, 2007).

'Manipadma', Brajkishor Verma, *Lorik Vijaya* (Kolkata: Sanskritik Parishad, third edn, 2009 [1970]).

Singh, Prafull Kumar and Naveen Chaudhary, 'Maun', *Manipadmak Patra* (Kolkata: Karnagoshthi, 2006).

Mishra, Anand and Govind Jha (ed.), *Varnratnakar* (Patna: Maithili Akademi, 1980).

Mishra, Anand and Mohan Bharadwaj (ed.), *Kriti Rajkamalak* (Patna: Maithili Akademi, second edn, 2006 ([1980]).

Mishra, Deep Narain, *Mithila Rajya Vimarsha* (Darbhanga: Santosh Prakashan, 2009).

Mishra, Girindra Mohan, *Kichhu Dekhal Kichhu Sunal* (Laheriasara:, Nava-Bharat Press, n.d.).

Mishra, Jayakant, *Maithili Sahityak Itihas* (Delhi: Sahitya Akademi, reprint, 2009 [1998]).

Mishra, Kishori Kant, *Chayanika* (Kolkata: Mithila Sanskritik Parishad, 2009).

Mishra, Mayanand, *Maithili Sahityak Itihas* (Supaul: Kishun Sankalp Lok, 2014).

Mishra, Panchanan, *Maithili Samaj* (Patna: Shekhar Prakashan, 2007).

Mishra, Shambhunath, *Maithilik Dadhichi Babu Bholalal Das* (Kolkata: Karnagoshthi, 1991).

Pandav, Madhyam (Bhim Nath Jha), *Parichayika* (Patna: Vaidehi Pustak Bhandar, 1978).

Pathak, Amaresh, *Maithili Upanyasak Aalochanatmak Adhyayan* (Patna: Aalok Prakashan, second edn, 2007 [1975]).

Putra, Maithili, 'Pradeep', *Nampat* (Darbhanga: Dr. Ramanarayan Jha, 2008).

Prasad, Raja Ram, *Katha Paridhi* (Darbhanga: Abhilasha Prakashan, 1997).

Prasad, Raja Ram, *Maithili Loknatya* (Darbhanga: Abhishek Prakashan, 2010).

Jha, Ramanand, 'Raman', *Maithili Sahitya O Rajneeti* (Madhubani: Akhiyasal Prakashan, 1994).

Jha, Ramanand (ed.), 'Raman', *Maithilik Aarambhik Katha* (Patna: Adheet Prakashan, 1998).

Jha, Ramanand, 'Raman', *Besahal* (Madhubani: Akhiyasal Prakashan, 2003).

Jha, Ramanand (ed.), 'Raman', *Maithilik Aarambhik Yatra Sahitya* (Madhubani: Akhiyasal Prakashan, 2009).

Jha, Ramanand (ed.), 'Raman', *George A. Grierson Geet Deenabhadrik O Geet Nevarak*, trs. Govind Jha (Madhubani: Akhiyasal Prakashan, 2010).

Jha, Lakshman, 'Sagar', *Uchair Baisu Kauwa* (Guwahati: Manju Pathak Memorial Trust, 2010).

Jha, Jayakant, 'Shrutdhar', *Maithili Bhasha Aa Sahitya* (Kolkata: Mithila Sanskritik Parishad, 1961).

Jha, Surendra (ed.), 'Suman', *Vidyapatikrit Purush Pariksha* (Patna: Maithili Akademi, second edn., 1988 [1983]).

Thakur, Ramlochan, *Apoorva* (Kolkata: Mithila Samad, 1996).

Thakur, Ramlochan, *Lakh Prashna Anootarit* (Babupali/Kolkata: Aroonodaya Prakashan, 2003).

Thakur, Ramlochan, *Maithili Lok Katha* (Babupali/Kolkata: Aroonodaya Prakashan, 2006).

Thakur, Upendra, *Mithilak Itihas* (Patna: 1992).

Thakur, Veena, *Itihas Darpan* (Darbhanga: Shri Ram Ratan Jha, 2008).

Viyogi, Taranand, *Desil Bayana Swatantrottar Maithili Katha* (Delhi: National Book Trust, 2007).

Hindi

Speeches, Articles, and Parts of Magazines and Periodicals

'Benipuri', Rambriksha, 'Vidyapati aur Hamara Kartabya', in *Mithilank* (ed.), Surendra Jha 'Suman' (Darbhanga: Mithila Mihir, 1936): 84–5.

Chatterjee, Suniti Kumar, 'Maithili Bhasha aur Sanskriti', in *Mithilank* (ed.), Surendra Jha 'Suman' (Darbhanga: Mithila Mihir, 1936), pp. 3–6.

Jha, Hetukar, *Lakshmishwar Singh Aur Hamara Samaj*. Maharaja Lakshmishwar Singh Memorial Lecture, Darbhanga, M.L.S.M. College (30 December 2009).

Jha, Hetukar, 'Chaudahavi–Pandrahavi Sadi Aur Uske Bad Mithila ki Samajik Stithi: Ek Samajshastriya Avalokan.' *Presidential Address, Second Bi-annual National Conference* (Darbhanga: Mithila Itihas Sansthan, 2011).

Presidential address of Amarnath Jha, 'Hindi Bhasha aur Sahitya', at the Abohar, 30th session of Akhil Bharatvarshiya Hindi-Sahitya-Sammelan (27–30 December 1941).

Books

Dikshit, Mathura Prasad, *Govind–Geetavali*. Ramlochan Sharan (ed.) (Laheria Sarai: Pustak Bhandar, n. d.)

Dwivedi, Hazari Prasad, *Hindi Sahitya Ka Aadikal* (Patna: Bihar Rashtra Bhasha Parishad, fourth edn, 1980 [1952]).

Dwivedi, Hazari Prasad, *Bhasha Sahitya aur Desh* (Delhi: Bharatiya Jnanpeeth, 1995).

Gorakhpuri, Firaq, *Urdu Bhasha aur Sahitya* (Lucknow: Uttar Pradesh Hindi Sansthan, 1962).

Hrischandra, Bhartendu, *Hindi Bhasha* (Patna: Khadagvilas Press, 1883).

Jha, Amarnath, *Vichardhara* (Allahabad: Kitab Mahal, 1948).

Sahay, Shiva Pujan, *Hindi Sahitya Aur Bihar*, Part-1 (Patna: Bihar Rashtra Bhasha Parishad, 1960).

Sharma, Ramawtar, *Parmarthdarshan*, trs. Harimohan Jha (Patna: Bihar Rashtra Bhasha Parishad, 1986).

Sharma, Radhavallabh, *Maithili Sanskar Geet* (Patna: Bihar Rashtra Bhasha Parishad, 1986).

Shrivastava, Virendra (ed.), *Kavikokil Vidyapatikrit Kirtilata* (Patna: Bihar Rashtra Bhasha Parishad, 1983).

Shukla, R.C., *Hindi Sahitya ka Itihas* (Kashi: Nagari Pracharini Sabha, reprint, 1990 [1929]).

Singh, Kripashankar, *Hindi–Urdu–Hindustani, Hindu Muslim Sampradayikta aur Aangrezi Raj 1800–1947* (Delhi: Prasangikta Prakashan, 1992).

Singh, Kumar Ganganand (eds), *Vidyapati–Padawali*, Part-1 (Patna: Bihar Rashtra Bhasha Parishad, 1972).

Singh, Kumar Ganganand (eds), *Vidyapati–Padawali*, Part-2 (Patna: Bihar Rashtra Bhasha Parishad, second edn, 2004 [1989]).

Singh, Lakshamipati (eds), *Vidyapati–Padawali*, Part-3 (Patna: Bihar Rashtra Bhasha Parishad, 1979).

Singh, Rambujhavan, *Hindi Sahitya Aur Bihar*, Part-V (Patna; Bihar Rashtra Bhasha Parishad, n.d.).

Tiwari, Hans Kumar, *Hindi Sahitya Aur Bihar*, Part 3 (Patna: Bihar Rashtra Bhasha Parishad, 1976).

English

Project Reports/Official Documents/Memorandums/Private Papers and Pamphlets

A Memorandum for Inclusion of Maithili in The Eighth Schedule of the Indian Constitution, submitted to the Honourable Prime Minister, Govt. of India, 7 May, Presented by Darbhanga, Vidyapati Seva Sansthan, Delhi, Akhil Bhartiya Mithila Sangh (Kolkata: Mithila Vikas Parishad, 2003).

Ahmad, Z.A. *National Language for India (A Symposium)* (Allahabad: Kitabistan, 1941).

C.W. J.C. No. 2263 of 1992, Binay Kumar Mishra Versus State of Bihar and others; C.W. J.C. No. 3379 of 1992, Praveen Kumar Jha and others Versus The state of Bihar and others; C.W. J.C. No. 3624 of 1992 Indra Kumar Thakur Versus the state of Bihar and others; C.W. J.C. No. 3669 of 1992 Chetana Samiti Versus the state of Bihar and others; C.W. J.C. No. 5160 of

1994, Narayan Jha and others Versus the state of Bihar and others; C.W. J.C. No. Navchetna through its secretary Satish Chandra Jha Versus the state of Bihar and others, Patna High Court Judgment, dated 30 October 2000.

Jha, Hetukar. *Nation-Building in a North Indian Region: The Case of Mithila* (Patna: A.N. Sinha Research Institute, 1976).

Memorial to His Excellency the Right Honourable Baron Sinha of Raipur, K.C., K.C.S.I., Governor of Bihar and Orissa From Maharajadhiraja of Darbhanga (Allahabad: The Pioneer Press, 1921).

Mishra, Dip Narain. *Emerging Pattern of Regionalism and National Integration: A Case Study of Mithila Raj Movement, Final Report (2002–2005)*, U.G.C. Supported Major Research Project in Political Science, No–F-5-3000/2001 (HRP) (Darbhanga: L.N.M.U., 2005).

Mishra, J., *The Case of Maithili before Sahitya Akademi* (New Delhi: 1963).

Mishra, Umesha, 'Foreword', in Proceedings of the Fourteenth All India Oriental Conference Darbhanga (Mithila), vol.–1, Mahamahopadhyaya Dr. Umesh Mishra, Local Secretary, XIV All India Oriental Conference, University of Allahabad (1949).

Ray, Rabindra, 'The Indianization of The Maithils.' *Project Report No. 29* (Allahabad: Govind Ballabh Pant Social Science Institute, 1987).

Report of the State Reorganisation Commission, Govt. of India, Publication Division (1955).

Singh, Janaki Nandan Singh, *Memorandum for the Formation of The Mithila State* (Darbhanga: Shri Janaki Nandan Singh, 1954).

Singh, U.N., P.K. Bose, and N. Rajaram, 'The Maithili Language Movement in North Bihar a Sociolinguistic Investigation.' *Department of Linguistics, Surat, South Gujarat University* (1985).

Sinha, Jayadhari, *Claims of Maithili for the Indian Constitution* (Darbhanga: Akhil Bharatiya Maithili Sahitya Parishad, 1967).

The Secretary, Maithili Sahitya Parishad, *The case of Maithili before the Patna University* (Darbhanga: Raj Press, 1933).

Speeches, Articles, Book Chapters and Essays in Magazines, Journals, and Periodicals

Amadutias's Johannes Christophorous, *Preface* in Cassiano Beligetti, *Alphabeticum Brahmanicum* (Rome: Italy, 1771).

Bailey, F.G., 'The Oriya Movement', *The Economic Weekly* (26 September 1959): 1331–8.

Bean, S., 'Linguistic Variation and the Caste System in South Asia', *Indian Linguistics*, vol. 35, no. 4 (1974).

Buchanan, Francis, *An Account of District of Purnea in 1809–10* (ed.) V.H. Jackson (Patna: Bihar and Orissa Research Society, 1928).

Buchanan, Francis, *An Account of the District of Bhagalpur in 1810–11* (Patna: Bihar and Orissa Research Society, 1939).

Burghart, Richard. 'A Quarrel in the Language Family: Agency and Representation of Speech in Mithila', *Modern Asian Studies*, vol. 27, no. 4 (October 1993): 761–804.

Chatterjee, P. 'Our Modernity', *Rotterdam/Dakar, South–South Exchange Programme for Research on the History of Development (SEPHIS) and the Council for the Development of Social Science Research in Africa (CODESRIA)* (1997).

Clark, Katerina and Michael Holquist, 'Marxism and the Philosophy of Language', in their (eds.), *Mikahil Bakhtin* (Cambridge, MA: Harvard University Press, 1984), pp. 212–37.

Cohn, Bernard S., 'The Command of Language and the Language of Command', in Ranjit Guha (ed.), *Subaltern Studies, Vol. IV* (New Delhi: Oxford University Press, 1985), pp. 276–329.

Cohn, Bernard S., 'The Census, Social Structure and Objectification in South Asia', in his *An Anthropologist among the Historians and other Essays* (Delhi: Oxford University Press, 1987), pp. 224–54.

Dua, H.R., 'Dimensions of Language Identity: Dynamics of Language Symbols and Functions', *Indian Journal of Linguistics*, no. 9 (1982).

Errington, J., 'Colonial Linguistics', *Annual Review of Anthropology*, vol. 30 (2001): 19–39

Friedrich, Paul, 'Language and Politics in India.' *Daedalus* (summer, 1962).

Ghosh, A., 'An Uncertain "coming of the Book" Early Print Cultures in Colonial India', *Book History*, vol. 6 (2003).

Heller, Monica, 'Language Choice, Social Institutions and Symbolic Domination', *Language in Society*, vol. 24, no. 3 (September 1995): 373–405.

Herder, Johann Gottfried, 'Treatise on the Origin of Language', in Michael N. Forster (ed.), *Herder Philosophical Writings* (Cambridge: Cambridge University Press, [1772]).

Home, education department, dated March 12, (Accessed at National Archives of India, New Delhi) 1856.

Home, educational department, dated 22 December, (Accessed at National Archives of India, New Delhi), 1859.

Hutton, W. H. (ed.), 'A Letter of Warren Hastings on the Civil Service of the East India Company', *English Historical Review*, vol. xliv. (1929).

Jha, Aniruddha, 'Maharajadhiraja Dr. Sir Kameshwar Singh', in Hetukar Jha (ed.), *Courage and Benevolence: Maharaja Kameshwar Singh (1907–1962)* (Darbhanga: Maharajadhiraja Kameshwar Singh Kalyani Foundation, 2007), pp. 414–24.

Jha, Hetukar, 'Elite–Mass Contradiction in Mithila in Historical Perspective', in Sachidananda and A.K. Lal (eds), *Elite and Development* (New Delhi: Concept, 1980).

Jha, Hetukar, *Man in Indian Tradition: Vidyapati's Discourse on Purusa* (New Delhi: Aryan Books International, 2002), pp. 1–32, 110–19.

Jha, Hetukar (ed.), 'Movement for Mithila State', in *Courage and Benevolence: Maharaja Kameshwar Singh (1907–1962)* (Darbhanga: Maharajadhiraja Kameshwar Singh Kalyani Foundation, 2007), pp. 133–47.

Jha, Hetukar, 'Lakshmishwar Singh (1858–1898) aur Hamara Samaj'. *Maharaja Lakshmishwar Singh Memorial Lecture* (Darbhanga: Maharaja Lakshmishwar Singh Memorial College, 30 December 2009).

Jha, Makhan, *Civilizational Regions of Mithila & Mahakoshal* (Delhi: Capital Publishing House, 1982), pp. 160–239.

Jha, Raj Chandra, 'Mithila Movement', in Sureshwar Jha (ed.), *Mithila Tradition and Change Essays in Honour of Pt. Tarakant Jha* (Darbhanga: Tarakant Jha Felicitation Committee, 2008).

Inden, R., 'Orientalist Constructions of India', *Modern Asian Studies*, vol. 20, no. 3 (1986): 401–46.

Kaviraj, Sudipta, 'Writing, Speaking, Being: Language and the Historical Formation of Identities in India', in Dagmar Hellmann Rajnaygam and Deitmar Rothermund (ed.), *Nationalstaat und sprachkonflikte in Sud-und Sudostasien* (Heidelberg: Sidasien Institut, 1992).

Kaviraj, Sudipta, 'The Imaginary Institution of India', in Partha Chatterjee and Gyandendra Pandey (eds), *Subaltern Studies, vol. VII* (New Delhi: Oxford University Press, 1992).

Kar, M., 'Assam's Language Questions in Retrospect', *Social Scientist*, vol. 4, no. 2 (September 1975): 21–35.

Kumar, Aishwarj, 'A Marginalized Voice in the History of Hindi', *Modern Asian Study*, vol. 47, no. 05 (September 2013): 1706–46.

Kumar, Krishna, 'Quest for Self-Identity: Cultural Consciousness and Education in Hindi Region, 1880–1950', *Economic and Political Weekly*, vol. 25, no. 23 (9 June 1990).

Lelyveld, David, 'Colonial Knowledge and the Fate of Hindustani', *Comparative Studies in Society and History*, vol. 35, no. 4 (October 1993).

Madan, T.N., 'Linguistic Diversity and National Unity: Dimensions of a Debate', in C.H. Hanumantha and P.C. Joshi (eds), *Reflections on Economic Development and Social Change* (Delhi: Allied, 1979), pp. 393–410.

Mishra, Harinath, 'Minority Language of Bihar', *Indian Nation* (22 February 1970).

'Opening Address of the Maharajadhiraja of Darbhanga at the Oriental Conference, Held at Benaras on the 31st December 1943' and his private correspondence and other speeches, in Hetukar Jha (ed.), *Courage and Benevolence: Maharaja Kameshwar Singh (1907–1962)* (Darbhanga: Maharajadhiraja Kameshwar Singh Kalyani Foundation, 2007), pp. 325–42.

Orsini, Francesca, 'What Did They Mean by 'Public'? Language Literature and the Politics of Nationalism'. *Economic and Political Weekly* (13 February 1999).

'Parliament and the Press by the Maharajadhiraja of Darbhanga Member Rajya Sabha Paper Read at The Seminar on Parliamentary Democracy' (December 1957). Hetukar Jha (ed.), *Courage and Benevolence: Maharaja Kameshwar Singh (1907–1962)* (Darbhanga: Maharajadhiraja Kameshwar Singh Kalyani Foundation, 2007), pp. 350–5.

Pollock, Sheldon, 'The Cosmopolitan Vernacular', *The Journal of Asian Studies*, vol. 57, no. 1 (February 1998): 6.

Pollock, Sheldon, 'India in the Vernacular Millennium: Literary Culture and Polity, 1000–1500'. *Daedalus*, vol. 127, no. 3, Early Modernities (Summer 1998): 41.

Pollock, Sheldon, 'Deep Orientalism Notes on Sanskrit and Power Beyond the Raj', in Peter van der Veer and Carol A. Breckenridge (eds), *Orientalism and the Postcolonial Predicament: Perspective on South Asia New Cultural Studies* (Pennsylvania: University of Pennsylvania Press, 1993).

Prasad, Ishvari Nandan, 'The Youngest Legislator of India The Biography of The Hon'ble Maharajadhiraja Sir Kameshwar Singh Bahadur, K.C.I.E. of Darbhanga', in Hetukar Jha (ed.), *Courage and Benevolence: Maharaja Kameshwar Singh (1907–1962)* (Darbhanga: Maharajadhiraja Kameshwar Singh Kalyani Foundation, 2007), pp. 388–411.

Proceedings of the Fourteenth All India Oriental Conference, vol. I, Darbhanga (Mithila), Mahamahopadhyaya Dr Umesh Mishra, M.A., D. LITT, Local Secretary, XIV All India Oriental Conference, University of Allahabad (1948): 1–17, 132–7, 153–205, 244–6.

Rai, Alok, 'Thinking through Hindi', in Rajeev Bhargava and Helmut Reifeld (eds), *Civil Society, Public Sphere and Citizenship, Dialogue and Perceptions* (New Delhi, Sage Publications, 2005).

Prasad, Rajaram, 'Rajan.' *Maithili Bhasha Andolanme Vidyapati Parvak Prasangikata, Vaidehi* (February 1989): 267–9.

Raju, A. Raghuram, 'Problematising Nationalism', *Economic and Political Weekly*, vol. 28, no. 27/28 (3–10 July 1993).

Sahoo, Pareshwar, 'Formation of Orissa as a Separate State', *Orissa Review* (April 2006): 67–9, accessed through http://orissa.gov.in/emagazine/Orissareview/April2006/engpdf/formation_of_orissa_as_separate.pdf accessed on 15 March 2013, at 12 am.

Sarangi, Asha, 'Enumeration and the Linguistic Identity Formation in Colonial North India', *Studies in History*, vol. 25, no. 2, n.s. (2009): 197–227.

Schwartzberg, Joseph, 'Factors in Linguistic Reorganization of Indian states', in Wallace (ed.), *Region and Nation in India* (New Delhi: American Institute of Indian Studies, 1985).

Seth, D.L., 'The Great Language Debate Politics of Metropolitan versus Vernacular India', in Upendra Baxi and Bhikhu Parekh (eds), *Crisis and Change in Contemporary India* (Delhi: Sage Publications, 1995).

Singh, Uday Narayan, 'Crises of Maithili Litterateurs', in *Muse India*, issue 12 (March–April 2007), accessed through http://www.museindia.com/viewarticle.asp?myr=2007 &issid =12&id=585 accessed on 28 August 2009.

Sinha, Jayadhari, 'Claim of Maithili as Language and Literature', Patna, *Searchlight* (5 April 1970).

Thakur, Manish Kumar, 'The Politics of Minority Languages: Some Reflections on Maithili Language Movement', *Journal of Social and Economic Development*, vol. IV, no. 2 (July–December 2002).

Thakur, Vidyanand, *Mithila*, part–First, Purnea, Shri Shankaranand Thakur, President, Maithili Sahitya Bhawan (1936), pp. 152–97.

The Notice of Amendment given by The Maharajadhiraja of Darbhanga on the 24th August 1947 and repeated on the 25th August 1947, in Hetukar Jha (ed.), *Courage and Benevolence: Maharaja Kameshwar Singh (1907–1962)* (Darbhanga: Maharajadhiraja Kameshwar Singh Kalyani Foundation, 2007), p. 140.

The speech of the Maharajadhiraja of Darbhanga in the Constituent Assembly, in Hetukar Jha (ed.), *Courage and Benevolence: Maharaja Kameshwar Singh (1907–1962)* (Darbhanga: Maharajadhiraja Kameshwar Singh Kalyani Foundation, 2007), pp. 141–2.

The Telegram sent by Ganganand Singh to the Secretary, Constituent Assembly of India, New Delhi on 12 July 1947 from Darbhanga and confirmed by post on 29 July 1947 from Delhi. See Jha, Hetukar (ed.), *Courage and Benevolence: Maharajadhiraja Kameshwar Singh 1907–1947* (Darbhanga: Maharajadhiraja Kameshwar Singh Kalyani Foundation, 2007), p. 136.

Washbrook, D., 'To Each a Language of His Own: Language, Culture and Society in Colonial India'. Penelope J. Coerfield (ed.), *Language History and Class* (Oxford: Blackwell, 1991).

Windhausen, John D., 'The Vernaculars, 1835–1839: A Third Medium for Indian Education', *Sociology of Education*, vol. 37, no. 3 (Spring 1964): 254–70.

Yang, Anand A. and James R. Hagen, 'Local Sources for the Study of Rural India: The Village Notes of Bihar'. *The Indian Economic and Social History Review*, vol. 13, no. 1 (January–March 1976).

Autobiographies/ Biographies, Felicitation Volumes, and Monographs

Jha, Hetukar, *Amarnatha Jha* (Delhi: Sahitya Akademi, 1997).

Jha, Hetukar, *Ganganath Jha*, Maithili trs. Ritunath Jha (Delhi: Sahitya Akademi, 2003).

Jha, Sureshwar (ed.), *Mithila Tradition and Change Essays in Honour of Pt. Tarakant Jha* (Darbhanga: Tarakant Jha Felicitation Committee, 2008).

Mishra, Jayadeva, *Chanda Jha* (Delhi: Sahitya Akademi, 1981).

Books

Aggarwal, N.K., *A Bibliography of Studies on Hindi Language and Linguistics* (Gurgaon: Indian Documentation Centre, 1978).

Alam, Muzaffar, *The Language of Political Islam in India, 1200–1800* (Delhi: Permanent Black, 2004).

Ambedkar, B.R., *Thoughts on Linguistic States* (Aligarh: Anand Sahitya Sadan, 1987).

Anderson, Benedict, *Imagined Communities: Reflections on the Origin and spread of Nationalism* (London: Verso, 1991).

Annamalai, E., *Managing Multilingualism in India: Political and Linguistic Manifestations* (Delhi: Sage Publications, 2001).

Aquil, Raziuddin and Partha Chatterjee (eds), *History in the Vernacular* (Ranikhet: Permanent Black, 2008).

Aquique, Md. *Economic History of Mithila* (New Delhi: Abhinav Publication, 1974).

Austin, Granville, *The Constitution of India: Cornerstone of a Nation* (New Delhi: Oxford University Press, 2009).

Ayer, Alfred Jules, *Language, Truth and Logic* (New York: Dover Publication, 1952).

Basu, Anathnath (ed.), *Report on the State of Education in Bengal (1835 and 1838) by William Adam* (Kolkata: University of Kolkata, 1941).

Basu, Aparna, *The Growth of Education and Political Development in India 1800–1920* (Delhi: Oxford University Press, 1974).

Basu, Sajal, *Regional Movements Politics of Language, Ethnicity, Identity* (New Delhi: Manohar Publication, 1992).

Bhargava, Rajeev and Helmut Reifeld (eds), *Civil Society, Public Sphere and Citizenship, Dialogue and Perceptions* (New Delhi: Sage Publications, 2005).

Bloomfield, L., *Language* (New York: Holt, 1933).

Bourdieu, Pierre, *Language and Symbolic Power* (Cambridge, MA: Harvard University Press, 1991).

Brass, Paul, *Language, Religion and Politics in North India* (Cambridge: Cambridge University Press, 1974).

Chakladar, Snehamoy, *Sociolinguistics: A Guide to Language Problem in India* (New Delhi: Mittal Publication, 1990).

Chandra, Sudhir, *The Oppressive Present, Literature and Social Consciousness in Colonial India* (Delhi: Oxford University Press, 1992).

Chatterjee, Partha, *Nation and Its Fragments* (Delhi: Oxford University Press, 1995).

Chatterji, Suniti Kumar, *Select Writings*, vol. I (New Delhi: Vikas Publishing House, 1978).

Chatterji, Suniti Kumar, *India: A Polyglot Nation and its Linguistic Problem Vis-à-vis National Integration* (Mumbai: Mahatma Gandhi Research Centre, 1973).

Chaudhary, Indra Kumar, *Some Aspects of Social Life of Medieval Mithila (1350–1750 A.D.)* (Patna: K. P. Jayaswal Research Institute, 1988).

Chaudhary, Radhakrishna, *A Survey of Maithili Literature* (Deoghar: Shanti Devi, 1976).

Chaudhary, Radhakrishna, *Mithila in the Age of Vidyapati* (Varanasi: Chaukhambha Orientalia, 1976).

Chomsky, Noam, *On Language* (New Delhi: Penguin Books, 2003).

Cohn, B.S., *Colonialism and Its Forms of Knowledge* (Delhi: Oxford University Press, 1986).

Cooper, R.L., *Language Planning and Social Change* (Cambridge: Cambridge University Press, 1989).

Dalmia, Vasudha, *The Nationalization of Hindu Traditions* (Delhi: Oxford University Press, 1997).

Dalton, Dennis, *Indian Idea of Freedom: Political Thought of Swami Vivekananda, Aurobindo Ghosh, Mahatma Gandhi and Rabindranath Tagore* (Cambridge, MA: The Academic Press, 1982).

Das, Sisir Kumar, *A History of Indian Literature 1800–1910: Western Impact, Indian Impact* (New Delhi: Sahitya Akademi, 1991).

Dasgupta, Jyotindra, *Language Conflict and National Development Group Politics and National Language Policy in India* (Mumbai: Oxford University Press, 1970).

Datta, Kali Kinkar (ed.), *The Comprehensive History of Bihar*, Part I and II (Patna: K.P. Jayaswal Research Institute, 1976).

Deshpande, Madhav, *Social Linguistic Attitudes in India* (Ann Arbor: Karoma, 1979).

Deutsch, K.W., *Nationalism and Social Communication: An Inquiry into the Foundations of Nationality* (Cambridge: MIT Press, 1953).

Diwakar, R.R., gen. ed., *Bihar Through the Ages* (Patna: K.P. Jayaswal Research Institute, 1959).

Dua, H.R., *Communication Policy and Language Planning* (Mysore: Yashoda Publications, 1991).

Edelman, Murray, *Political Language: Words That Succeed and Policies That Fail*, New York, Academic Press, 1977.

Edwards, John, *Language Society and Identity* (London: Basil Blackwell in association with Andre Deutsch, 1985).

Fallon, S.W., *A New Hindustani—English Dictionary, Hindustani Literature and Folk Lore* (Benaras: The Medical Hall Press, 1879).

Fishman, Joshua, *Readings in the Sociology of Language* (The Hague: Mouton, 1968).

Fishman, Joshua (ed.), *Language Modernization and Planning in Advance in Language Planning* (The Hague: Montou, 1974).

Foster, William (ed.), *The Embassy of Sir Thomas Roe to India, 1615–19* (Cambridge: Cambridge University Press, 1926).

Foucault, Michel, *Language, Counter memory and Practice: Selected Essays and Interviews*, trs. D. Bouchard and Sherry Simon (New Haven: Cornell University Press, 1977).

Foucault, Michel, *The Order of Things* (New York : Vintage, 1973).

Gandhi, Mohandas Karamchand, *Thoughts on National Language* (Ahmedabad: Navajivan Publishing House, 1956).

Grierson, George, *Seven Grammars of the Dialects and Subdialects of the Bihari Language, 1884.*

Grierson, George, *Linguistic Survey of India* (Low Price Publications, 1994).

Grierson, George, *An Introduction to the Maithili Language of North Bihar* (Kolkata: Asiatic Society, 1881).

Grierson, George, *Linguistic Survey of India Vol. I, Part I* (Delhi: Motilal Banarsidass, reprint, 1967 [1927]).

Geetha, K.R., *A Classified Bibliography of Linguistic Research on Indian Languages, vol.1 (Hindi Speaking States)* (Mysore: Central Institute of Indian Languages, 1983).

Halhed, N., *A Grammar of the Bengali Language* (Hooghly: reprint, 1969 [1778]).

Henningham, Stephen, *A Great Estate and Its Landlords in Colonial India, Darbhanga 1860–1942* (New Delhi: Oxford University Press, 1990).

Huppe, Bernard F., *Logic and Language* (New York: Alfred A. Knopf, 1956).

Hudson, Kenneth, *Language of Modern Politics* (London: Macmillan Press, 1980).

Hutchinson, John and Anthony D. Smith, *Nationalism* (Oxford: Oxford University Press, 2000).

Inden, Ronald, *Imaginary India* (Oxford: Basil Blackwell, 1990).

Jha, Chanda, 'Vijnapan', in *Purush Paiksha* (Darbhanga: Darbhanga Raj Press, 1888).

Jha, Harimohan, *Trends of Linguistic Analysis in Indian Philosophy* (Varanasi: Chaukhambha Orientalia, 1981).

Jha, Hetukar, *Social Structure of Indian Villages: A Study of Rural Bihar* (New Delhi: Sage Publications, 1991).

Jha, Hetukar (ed.), *A Glimpse of Tirhut in the Second Half of the Nineteenth Century: Riaz-i-Tirhut of Ayodhya Prasad "Bahar"*, Kameshwar Singh Bihar

Heritage Series–3 (Darbhanga: Maharajadhiraja Kameshwar Singh Kalyani Foundation, 1997).

Jha, Hetukar (ed.), *Mithila in the Nineteenth Century: Aina-i-Tirhut of Bihari Lal 'Fitrat'*, Kameshwar Singh Bihar Heritage Series 5 (Darbhanga Maharajadhiraja Kameshwar Singh Kalyani Foundation, 2001).

Jha, Hetukar (ed.), *Tirhut in Early Twentieth Century: Mithila Darpan of Ras Bihari Lal Das*, Kameshwar Singh Bihar Heritage Series 8 (Darbhanga: Maharajadhiraja Kameshwar Singh Kalyani Foundation, 2005).

Jha, Hetukar and Vednath Jha (eds), *Maithili Chrestomathy and Vocabulary by George A. Grierson* (Darbhanga: Maharjadhiraja Kameshwar Singh Kalyani Foundation, 2009).

Jha, Hira Kant, *Growth and Problems of Printing Industry* (New Delhi: Inter-India Publications, 1986).

Jha, J.C., *Migration and Achievements of Mithila Panditas* (Patna: Janaki Prakashan, 1991).

Jha, Jata Shankar, *History of Darbhanga Raj* (Patna; K.P. Jayaswal Research Institute, 1972).

Jha, Jata Shankar, *Biography of an Indian Patriot Maharaja Lakshmishwar Singh of Darbhanga* (Patna: Maharaja Lakshmishwar Singh Smarak Samiti, 1972).

Jha, Jata Shankar, *Beginnings of Modern Education in Mithila* (Patna: K. P. Jayaswal Research Institute, 1972).

Jha, Jata Shankar, *Education in Bihar* (Patna: K.P. Jayaswal Research Institute, 1979).

Jha, Lakshman, *Mithila A Union Republic* (Darbhanga: Mithila Mandal, 1952).

Jha, Lakshman, *Mithila in India* (Darbhanga; Mithila Mandal, 1953).

Jha, Pankaj Kumar, *The Colonial Periphery Imagining Mithila* (Patna: Janaki Prakashan, 2002).

Jha, Shailendra Kumar, *History of University Legislations in Bihar (1917–1985)* (Patna: K.P. Jayaswal Research Institute, 1991).

Jha, Shashi Shekhar, *Political Elite in Bihar* (Mumbai: Vora & Co. Publishers, 1972).

Jha, Subhadra, *The Formation of Maithili Language* (London: Luzac, 1958).

Jha, Sunil Kumar, *Maithili Some Aspects of Its Phonetics and Phonology* (Delhi: Motilal Banarsidas, 2001).

Jones, M., *Clive of India* (London: Constable and Robinson Ltd., 1974).

Karat, Prakash, *Language and Nationality Politics in India* (Delhi: Orient Longman, 1973).

Keer, Dhananjay, *Veer Savarakar* (Mumbai: Popular Prakashan, 1966).

Kesavan, B.S., *Origins of Printing and Publishing in Hindi Heartland* (Delhi: National Book Trust, 1997).

King, Christopher, *One Language Two Scripts: The Hindi Movement in Nineteenth Century North India* (Mumbai: Oxford University Press, 1994).

Kumar, Krishna, *The Political Agenda of Education* (New Delhi: Sage Publications, 1991).

Lohia, Ram Manohar, *Language* (Hyderabad: Ram Manohar Lohia Nyas, 1986).

Lukes, Steven, *Power* (Oxford: Basil Blackwell, 1986).

Majeed, Javed, *Ungoverned Imaginings: James Mills the History of British India and Orientalism* (Oxford: Clarendon Press, 1992).

Mathew, J. and S.G. Kalpana, *A Classified State Bibliography of Linguistic Research on Indian Languages*, Vol. V (Mysore: Central Institute of Indian Languages, 1986).

Matilal, Bimal Krishna, *Logic Language and Reality Introduction to Indian Philosophical Studies* (Delhi: Motilal Banarsidas, 1985).

Mir, Farina, *The Social Space of Language : Vernacular Culture in British Colonial Punjab* (University of California Press, 2010).

Mishra, Jayakant, *A History of Maithili Literature*, vol. II (Allahabad: Tirbhukti Publications, 1950).

Mitchell, Lisa, *Language Emotions and Politics in South India* (Ranikhet: Permanent Black, 2010).

Murray, Denise, *Knowledge Machines: Language and Information in a Technological Society* (Wesley Pub. Co., 1995).

Nandy, Ashis, *The Intimate Enemy Loss and Recovery of Self under Colonialism* (Delhi: Oxford University Press, sixth impression, 1992 [1983]).

Naregal, Veena, *Language Politics, Elites and the Public Sphere* (New Delhi: Permanent Black, 2001).

Nayar, Baldev Raj, *National Communication and the Language Policy in India* (New York: Fredrick A. Prager, 1969).

Nigam, R.C., *India: Language Handbook on Mother Tongues in Census* (New Delhi: Ministry of Home Affairs, 1972).

Ojha, P.N., *History of the Indian National Congress in Bihar 1885–1985* (Patna: K. P. Jayaswal Research Institute, 1985).

Orsini, Francesca, *The Hindi Public Sphere: Language and Literature in the Age of Nationalism* (Delhi: Oxford University Press, 2002).

Offredi, M., *Language Versus Dialect* (Delhi: Manohar Publishers and Distributors, 1990).

Page, R.B.L., *The National Language Question, Linguistic problems of Newly Independent States* (Oxford: Oxford University Press, 1964).

Paul, Bimal Chandra, *Mithila Land and the Peoples* (Madhyamgram: 24-Parganas, Paulami Publication, 1993).

Phadke, Y.D., *Politics and Language* (Mumbai: Himalaya Publishing House, 1977).

Phillipson, Robert, *Linguistic Imperialism* (Oxford: Oxford University Press, 1992).

Prakash, Gyan, *Another Reason: Science and the Imagination of Modern India* (Princeton: Princeton University Press, 1999).

Rahman, Tariq, *Language and Politics in Pakistan* (New Delhi: Orient Longman, 2007).

Rai, Alok, *Hindi Nationalism* (New Delhi: Orient Longman, 2001).

Rai, Amrit, *A House Divided: The Origin and Development of Hindi–Urdu* (Delhi: Oxford University Press, 1991).

Ramaswami, Sumathi, *Passion of the Tongue Devotion in Tamil India 1891–1970* (California: University of California Press, 1997).

Ramaswami, Sumathi, *Beyond Appearance; Visual Practices and Ideologies in Modern India* (New Delhi: Sage Publications, 2003).

Ramaswami, Sumathi, *Fabulous Geography, Catastrophic Histories Lost Land of Lemuria* (Delhi: Permanent Black, 2005).

Ram, Mohan, *Hindi against India: Meaning of DMK* (New Delhi: Rachna Prakashan, 1968).

Rao, D.S., *Five Decades: The National Academy of Letters, India: A Short History of Sahitya Akademi* (Delhi: Sahitya Akademi, 2004).

Robinson, Francis, *Separatism among Indian Muslims the Politics of United Province's Muslims 1860–1925* (Delhi: Oxford University Press, 1993).

Roy, Naresh Chandra, *Federalism and Linguistic States* (Kolkata: Firma K. L. Mukhopadhyay, 1962).

Rudolph, Llyod I. and Susanne H. Rudolph, *The Modernity of Tradition: Political Development in India* (Chicago: Chicago University Press, 1967).

Said, E., *Orientalism* (New York: Pantheon Books, 1978).

Sarangi, Asha (ed.), *Language and Politics in India* (Delhi: Oxford University Press, 2009).

Schwartzberg, Joseph E. *A Historical Atlas of South Asia*, Second Impression (New York: Oxford University Press, 1992).

Scott, James C., *Weapons of the Weak: Everyday Forms of Peasant Resistance* (New Haven: Yale University Press, 1985).

Seal, Anil, *The Emergence of Indian Nationalism: Competition and Collaboration in Latter Nineteenth Century* (Cambridge: Cambridge University Press, 1968).

Sharda, B.A., *A Directory of Institutions in Language and Literature in India* (Mysore: Central Institute of Indian Languages, 1984).

Sharma, J. Shakuntala, *Classified Bibliography of Linguistic Dissertation on Indian Languages*, Section 4 (Mysore: Central Institute of Indian Languages, 1978).

Shapiro, M.C. and H.C. Schiffman, *Language and Society in South Asia* (Washington: University of Washington, 1975).

Singh, K.S. and S. Manoharan, *Languages and Scripts–People of Indian National Series*, vol. 9 (New Delhi: Oxford University Press, 1993).

Singh, S.N., *History of Tirhut* (Kolkata: The Baptist Mission Press, 1922).

Singh, U.N., *The Maithili Language Movement: Successes and Failures* (Mysore: Central Institute of Indian Language, 1980).

Tarachand, *The Problem of Hindustani* (Allahabad: Indian Periodical Ltd., 1944).

Terry, E., *A Voyage to East India* (Salisbury: W. Cater; S. Hayes; J. Wilkie; and E. Easton, 1777).

Thakur, Upendra Thakur, *History of Mithila* (Darbhanga: Mithila Research Institute, 1988).

Thakur, Upendra Thakur, *Aspects of Society and Economy of Medieval Mithila* (Patna: Janaki Prakashan, 1989).

Trautman, T.R., *Aryans and the British India* (California: University of California Press, 1927).

Viswanathan, Gauri, *Masks of Conquest: Literary Study and British Rule in India* (London: Faber and Faber, 1989).

Volosinov, V.N., 'Marxism and the Philosophy of Language', trs., Ladislav Matejika and I.R. Titunik (New York: Seminar Press, 1973).

Vossler, K., *The Spirit of Language in Civilization* (London: Routledge, 1932).

Washbrook, David and Penelope Corfield, *Language, History, Class* (Oxford: Blackwell, 1991).

Watson, Seton H., *Language and National Consciousness* (London: British Academy, 1981).

Yadav, R.K., *The Indian Language Problem: A Comparative Study* (Delhi: National Publishing House, 1966).

Newspapers

Searchlight, English Daily, Patna (1967–71).

Indian Nation, English Daily, Patna (1967–71).

Mithila Samad, Maithili Daily, Kolkata (2012).

Web Sources

'Mithila Vibhuti'. http://www.mithiladainik.in/2008/07/blog-post_29.html, accessed on 26 August 2017.

'Anubhuti: Bhartendu Harischandra—Matri Bhasha ke Prati', http://www.anubhuti-hindi.org/dohe/bhartendu.htm, accessed on 26 August 2017.

'Essentials of Hindutva', http://savarkar.org/en//Encyc/2017/5/23/Essentials-of-Hindutva.html, accessed on 26 August 2017.

'Johann Gottfried Herder: Treatise on the Origin of Language', http://www.marxists.org/archive/herder/1772/origins-language.htm, accessed on 26 August 2017.

'Muse India Archives: Udaya Narayana Singh—Crises of Maithili Litterateurs', http://www.museindia.com/viewarticle.asp?myr=2007&issid=12&id=585, accessed on 26 August 2017.

'Orissa Review—April 2006: Formation of Orissa as a Separate State', http://magazines.odisha.gov.in/Orissareview/April2006/engpdf/formation_of_orissa_as_separate.pdf, accessed on 26 August 2017.

Index

About the Author

MITHILESH KUMAR JHA teaches political science in the Department of Humanities and Social Sciences, Indian Institute of Technology, Guwahati, India. He works around the areas of modern Indian political thought, political thought in comparative perspective, political theory, Indian politics, especially language, and related issues of state formation in modern India. He is the recipient of the Charles Wallace Scholarship, 2012. At present, he is working on a project on social and political imaginaries in early twentieth-century Mithila.

333 index